# Lecture Notes in Computer Science 12497

More information about this series at http://www.springer.com/series/7409

Anne-Gwenn Bosser · David E. Millard ·
Charlie Hargood (Eds.)

# Interactive Storytelling

13th International Conference
on Interactive Digital Storytelling, ICIDS 2020
Bournemouth, UK, November 3–6, 2020
Proceedings

 Springer

*Editors*
Anne-Gwenn Bosser
Ecole Nationale d'Ingénieurs de Brest
Brest, France

David E. Millard ⓘ
University of Southampton
Southampton, UK

Charlie Hargood ⓘ
Creative Technology
Bournemouth University
Poole, Dorset, UK

ISSN 0302-9743 ISSN 1611-3349 (electronic)
Lecture Notes in Computer Science
ISBN 978-3-030-62515-3 ISBN 978-3-030-62516-0 (eBook)
https://doi.org/10.1007/978-3-030-62516-0

LNCS Sublibrary: SL3 – Information Systems and Applications, incl. Internet/Web, and HCI

This Springer imprint is published by the registered company Springer Nature Switzerland AG
The registered company address is: Gewerbestrasse 11, 6330 Cham, Switzerland

# Preface

This volume constitutes the proceedings of the 13th International Conference on Interactive Digital Storytelling (ICIDS 2020). ICIDS is the premier conference for researchers and practitioners in the foundations, development, and study of interactive narratives and their applications. Authors and participants from varied backgrounds attend this venue to share theoretical, technological, and applied design practices. The annual conference is a dynamic and stimulating interdisciplinary gathering that combines computational narratology, narrative systems, storytelling technology, humanities-inspired theoretical inquiry, empirical research, and artistic expression.

This year's conference has been built around the central theme of "Interactive Digital Narrative Scholarship" – this builds upon a recurrent issue in recent years of the conference which has sought to define the methodologies, scholarly, and scientific basis of Interactive Digital Narrative as an academic discipline. From earlier international joint efforts to integrate research from multiple fields of study to today's endeavors by researchers to provide scholarly works of reference, the conversation on how to advance Interactive Storytelling research as a discipline, with its own epistemology, is a thread that links each ICIDS edition to the next. This year, to emphasize our central theme, we used a dedicated panel in order to explore multiple points of view as well as to encourage audience participation.

These proceedings reflect our conversation as we continue to define the discipline of Interactive Digital Narrative scholarship, anchor the community around it, and work towards rigorously refining the terminology, theory, and methodologies within our field. We have structured the discussion around four main tracks: Narrative Systems (covering technological research from narrative AI to authoring tools), Interactive Narrative Theory (exploring narratological models and literary approaches), Interactive Narrative Impact and Applications (describing the impact of interactive narrative on society and novel applications), and Interactive Narrative Research Discipline and Contemporary Practice (presenting new philosophies and methodologies for research and teaching).

ICIDS 2020 should have been hosted by its organizer, the Department of Creative Technology of Bournemouth University, UK. Due to the worldwide pandemic of COVID-19, the scientific conference, like many others this year, took place online in an alternate format: research papers were presented and discussed during thematic panels in order to favor interaction. These were organized around three keynotes, which provided focus points during the most shared hours of the day across different timezones. Demonstrations (descriptions included in these proceedings) and a virtual Arts Exhibit featuring more than 30 installations showcased exciting novel work.

Despite the ongoing worldwide turmoil in the months leading to the conference, we received 70 paper submissions (4 posters, 17 short papers, and 49 full papers). Following the review process, the conference accepted 15 full papers, 8 short papers, and 5 posters, including full or short papers which have been resubmitted in the short paper or the poster category. The acceptance rate for full papers was thus 30.61%.

Building on the experience of previous years, the review process was strictly double-blind, used a structured and detailed review form, and included an extended discussion phase between the reviewers, steered by our area chairs, to attempt to build a consensus opinion. A minimum of three reviews per paper were requested before the decision, with additional reviews solicited on the recommendations of reviewers, or in the light of their discussions. We want to thank our area chairs for their hard work and participation in the meta-reviews process: Fred Charles, James Cole, Sarah Harmon, Sandy Louchart, Valentina Nisi, Catia Prandi, Anastasia Salter, and Henrik Schønau Fog.

Finally we want to express our gratitude to all the members of our research community who accepted to serve as reviewers this year, as we recognize the difficulties many of us will have been facing in our personal lives. Their commitment to providing high-quality reviews and constructive and insightful discussions is a credit to our community.

November 2020

Anne-Gwenn Bosser
David E. Millard
Charlie Hargood

# ARDIN, the Association for Research in Digital Interactive Narratives

ARDIN's purpose is to support research in Interactive Digital Narratives (IDN), in a wide range of forms, be that video and computer games, interactive documentaries and fiction, journalistic interactives, art projects, educational titles, transmedia, virtual reality and augmented reality titles, or any emerging novel forms of IDN.

ARDIN provides a home for an interdisciplinary community and for various activities that connect, support, grow, and validate said community. The long-term vision for the suite of activities hosted by ARDIN includes membership services such as a community platform, newsletters, job postings, and support for local gatherings, but also conferences, publication opportunities, research fellowships, and academic/professional awards.

ICIDS is the main academic conference of ARDIN. Additional international and local conferences are welcome to join the organization. The Zip-Scene conference, focused on eastern Europe, is the first associated conference.

Diversity is important to ARDIN. The organization will strive towards gender balance and the representation of different people from different origins. Diversity also means to represent scholars at different levels of their careers.

No ARDIN member shall discriminate against any other ARDIN member or others outside of the organization in any way, including but not limited to gender, nationality, race, religion, sexuality, or ability. Discrimination against these principles will not be tolerated and membership in ARDIN can be withdrawn based on evidence of such behavior.

The association is incorporated as a legal entity in Amsterdam, The Netherlands. First proposed during the ICIDS 2017 conference in Madeira, Portugal, the association was officially announced at ICIDS 2018 in Dublin, Ireland. During its foundational year, members of the former ICIDS Steering Committee continued to serve as the ARDIN board as approved by the first general assembly at ICIDS 2018. The current board structure and membership were approved at the second general assembly at ICIDS 2019 in Utah, USA, and as of September 2020, ARDIN has more than 170 members. More information about ARDIN can be found at https://ardin.online/.

# Organization

## Organization Committee

### General Chair

Charlie Hargood     Bournemouth University, UK

### Program Committee Chairs

Anne-Gwenn Bosser   ENIB, Lab-STICC, France
David E. Millard    University of Southampton, UK

### Art Exhibits Chairs

Jim Pope       Bournemouth University, UK
María Cecilia Reyes    CNR-ITD, Italy

### Publicity Chair

Dene Grigar      Washington State University Vancouver, USA

### Proceedings Chair

Alex Mitchell      National University of Singapore, Singapore

### Workshop Chair

Sam Brooker      University of Richmond, UK

### Demo Chair

James Ryan      Carleton College, USA

### Doctoral Consortium Chair

Ulrike Spierling     RheinMain University of Applied Sciences, Germany

### Special Issue Chair

Christos Gatzidis    Bournemouth University, UK

# Virtual Chairs

Hartmut Koenitz          University of Amsterdam, The Netherlands
Rebecca Rouse            University of Skövde, Sweden

# Local Chairs

Vedad Hulusic           Bournemouth University, UK
Huiwen Zhao             Bournemouth University, UK

# ARDIN Officers and Board

### Executive Board

Hartmut Koenitz (President)   University of Amsterdam, The Netherlands
Frank Nack (Treasurer)        University of Amsterdam, The Netherlands
Lissa Holloway-Attaway        University of Skövde, Sweden
Alex Mitchell                 National University of Singapore, Singapore
Rebecca Rouse                 University of Skövde, Sweden

### General Board

Ágnes Bakk                    Moholy-Nagy University of Art and Design, Hungary
Luis Bruni                    Aalborg University, Denmark
Clara Fernandez-Vara          New York University, USA
Josh Fisher                   Columbia College Chicago, USA
Andrew Gordon                 University of Southern California, USA
Mads Haahr                    Trinity College Dublin, Ireland
Michael Mateas                University of California, Santa Cruz, USA
Valentina Nisi                University of Madeira, Portugal, and Carnegie Mellon
                                University, USA
Mirjam Palosaari Eladhari     Södertörn University, Sweden
Tess Tanenbaum                University of California, Irvine, USA
David Thue                    Carleton University, Canada, and Reykjavik
                                University, Iceland

# Program Committee Area Chairs

### Narrative Systems

Fred Charles            Bournemouth University, UK
Sarah Harmon            Bowdoin College, USA

### Interactive Narrative Theory

Anastasia Salter        University of Central Florida, USA
James Cole              Arts University Bournemouth, UK

## IDN Impact and Applications

Valentina Nisi          University of Madeira, Portugal, and Carnegie Mellon
                        University, USA
Catia Prandi            University of Bologna, Italy

## IDN Research Discipline

Sandy Louchart          The Glasgow School of Art, UK
Henrik Schønau Fog      Aalborg University, Denmark

## Program Committee

Panos Amelidis              Bournemouth University, UK
Ruth Aylett                 Heriot-Watt University, UK
Sasha Azad                  North Carolina State University, USA
Sojung Bahng                Monash University, Australia
Ágnes Karolina Bakk         Moholy-Nagy University of Art and Design, Hungary
Paulo Bala                  Madeira Interactive Technologies Institute, Portugal
Jonathan Barbara            Saint Martin's Institute of Higher Education, Malta
Matthew Barr                University of Glasgow, UK
Nicole Basaraba             Trinity College Dublin, Ireland
Mark Bernstein              Eastgate Systems, Inc., USA
Tom Blount                  University of Southampton, UK
Beth Cardier                Sirius-Beta, Inc., USA
Rogelio E. Cardona-Rivera   The University of Utah, USA
Elin Carstensdottir         University of California, Santa Cruz, USA
Miguel Carvalhais           Universidade do Porto, Portugal
Deborah Castro              Erasmus University Rotterdam, The Netherlands
Marc Cavazza                University of Greenwich, UK
Chiara Ceccarini            University of Bologna, Italy
Vanessa Cesário             ITI/LARSys, Portugal
Ronan Champagnat            La Rochelle Université, France
Yun-Gyung Cheong            Sungkyunkwan University, South Korea
Marianna Ciancia            Politecnico di Milano, Italy
Nuno N. Correia             University of Greenwich, UK, and ITI/LARSyS,
                            Portgual
Chris Crawford              Storytron, Inc., USA
Mara Dionisio               Madeira Interactive Technologies Institute, Portugal
Maria José Ferreira         Universidade de Lisboa, Portugal
Mark Finlayson              Florida International University, USA
Joshua Fisher               Georgia Institute of Technology, USA
Christos Gatzidis           Bournemouth University, UK
Andrew Gordon               University of Southern California, USA
Daniel Green                Bournemouth University, UK
Dene Grigar                 Washington State University, USA
Jessica Hammer              Carnegie Mellon University, USA
Brent Harrison              University of Kentucky, USA

| | |
|---|---|
| Catherine Havasi | Massachusetts Institute of Technology, USA |
| Lissa Holloway-Attaway | University of Skövde, Sweden |
| Clare J. Hooper | University of Southampton, UK |
| Vedad Hulusic | Bournemouth University, UK |
| Dennis Jansen | Utrecht University, The Netherlands |
| Akrivi Katifori | University of Athens, Greece |
| Geoff Kaufman | Carnegie Mellon University, USA |
| Erica Kleinman | Northeastern University, USA |
| Andrew Klobucar | New Jersey Institute of Technology, USA |
| Hartmut Koenitz | University of Amsterdam, The Netherlands |
| Max Kreminski | University of California, Santa Cruz, USA |
| Ben Kybartas | McGill University, Canada |
| Bjarke Alexander Larsen | Aalborg University, Denmark |
| Boyang Li | Baidu Research Institute, USA |
| Vincenzo Lombardo | Università di Torino, Italy |
| Domitile Lourdeaux | Université Technologique de Compiègne, France |
| Ilaria Mariani | Politecnico di Milano, Italy |
| Chris Martens | North Carolina State University, USA |
| Alex Mitchell | National University of Singapore, Singapore |
| John Murray | University of Central Florida, USA |
| Frank Nack | University of Amsterdam, The Netherlands |
| Valentina Nisi | University of Madeira, Portugal, and Carnegie Mellon University, USA |
| Michael Nitsche | Georgia Institute of Technology, USA |
| Sandra Olim | Madeira Interactive Technology Institute, Portugal |
| Ethel Ong | De La Salle University, Philippines |
| Federico Peinado | Universidad Complutense de Madrid, Spain |
| Andrew Perkis | Norwegian University of Science and Technology, Norway |
| Antonio Pizzo | Université di Torino, Italy |
| Jonathan Rowe | North Carolina State University, USA |
| Sabrina Scuri | Madeira Interactive Technologies Institute, Portugal |
| Digdem Sezen | Istanbul University, Turkey |
| Jesse Smith | University of California, Davis, USA |
| Ulrike Spierling | RheinMain University of Applied Sciences, Germany |
| Alina Striner | Centrum Wiskunde & Informatica, The Netherlands |
| Adam Summerville | Cal Poly Pomona, USA |
| Nicolas Szilas | University of Geneva, Switzerland |
| Mariet Theune | University of Twente, The Netherlands |
| Mattia Thibault | Tampere University, Finland |
| David Thue | Carleton University, Canada |
| Emmett Tomai | The University of Texas at Rio Grande Valley, USA |
| Romana Turina | Arts University Bournemouth, UK |
| Stephen Ware | University of Kentucky, USA |
| Mark Weal | University of Southampton, UK |
| Hui-Yin Wu | Université de Côte d'Azur, Inria, France |

Nelson Zagalo            University of Aveiro, Portugal
Huiwen Zhao              Bournemouth University, UK

## Additional Reviewers

Jason Alonso
Alexander Card
Asim Hameed

# Contents

**Interactive Digital Narrative Scholarship**

ICIDS2020 Panel: Building the Discipline of Interactive
Digital Narratives . . . . . . . . . . . . . . . . . . . . . . . . . . . . . . . . . . . . . . . .     3
    *Mark Bernstein, Mirjam Palosaari Eladhari, Hartmut Koenitz,*
    *Sandy Louchart, Frank Nack, Chris Martens, Giulia Carla Rossi,*
    *Anne-Gwenn Bosser, and David E. Millard*

**Narrative Systems**

*Letters to José*: A Design Case for Building Tangible
Interactive Narratives. . . . . . . . . . . . . . . . . . . . . . . . . . . . . . . . . . . . . .    15
    *Daniel Echeverri and Huaxin Wei*

Embedded Narratives in Procedurally Generated Environments . . . . . . . . . . .    30
    *Thomas Lund Nielsen, Eoin Ivan Rafferty, Henrik Schoenau-Fog,*
    *and George Palamas*

Crafting Interactive Narrative Games with Adversarial Planning Agents
from Simulations. . . . . . . . . . . . . . . . . . . . . . . . . . . . . . . . . . . . . . . . . .    44
    *Chris Miller, Mayank Dighe, Chris Martens, and Arnav Jhala*

A Systematic Analysis of User Experience Dimensions for Interactive
Digital Narratives . . . . . . . . . . . . . . . . . . . . . . . . . . . . . . . . . . . . . . . . .    58
    *Ashwathy T. Revi, David E. Millard, and Stuart E. Middleton*

Digital Storytelling in a Museum Application Using the Web of Things . . . .    75
    *Mortaza Alinam, Luca Ciotoli, Frosina Koceva, and Ilaria Torre*

User Testing Persuasive Interactive Web Documentaries:
An Empirical Study. . . . . . . . . . . . . . . . . . . . . . . . . . . . . . . . . . . . . . . . .    83
    *Nicole Basaraba, Owen Conlan, Jennifer Edmond, and Peter Arnds*

Towards the Emergent Theatre: A Novel Approach for Creating Live
Emergent Narratives Using Finite State Machines . . . . . . . . . . . . . . . . . . .    92
    *Craig Paul Green, Lars Erik Holmquist, and Steve Gibson*

A Novel Design Pipeline for Authoring Tools . . . . . . . . . . . . . . . . . . . . . .   102
    *Daniel Green, Charlie Hargood, and Fred Charles*

Toward a Block-Based Programming Approach to Interactive Storytelling
for Upper Elementary Students . . . . . . . . . . . . . . . . . . . . . . . . . . . . . . . .     111
   Andy Smith, Bradford Mott, Sandra Taylor, Aleata Hubbard-Cheuoua,
   James Minogue, Kevin Oliver, and Cathy Ringstaff

Twine and DooM as Authoring Tools in Teaching IDN Design
of LudoNarrative Dissonance . . . . . . . . . . . . . . . . . . . . . . . . . . . . . . . .     120
   Jonathan Barbara

A Comparison of Children's Narrative Expressions in Enactment
and Writing . . . . . . . . . . . . . . . . . . . . . . . . . . . . . . . . . . . . . . . . . . . .     125
   Niloofar Zarei, Francis Quek, Sharon Lynn Chu, and Sarah Anne Brown

**Interactive Narrative Theory**

GFI: A Formal Approach to Narrative Design and Game Research . . . . . . . .     133
   Rogelio E. Cardona-Rivera, José P. Zagal, and Michael S. Debus

Weird and Wonderful: How Experimental Film Narratives Can Inform
Interactive Digital Narratives . . . . . . . . . . . . . . . . . . . . . . . . . . . . . . . .     149
   Chris Hales

"How Do I Restart This Thing?" Repeat Experience and Resistance
to Closure in Rewind Storygames . . . . . . . . . . . . . . . . . . . . . . . . . . . . .     164
   Alex Mitchell and Liting Kway

The Case for Invisibility: Understanding and Improving Agency in Black
Mirror's Bandersnatch and Other Interactive Digital Narrative Works . . . . . .     178
   Anna Marie Rezk and Mads Haahr

Dramatic Narrative Logics: Integrating Drama into Storygames
with Operational Logics . . . . . . . . . . . . . . . . . . . . . . . . . . . . . . . . . . . .     190
   Kenneth Tan and Alex Mitchell

When the Fourth Layer Meets the Fourth Wall: The Case for Critical
Game Retellings . . . . . . . . . . . . . . . . . . . . . . . . . . . . . . . . . . . . . . . . . .     203
   Steven Sych

What Might an Action do? Toward a Grounded View of Actions
in Interactive Storytelling . . . . . . . . . . . . . . . . . . . . . . . . . . . . . . . . . . .     212
   David Thue

Towards Gestural Specificity in Interactive Digital Literary Narratives . . . . . .     221
   Serge Bouchardon

**Interactive Narrative Impact and Applications**

Capturing User Emotions in Interactive Stories: Comparing a Diegetic
and a Non-diegetic Approach to Self-reporting Emotion. . . . . . . . . . . . . .     229
  Sarah Anne Brown, Cheryl Resch, Vanessa Han,
  Srividya Vaishnavi Surampudi, Pratyusha Karanam,
  and Sharon Lynn Chu

Interpretive Play and the Player Psychology of Optimal
Arousal Regulation . . . . . . . . . . . . . . . . . . . . . . . . . . . . . . . . . . . . . . . .     243
  Matthew Higgins and Peter Howell

The Procedural Nature of Interactive Digital Narratives and Early Literacy. . .     258
  Cristina Sylla and Maitê Gil

Vim: A Tangible Energy Story . . . . . . . . . . . . . . . . . . . . . . . . . . . . . . . .     271
  Skye Doherty, Stephen Snow, Kathleen Jennings, Ben Rose,
  Ben Matthews, and Stephen Viller

Tale of T(r)ails: The Design of an AR Comic Book for an Animal
Welfare Transmedia . . . . . . . . . . . . . . . . . . . . . . . . . . . . . . . . . . . . . . .     281
  Mara Dionisio, Paulo Bala, Sarah Oliveira, and Valentina Nisi

**The Interactive Narrative Research Discipline
and Contemporary Practice**

Circuits, Cycles, Configurations: An Interaction Model of Web Comics . . . . .     287
  Alessio Antonini, Sam Brooker, and Francesca Benatti

Archiving Interactive Narratives at the British Library . . . . . . . . . . . . . . . .     300
  Lynda Clark, Giulia Carla Rossi, and Stella Wisdom

Gated Story Structure and Dramatic Agency in Sam Barlow's Telling Lies. . .     314
  T. M. Gasque, Kevin Tang, Brad Rittenhouse, and Janet Murray

Magic and Immersion in VR . . . . . . . . . . . . . . . . . . . . . . . . . . . . . . . . .     327
  Ágnes Karolina Bakk

**Demonstrations**

Honey, I'm Home: An Adventure Game with Procedurally Generated
Narrative Puzzles . . . . . . . . . . . . . . . . . . . . . . . . . . . . . . . . . . . . . . . . .     335
  Lilian Morgan and Mads Haahr

A Natural History Museum Experience: Memories of Carvalhal's
Palace – Turning Point . . . . . . . . . . . . . . . . . . . . . . . . . . . . . . . . . . . . .     339
  Vanessa Cesário, Sandra Olim, and Valentina Nisi

Ares 2036: Exploring the Space of Rapid Prototyping for Transformative
Interactive Storytelling. . . . . . . . . . . . . . . . . . . . . . . . . . . . . . . . . . . . .    344
    Christian Roth and Julie Dacanay

The Story Maker - An Authoring Tool for Multimedia-Rich Interactive
Narratives . . . . . . . . . . . . . . . . . . . . . . . . . . . . . . . . . . . . . . . . . . . . . .    349
    Ektor Vrettakis, Christos Lougiakis, Akrivi Katifori, Vassilis Kourtis,
    Stamatis Christoforidis, Manos Karvounis, and Yannis Ioanidis

Using Reverse Interactive Audio Systems (RIAS) to Direct Attention
in Virtual Reality Narrative Practices: A Case Study . . . . . . . . . . . . . . . . . .    353
    Aletta J. Steynberg

Tell a Tail 360°: Immersive Storytelling on Animal Welfare. . . . . . . . . . . . .    357
    Paulo Bala, Mara Dionisio, Tânia Andrade, and Valentina Nisi

Digital Narrative, Documents and Interactive Public History. . . . . . . . . . . . .    361
    Tristan Revells and Yuzhu Chai

**Author Index** . . . . . . . . . . . . . . . . . . . . . . . . . . . . . . . . . . . . . . . . . . .    365

# Interactive Digital Narrative Scholarship

# ICIDS2020 Panel: Building the Discipline of Interactive Digital Narratives

Mark Bernstein[1], Mirjam Palosaari Eladhari[2], Hartmut Koenitz[3], Sandy Louchart[4], Frank Nack[3], Chris Martens[5], Giulia Carla Rossi[6], Anne-Gwenn Bosser[7], and David E. Millard[8(✉)]

[1] Eastgate Systems, Inc., 134 Main Street, Watertown, MA, USA
bernstein@eastgate.com
[2] Stockholm University, Stockholm, Sweden
mirjam@dsv.su.se
[3] University of Amsterdam, Amsterdam, The Netherlands
{h.a.koenitz,nack}@uva.nl
[4] Glasgow School of Art, Glasgow, UK
s.louchart@gsa.ac.uk
[5] North Carolina State University, Raleigh, NC, USA
contextadventure@gmail.com
[6] The British Library, London, UK
GiuliaCarla.Rossi@bl.uk
[7] ENIB - Lab-STICC UMR CNRS 6285, Brest, France
anne-gwenn.bosser@enib.fr
[8] The University of Southampton, Southampton, UK
dem@soton.ac.uk

## 1 Introduction

Building our discipline has been an ongoing discussion since the early days of ICIDS. From earlier international joint efforts to integrate research from multiple fields of study to today's endeavours by researchers to provide scholarly works of reference, the discussion on how to continue building Interactive Digital Narratives as a discipline with its own vocabulary, scope, evaluation and methods is far from over. This year, we have chosen to continue this discussion through a panel in order to explore what are the epistemological implications of the multiple disciplinary roots of our field, and what are the next steps we should take as a community.

The aim of this panel is to continue the conversation on how to build the discipline, to look beyond ICIDS for inspiration and advice, and to invite a broad section of the community to become involved. Our panelists represent the long view of Interactive Digital Narrative as a discipline, both in terms of its history and relation to other disciplines and its long term future and preservation. In addition they propose new initiatives to capture the knowledge of the discipline and create new community resources.

Programme Co-Chairs Anne-Gwenn Bosser and David Millard are the moderators of the panel and editors of this joint paper. In it we asked each of our

© Springer Nature Switzerland AG 2020
A.-G. Bosser et al. (Eds.): ICIDS 2020, LNCS 12497, pp. 3–11, 2020.
https://doi.org/10.1007/978-3-030-62516-0_1

panelists to introduce themselves and gave them the opportunity to outline their positions.

## 2  Panelist: Mark Bernstein

*Mark Bernstein graduated from Swarthmore College and received his doctorate in Chemistry from Harvard in 1983. After three years at DuPont Central Research, he returned to Eastgate Systems, a software development startup he had founded in graduate school with five Swarthmore friends. He has been closely associated with the ACM Hypertext Conference from its foundation in 1987, and has been program chair of that conference (twice), of ACM WikiSym, and of ACM Web Science. His most recent digital story is Those Trojan Girls [8] and his most recent book is Intertwingled [4].*

### 2.1  Position Statement

Over the years, I have been program chair of four computer science conferences and have served in various roles on the program committees of dozens more. I have attended nearly every instance of the ACM Hypertext Conference from its start in 1987 through the present, an era in which that discipline went from wild exuberance to despair and on to what appears to be an incipient revival. I've attended lots of conferences in a variety of disciplines. I was trained as a physical chemist and continue to regard the practices and ethics of the physical sciences as a baseline.

**Ambition.** A thriving discipline is ambitious. It addresses difficult, consequential problems, and it expects them to be solved. Crucially, a healthy discipline expects that its own members will find the answers. *Hypertext 87* mattered because it gathered just about everyone who did research in the field; you knew the names on the name badges from papers you had read, but few of us had seen these researchers before.

Interactive digital storytelling often spends its time reporting on the work of industrial practice [10] or promoting its knowledge of methods for enhancing business productivity [8].

In point of fact, digital storytelling does address difficult and consequential problems, but its practitioners seldom talk about them. Narrative is indispensable and complicated. Much of what we know about narrative – narratology, discourse, construction of meaning, mediation – was (pace Laurel [9]) learned only recently. Interactive and generated narrative give us, for the first time, the chance to read stories that are not completely human. The core disaster of the short 20th century can be read as a determined attack on narrative truth. If we can put an end to that, we need no further ambition; if not, we have no future [4].

**Rigor and Scholarship.** Because a prospering discipline is confident that its work will be read, its papers need not excessively cite their authors' past works and repeat idiosyncratic notation and terminology. It is understood that everyone else in the discipline knows its literature.

In the 20th century, program committees met in person and discussed each paper in considerable depth. Minor flaws in scholarship received censure, major omissions earned rejection. No one, after attending one of those meetings, wanted to be the author of a paper over which the worthies of the field shook their heads and sighed. Nor would one want to be an erring reviewer whose comments were cursory or who had overlook a blunder. The switch to email and EasyChair has saved lots of money and travel, but has often encouraged bad behavior.

For several hypertext conferences in the early years, and for Web Science 2013, I read nearly every submitted paper. I heartily recommend this useful exercise; it is the best way to discover widespread misunderstandings and methodological errors [3].

**Passion and Mission.** Flourishing disciplines are serious: they may address topics that most people consider esoteric, but those topics – Southwestern Archeology [13] or the fall of Rome [12] matter deeply. Keeping the literature uncontaminated is therefore a serious business: if you publish a bad paper, someday a bridge might collapse.

Conferences at the intersection of art and technology confront two intractable problems. First, of course, is the Two Cultures problem in its general form, and specifically the belief that "art" is either childish or an inspired gift. If stories are for children or primitive peoples, then it's hard for their study to matter. If creation requires inspiration, we can dismiss our own failures by blaming them on G-d or the muse. In addition, it is tempting to regard the intersection of science and humanities as a site of a merely economic transaction. Such mercenary motivations distract the discipline from its proper goal, which is (of course) *to follow knowledge like a sinking star beyond the utmost bound of human thought.*

**Tension.** Passionate opinions about ambitious domains lead to tension, and tension is the mark of a vigorous discipline. When ambition is lost, tension dissipates; it may seem for a time that everyone is finally getting along but, in reality, this is a sign of decay. Without passion, of course, tension becomes mere academic politics.

**Dialogue.** In healthy disciplines, papers and monographs exist in dialogue and argue with each other across the years. The best way to advance a cause and to resolve tension is to do the work.

Readercon[1] chiefly studies fantastika—contemporary fiction that departs from reality [5]. Many of its participants advance premises in the form of stories and novels which their colleagues and rivals read as a matter of course—and to which they in turn reply through their own stories and novels. The past decade has, for example, seen an extended discussion of the proper approach to "alien" in SF and horror, carried forth in critical works and lectures, in panels, and especially in novels.

---

[1] Readercon: The conference on imaginative literature. https://readercon.org.

**Polish and Writing.** Contributors to an energetic discipline take pains over their work because the work matters, because everyone who matters will read it, because the readers are passionate, and because sloppiness and obscurity will top them no good. Too much polish is pernicious:

> Always look for invention first, and after that, for such execution as will help the invention, and as the inventor is capable of without painful effort, and no more. Above all, demand no refinement of execution where there is no thought, for that is slaves' work, unredeemed [6].

We don't need clever wordplay or eloquent rhetoric, and we understand that students working in their second or third language may not always express themselves perfectly. Prefer clear statement and clean methodology. Avoid clinical experiments where the conclusion is pre-ordained. If your statistics won't be significant, adopt other methods.

## 3   Panelist: Hartmut Koenitz

Note: Hartmut is writing with Mirjam Palsaari Eladhari, Sandy Louchart, and Frank Nack, as part of the INDCOR encyclopaedia project.

*Hartmut Koenitz is a visiting researcher at the Informatics Institute of the University of Amsterdam. Previously he was Professor for Interactive Narrative Design at HKU. He holds a PhD from the Georgia Institute of Technology on the theory and practice of Interactive Digital Narrative. His research interests are at the intersection of art, culture, history, and technology. Hartmut has published over 50 scholarly publications and several books, including the co-edited volume Interactive Digital Narrative – history, theory and practice (Routledge 2015). He is the creator of the ASAPS authoring tool, which has been used to create more than 150 works, including Breaking Points (available via the iTunes Store for iPad) and Occupy Istanbul, a game on the Gezi park protests in Istanbul 2013. Since November 2019, Hartmut is the president of ARDIN, the Association for Research in Digital Interactive Narratives. He is the chair of the EU COST Action INDCOR (CA18230 - Interactive Narrative Design for Complexity Representations). He is also a visual artist, and his works have been shown in Atlanta, Paris, Istanbul, Seoul, Copenhagen and Porto.*

### 3.1   Position Statement

The lack of a shared vocabulary is a longstanding issue of the field of interactive digital storytelling that has been compared to the biblical metaphor of the "Babylonian confusio" [8]. Scholars and practitioners concerned with the topic of interactive digital narratives originate in a number of different fields, including literature studies, film studies, computer sciences and many more. All of these fields have associated specific vocabulary, which is often not immediately accessible to "outsiders". The issue is further aggravated by the fact that many common terms used in interactive digital narratives research – such as "narrative", "plot" or "story" – have a both a common meaning in everyday conversation and a specific one in scholarly and professional contexts.

This issue manifests as a considerable obstacle to productive work, especially in interdisciplinary settings, for example in the multinational research network INDCOR (Interactive Narrative Design for COmplexity Representations) which brings together an interdisciplinary network of scholars from over 30 countries. INDCOR builds on the foundations laid by earlier projects such as IRIS [1] and RIDERS[2], but is specifically concerned with the application of interactive digital narratives for the representation of complex topics such as global warming, or the worldwide refugee crisis. Here, a shared vocabulary is a necessity in order to enable scholars and practitioners from various disciplines to meaningfully contribute to the project. In addition, the question of vocabulary is a crucial element in the networks' intention to improve the understanding of IDN in society at large.

**An Analytical Basis.** The purpose and nature of a shared vocabulary is that key terminology is understood across a multidisciplinary field. It does not mean that all differences in meaning or historical context would simply disappear, but that explicit connections will enable scholars to better understand (and even disagree with) each other and productively work together. In order to enable such a shared understanding, an overarching analytical perspective is necessary. This is an insight driven home by our own experience in the INDCOR project, where it became apparent quickly that without it, a shared vocabulary would simply replicate the existing babylonian confusion. In ongoing work and subsequent meetings in Vienna and online the SPP (System Process Product) model [7] was the one singled out to function as a starting point for connecting the four pillars that are expressed as workgroups in INDCOR (design and development, conceptual development, evaluation and societal context). Hence, the SPP structure is used as a central element in a taxonomy underlying the shared vocabulary.

**The Encyclopedic Approach.** Most importantly, the concept of a shared vocabulary should be made available for the whole community, so it can serve as a hub for knowledge exchange and an important step in building a field accessible also to newcomers and related disciplines. Examples for such hubs exist in the form of online encyclopedias. In the scholarly realm, two particularly successful examples are the Living Handbook of Narratology[3] and the Stanford Encyclopedia of Philosophy[4]. We aim to follow the example set by these projects in creating a high-quality resource for the community. This means the creation of an organization similar to an academic journal with an editorial board, a thorough review process and entries which are recognized as peer-reviewed publications.

---

[2] Riders Project, http://www.riders-project.net.

[3] Hühn, P., et al.: The Living Handbook of Narratology, http://www.lhn.uni-hamburg.de.

[4] Stanford Encyclopedia of Philosophy, https://plato.stanford.edu/.

The proposed content structure of the Encyclopedia of IDN will need to evolve in tandem with the INDCOR project and developments in the research community. In general, entries are guided by the principles of multi-entry and interlinked dependencies. The components of information that we are using as a starting point for encyclopedia entries include two main types:

- **Concept** (central to IDN)
  - alternative names for concept
  - relation to SPP-based taxonomy
  - definition
  - background
  - precursors
  - custom sections for specific concept
  - bibliography

- **IDN** (a specific work)
  - precursors
  - underlying system
  - audience-facing elements (including interaction, audience feedback, discourse, cinematography, lighting etc.)
  - media specificity and traditions
  - reception

The following terms are meant as a foundation for the encyclopedia, covering central concepts in the IDN community. The list is selected from a longer one developed by INDCOR project's WG2, but by no means exhaustive and intended to grow over time.

| | | |
|---|---|---|
| Affordance | Interactor | Plot |
| Agency | Interaction model | Process |
| Asset | Interactivity | Procedurality |
| Audience | Instantiation | Protostory |
| Author | Meaning(-making) | Reflexivity |
| Authoring tool/system | Media specificity | Replayability |
| Beat | Narration | Representation |
| Character | Narrative | Re-telling |
| Cognitive Model | Narrative complexity | Scaffolding |
| Discourse | Narrative design | Scripting (internal and external) |
| Embodiment | Narrative architect | Simulation |
| Emergent narrative | Narrative Game mechanics | Story |
| Environmental storytelling | Narrative product | Story architecture |
| Event | Narrator | Transformation |
| IDN | Participation | |
| Immersion | Performance | |

The group of chairs of the IDNCOR project (nine scholars originating in different disciplines, gender-balanced and at different career stages) will act as the initial editorial board, soliciting entries from authors inside the project and the community at large. This board will be inviting additional experts from the field to assure a diversity of perspectives and a high level of quality content also for topics outside their core expertise. The aim is to make the encyclopedia a sustainable communal endeavor.

**Conclusion.** In this position statement, we have introduced INDCOR's encyclopedia project, designed to provide a shared vocabulary for field of interactive digital narrative research and practice. We invite the research community to partake in this endeavour.

# 4  Panelist: Chris Martens

*Dr. Chris Martens is an Assistant Professor in Computer Science at North Carolina State University. They work on formal models and authoring tools for generative and interactive narratives. They are a recipient of an NSF CAREER Award on narrative generation for comprehension of privacy policies, and won the 2019 ICIDS Best Paper Award for theoretical developments synthesizing interaction in live performances and digital contexts.*

# 5  Panelist: Giulia Carla Rossi

*Giulia Carla Rossi is Curator for Digital Publications at the British Library. With a background in eBook production and digital publishing, her current work focuses on UK emerging formats, publications produced for mobile devices and interactive narratives. She is interested in interactive storytelling, net art and how new forms of creating and consuming content are challenging existing practices in collecting institutions.*

## 5.1  Position Statement

While preservation might be perceived as a field solely focused on safeguarding the past for the future, digital preservation needs to consider future formats as well as past ones, and the impact new technologies might have on current policies. Born-digital publications such as interactive narratives inherit the challenges and requirements related to technology preservation. The speed at which technology develops and gets picked up – but also the speed at which it decays and gets abandoned – compared to the pace at which digital preservation technology progresses forces collecting institutions into a reactive position. A reaction that needs to be rapid and timely in order to respond to the short life span of digital formats and to avoid losing content that doesn't have a print counterpart.

This challenge can also be interpreted as a positive sign of growth in the interactive digital storytelling field. While the variety of formats and the use of proprietary software might introduce difficulties from a preservation perspective, non-standard formats also indicate a rise in creativity and innovation. The "democratization" of interactive writing tools, through a surge in freely available online tools requiring limited or no coding experience, helped remove the main obstacles to free game creation [2]. It also facilitated the collection of a varied sample of interactive fiction for the UK Web Archive Interactive Narratives collection[5] - many of its narratives are slice-of-life vignettes by groups often marginalised in the mainstream video game industry, which adds a social history value to the preservation of these publications.

Collecting interactive publications at scale has also proven to be a challenge to cultural institutions. The individuality and diversity of formats makes necessary a targeted and selective approach to collecting, compared to a more comprehensive method that could be used for standardised formats. The costs associated with digital preservation can also present an obstacle – these include different aspects of the collection management lifecycle, like storage, staff training, maintenance and access solutions. It's not enough to just collect files for a publication, if there is no way to ensure preservation over the long term and provide meaningful access. However, not preserving can also be costly: in terms of cultural loss, surely, but also financially, as it's often more expensive to preserve a format once it's at risk [11]. Preventive measures can indeed be more cost effective than reactive measures and extend the life of collection items. But how to anticipate new technologies?

It's extremely important for collecting organisations to be aware of changes in the models, tools, platforms and formats used by creators to produce content and make it available to the public. This is especially difficult when dealing with new and emerging media, due to the fast moving environment they are created in, and the fact that traditional channels used to gather information for other collections are not as effective in this situation. Approaching this work as an interdisciplinary and cross-sector collaboration has proven to be a successful strategy. Collecting institutions can benefit from the support and expertise of creative industries and researchers in the field, as well as other institutions working on similar challenges.

The UK Web Archive Interactive Narratives collection was established by Lynda Clark, during a post-doctoral placement at the British Library around emerging formats and interactive fiction. The fact that Clark had first-hand experience of writing interactive fiction helped build the collection, as, when trying to capture her own works, narratives could be tweaked and adjusted to test archiving tools. Direct contact with publishers and developers of the works we archived, like inkle and Editions at Play, also significantly facilitated our task, granting us unmediated support from the creators as well as an insight

---

[5] UKWA: Interactive Narratives collection.
https://www.webarchive.org.uk/en/ukwa/collection/1836.

into context and authorial intent – both valuable when deciding what to collect in terms of contextual materials.

While there are many challenges associated with this work, there is value in collecting and preserving these complex digital publications. The anticipated need and interest for this collection is for people working in the new digital media field. Writers, creators and researchers will have access to past examples of digital storytelling, and can gain an insight into the context in which these were originally produced and how the field has since evolved. This can help creators in their future work and provide a valuable contribution to developing Interactive Digital Narrative as a discipline.

# References

1. Cavazza, M., et al.: The IRIS network of excellence: integrating research in interactive storytelling. In: Spierling, U., Szilas, N. (eds.) ICIDS 2008. LNCS, vol. 5334, pp. 14–19. Springer, Heidelberg (2008). https://doi.org/10.1007/978-3-540-89454-4_3
2. Anthropy, A.: Rise of the Videogame Zinesters : How Freaks, Normals, Amateurs, Artists, Dreamers, Drop-outs, Queers, Housewives Are Taking Back an Art Form: How ... People Like You Are Taking Back an Art Form, illustrated edition edn. Seven Stories Press, New York (2012)
3. Bergstrom, C.: Calling Bullshit: The Art of Skepticism in a Data-Driven World, illustrated edition edn. Penguin Random House, New York (2020)
4. Bernstein, M.: Hypertext in the age of trump. In: Intertwingled. Eastgate Systems, Watertown (2019). https://www.eastgate.com/Tinderbox/Intertwingled.html
5. Clute, J.: Pardon This Intrusion: Fantastika in the World Storm, 1st edn. Beccon Publications, Essex (2011)
6. Harrington, P.: Chapter 6. In: The Stones of Venice, vol. 2. Smith, Elder & Co. London (1873)
7. Koenitz, H.: Towards a Specific Theory of Interactive Digital Narrative. In: Interactive Digital Narrative, pp. 91–105. Taylor and Francis/Routledge (2015). https://doi.org/10.4324/9781315769189-8. https://www.taylorfrancis.com/
8. Koenitz, H., Eladhari, M.P.: Challenges of IDN research and teaching. In: Cardona-Rivera, R.E., Sullivan, A., Young, R.M. (eds.) ICIDS 2019. LNCS, vol. 11869, pp. 26–39. Springer, Cham (2019). https://doi.org/10.1007/978-3-030-33894-7_4
9. Laurel, B. (ed.): The Art of Human-Computer Interface Design, 1st edn. Addison-Wesley Professional, Reading (1990)
10. Mu, C.: Is "Citizen Kane" moment coming? - a research on Chinese VR documentary practice and storytelling. In: Cardona-Rivera, R.E., Sullivan, A., Young, R.M. (eds.) ICIDS 2019. LNCS, vol. 11869, pp. 40–44. Springer, Cham (2019). https://doi.org/10.1007/978-3-030-33894-7_5
11. Ranger, J.: Three Views Of Digital Preservation (2014). https://blog.weareavp.com/three-views-of-digital-preservation
12. Ward-Perkins, B.: The Fall of Rome: And the End of Civilization, New edition edn. OUP, Oxford (2006)
13. Woodbury, R.: 60 Sixty Years of Southwestern Archaeology : A History of the Pecos Conference. University of New Mexico Press, Albuquerque (1993). https://www.abebooks.com/first-edition/sixty-years-southwestern-archaeology-history-Pecos/5628786047/bd

# Narrative Systems

# *Letters to José*: A Design Case for Building Tangible Interactive Narratives

Daniel Echeverri and Huaxin Wei[✉]

School of Design, The Hong Kong Polytechnic University, Hung Hom, Kowloon, Hong Kong
17901330r@connect.polyu.hk, huaxin.wei@polyu.edu.hk

**Abstract.** The field of interactive digital storytelling has been largely focused on screen-based, algorithm-driven narrative systems. While a considerable number of tools, models and experimental cases have been built to explore different aspects of the narrative and system design, very few of them are applicable for the category of tangible narratives. This paper presents a design case, *Letters to José*, to contribute to the body of works in tangible storytelling. Conducted through a research through design process, the building and evaluation of this case reveals key design aspects and considerations for authoring tangibles narratives, as well as the interactive narrative experience it brings. From the design process and the study findings, we identify a critical design category – artifacts for storytelling – whose characteristics and roles in an interactive narrative system are discussed. In reflecting the decision-makings, we address the complex design problems for building tangible interactive narratives.

**Keywords:** Tangible narrative · Artifacts for storytelling · Interactive narrative · Tangible interaction · Research through design · *Letters to josé*

## 1 Introduction

This paper presents *Letters to José*, a tangible interactive story implemented in a physical-digital hybrid system enabled with multimodal interactions. We introduce the making of this tangible story, discuss the experiences the story brings, and reflect on the lessons and implications that can contribute to authoring of tangible narratives. Using a research through design method, we approach interactive digital narrative (IDN) from a material, physical angle in order to explore more varied experiential qualities than those brought by conventional screen-based forms of narrative. We are particularly interested in how physical artifacts can support the interactive engagement with a narrative, as well as those motives, factors, and mechanisms that lead to enjoyment of a narrative.

With a goal of expanding the understanding of tangible narrative, we contribute a fully implemented design case, *Letters to José*, to the repository of IDNs and the limited body of works of tangible narratives. Our design and evaluation affirm that physical artifacts and narrative structure play an important role in supporting enjoyable narrative experience. Methodologically, we also introduce Research through Design as an approach to the practice of IDN to bridge better between research and design.

© Springer Nature Switzerland AG 2020
A.-G. Bosser et al. (Eds.): ICIDS 2020, LNCS 12497, pp. 15–29, 2020.
https://doi.org/10.1007/978-3-030-62516-0_2

Ultimately, we hope to contribute to the "kaleidoscopic view" of IDN advocated by Janet Murray [27], by demonstrating artifact-based tangible narratives as a promising IDN form.

## 2 Related Work

Interactive Digital Narratives (IDN) are "a form of expression enabled and defined by digital media that tightly integrates interactivity and narrative as a flexible cognitive frame" [18]. We consider Tangible Narratives (TN) are a form of IDN because they well fulfill the definition. However, the interaction process in TN is not limited to screen-based interface like in most existing IDNs. Instead, different tangible physical artifacts are mapped to distinct aspects of the narrative [6] and tangible interaction technology is tightly knitted into a structure that involves a plot, different characters, and other narrative elements [14]. Here we will review the current status quo of TN and the related works that provide us theoretical basis and design inspirations.

### 2.1 The 'Implicit' Tangible Narrative

In a recent paper discussing disciplinary research directions of interactive digital narrative (IDN), Koenitz and Eladhari [19] list a number of recent interactive stories as substantial achievements, such as *Façade* [21], all of which are screen-based works. Not only do we not see enough cases and working prototypes of tangible stories in general, but we do not see much updated theoretical discussion on newer forms of interactive narrative – including tangible stories, in the community of IDN. This can be due to the first of five critical challenges identified by Koenitz and Eladhari [19], which is the "dependency on legacy analytical framework". They explain that the field largely inherits theoretical instruments from "earlier mediated forms of narrative" and the views are bound to be limited.

The situation is not optimal, either, in the design and development of authoring tools for IDN. We can hardly identify tools and models applicable for story applications that are not screen-based and/or built with embodied tangible interactions. In their conclusion of a survey of 300 tools, Shibolet et al. [35] stress that "interaction models and user experience with narrative design – particularly through embodied/gestural interfaces" are "at best implicit in IDN-specific authoring tools".

As of the time of this writing, there is not even a single cohesive definition of what a tangible narrative is. The terms *tangible narrative* and *tangible interactive narrative* seem to be interchangeable, the former being used in most influential works. Tangible narratives are sometimes denoted from the system perspective as *Tangible Storytelling systems* [42], *Tangible and Embodied storytelling* systems [3], or *Tangible Spatial narratives* [23]. They are also framed from the practice of storytelling as *Tangible and Interactive Storytelling* [13] or *Object-based Tangible Storytelling* [41]. Tangible narratives are also implicitly referred to, from the perspective of tangible interaction and interface design, as tangible platforms [23, 39], environments [1], or simply tangible interfaces that support a narrative [4, 5, 22, 24, 25, 34, 40].

As Koenitz and Eladhari [19] rightly point out for IDN as an emerging discipline, "we should seize the opportunity to not only change the object of inquiry, but also our instruments to measure them in order to understand specific characteristics and enable novel insights". In this light, we take an adventure and explore the potential of embodied tangible interaction for constructing novel interactive narrative experiences.

## 2.2 Previous Work in Tangible Narrative

In our work, we draw insights from literature both within and beyond IDN. For narrative structure, we borrow from narratology some of the principles of interactive narrative proposed by Marie-Laure Ryan [33]. For interaction design, we ground part of our theoretical basis in the early work of Hiroshi Ishii [16, 44] and other works that contributed to the foundations of Tangible Interaction (e.g., [9, 15, 17, 22]). We also consider perspectives from the study of play and games (e.g., [45]) and of different forms of interactive storytelling (e.g., [26]). Lastly and importantly, we draw insights from existing design cases (e.g., [5, 13, 41]) and from frameworks that intend to facilitate the creation of TN [6, 14]). What follows is a set of key concepts and frameworks that helped build our understanding and theoretical foundation of TN.

*Diegetic Objects:* Holmquist et al. [15] discussed the idea of heightening the sense of involvement by providing *physical, diegetic objects* – some computationally enhanced – that represent important parts of the narrative. They explored the narrative's expressive aspects by situating the player in different perspectives of the story. In a similar approach, Mazalek et al. [22] presented a method that considered cooperative and social interactive experiences in the form of *viewpoints*. These viewpoints allow the user to interact and modify a linear narrative in a shared space.

*Cognitive Hyperlinks.* Tanenbaum et al. [41] introduced *Reading Glove*, an interactive narrative system that makes use of RFID-enabled gloves to bound a digital narrative to physical objects. Their work introduced the notion of *cognitive hyperlinks* – "reoccurring themes, characters, locations, and other literary elements that help a reader to make sense of the structure of a story".

*Defining Tangible Narrative.* Even though most authors root varied tangible narratives in the different relationships between what is physical, what is virtual, and what they represent of the narrative, they come short in defining them. Harley et al. [14] provided a simple yet vital characterization of TN: "tangible interaction technology is understood as a *necessary component* of the narrative or its construction" and "the resulting narrative *will include* at least one of the following: plot, character, or setting" (emphasis added) [14]. This characterization is supplemented by the system view provided by Catala et al. [3]: "tangible and embodied storytelling systems rely less on computational story modeling, and instead focus primarily on free story creation and play". They pointed out that "ideally, a system should combine the affordances of both modalities, this is, provide physical interaction and a good story" [3]. Considering the above, within our work we frame TN as *hybrid interactive experiences representing the structured sequence of events in a story by digitally bounding and mapping narrative content to one or more physical artifacts and environments.*

## 3 A Research Through Design Approach

Building a tangible system requires knowledge and skills from both design and tangible interaction, the latter being an established area in the field of human-computer interaction (HCI). Building a tangible story, consequently, is significantly different from creating self-contained software that usually run as an interactive story on the screen. We thus turn to practice-based design and HCI research and adopt the method of research through design to guide the overarching research process.

As Frayling [10] observes, research is transversal to all practices, among them, art and design. The relationship between research with design and art can be understood from three perspectives: *research into art and design*, *research for art and design*, and *research through art and design (RtD)*. We choose the perspective of RtD because it includes materials research, technical experimentation, as well as action research and practical experiments [10]. Introducing this perspective into HCI research, Zimmerman and Forlizzi [46] define Research through Design as "an approach to conducting scholarly research that employs the methods, practices, and processes of design practice with the intention of generating new knowledge". As practice-based research, the approach of RtD is adopted not only to many topics of HCI [20], but also to "many worlds of design" [12]. An author of tangible narrative is bound to work in the intersection of IDN and HCI; we therefore believe RtD will benefit our research and design process.

An important characteristic of RtD is that it does not intend to build knowledge *for* the making of an artifact, but to build knowledge *through* the process of designing the artifact. This requires rigorous and meticulous documentation of the design process. For instance, we created prototypes with different levels of detail and functionalities to explore specific aspects of the experience. The true value of these prototypes, more than experimental platforms to "try something", lies in the annotated observations and insights documented as written ideas, self-addressed notes, conceptual maps, sketches, and diagrams, which formed our autoethnographic journals. Through these, we established a way of systematically creating evidence of the research process, and generated new theory grounded on the findings that led to the iteration of the experimental work.

## 4  Designing *Letters to José*

*Letters to José* is a true story based on a series of letters sent in a late 1940s' Colombia, which were addressed to José, a fresh army recruit, by Jesús, a young medical student and José's brother. Among the letters, there was a noteworthy chronological gap of around six months on each; perhaps several more were sent and received but got lost over time, with only 27 remaining. There is no written record of José's responses since many of the material memories of Jesús, including letters and photos, were gradually discarded after he passed away in 1998. Nonetheless, the remaining letters preserved a sense of order in the matters and events discussed. These family letters, perhaps by fate, eventually fell into the hands of the lead author of this paper, who is José's grandnephew and also Jesús's grandson.

The design project in this research is thus a process of transforming these letters into an interactive experience. The project first went through several preparatory steps including transcribing – from handwritten and typed texts to digital texts – and translating – from Spanish to English. It then entered the first phase to organize the texts into a coherent story and form a narrative structure. With the story roughly assembled, the next phase – editing and scripting – was focused on "making sense" of what the story meant through a long editing process that paid particular attention to how interactivity could support specific narrative events. Once the detailed structure with the scripted actions was completed, the phase of crafting and prototyping started, leading to the final narrative product underlain by a tangible interface system. The following provides more details of the organizing phase and the editing and scripting phase.

## 4.1 Organizing and Structuring

With a preliminary translation completed, the content of the letters was arranged by the timeline with all the events between 1948 and 1957. To keep the narrative concise and manageable, only those events between 1948 and 1952 were integrated into three major character arcs. The first arc describes Jesús studying to become a doctor. The second arc portrays Jesús's life as a medical intern. The third and final arc depicts Jesús's life as a family man. Each character arc does not follow the traditional three-act structure. Instead, *Letters to José* is a character-driven narrative where the storyline follows the gradual transition from student into doctor and family man. This transition motivates the interactor to explore events and characters and progress with the story.

Once an overarching structure is established, each letter was broken down into its corresponding chronological events, and grouped into short texts – labeled as $S$ content, as in *story content*. Along with the three main character arcs, a series of secondary arcs were created based on the anecdotes shared by Jesús about the life of other family members. These secondary arcs are not confined to one main character arc, but transverse to the entire narrative. This two-level structure allows the interactor to track crucial events that begin and end in the same secondary character arc.

To facilitate the tracking and understanding of each event, we decided to introduce an expositional type of content to the main narrative structure with three purposes: *expectation (e)*, *dilemma (d)*, or *context (c)*. These *exposition* contents are labeled as $E$ content. Exposition with expectation $E(e)$ intends to generate an expectation of what will happen in each major character arc. Exposition with dilemma $E(d)$ intends to develop an active response – in the form of choice – from the interactor. Finally, exposition with context $E(c)$ provides the interactor with a clarification of the connections between events. Table 1 shows some examples of these coded contents.

In its final form, *Letters to José* is a hybrid between a non-linear and a linear narrative. It is non-linear because the narrative structure allows the interactor to deviate in the secondary arcs. The structure of *Letters to José* is a combination of two types of structures – the maze structure and the vector-with-side-branches structure in Ryan's [32] typology of structures of interactive narrativity, which we call *mixed-maze* structure. According to Ryan, a maze structure includes multiple paths with a common starting and ending points, whereas a vector structure has a main path with side branches.

**Table 1.** Content fragments of the script of *Letters to José*.

| Text | Content | Directs to |
|------|---------|-----------|
| *O(i.1)* | <u>Sign</u>: Touch the words "Bogotá or Cali" | *S(L.1A)*→ |
| *S(L.1A)* | <u>Audio clip</u>: *After many days of not writing for reasons that will become clear later, it is a pleasure to take this time to write you a letter as I have many things to tell you* | *O(a.1)*→ |
| *O(a.1)* | <u>Audio clip</u>: *Read the text on the right panel, look for the light, and then pose and place the Puppet to continue* | *O(i.2)*→ *E(c.1A)*→ |
| *E(c.1A)* | <u>Text</u>: A whole year went faster than anyone expected. This was the beginning of the 1950s, just when José started working training pilots | *O(i.2)*→ |

## 4.2 Editing and Scripting

**Editing.** With the above basic structure defined, many of the missing gaps of the story were filled in with narrative information obtained through background research and an interview with José. We noticed that the length of the final story was too long to be presented as an interactive narrative, given the limited attention span of people and the high cognitive load of experiencing a story like *Letters to José*. It thus became necessary to edit a new version that fit the needs of the experience better. With this in mind, the story was revised for length, clarity, and order. Editing in this round focused on creating a chronologically organized narrative of each chapter while considering possible interactive and scripting needs. For example, several sentences were re-written or combined, prioritizing authoring creativity to absolute loyalty to the original autobiographical texts. Other fragments were removed, merged with others, or grouped into new ones.

**Scripting.** Previously when organizing *Letters to José* as a *mixed maze* structure, common points (e.g., anecdotes of a certain family member) in each letter's events were identified and links were built among them. These links could lead to other *exposition* or *story* contents and thus help create side branches. These branches are moments in which the reader can explore the storyworld with a clear way to return to the main storyline. In most cases, they are secondary character arcs that provide context between events.

At this point, however, the narrative structure was still 'static' without a strong sense of direction for the interactor. We thus created the third type of content – after story content and exposition content and call it *operation* (*O*) content. Their function can be informing – or *O(i)* or describing an action – or *O(a)* (see Table 1). *Informative* contents, as interface elements, address the interactor, advise, and guide, how the interactor can act. Meanwhile, *action* contents provide feedback and then introduce possible actions. Both *action* and *informative* contents connect transversely with *exposition* or *story* contents. *Action* and *informative* contents are cognitive affordances that provide spatial and performative information. They direct the interactor towards auditive or visual cues that intend to trigger new narrative fragments.

Unlike *story* or *exposition* contents described above, *action* and *information* contents have a specific syntax. They should point to a location inside a physical place (i.e., the represented storyworld), and they should identify the object on which the interactor can act and/or describe the possible outcome of that action. The final step in creating the narrative was to script the different links between *story* contents, *exposition* contents, and *operation* contents. Scripting in this design project, therefore, means both script writing of the operational texts and system scripting in order to create linkage between text nodes just like in a hypertext. Figure 1 depicts the overall narrative structure with varied types of contents.

Looking at Ryan's [31] characterization of plots, *Letters to José* can be described as an epistemic plot that is a superposition of two lines of stories. On the one hand, one story is the small events told by the letters, centered around Jesús's life. On the other hand, another story is the narrative events intended to lead the interactor to discover and explore other side events. In epistemic plots, the desire to know is the key to engage the interactor [31]. This kind of narrative experience allows people to engage with the story as actors and spectators at the same time.

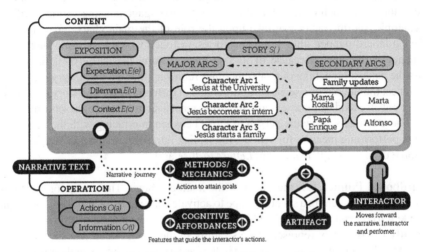

**Fig. 1.** Narrative structure of *Letter to José*.

### 4.3   Crafting and Prototyping

We decided to explore in *Letters to José* the under-researched physical-digital hybrid form in creating our tangible interactive story. After implementing three iterations of prototypes with various combinations of form factors and interaction mechanisms, *Letters to José* is finally presented as three interactive, multimodal, unfolding paper worlds that combine unique paper mechanisms with different visual, performative, and auditory modes (Fig. 2)

Each paper world houses a BareConductive *Touch Board (TB)* paired to a *NodeMCU ESP8266* – both Arduino-based microcontrollers. The TB handles touch events using capacitive electrodes connected to graphics screen-printed with conductive paint. The NodeMCU controls a module that reads RFID tags in different artifacts. It also controls

**Fig. 2.** General overview of the set-up of *Letters to José*. On the left, Chapter 1 and 3, to the right Chapter 2. On the bottom, to the left, the Puppet; in the center, the Family Cards.

photocells, reed-switches, and a thermistor. Upon touching, reading a tag, or triggering any sensor, the TB plays an audio clip. With the *ESP8266*, each paper world *talks* to each other using though the *User Datagram Protocol* (UDP).

Every paper world is divided into separate panels, which are both the interface and the stage of the story. Each panel offers different ways to engage in using various artifacts. For example, the interactor can take upon the role of the main character represented in the cardboard puppet, unlock hidden stories, or touch words to activate short audio fragments of the story. Because of its non-linear nature, the narrative is distributed across the panels, branching out, or sometimes returning into the main storyline. In this experience, the interactor's senses are stimulated in different ways; the story is told by a narrator but also read by the interactor, materials react to actions, and light sets timing and pace. These artifacts allow the person to move between interfacing with the interactive system, performing meaningful actions, immersing into the narrative, and back.

Some of the artifacts featured in *Letters to José* are:

- **Cardboard Puppet.** It is the avatar of the main character. The interactor must pose the Puppet by matching a specific shape to activate each narrative fragment. A magnet inside it triggers a reed-switch, which ultimately activates an audio clip.
- **Family Cards.** They represent José's family in the story. When placed close to an RFID module in a paper world, the tag in the card triggers a clip about their life. When a pull-out tab in the card is pulled, the face of the character is revealed.
- **Paper Flower.** The flower is unveiled using a fold-out mechanism. There is a 0402 surface-mount LED at the end of the flower's pistil. When the interactor blows the flower, the variation in the voltage of the LED triggers the audio clip to play.

## 5   Experiencing *Letters to José*

To observe how people are engaged with *Letters to José* and react to this unique form of tangible narrative, we conducted a small-scale study with twelve participants, using concurrent (quantitative and qualitative data were collected at the same time) and embedded (the quantitative data informed the qualitative methodology) exploratory mixed methods, in Creswell and Plano Clark's terms [7]. The main goal of the study was to investigate participants' phenomenological experiences and understand the motives, factors, and mechanisms that led them to enjoy the narrative. While most of this information can be gathered qualitatively, we decided to deploy three existing quantitative surveys as an aid simply gauging the high-level quality of *Letters to José*, in the areas of engagement, narrative transportation, and agency. The emphasis of the study, however, was placed on the qualitative component of the data, which is also the main source for us to derive knowledge in people's subjective experiences of tangible narratives.

## 5.1  Study Design

**Participants and Procedure.** The participant sample was based on a convenience sample recruited at our university. No reward or benefit was offered to the participants. All twelve participants were students – between 18 to 44 years old – from different academic programs; seven were women and five were men. Eleven out of twelve participants were non-native English speakers from regions, however, where English is recognized as an official language. Five opted to individually interact with the narrative, while seven participants did it in two separate groups, one group with three participants, and one with four. In both groups, the participants were friends or classmates.

After giving their written consent, the participants were instructed on how to interact with the narrative. For the participants to gain the best experience and for the benefit of their time and attention, they freely interacted with Chapters 2 and 3 of *Letters to José*, following the instructions relayed by the audio clips, while the researcher observing on the side and taking notes. Once completing the experience, the participants individually answered three open-ended questions in written form. Next, they individually completed three short questionnaires, each measuring the level of agreement concerning different aspects of their experience. The session was then concluded with a semi-structured interview that focused on the experiential aspects of the narrative with particular attention to play, performance, and interactivity. A typical session lasted from 45 to 55 min, of which around 25 min were spent on experiencing the narrative.

**Data collection and analysis.** As mentioned above, participants responded to three instruments. The first one was the open-ended questionnaire with three questions sought to quickly recall and rationalize some of the most recent and relevant aspects of their experience. The second one was a set of three questionnaires with slight appropriation to our study context: 1) the User Engagement Scale (UES-SF) [28], 2) the Transportation Scale (TS-SF) on aspects related to being immersed in the narrative [2], and 3) the Sense of Agency Rating Scale (SOAR) that measures subjective alterations to the participants' sense of agency [30]. The last instrument was semi-structured interview, which was recorded in audio and transcribed to textual notes.

For data analysis, we only used the quantitative results – from the set of surveys and a timed-log – as a relative reference for each participant's levels of engagement, transportation, and sense of agency. The main analysis focused on qualitative data from participants' written answers, the researcher's notes, and statements from semi-structured interviews. We followed an abductive approach to our analysis by combining inductive coding (a list of a-priori codes) with an interpretative procedure based on Smith et al.'s [37] *Interpretative Phenomenological Analysis* (IPA).

## 5.2   Study Results

Using both inductive and deductive processes in our data coding, we identified five categories of themes. Through an inductive process, two categories emerged: the phenomenological experience, or what shaped the participant's subjective experiences, and the sensorial materiality, or the relationship between materialities and the participant's senses. Using a deductive process, three categories emerged: 1) the presentation, or how the participants understood the relationships between form and materiality, 2) the system, or how they interacted with the digital artifact, and 3) the narrative, or how the story elicited affective and cognitive responses. In general, our observations and comments from the participants suggest that the experience of *Letters to José* was quite positive and unique compared to other interactive narratives. Both physical artifacts and narrative content presented in our chosen narrative structure stimulated the participant's perception and imagination and created enjoyment.

**Phenomenological Experience.** In this category, the analysis identified such subjective aspects as curiosity, enjoyment, exploration, and frustration. For instance, the participants felt curious when they acted by chance and unintentionally but found hidden surprises or entered a plot branch. Most participants expressed that they enjoyed the experience for different reasons; for example, because they were able to act, play, and unfold the narrative through physical, ludic actions, or because the narrative stimulated their imagination by the visual and audio cues. Like how Participant 16L commented on manipulating objects: *"the part where I had to place or pull objects [was] fascinating since it helped me visualize the real scenario"*. On the other hand, the participants generally described three types of frustration: cognitive (e.g., language limitations), narrative (e.g., lack of context), or perceptual (e.g., missing audio cues). These negatively affected the enjoyment of the experience. From a purely phenomenological point of view, the participants' lived experience also influenced their comprehension of the narrative. In a related manner, meaning-making was reinforced (or hindered) by the coherence (lack thereof) between the representation of the storyworld, the understanding of the story events, and the actions they could perform.

**Sensorial Materiality.** In this category, the analysis focused on the way particular material aspects of the experience, such as radiating light, speech and soundscape, and material qualities of the artifacts were perceived by the participants' senses. The participants expressed that the sound drove most of their interactions, while light supported many of the instructions relayed audibly. Their sense of touch allowed them to not only feel directly involved with both the narrative and the control aspects of the experience, but also appreciate different aesthetic characteristics of the narrative system. Such characteristics as the visual features, soundscape and the material qualities of the panels were aesthetically pleasing to the participants. Among the most interesting findings is the primacy of sound over other perceivable modalities, sometimes leading to the loss of attention. Nevertheless, the modality of sound was also one of the most enjoyable aspects of the experience because it helped trigger the participant's imagination.

**Interactive Narrative Experience.** Here the analysis focused on the effects brought by the set of design elements that form the ontology of the interactive narrative system.

These elements come from presentation design (– mostly related to interface design but also including performance logic design), story design, and system design. Most participants agreed that the overall agency is limited in terms of the actions they could do. However, they were satisfied that they could control the story's progression and influence the way the narrative unfolded by taking mostly spontaneous actions in their physical performance. There were moments in which they planned their actions out of curiosity, or as an answer to a prompt of the system. The different mechanics of the narrative system made sense to most of the participants, as they were able to gradually internalize them along the way. Crucially, the participants attributed their story comprehension to the artifacts that helped establish a narrative context and the two-level mixed-maze narrative structure that made them feel curious to explore the narrative. Additionally, the first-person narration made some participants feel empathetic towards the main character of the story, leading to a sense of amazement, introspection, and sometimes emotionally connected to specific narrative events. For example, Participant 04B commented: "*I remember… one of the family cards… says: never be too late to contact your mom. And it's a little bit touching to me. It reminds me to spend more time with my parents*". In a case like this, an interactor identifies with the character because of similar life experiences. They felt rewarded because the experience stimulated their senses and it was *their* active participation that allowed the story to unfold.

## 6 Discussion

**Artifacts for Interactive Storytelling.** With reflections of the design process as well as the study results, we identified *artifacts* as a critical design category for tangible narratives with three primary qualities revealed in our research and design. The three qualities are: *a position in time and space (diegesis)*, *a relationship between representation and action (embodiment)*, and *its role in the narrative system (function)*. Both diegesis and embodiment are gradual qualities complemented by the artifact's function in the narrative system. The higher the value of diegesis (diegetic, transdiegetic, or extradiegetic) and embodiment (full, coupled, or non-graspable) in these qualities in the artifacts of a narrative system, the more tangible they are, and the closer their representation is to the story. In real world, artifacts are objects with unique communicative and semiotic purposes. In a tangible narrative system, artifacts have concrete meanings; they can variably represent a character of the story, a function of the system, a tool, or everything at the same time. Our study findings showed that participants responded to the artifacts in *Letters to José* not only on how they worked in the narrative but also on how they stimulated their senses through the visual, tactile, or even auditive features.

In other words, artifacts for storytelling must have a position in time and space, establish a relationship between what represents and the possible actions, and assume one or more roles in the narrative. As suggested in our study findings, *artifacts* in *Letters to José* had various impacts in the phenomenological experience of the participants; they can drive their comprehension of the story, support their curiosity and interest in the narrative, and provide and constrain their agency. The Puppet in *Letters to José*, for example, can be characterized differently. It is fully diegetic because, as an artifact, it represents the likeness of the main character in the storyworld and the real world. However, it is fully embodied because it not only can be posed, so it looks like it is driving a car or sleeping in the bed, but also can trigger sound in another part of the presentation space. Finally, the Puppet can also be transdiegetic when used only as a mediator between the tutorial and the interactor. Its function in all the cases described above, is exploratory because its operation does not alter the narrative in any way.

**Designing Hybrid (Physical-Digital) Narrative Systems.** We have discussed above the role of physical artifacts in a narrative system. When it comes to placing artifacts in a hybrid system, there are a few design lessons we learned from both our process and the literature. *First,* consider the artifacts' materiality, not only its tangible aspects but also the way the artifact is perceived by other senses [29]; they can vibrate, emit sound, have different textures, or even produce a smell. Sometimes this materiality can set the conceptual context of the storyworld or stimulate the imagination of the interactor. All these aspects might contribute towards adding meaning to the artifact in the context of the narrative, as seen both in *Letters to José* and examples in literature (e.g., [36, 43]). *Second*, have a clear understanding of the possible roles of the artifact. This is because interaction through artifacts in a narrative is usually less rational or pragmatic, allowing for playful and fun methods of interaction, again as seen both in our study and examples in literature (e.g., [8, 11, 38]). *Third*, the dual role of the artifact as an 'input' that triggers digital content and an 'output' that expresses digital content [16, 44] can be an interesting resource that authors and designers of hybrid systems can take advantage of.

## 7 Conclusion and Future Work

*Letters to José* is at the same time a tangible story and a research through design project, through which we explored various design aspects and experiential qualities of tangible narrative. Within the scope of this paper, we presented the structural considerations of *Letters to José* and briefly discussed some of the most relevant findings of a study that sought to investigate participants' experiences with *Letters to José*. One of the key findings is that it is of vital importance to organically integrate ludic actions with designed stimulation of the interactor's imagination through different modalities and materialities in interactive storytelling. In reflecting our research through design, we identified the critical design category of *artifacts for storytelling* and discussed extensively on their characteristics and roles in supporting the narrative experience. We also demonstrated a series of decision-makings to address complex problems related to shaping interactive experiences in the context of tangible narratives.

Although our study showed positive reception of *Letters to José*, more work needs to be done in order to derive more generalized findings for researchers and practitioners in IDN. In the immediate future, we plan to refine the categories of the current study results, with reference to our design annotations along the making process, so to elicit a set of critical constructs for an authoring model for tangible narrative systems. We also plan to further refine the categories related to artifacts and materiality and derive principles regarding physical design for TN.

Ultimately, our ideal tangible narratives, located in the broader realm of IDN, must illustrate non-competitive, self-expressive play that provides greater agency, use system mechanics to exploration the narrative world, prioritize narrative aesthetics over win/lose states and foster immersion through narrative pleasure, but above all the mediation of artifacts that support the storytelling process.

**Acknowledgements.** We would like to thank Dr. Cedric van Eenoo for his valuable input and the participants for their time and insights. We would also like to acknowledge Rafael Reyes-Ruiz for his help in translating, editing, and proofing of *Letters to José*. This research was supported by School of Design at The Hong Kong Polytechnic University and funded by the Hong Kong Ph.D. Fellowship of the Hong Kong Research Grants Council.

# References

1. Alves, A., Lopes, R., Matos, P., Velho, L., Silva, D.: Reactoon: storytelling in a tangible environment. In: 2010 Third IEEE International Conference on Digital Game and Intelligent Toy Enhanced Learning, pp. 161–165. IEEE, Kaohsiung, Taiwan (2010). https://doi.org/10.1109/DIGITEL.2010.28
2. Appel, M., et al.: The transportation scale-short form (TS–SF). Media Psychol. **18**(2), 243–266 (2015). https://doi.org/10.1080/15213269.2014.987400
3. Catala, A., Theune, M., Sylla, C., Ribeiro, P.: Bringing together interactive digital storytelling with tangible interaction: challenges and opportunities. In: Nunes, N., Oakley, I., Nisi, V. (eds.) ICIDS 2017. LNCS, vol. 10690, pp. 395–398. Springer, Cham (2017). https://doi.org/10.1007/978-3-319-71027-3_51
4. Chenzira, A., Chen, Y., Mazalek, A.: RENATI: recontextualizing narratives for tangible interfaces. In: Proceedings of the 2nd International Conference on Tangible and Embedded Interaction - TEI'2008, p. 147. ACM Press, Bonn, Germany (2008). https://doi.org/10.1145/1347390.1347423
5. Chu, J.H.: Designing tangible interfaces to support expression and sensemaking in interactive narratives. In: Proceeding of TEI 2015, pp. 457–460. ACM Press, Stanford, CA, US (2015). https://doi.org/10.1145/2677199.2693161
6. Chu, J.H.: Embodied Engagement with Narrative: a Design Framework for Presenting Cultural Heritage Artifacts with Digital Media. Georgia Institute of Technology (2018)
7. Creswell, J.W., Plano Clark, V.L.: Designing and Conducting Mixed Methods Research. SAGE Publications, Thousand Oaks, Calif (2007)
8. Feltham, F., Vetere, F., Wensveen, S.: Designing tangible artefacts for playful interactions and dialogues. In: Proceedings of the 2007 Conference on Designing Pleasurable Products and Interfaces - DPPI'2007, p. 61. ACM Press, Helsinki, Finland (2007). https://doi.org/10.1145/1314161.1314167
9. Fishkin, K.P.: A taxonomy for and analysis of tangible interfaces. Pers. Ubiquitous Comput. **8**(5), 347–358 (2004). https://doi.org/10.1007/s00779-004-0297-4
10. Frayling, C.: Royal college of art research papers Vol 1 No 1 1993/4: research in art and design. Royal College of Art, London, United Kingdom (1993)
11. Gaver, W.: Curious Things for Curious People. University of London, London, United Kingdom, Goldsmiths (2007)
12. Gaver, W.: What should we expect from research through design? In: Proceedings of the SIGCHI Conference on Human Factors in Computing Systems, pp. 937–946. ACM, Austin, Texas (2012)

13. Gupta, S.: Shiva's Rangoli: Tangible and Interactive Storytelling in Ambient Environments. University of California, Irvine (2018)
14. Harley, D., Chu, J.H., Kwan, J., Mazalek, A.: Towards a framework for tangible narratives. In: Proceedings of TEI'2016, pp. 62–69. ACM Press, Eindhoven, Netherlands (2016). https://doi.org/10.1145/2839462.2839471
15. Holmquist, L.E., Helander, M., Dixon, S.: Every object tells a story: physical interfaces for digital storytelling. In: Proceedings of the NordiCHI (2000)
16. Ishii, H., Ullmer, B.: Tangible bits: towards seamless interfaces between people, bits and atoms. In: Proceedings of CHI'1997, pp. 234–241. ACM Press, Atlanta, GA, US (1997). https://doi.org/10.1145/258549.258715
17. Jacob, R.J., et al.: Reality-based interaction: a framework for post-WIMP interfaces. In: Proceedings of the SIGCHI Conference on Human Factors in Computing Systems, pp. 201–210. ACM, Florence, Italy (2008)
18. Koenitz, H.: Towards a specific theory of interactive digital narrative. In: Koenitz, H., et al. (eds.) Interactive Digital Narrative: History, Theory and Practice, pp. 91–105. Routledge, United Kingdom (2015). https://doi.org/10.4324/9781315769189
19. Koenitz, H., Eladhari, M.P.: Challenges of IDN research and teaching. In: Cardona-Rivera, R.E., Sullivan, A., Young, R.M. (eds.) ICIDS 2019. LNCS, vol. 11869, pp. 26–39. Springer, Cham (2019). https://doi.org/10.1007/978-3-030-33894-7_4
20. Kuutti, K., Bannon, L.J.: The turn to practice in HCI: towards a research agenda. In: Proceedings of CHI 2014, pp. 3543–3552. ACM Press, Toronto, Ontario, Canada (2014). https://doi.org/10.1145/2556288.2557111
21. Mateas, M., Stern, A.: Façade: an experiment in building a fully-realized interactive drama. In: Game Developers Conference, vol. 2, pp. 4–8 (2003)
22. Mazalek, A., Davenport, G., Ishii, H.: Tangible viewpoints: a physical approach to multimedia stories. In: Proceedings of the Tenth ACM International Conference on Multimedia, pp. 153–160. ACM (2002)
23. Mazalek, A., Davenport, G.: A tangible platform for documenting experiences and sharing multimedia stories. In: Proceedings of the 2003 ACM SIGMM Workshop on Experiential Telepresence - ETP'2003, pp. 105–109. ACM Press, Berkeley, California (2003). https://doi.org/10.1145/982484.982505
24. Mazalek, A.: Tangible narratives: emerging interfaces for digital storytelling and machinima. In: Lowood, H., Nitsche, M. (eds.) The Machinima Reader, pp. 91–110. The MIT Press (2011). https://doi.org/10.7551/mitpress/9780262015332.003.0007
25. Moher, T., et al.: StoryGrid: a tangible interface for student expression. In: CHI'2005 Extended Abstracts on Human Factors in Computing Systems, pp. 1669–1672. ACM (2005)
26. Montfort, N.: Toward a theory of interactive fiction. In: IF Theory Reader, pp. 25–58 Lulu.com, Boston, MA, US (2011)
27. Murray, J.H.: Research into interactive digital narrative: a kaleidoscopic view. In: Rouse, R., Koenitz, H., Haahr, M. (eds.) ICIDS 2018. LNCS, vol. 11318, pp. 3–17. Springer, Cham (2018). https://doi.org/10.1007/978-3-030-04028-4_1
28. O'Brien, H.L., et al.: A practical approach to measuring user engagement with the refined user engagement scale (UES) and new UES short form. Int. J. Hum.-Comput. Stud. **112**, 28–39 (2018). https://doi.org/10.1016/j.ijhcs.2018.01.004
29. Petrelli, D., Soranzo, A., Ciolfi, L., Reidy, J.: Exploring the aesthetics of tangible interaction: experiments on the perception of hybrid objects. In: Proceedings of the TEI'2016, pp. 100–108. ACM Press, Eindhoven, Netherlands (2016). https://doi.org/10.1145/2839462.2839478
30. Pritchard, S.C., Zopf, R., Polito, V., Kaplan, D.M., Williams, M.A.: Non-hierarchical influence of visual form, touch, and position cues on embodiment, agency, and presence in virtual reality. Front. Psychol. **7**, 1649 (2016). https://doi.org/10.3389/fpsyg.2016.01649

31. Ryan, M.-L.: Interactive narrative, plot types, and interpersonal relations. In: Spierling, U., Szilas, N. (eds.) ICIDS 2008. LNCS, vol. 5334, pp. 6–13. Springer, Heidelberg (2008). https://doi.org/10.1007/978-3-540-89454-4_2

32. Ryan, M.-L.: Narrative As Virtual Reality: Immersion and Interactivity in Literature and Electronic Media. Johns Hopkins University Press, Baltimore (2001)

33. Ryan, M.-L.: From narrative games to playable stories: toward a poetics of interactive narrative. Storyworlds: J. Narrative Stud. **1**, 43–59 (2009)

34. Shen, Y.T., Mazalek, A.: PuzzleTale: a tangible puzzle game for interactive storytelling. ACM Comput. Entertainment **8**(2), 1–15 (2010). https://doi.org/10.1145/1899687.1899693

35. Shibolet, Y., Knoller, N., Koenitz, H.: A framework for classifying and describing authoring tools for interactive digital narrative. In: Rouse, R., Koenitz, H., Haahr, M. (eds.) ICIDS 2018. LNCS, vol. 11318, pp. 523–533. Springer, Cham (2018). https://doi.org/10.1007/978-3-030-04028-4_61

36. Sieland, S.S.: The reciprocation of materialized imagination. In: Brown, S., Tateo, L. (eds.) The Method of Imagination, pp. 83–116. IAP, Charlotte, NC, USA (2018)

37. Smith, J., et al.: Doing interpretative phenomenological analysis. In: Murray, M., Chamberlain, K. (eds.) Qualitative Health Psychology: Theories and Methods, pp. 218–240. SAGE Publications Ltd, London, UK (1999)

38. Sullivan, A., McCoy, J.A., Hendricks, S., Williams, B.: Loominary: crafting tangible artifacts from player narrative. In: Proceedings of the Twelfth International Conference on Tangible, Embedded, and Embodied Interaction-TEI'2018, pp. 443–450. ACM Press, Stockholm, Sweden (2018). https://doi.org/10.1145/3173225.3173249

39. Sylla, C., Gonçalves, S., Brito, P., Branco, P., Coutinho, C.: A tangible platform for mixing and remixing narratives. In: Reidsma, D., Katayose, H., Nijholt, A. (eds.) ACE 2013. LNCS, vol. 8253, pp. 630–633. Springer, Cham (2013). https://doi.org/10.1007/978-3-319-03161-3_69

40. Sylla, C., Branco, P., Coutinho, C., Coquet, E., Skaroupka, D.: TOK: a tangible interface for storytelling. In: Proceedings of CHI 2011, pp. 1363–1368. ACM Press, Vancouver, BC, Canada (2011). https://doi.org/10.1145/1979742.1979775

41. Tanenbaum, J., Tanenbaum, K., Antle, A.: The reading glove: designing interactions for object-based tangible storytelling. In: Proceedings of the 1st Augmented Human International Conference, p. 9. ACM, Megève, France (2010)

42. Tanenbaum, K., Hatala, M., Tanenbaum, J., Wakkary, R., Antle, A.: A case study of intended versus actual experience of adaptivity in a tangible storytelling system. User Model. User-Adap. Inter. **24**(3), 175–217 (2013). https://doi.org/10.1007/s11257-013-9140-9

43. Tek-Jin, N., Kim, C.: Design by tangible stories: enriching interactive everyday products with ludic value. Int. J. Des. **5**, 1 (2011)

44. Ullmer, B., Ishii, H.: Emerging frameworks for tangible user interfaces. IBM Syst. J. **39**(3.4), 915–931 (2000). https://doi.org/10.1147/sj.393.0915

45. Wardrip-Fruin, N.: Playable media and textual instruments. In: Gendolla, P., Schäfer, J. (eds.) The Aesthetics of Net Literature. Transcript-Verlag, Bielefeld, Germnay (2007). https://doi.org/10.14361/9783839404935-010

46. Zimmerman, J., Forlizzi, J.: Research through design in HCI. In: Olson, J.S., Kellogg, W.A. (eds.) Ways of Knowing in HCI. LNCS, pp. 167–189. Springer, New York (2014). https://doi.org/10.1007/978-3-1-4939-0378-8_8

# Embedded Narratives in Procedurally Generated Environments

Thomas Lund Nielsen, Eoin Ivan Rafferty, Henrik Schoenau-Fog$^{(\boxtimes)}$(iD),
and George Palamas(iD)

Department of Architecture, Design, and Media Technology,
Aalborg University Copenhagen, Copenhagen, Denmark
hsf@create.aau.dk

**Abstract.** Procedural Content Generation can help alleviate the workloads of designers, with the drawback of reducing their control over the
final product. At the same time, many games have a growing focus on
conveying a narrative using environmental storytelling which requires a
high degree of control to embed in a virtual environment. This paper
seeks to reconcile the apparent conflict in these two approaches, and
explores a method in which Procedural Content Generation can be used
to create virtual environments with embedded narratives. This is done
using a Space-Time Drama Manager to dynamically place narrative elements in the virtual environment. A prototype game was developed and
evaluated in a between-groups test (n = 69). Participants in the control condition all experienced the same environment, while those in the
experimental condition each experienced a different procedurally generated environment. No significant difference was found for any of the
measures. This was attributed to the fact that it is possible to convey an
embedded narrative consistently to players, even when the environment
which contains the narrative elements is procedurally generated, yielding
a different experience for each participant.

**Keywords:** Procedural Content Generation · Environmental
Storytelling · Embedded narratives · Narrative experience ·
Space-Time Drama Manager

## 1 Introduction

Procedural content generation (PCG) is becoming an apparent approach of the
Games industry. Many games use PCG for creating and distributing vegetation,
which is time-consuming manual labour if done by hand. In some cases, rather
than aiding and augmenting the workflow of artists and designers, PCG can
remove the need for them in the development pipeline entirely. This could make
the production of games "faster and cheaper" [25]. Using PCG to create game
assets and levels has allowed small development teams to produce successful,
ambitious and content-rich games. For example, game developer Notch used
PCG to develop *Minecraft* [18] as a single-man team.

© Springer Nature Switzerland AG 2020
A.-G. Bosser et al. (Eds.): ICIDS 2020, LNCS 12497, pp. 30–43, 2020.
https://doi.org/10.1007/978-3-030-62516-0_3

However, those environments need to contain highly engaging content and still uphold coherency as explored by Nenad [20]. One aspect which has been overlooked thus far is that of a game's narrative. Most games have some form of narrative, whether it is a simple short background, or an integral part of the game experience. Even in non-story driven games, for example simulation games like The Sims [17], a narrative can emerge. That is to say, a game's narrative does not need to be explicitly told or even planned and written [1].

Explicit methods, such as text and dialogue, are often used to tell a story in a game. These methods are generally unambiguous and lead to the player interpreting the story as per the author's intention. Game stories told this way are often supported by the environment, which is generally hand-crafted to support that narrative. Many story-focused AAA games, such as the *Uncharted* series [19] use this approach. A game like *Marvel's Spider-Man* [12], which relies heavily on procedural tools, needs hand-crafted environments to some degree for story focused elements of the game [23].

When discussing narratives in games a large part comes down to the large elaborate environments in which the characters roam. Games also offer many other possibilities to the user including the mechanics and rules of the game and these parts must also not be forgotten when discerning the narrative possibilities a game offer [16]. In this paper however, the main focus will be on the Virtual Environment (VE) and how this affects the narrative as the PCG will affect the VE and in turn might impact the narrative.

## 2   Background

Historically, storytelling has mostly been viewed in terms of time, i.e. the timing of events in the story (e.g. [22]). However, in a game, not only the time but also the space plays an important role in the storytelling. Due to the existence of a perceivable environment in which the player roams, the environment does not only serve as a container, but can be used to enhance the narrative or even serve as the main actor in the storytelling process, i.e. environmental storytelling (ES) [2,10,29].

Environmental Storytelling originates from Carson [7,8] but is especially known by the definitions from Jenkins [13]. Here ES is defined as different ways of utilising the VE to convey the narrative. In particular Jenkins defined four different types.

– **Evoked narratives** - An existing narrative or diegesis is enhanced by the details in the VE.
– **Enacted narratives** - The player and their character is put centre stage. Here the micro narratives that are created by the player's actions contribute to the overall narrative.
– **Embedded narratives** - Utilises the player's ability to construct the narrative themselves based on the details presented to them

– **Emergent narratives** - The player can construct their own narrative based on encountered events and props in the diegesis. The game does not offer a specific story but instead makes it possible for the player to make stories based on their actions within the game.

Embedded narratives are interesting in terms of PCG as the VE itself contributes to the telling of the narrative and thus, changing this could dramatically change the narrative the player experience.

## 2.1  Embedded Narratives

Embedded narratives can take centre stage or be a supplement tool to game designers. Some games rely almost solely on embedded narratives and they require a high level of comprehension from the player. More often, embedded narratives are used in conjunction with other modes of storytelling. Popular games such as the Uncharted series [19] makes use of this a lot. The attentive player will notice details in the space design that reveals clues of past events and these might be confirmed by the characters after some time with dialogue or cut scenes. Other popular games such as *Portal* [28] and *Half-Life 2* [27] use embedded narratives to reveal narrative information, or hint at sub-plots, which are not provided by the game's narrator. In some cases these embedded narratives even help teach the player game mechanics and concepts.

Embedded narratives can be seen in many popular "walking simulator" style games, such as *Firewatch* [6] or *Gone Home* [11]. In such games, the player wanders around open spaces that are designed to contain valuable pieces of narrative information. Often, they also make use of different kinds of dialogue to express the thoughts of the characters and thus underline the meaning of the pieces. Embedded narratives can however stand on their own as touched upon above, but it does open up for a lot interpretation by the receivers. As an example, the game company Invisible Walls [3] developed the game *Aporia: Beyond the Valley*, with which they researched whether the "open-ended" format of these kinds of ES games affects the engagement and continuation desire of the player [3].

Telling a story exclusively trough the space design puts a lot of strain on the player and might end up yielding totally different narrative experiences from player to player as ES is more of a bottom-up process for the player compared to classic storytelling.

This relationship is addressed by Bruni and Baceviciute [4] as they propose the notion of the *Author-Audience Distance* (AAD) which is a measure of the interpretation gap that occurs between the author and the receiver when telling a narrative. On this continuum, larger levels of abstraction yields more ways the narrative can be interpreted versus smaller levels of abstraction where the narrative is more precise and thoroughly explained (didascalic) thus diminishing the gap between the author and receiver (illustrated in Fig. 1). When designing a narrative it is good to have the level of abstraction in mind, and in terms of ES, and especially in the case of embedded narratives, it is preferred to create a narrative with low abstraction levels as otherwise some users might have the intended interpretation but many others might have different ones. This is of course dependent on whether such a gap in interpretation is wanted or not.

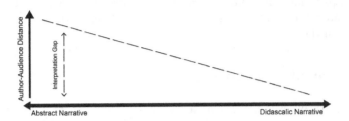

**Fig. 1.** Illustration of the Author-Audience Distance as created by Bruni and Baceviciute [4]

**Staged Areas.** An important part of embedded narratives is the use of *Staged Areas* [13]. A staged area (SA) is a place in the VE that has been designed to specifically convey a part of the narrative. Instead of designing the entire space as an embedded narrative, the game designers instead design smaller specific areas that the player can discover and by that discovery gain more information about the narrative itself. These areas then become equivalent to an event in a classic narrative. So where a writer would repeat specific events or pieces of information to underline the importance, the game designer can create multiple SAs or have the same information in multiple of the SAs of an embedded narrative. In regards to the PCG approach this paper has, the usage of SAs are important as they can potentially serve as a great tool in keeping narrative information similar across different VEs. Designers could hand-craft a number of SAs, which could then be used to populate the generated environment. This maintains some level of designer control, but could still alleviate the workload by allowing designers to focus on key narrative areas, rather than the entire environment.

The use of PCG environments seems to clash on a fairly fundamental level with the use of ES. Jenkins [13] argues that space plays a major role in storytelling in games, and using PCG to create a game environment takes away a lot of control over that space which authors and developers generally desire. It is perhaps therefore that not many narrative-focused games rely heavily on PCG [21].

## 2.2  Procedural Content Generation

In order to create VEs with PCG, it is firstly important to understand how environments are represented by game engines. This study is focused on outdoor environments, known as terrains or landscapes. These are represented most often using a 2D greyscale texture known as a heightmap, though other forms of

VE such as a building interior would be represented with a different data structure. Terrains can be procedurally generated by creating these heightmaps using gradient noise or algorithms such as diamond-square [25]. In addition to the heightmap, further structures are used to represent terrains, such as splatmaps or alpha maps to identify what materials are painted on the surface at different locations, and detail maps to identify where objects such as trees, rocks, or grass are located on the map.

## 3   Experimental Setup

A specific narrative was created as a backstory, and from that five SAs were designed to convey the important parts. The specific story, in this case, is that the player arrives at a seemingly deserted island. As the SAs were the only method for conveying the narrative they included props, logos, and other information that would convey what had happened and what was happening on this island. The first SAs would point towards a military presence but later SAs would reveal that the military had disappeared. The SAs were therefore encountered in a certain order for the presented information to make sense.

A terrain generator was created using the Unity engine [26]. This generator used multiple layers of Perlin noise to create a natural-seeming terrain. Voronoi tessellation was used to create a number of peaks around the terrain, giving designers control of the generation so they could ensure that there would be a number of hills and valleys generated (see Fig. 2). Furthermore, a fall-off map was used to ensure that the heightmap values would approach zero towards the edge of the texture, ensuring that the generated terrains could function as an island, as required by the narrative.

To further enhance the visuals of the terrain, a number of simple erosion simulations were included, which would break up the repetitive patterns of the noise by simulating erosion from rain, rivers, tides and landslides. Splat maps were populated based on the heightmap, so that areas with different heights and slopes would have different materials applied. Likewise, trees and other details were added to the environment using similar height and slope constraints.

**Fig. 2.** Sample terrains generated with Perlin noise, Voronoi tessellation, and Midpoint Displacement with Diamond-Square

To guide the players, a number of points of interest - or *Wienies* [14] - was implemented to ensure they would have a sense of direction that could also be used to determine where the SAs could be spawned (see Fig. 3). By using a Space-Time Drama Manager (STDM) similar to the one described by Schoenau-Fog [24] we could dynamically embed the SAs in the environment no matter where the player was and in the right order to uphold the right narrative sequence of events.

**Fig. 3.** The two points of interest (Wienies) that was used to guide the players

## 4   Methods

To examine if changing the space in which an embedded narrative takes place affects the players, a between-groups evaluation was used. In the control condition, participants experienced an embedded narrative in an environment that is generated with a parametric PCG system, which at runtime has a single dimension of control, i.e. a random seed. This random seed can be used to reproduce environments, and to ensure that participants in this condition experience the same environment as each other i.e. factors such as the topography of the landscape, the distribution of foliage, etc. will remain the same for all participants.

In the experimental condition, participants were presented with a similar VE, also containing an embedded narrative. However in this case the environment was generated from a different random seed for each participant. This means that no two participants would experience the same environment in this condition. For both conditions apply, that the five SAs were created in advance and dynamically placed in the VE. For the control condition, each SA would automatically be placed in the approximately same places as the VE was the same and thus the parameters for the STDM would be the same ultimately yielding the same output if the participants took similar paths (as guided by the wienies).

Previous research like Connor, Greig, and Kruse [9] has compared a procedurally generated environment to a human-designed one. For this paper however, we want to inspect how the difference in VEs across participants affects the experience. Similarly, that project tested the effect on players' immersion whereas we argue the engagement in the narrative is a more suitable measure. To further expand, we also want knowledge about the narrative understanding to see if it is possible to tell a coherent narrative for individual players and whether that the narrative understanding is consistent between players.

All data was gathered via a post-game questionnaire. The methods were pilot tested to ensure the questionnaire yielded the correct results and the prototype functioned as expected. Participants were provided with a link to a website which hosts the application. When launching the application, participants will be randomly assigned to either the control or experimental condition. The random distribution should result in approximately equal numbers of participants in each condition. Once the game was finished, participants were redirected to an online questionnaire, which kept a record of what random seed they had so that the answers in the questionnaire could be associated to the condition they experienced. The questionnaire consists of three sections, which are outlined below:

**1. Narrative Engagement.** The first section of the questionnaire consists of nine Likert items adapted from Busselle and Bilandzic [5]'s Narrative Engagement Questionnaire. This will first and foremost point towards the narrative engagement of the participants but the part concerning narrative understanding will also be used together with the results from Sect. 3.

**2. Narrative Tension.** The second section is a Likert scale concerning the tension in the narrative. This consists of six Likert items that address the progression of the narrative and the participant's attention over time and whether we succeeded in creating suspense. This can then be used to point towards narrative coherency as players would not be able to experience tension in the narrative without also experiencing some level of coherency.

**3. Narrative Coherency.** This section consists of questions about the specific details of the narrative regarding the game experience. There are two questions for each key piece of information, while two are "dummy questions", which ask about non-existent narrative elements. These dummy questions should help indicate if participants have properly understood the narrative (i.e. can identify that these elements were not present), and that they are truthfully responding to the questionnaire. This method has been used in a previous study which was also concerned with participants noticing narrative elements in a VE [15].

These questions are first asked in an open-ended format, followed by multiple-choice. This way the participant will first give their own unbiased understanding of the narrative, before giving an answer that may be biased by the options presented. From the narrative we specified three pieces of key information that the players should be able to get from encountering all the SAs and in the right order. The Key information was:

- There were military personnel at the island at some point

- Something bad happened to them
- There is now a cult on the island

There were multiple dependent variables. For the narrative understanding part there were 8 questions, two for each piece of key information and two dummy questions not concerning any of it. The possible answers and their rank can be seen in Table 1. These ranks will then be summed for each of the pieces of the key information and dummy questions, resulting in a score for each piece of information as well as a collective one for all 8 questions.

**Table 1.** The specific questions asked and the possible answers to those questions, ranked according to how close to the intended meaning they are, i.e. rank 3 answer is the authors intend and rank 2 and 1 are further and further away. The number in the parenthesis indicates what key piece of information that question refers to (1 = The military was on the island; 2 = Something bad happened to them; 3 = There is a cult on the island now; m = misleading)

| Question | Rank 3 | Rank 2 | Rank 1 |
|---|---|---|---|
| Why is the island hidden on maps? (1) | It is government property | It is private property | It is undiscovered |
| Is there anyone else on the island? (3) | Yes | Could be | No |
| Where did the skeletons come from? (m) | I did not see any skeletons | The former inhabitants | Animals |
| Who built the radio tower? (1) | The military | A private company | Natives to the island |
| Where are the ones who built the radio tower now? (2) | Still on the island | Dead | They left the island |
| Why is so much stuff left on the island? (2) | No one left | Everyone left in a hurry | It was useless |
| Who killed the former inhabitants on the island? (m) | They are not dead | A cult | The government |
| Who set fire to the boat? (3) | A cult | The military | It was an accident |

For all applicable scales, Anderson-Darling and Levene's tests were used to determine if the data could be treated as parametric. If the data were non-normal, the data would be log-transformed and tested again for normality. If the data were parametric, they were evaluated with an independent t-test, otherwise with Mann-Whitney U.

## 4.1 Findings

The prototype used for the evaluation was a browser-based game hosted on Itch.io (https://raffba.itch.io/med10). The game was distributed through multiple groups on Facebook to gather as many participants as possible. The application was available for testing for 6 days in the spring of 2020. Over this span of time, 69 participants completed the game and answered the questionnaire. All participants were randomly assigned either the control or the experimental condition which resulted in 37 (29 male, 7 female, 1 other) in the control condition and 32 (24 male, 8 female) in the experimental condition. Both groups has a similar average age of 28.9 for the control and 28.6 for the experimental condition.

**Narrative Understanding.** The log transformed data from the control condition were normally distributed ($\alpha = 0.05$, $A^2 = 0.519$, $A^2 < 0.722$), though the data from the experimental condition were not ($\alpha = 0.05, A^2 = 1.629, A^2 > 0.715$). Therefore the data could not be treated as parametric. Mann-Whitney U indicated that there was no significant difference in understanding between conditions ($U = 467, p = 0.06, r = -0.18$) (see Table 2 and Fig. 4).

**Overall Narrative Engagement.** The summed results from the engagement scale for the control condition were normally distributed ($\alpha = 0.05, A^2 = 0.516, A^2 < 0.722$), as were the data from the experimental condition ($\alpha = 0.05, A^2 = 0.287, A^2 < 0.715$). Levene's test indicated that the difference in variance between conditions was approximately zero, $F(36, 31) = 0.014, p = 0.91$. Therefore the data could be treated as parametric. An independent t-test indicated no significant difference in narrative engagement between conditions ($t = -0.98, p = 0.33, r = 0.12$). See Table 3 for descriptive statistics and Fig. 4 for distributions and box plots.

**Narrative Coherency.** An Anderson-Darling test indicated that the log-transformed data of narrative coherency were neither normally distributed in the control condition ($\alpha = 0.05$, $A^2 = 2.057, A^2 > 0.722$) nor the experimental condition ($\alpha = 0.05$, $A^2 = 1.323, A^2 > 0.715$). However Levene's test did show that the difference in variance between the conditions was approximately zero, $F(36, 31) = 0.292, p = 0.59$. Since the data were not parametric, Mann-Whitney U was used to test the narrative coherency section. This test indicated that between the control group ($Mdn = 15$) and the experimental group ($Mdn = 15$) there was no significant difference in narrative coherency ($U = 533.5, p = 0.24, r = -0.08$). See Table 4 for descriptive statistics and Fig. 5 for distribution and box plots.

From these results a lot of interesting findings can be extracted. Most noticeable is how none of the inferential statistics returned significant results. When comparing the narrative engagement the two samples have equal variances and

**Table 2.** Descriptive statistics of narrative understanding

| Condition | N | Mean rank | Std dev | Median | Sum of ranks |
|---|---|---|---|---|---|
| Control | 37 | 9.513 | 3.576 | 9 | 352 |
| Experimental | 32 | 10.687 | 3.876 | 12 | 342 |
| Total | 69 | | | | |

**Table 3.** Descriptive statistics of narrative engagement

| Condition | N | Mean rank | Std dev | Median | Sum of ranks |
|---|---|---|---|---|---|
| Control | 37 | 24.108 | 5.774 | 25 | 892 |
| Experimental | 32 | 29.469 | 5.562 | 25 | 815 |
| Total | 69 | | | | |

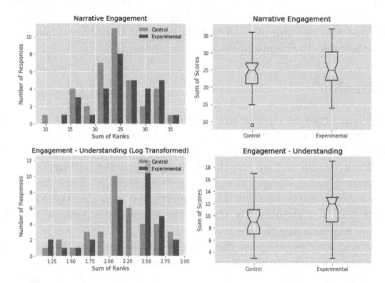

**Fig. 4.** Distribution (Log-transformed) and box plot of narrative understanding (bottom). Despite not having significant results, the distribution indicate a higher mean in the experimental condition. Distribution and box plot of collected narrative engagement (top)

**Table 4.** Descriptive statistics of narrative coherency

| Condition | N | Mean rank | Std dev | Median | Sum of ranks |
|---|---|---|---|---|---|
| Control | 37 | 14.135 | 4.816 | 15 | 523 |
| Experimental | 32 | 15.031 | 4.398 | 15 | 481 |
| Total | 69 | | | | |

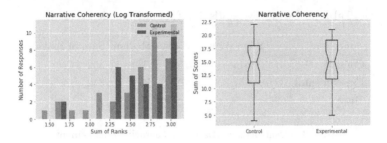

**Fig. 5.** Distribution and box plot of narrative coherency

the independent t-test also shows that there is no significant difference in narrative engagement between them.

For the narrative coherency, the variances are once again equal between the groups and the Mann-Whitney U also showed no significant difference. This indicates that the two groups had similar levels of narrative coherency when analysing the ranks in the multiple-choice questions.

## 5   Discussion

All the data analysis was performed between the two groups to examine how experiencing a different VE influences narrative engagement, tension (suspense), and understanding in players. None of the comparisons between groups yielded any significant results and we can therefore not reject the null hypothesis stating that *there is not a significant difference in engagement levels and narrative coherency between the two groups.* This suggests that changing the VE for every participant does not significantly change the narrative experience on average compared to experiencing the same one.

For the narrative engagement the Levene's test shows that the variances are equal. Beyond checking if the data were parametric, it was important to look for a difference in variance, as it would indicate that the difference in the VEs would mean a difference in the experience for the participants. That this is not the case is interesting, and using different procedurally generated environments cannot be said to influence the narrative engagement of the player.

For the narrative coherency also no significant difference was found showing an equal level between the two groups when looking at the multiple-choice questions. The box plots of the different key pieces of information and the summed responses also shows that the variance is the same for the two groups. This is interesting because for the experimental condition the participants did not experience the same VE, but that did not affect the narrative to such a large degree that it meant a lower narrative understanding. One sub-scale from the narrative engagement measure was similarly about the narrative understanding; looking at this sub-scale also reveals no significant difference. It does however return a low p-value of 0.06 which could indicate a type-II error. By looking at the box plot it can be seen that had the results been significant it would have been in favour of the experimental condition. The reason for a better narrative understanding in this condition might be because the chosen random seed for the control condition actually is not as representative as we thought, and therefore it is more a matter of this yielding lower results, than the experimental yielding higher. This however, can not be proven from these results. It is also worth mentioning that the overall narrative coherency scale is in the range of 0 to 24. The box plots show that in both conditions, 75% of participants scored above 12, meaning that despite the broad distribution, there was a generally high level of narrative understanding.

The aim here was to detect any significant impacts changing the VE for each player would have. Not finding any difference is evidence that it is possible to utilise ES even in an ever changing environment without impacting the engagement and narrative coherency for the player.

The method for measuring the narrative coherency seemed to work as intended. No analysis of how many changed their answer when faced with the choice was made as this would not have added any valuable information. Here we were only interested in the specifics of whether they got the right understanding or not, which an answer to the multiple choice question would reveal, but having them give their own answer first enabled them to consider their own interpretation before being faced with the choice which would be less likely to bias them when choosing the answers.

These multiple-choice questions introduce some biases. They are formulated by the narrative designers, who of course have the "right" interpretation of the narrative in mind when making the questions. Perhaps a better solution would have been to run a preliminary test of narrative coherence with qualitative responses, which would have been coded to generate the multiple-choice items.

# 6   Conclusion

This project developed a prototype game with a PCG environment and an embedded narrative. The results in the between-subject test showed that there was no significant difference in the narrative experience between players all experiencing the same virtual environment (VE) and players all experiencing different VEs. Furthermore, similar levels of variance of narrative coherency, narrative tension, and narrative understanding across conditions indicate that there was external consistency between participants. This shows that it is possible to dynamically embed a narrative in the space of a game and still uphold similar levels of narrative engagement and coherency in all participants regardless of which environment they experience.

Though it is difficult to infer a lot in regards to specific levels of these measures compared to more classical designed game spaces it does show promise for the combination of techniques of Procedural Content Generation (PCG) and Environmental Storytelling (ES).

There are many different methods which can be used for PCG, but a constraint-based PCG system allows designers to specify high-level requirements for the environment, which is well suited to being combined with ES and embedded narratives. This allows designers to still specify requirements for the environment, while reducing the amount of time needed to craft expansive worlds, allowing them to focus on the finer detail of important narrative elements and SAs. Furthermore, this opens up possibilities for enhanced replayability for narrative games in PCG environments.

# References

1. Aylett, R., Louchart, S.: Being there: participants and spectators in interactive narrative. In: Cavazza, M., Donikian, S. (eds.) ICVS 2007. LNCS, vol. 4871, pp. 117–128. Springer, Heidelberg (2007). https://doi.org/10.1007/978-3-540-77039-8_10
2. Baynham, M.: Narratives in space and time: beyond "backdrop" accounts of narrative orientation. Narrat. Inq. **13**(2), 347–366 (2003)
3. Bevensee, S.H., Dahlsgaard Boisen, K.A., Olsen, M.P., Schoenau-Fog, H., Bruni, L.E.: Aporia – exploring continuation desire in a game focused on environmental storytelling. In: Oyarzun, D., Peinado, F., Young, R.M., Elizalde, A., Méndez, G. (eds.) ICIDS 2012. LNCS, vol. 7648, pp. 42–47. Springer, Heidelberg (2012). https://doi.org/10.1007/978-3-642-34851-8_4
4. Bruni, L.E., Baceviciute, S.: Narrative intelligibility and closure in interactive systems. In: Koenitz, H., Sezen, T.I., Ferri, G., Haahr, M., Sezen, D., Ç atak, G. (eds.) ICIDS 2013. LNCS, vol. 8230, pp. 13–24. Springer, Cham (2013). https://doi.org/10.1007/978-3-319-02756-2_2
5. Busselle, R., Bilandzic, H.: Measuring narrative engagement. Media Psychol. **12**(4), 321–347 (2009). https://doi.org/10.1080/15213260903287259
6. Santo, C.: Firewatch. Campo Santo Ç atar (2016)
7. Carson, D.: Environmental storytelling: creating immersive 3D worlds using lessons learned from the theme park industry (2000). https://tinyurl.com/ybj6vrcm. Accessed 8 Mar 2020
8. Carson, D.: Environmental storytelling, part ii: bringing theme park environment design techniques to the virtual world (2020). https://tinyurl.com/yca4kd9s. Accessed 8 Mar 2020
9. Connor, A.M., Greig, T.J., Kruse, J.: Evaluating the impact of procedurally generated content on game immersion. Comput. Games J. **6**(4), 209–225 (2017). https://doi.org/10.1007/s40869-017-0043-6
10. Fina, A.D.: Crossing borders: time, space, and disorientation in narrative. Narrat. Inq. **13**(2), 367–391 (2003)
11. Fullbright: Gone Home. The Fullbright Company (2013)
12. Insomniac Games: Marvel's Spider-Man. Sony Interactive Entertainment (2018)
13. Jenkins, H.: Game design as narrative architecture. In: Ardrip-Fruin, N., Harrigan, P. (eds.) First Person: New Media as Story, Performance, and Game, pp. 118–130. MIT Press, Cambridge (2004)
14. Korkihort, J.: The Origin of the Disneyland Wienie. MousePlanet (2016). https://tinyurl.com/y7gplufe. Accessed 13 Mar 2020
15. Kvisgaard, A., et al.: Frames to zones: applying mise-en-scène techniques in cinematic virtual reality. In: 2019 IEEE 5th Workshop on Everyday Virtual Reality, WEVR 2019, 23-03-2019. IEEE, United States (2019). https://doi.org/10.1109/WEVR.2019.8809592

16. Larsen, B.A., Schoenau-Fog, H.: The narrative quality of game mechanics. In: Nack, F., Gordon, A.S. (eds.) ICIDS 2016. LNCS, vol. 10045, pp. 61–72. Springer, Cham (2016). https://doi.org/10.1007/978-3-319-48279-8_6
17. Maxis: The Sims 4. Electronic Arts (2014)
18. Mojang: Minecraft. Mojang and Microsoft Studios (2011)
19. Naughty Dog: Uncharted. Sony Interactive Entertainment (2007–2017)
20. Nenad, M.: Designing game worlds. Coherence in the design of open world games through procedural generation techniques, pp. 353–363 (2018). https://doi.org/10.1145/3270316.3270319
21. Portnow, J., Floyd, D.: Procedural generation - how games create infinite worlds - extra credits (2015). https://www.youtube.com/watch?v=TgbuWfGeG2o. Accessed 11 Feb 2020
22. Ricoeur, P.: Narrative time. Crit. Inq. **7**(1), 169–190 (1980)
23. Santiago, D.: Procedurally crafting manhattan for "Marvel's Spider-Man". GDC (2019). https://www.gdcvault.com/play/1025765/Procedurally-Crafting-Manhattan-for-Marvel. Accessed 11 Feb 2020
24. Schoenau-Fog, H.: Adaptive storyworlds: utilizing the space-time continuum in interactive digital storytelling. In: Schoenau-Fog, H., Bruni, L.E., Louchart, S., Baceviciute, S. (eds.) ICIDS 2015. LNCS, vol. 9445, pp. 58–65. Springer, Cham (2015). https://doi.org/10.1007/978-3-319-27036-4_6
25. Shaker, N., Togelius, J., Nelson, M.J.: Procedural Content Generation in Games. Springer, Cham (2016). https://doi.org/10.1007/978-3-319-42716-4
26. Unity Technologies: Unity (2020). https://unity.com
27. Valve: Half-Life 2. Valve Corporation (2004)
28. Valve: Portal. Valve Corporation (2007)
29. Zakowski, S.: Environmental storytelling, ideologies and quantum physics: narrative space and the bioshock games. In: DiGRA/FDG &# 3916 - Proceedings of the First International Joint Conference of DiGRA and FDG. Digital Games Research Association and Society for the Advancement of the Science of Digital Games, Dundee, Scotland (2016)

# Crafting Interactive Narrative Games
# with Adversarial Planning Agents
# from Simulations

Chris Miller[✉], Mayank Dighe, Chris Martens, and Arnav Jhala

North Carolina State University, Raleigh, USA
{cwmille6,mdighe,ahjhala}@ncsu.edu, martens@csc.ncsu.edu

**Abstract.** This paper describes Adversario, an implemented system for creating interactive narrative games centered around an adversarial planner directing autonomous agents to achieve goals that conflict with player goals. Through our implementation, we present a novel framework for creating interactive narrative games wherein the autonomous agents guided by the adversarial planner have rich and varied attributes derived from a complex social simulation. By doing this, we show that it is possible to craft interactive narrative games with a set of carefully curated domain actions to produce interactions in a procedurally generated world with rich characters. Our system bridges several gaps between interactive narrative game design, procedural content generation, and classical AI planning. We demonstrate this by transforming a simulation-planning based narrative generation system into a system for streamlining the process of crafting interactive narrative games involving rich procedurally generated agents.

## 1 Introduction

This paper describes the development of the interactive narrative game Adversario wherein the core game mechanic revolves around the player competing against a real-time adversarial planner controlling several autonomous agents. Two key distinguishing features of Adversario are: 1) each agent (including the player) is procedurally generated with detailed personalities and relationships with other agents derived from an underlying social simulation and 2) generated plans are re-evaluated each turn of the game allowing for an adaptive adversarial planner. The real-time nature of the adversarial planner, the richness of character information, and our framework for streamlining the communication between the playable game and its underlying AI planner allow for the generation of interactive narrative game levels and character behaviors that are dynamic, adaptive, and varied. We present this system as a novel application of AI planning and procedural content (PCG) generation in crafting interactive narrative games that also aims to address the need for PCG in games at run time [8,14]. We have consciously chosen to incorporate AI planning techniques in the design of this system since previous research has shown that planning

© Springer Nature Switzerland AG 2020
A.-G. Bosser et al. (Eds.): ICIDS 2020, LNCS 12497, pp. 44–57, 2020.
https://doi.org/10.1007/978-3-030-62516-0_4

techniques are well-suited for story generation and interactive narrative experiences [3,14,20,22]. This has been demonstrated in several commercial games and more fully-realized academic virtual environments for interactive narrative experiences [1,2,11–13,17].

Adversario has been developed with Miller et al.'s Stories of the Town [10] as its simulation engine with the purpose of redesigning the system to support a more interactive and accessible application domain; in this case interactive narrative games. In its current implementation, Adversario utilizes planning techniques based on Glaive, a state-space narrative planner [18], to maintain narrative coherence. It uses a custom implementation of Talk of the Town, a richly detailed social simulation for domain generation that is input to the planner [15,18]. The Stories of the Town system [10] provides a framework for extracting information from a complex social simulation, representing that information in a way compatible with a classical AI plan solver, and translating derived planning problem solutions into a specific format (e.g. narratives). Adversario illustrates a new, modularized application domain for Stories of the Town's simulation-planning based narrative generation that allows for more interactive engagement with the underlying complex simulation/planning system via an interactive narrative game.

## 2 Related Work

### 2.1 Stories of the Town

Stories of the Town is described as a system that automatically generates narratives by recombining three distinct approaches to narrative generation: simulation, narrative planning, and context-free grammars [10]. Examples of these approaches include Talk of the Town, Glaive, and Tracery with the first two being directly incorporated into Stories of the Town [4,5,15,18].

Stories of the Town's narrative generation process begins by running an instance of the Talk of the Town simulation. This simulation runs until a predetermined amount of data (e.g. character relationships, number of characters, etc.) has been generated. This data is then extracted from the simulation as local JSON files which can be easily referenced in various stages of the narrative generation process. Once processed, this data is reformulated as a planning problem description compatible with Glaive which subsequently returns a solution to the planning problem as a series of discrete action steps to reach a set of narrative goals. Lastly, narratives are generated by using the PCFG to expand each solution step as well-structured sentences resulting in a coherent (at least in terms of causal relationships for a planner), semantically well-structured story.

### 2.2 The Best Laid Plans

The Best Laid Plans is an interactive narrative adventure game wherein the player assumes the role of a goblin minion tasked with successfully completing its mission of retrieving a particular item in spite of NPCs who thwart the player's plans while attempting to achieve their own goals [19].

There are however a few key differences between Adversario and The Best Laid Plans. In The Best Laid Plans, the player constructs and provides a *complete plan* to the adversarial planner and *the planner only begins crafting opposing plans once it has access to the player's complete plan.* Essentially, in The Best Laid Plans, the adversarial planner plans against a complete plan that does not change while it generates an opposing plan. In Adversario however, adversarial plans are reevaluated each time the player executes an action capable of affecting the current iteration of the adversarial plan. This is possible because in Adversario the AI planner does not take a complete plan as input but instead checks the current state of the game as agents affect the game at each discrete timestep. Secondly, the agents in The Best Laid Plans are all predetermined. In Adversario however, agents are supplemented with various attributes such as personalities and relationships with other characters derived from the rich simulation history present in Stories of the Town [10]. These personalities and relationships, which also change with each instantiation of the game, directly influence the range of actions each individual agent may pursue. As we will show, this results in a game in which the actions agents take to foil the player's plans and the player's range of successful strategies for winning the game can change with each playthrough.

### 2.3   Reactive Planning for Drama Management

It should be noted that Adversario is not the first system to set out to incorporate plan-based AI behaviors in dynamic, interactive game environments [7,9,21]. Façade is a well-known example of one such system wherein the player is thrust into an evolving and adaptive narrative involving themselves and two other NPCs [9]. Adversario has several commonalities with these systems including adaptive planning, a dynamic and interactive environment, and a hierarchical system for managing its game state in in coordination with an underlying planner. However, Adversario goes beyond these commonalities by also incorporating a richer variety of game state information derived from Stories of the Town into the instantiation of each game session. Character personalities and relationships change with each play of the game allowing for each exploration of the dynamic game environment to lead to new situations and, ultimately, interactive narrative experiences. Addtionally, it does this from the perspective of an adversarial planning game.

## 3   Game Design

### 3.1   Gameplay

In Adversario, the player assumes the role of an unnamed hero tasked with collecting as many shards as possible. Throughout the course of the game, the player competes against several other AI agents being orchestrated by the main

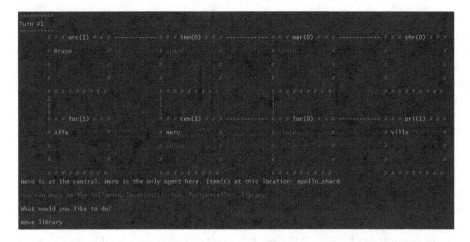

**Fig. 1.** A section of Adversario's interface. At the start of each turn the player is presented with the current state of the game via a map and supplementary text describing the player's current location and possessions. This is also the interface through which the player performs actions.

adversary simply called *Villain*. Similar to the player, the ultimate goal of the main adversary and their minions is to collect as many shards as possible. The player and AI agents have access to a range of actions—some of which can only be performed when a character has fulfilled certain preconditions and some of which can only be performed by the player or only by a NPC. Regardless, all actions affect the state of the game in some way.

Gameplay takes place on a map of various connected regions which may contain items and also serve as markers for each agent's location at each state of the game as shown in Fig. 1. The game proceeds in a turn-based fashion with the player being able to take one action at the start of each turn. Actions available to the player include, but are not limited to, moving from one place to another, retrieving an item at the player's current location, and using a held item. After the player performs their action for that turn, the AI planner then instructs one of the NPCs to perform an action. Thus, the player and the collective adversaries both execute no more than one action per turn. The effects of an agent's actions are reflected immediately in the game world such that the player's action at the beginning of a turn may result in the planner being forced to change its plan in that same turn (e.g. if the player used up an item the adversary was planning to use). The game progresses in this alternating cycle of player and AI actions until all of the shards have been collected.

## 3.2   Characters

One of the key, motivating design factors of Adversario is having autonomous agents with complex and varied attributes capable of affecting gameplay in noticeable ways in each playthrough. This is in part possible due to the amount of information extracted from characters in Stories of the Town [10]. Additionally, rather than having these attributes randomly generated from a corpus of possible attributes, we now have access to a simulation history which can be used to trace the development of particular character attributes. This ultimately allows for each iteration of Adversario to utilize character information from simulated characters with detailed histories describing the development of their attributes and relationships with other agents.

Rather than instantiating each agent in Adversario as a direct instantiation of a character from Stories of the Town, we instead assign each agent (including the player) a *persona*. In the context of Adversario, a persona represents the character from Stories of the Town from which an agent derives all of their personality and relationship attributes. Namely, if the player's persona is John Davis, the player will assume all of John Davis' attributes while still retaining their in-game title of "Hero". Figure 2 illustrates a character profile for the hero who has assumed the persona of Alan Rossler. The main reason for us choosing this representation is to allow the representation and description of characters in the narrative planner and game to focus more on their roles as opposed to whoever happens to be their persona each playthrough. Each agent in Adversario is assigned a persona at the beginning of the game based on the results of a network analysis process detailed in Sect. 4.2.

**Fig. 2.** A minimal character profile for the player who starts the game with the title of 'Hero'. In this instance, the hero assumes the persona of a character from Stories of the Town named Alan Rossler and inherits all of their attributes (e.g. personality, relationships, occupation).

## 4    Game Architecture

Figure 3 illustrates the general architecture and process workflow of the Adversario system. In this section we describe each module of the system in detail and how each relates to the game.

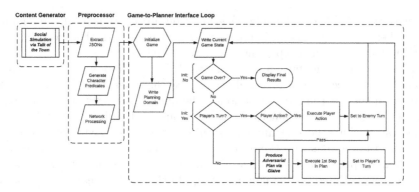

**Fig. 3.** Architecture and process flow of the Adversario system. The system can be described through the processes of three modules: a content generator, a preprocessor, and a game-to-planner interface.

**Content Generator:** The content generator is the default starting point of Adversario. The content generator runs the standard social simulation in Stories of the Town. This process simulates characters existing within a simulated town and ultimately generates a large collection of events and characters with attributes developed during the simulation. Once this simulation halts, the simulation is handled by the preprocessor.

**Preprocessor:** Adversario's preprocessor represents one of our main contributions towards developing a framework for mapping data from a social simulation to an interactive narrative game that incorporates that data. The preprocessor begins by extracting character information from Stories of the Town's implementation of Talk of the Town as easily referencible lists (e.g. JSONs) [10,15]. The preprocessor then prepares for this information to be utilized by Adversario's narrative planner (i.e. Glaive) by mapping each character's attributes to first-order logic predicates and storing these predicates in local files [18]. Listing 1.1 shows an excerpt from such a generated file.

```
(occupations Alfred_Beiner engineer)
(attracted_to_women Alfred_Beiner)
(adult Alfred_Beiner)
(likes Alfred_Beiner Wanda_Dier)
(male Alfred_Beiner)
```

**Listing 1.1.** Excerpt of a PDDL predicate file for a simulated character named Alfred Beiner.

The last step of the preprocessor before the game is initialized is the creation and analysis of a network constructed of characters from the content generator. Each character is represented as a node in a multigraph—a graph in which nodes can have more than one edge. As each character node is processed, graph edges are added whenever a character possesses an attribute that relates to another character. For example, with the predicate *(likes A B)*, an edge is added from A to $B$ with the label *likes*. The network generation process thus results in a multi-graph wherein each character is represented as a node with their relationships to other characters being represented as directed edges.

An important contribution of the network is that it provides a more systematic way to decide how to handle simulated character data. Upon creation, information such as the number of nodes, the number of edges, which node has the most edges, etc., is output to the game's console. This information provides useful insights into the vast amount of information generated. The density of edges for example illustrate the overall connectedness of the various characters generated. In particular, we utilize this network to determine how to assign agent personas. Based on the number of agents that will appear in Adversario, say $n$ characters, we process the network to find the $n$ characters with the most amount of inward and outward edges. In context, these $n$ character nodes represent the characters with the most relationships with other characters. Of these $n$ characters, we term the *most influenced* character to be the character with the most outward edges and the *most influential* character to be the character with the most inward edges. The reason for this representation is apparent from the observation that *(likes A B)* with a directed edge from $A$ to $B$ describes character $B$ as exhibiting some property or history that influenced $A$ to like $B$. With this information, the player's agent in Adversario is assigned a persona based on the most influenced character and the main antagonist is assigned theirs based on the most influential character. The reason for this assignment is motivated by fostering the AI planner's ability to pursue certain actions being directly impacted by other agents' relationships with that agent. The remaining agents in the game are assigned their personas from the remaining set of $n$ characters.

**Game-to-Planner Interface:** The game-to-planner interface (G2PI) module represents the second unique contribution of our system's architecture. The G2PI module provides a structured framework for constant communication between the front-end interactive narrative game, the game logic and state representation, and the underlying narrative planner. In essence, this module translates game state information from the playable game to the narrative planner and vice-versa. In practice, this allows the adversarial planner to generate plans based on the current state of the game and have these planned actions' effects reflected back in the playable game as they are executed.

Before entering the main game loop, the game is initialized by assigning characters' personas, generating item and character locations, etc. This process generates the initial state of the game. The next step in the G2PI module is the writing and outputting of a planning domain file for Glaive [18]. In order to produce solutions for solving narrative planning problems, Glaive takes as input two distinct files: a problem definition and a domain description. The problem definition describes the instance of a problem to be solved by the planner whereas the domain description states the actions, objects, and constants that exist in any narrative problem being solved. Similar to early planning systems, actions in Glaive are defined primarily in terms of preconditions and effects and can be reused for multiple purposes in generated plans [6,16].

Adversario's G2PI module expedites communication and consistency between the narrative planner and application domain. A clear example of this is that in Adversario, all information passed to the narrative planner is written automatically as the user defines the game logic. Whenever users define new actions for the interactive narrative game in Adversario, each type of object (e.g. agent, item, location) involved in that action is marked as a parameter for a Planning Domain Definition Language (PDDL) action. At the same time, users are also required to pass the preconditions and effects of their new action. Listing 1.2 illustrates an example for an action defined in the game. With this information being supplied while the game logic is being defined, users are effectively writing the planning domain as they write the game's logic without being required to separately define each or continue to check for consistency between the planner and the interactive game.

```
(:action move
    :parameters (?char - character ?from - location ?to - location )
    :precondition (and ( at ?char ?from )
                       (adjacent ?from ?to )
        . . .
    :effect (and ( at ?char ?to )
                ( not ( at ?char ?from )
        . . .
```

**Listing 1.2.** Excerpt of a PDDL action description for the action 'move'. In the interactive narrative game and the planner, the action describes a character moving from one location to another.

The next process in the G2PI module is essentially the starting point for the main game loop. In the *Write Current Game State* process, all state information about the current game session is output as a problem definition file—this is the other input file that Glaive requires. As aforementioned, the problem definition describes the specific instance of a problem to be solved and is represented as a list of first-order logic predicates. Here, we also define the ultimate end goal for the planner as having all of the shards collected. *Essentially, this process exports each state of the game as a problem that the planner must solve.* Game state information includes the locations of agents, the locations of items, any items an agent possesses, etc., as shown in Listing 1.3. This process forms a core part of the G2PI module as it provides a method for the narrative planner to be logically in sync with the actual game being played.

```
( at Hero central )
( has Villain zeus_shard )
( adjacent central inn )
( item_at hera_shard market )
( friends Villain Alfa )
( enemies Hero Villain )
```

**Listing 1.3.** Excerpt of a problem definition describing the current game state for the eventual problem to be solved by the narrative planner.

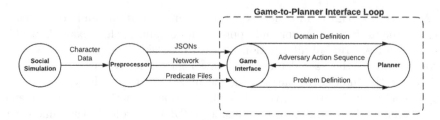

**Fig. 4.** A simplified illustration of Adversario's dataflow. Character information is passed from a social simulation to a preprocessor which outputs several forms of data for the interactive narrative game to utilize. This information is handled by the overall game-to-planner interface which communicates between the forward-facing game's logic and the underlying narrative planner.

Once the game state is written, the game checks if the game has been declared to be over. In Adversario, the game is declared to be over when all of the shards have been collected. When this happens, the game loop is halted and final results are displayed to the player. If the game proceeds however, the game then checks whose turn it is. If it is the player's turn, they are allowed to input an action via a shell terminal and the game then executes that action, ends the player's turn, and re-enters the game loop by writing the updated current game state. As shown in Fig. 3, players are also able to skip their turn thereby switching to the enemy's turn without taking an action. When it is the enemy's turn however, this process changes. The enemy's turn begins by using Glaive to produce a solution to the planning problem definition generated at the top of each game loop cycle. This problem definition is used as input along with the domain definition generated in the 2nd step of the G2PI module. (Note that the domain definition file is only generated once since it does not change throughout the course of the game.) Now that Glaive has knowledge of the current state of the game, the types of actions agents can perform, and has a well-defined goal of every shard being taken by some agent (incl. the player), Glaive returns a planning problem solution describing how to manipulate agents (except for the player since the planner does not control them) to achieve its goal. Listing 1.4 is an excerpt of a solution from one turn of an example game.

```
(:steps (take Bravo ares_shard townhall)
        (move Bravo townhall library)
        (take Bravo zeus_shard library)
        (take Alfa demeter_shard market)
        (move Alfa market fortuneteller)
        (bestow Alfa demeter_shard Villain fortuneteller)
        ...
```

**Listing 1.4.** Excerpt of a generated solution for allowing the adversary to accomplish its goal. The action sequence involves two agents, Bravo and Alfa, moving, taking, and giving items throughout the game.

In order to prevent the adversary from completing the game too quickly, we then instruct the game to execute *only the 1st step of a returned solution*. The instructed agent then completes this action, the next turn is set to the player's turn, and the process returns back to the top of the game loop wherein the updated game state is written. If the planner does not return a solution or exceeds our predetermined solving time however, the enemy's turn is skipped and the player regains control of the game.

**The Overall Architecture:** With all of the information presented above, we now summarize the overall architecture and process flow of the Adversario system. This simplified architecture is illustrated in Fig. 4. Adversario begins by running a **content generator** built upon Stories of the Town's implementation of Talk of the Town [10,15]. This content generation module generates a set of characters with detailed attributes spanning personalities and relationships. This information is then passed to a **preprocessor** that extracts this information in various forms (e.g. JSONs, specialized predicate files) and generates and analyzes a network of these characters to determine which characters should be utilized in the interactive narrative game. In practice, this network analysis determines each game agent's persona (i.e. the character from which that agent will derive specific relationships and attributes). The game is then initialized— a process which determines the location of agents, items, etc. This constitutes the first step of the **game-to-planner interface**. Around this same time, the types of actions and objects available in the interactive game are *automatically* processed to generate a planning domain file compatible with a PDDL planner (in this case Glaive) [18].

From this point, users enter the main game loop cycle which always starts with writing the current state of the game as a problem definition file which describes the current state as a series of first-order logic predicates. This step allows the planner to be in sync with the actual playable game. The game alternates between player and enemy turns until the end goal of the game (i.e. having all of the shards being collected) is achieved. On the player's turn, the player is able to execute at most one action which will immediately affect the game's state. This action is then processed, the next turn is set to the enemy's turn, and gameplay resumes from the top of the game loop. On the enemy's turn, the current state of the game and range of actions available to planning agents (not including the player) are passed to Glaive via the problem definition and domain definition files respectively. Glaive then returns a sequence of action steps describing how to instruct agents to achieve the end goal of the game based on the current state of the game. The first step of this returned plan is then executed by the respective agent and gameplay resumes from the top of the game cycle with it now being the player's turn. In the event that the planner fails to return a solution or exceeds a predetermined solving time, the enemy's turn is skipped. The game checks for whether or not every shard in the game has been collected at the top of each turn and if so, the game loop is exited and final results are displayed to the player.

# 5   Results

In this section we present a gameplay session from Adversario and reflect on our current implementation of Adversario.

The *CONVINCE* and *FEUD* actions share an identical color due to the fact that these actions are distinctly different from the other actions—*these actions can only be executed if two agents' personas have certain relationships with each other*. For example, *CONVINCE* can only be performed if the player tries to perform the action with an agent who likes them (i.e. *(likes agent player)*). Given that these attributes are derived from personas which change each instantiation of the game, this action might not always be available to the player. *CONVINCE* also has a side-effect that can foster even more interesting behaviors. When the player convinces another agent, they not only receive an item from that agent but that agent might also start a feud with another agent. Similar to *CONVINCE*, *FEUD* also requires specific relationship conditions to be met in order for it to be performed. In this case, *FEUD* can only be performed if an agent has been convinced by the player *and* if there exists another agent that the instigating agent is enemies with (i.e. *(enemies instigator other)*).

Figure 5 illustrates an actual gameplay session from Adversario via a series of tables. The tables should be read left-to-right, top-to-bottom. The first table contains a legend for the subsequent tables. In the subsequent tables, each column corresponds to a turn and each row corresponds to an agent. The player is depicted as the agent in the first row of agents. The highlighted column shows the current turn number along with that agent's executed action on that turn. The remaining columns describe each agent's (except for the player's) actions for the next four turns. It should be noted that in the actual game, the player is not provided with any information describing other agents' future actions; namely the player can only assume what other agents might do. It is only for illustrative development and research purposes that we explicitly provide this information.

Actions that involve two agents (e.g. giving and stealing) are highlighted with a different color shared between the two agents involved when that action is executed. In the game shown in Fig. 5, there are six shards to be collected. The game ends once all six shards have been collected. Through the figure, one can also see how subsequent plan steps change as the player interacts with the game. Even as the player moves from one location to another, the adversarial planner reevaluates its plans. As mentioned in the game's implementation, it can be seen that adversarial plans do not change when the player does not perform an action (e.g. T5).

In its current form, Adversario accomplishes the goals that we set out to achieve. The game supports the instantiation of agents who derive their attributes from a social simulation while also allowing these derived attributes to directly impact gameplay and the underlying planner. As the player takes actions in the game, the planner continuously adapts to the current state of the game in order to discover new ways to obstruct the player whose goals directly conflict with those of the planner. In essence, we have successfully implemented an interactive narrative game featuring real-time adversarial planning and detailed

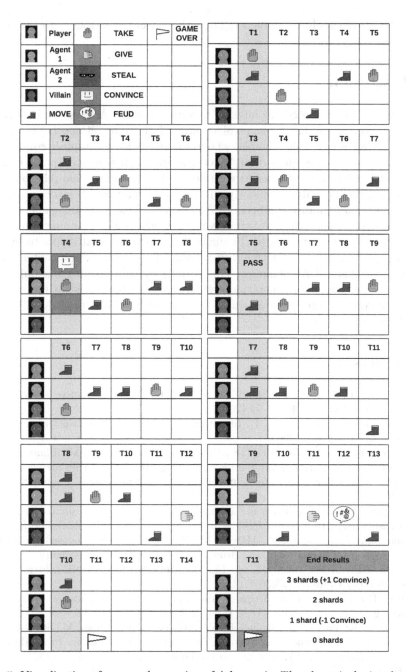

**Fig. 5.** Visualization of a gameplay session of Adversario. The player is depicted as the agent in the first row of agents with all of the remaining agents being controlled by the adversarial planner. Different icons correspond to different actions that agents take or plan to take at each turn. These actions are Move, Take, Give, Steal, Convince, Feud, and Game Over.

agent attributes capable of influencing how the player can engage with the game and its agents' behaviors.

## 6   Discussion

In this paper, we presented our interactive narrative game Adversario. In Adversario, the core game mechanic revolves around the interactions between the player and an adversarial planner who both strive to accomplish competing goals. The two main design goals of Adversario are: 1) allowing each procedurally generated agent to be instantiated with detailed personalities and relationships with other agents capable of directly affecting gameplay and 2) incorporating a framework for communication between Adversario's forward-facing game and its narrative planner such that real-time, adaptive, adversarial planning is feasible in an interactive narrative game. In summation, Adversario attempts to bridge several gaps between interactive narrative game design, procedural content generation, and classical AI planning. This is done by transforming a simulation-planning based narrative generation system into a system for streamlining the process of crafting interactive narrative games involving rich procedurally generated agents.

## References

1. Cavazza, M., Charles, F., Mead, S.J.: Character-based interactive storytelling. IEEE Intell. Syst. **17**(4), 17–24 (2002)
2. Champandard, A., Verweij, T., Straatman, R.: Killzone 2 multiplayer bots. In: Game AI Conference (2009)
3. Charles, F., Lozano, M., Mead, S., Bisquerra, A.F., Cavazza, M.: Planning formalisms and authoring in interactive storytelling. In: Technologies for Interactive Digital Storytelling and Entertainment, TIDSE 03 Proceedings. Fraunhofer IRB Verlag (2003)
4. Compton, K., Filstrup, B., et al.: Tracery: approachable story grammar authoring for casual users. In: Seventh Intelligent Narrative Technologies Workshop (2014)
5. Compton, K., Kybartas, B., Mateas, M.: Tracery: an author-focused generative text tool. In: Schoenau-Fog, H., Bruni, L.E., Louchart, S., Baceviciute, S. (eds.) ICIDS 2015. LNCS, vol. 9445, pp. 154–161. Springer, Cham (2015). https://doi.org/10.1007/978-3-319-27036-4_14
6. Fikes, R.E., Nilsson, N.J.: Strips: a new approach to the application of theorem proving to problem solving. Artif. Intell. **2**(3–4), 189–208 (1971)
7. Garbe, J., Kreminski, M., Samuel, B., Wardrip-Fruin, N., Mateas, M.: StoryAssembler: an engine for generating dynamic choice-driven narratives. In: Proceedings of the 14th International Conference on the Foundations of Digital Games, pp. 1–10 (2019)
8. Levine, K.: Narrative legos. In: Game Developers Conference (2014)
9. Mateas, M., Stern, A.: Structuring content in the façade interactive drama architecture. In: AIIDE, pp. 93–98 (2005)

10. Miller, C., Dighe, M., Martens, C., Jhala, A.: Stories of the town: balancing character autonomy and coherent narrative in procedurally generated worlds. In: Proceedings of the 14th International Conference on the Foundations of Digital Games, pp. 1–9 (2019)

11. Orkin, J.: Three states and a plan: the AI of fear. In: Game Developers Conference, vol. 2006, p. 4 (2006)

12. Pizzi, D., Charles, F., Lugrin, J.-L., Cavazza, M.: Interactive storytelling with literary feelings. In: Paiva, A.C.R., Prada, R., Picard, R.W. (eds.) ACII 2007. LNCS, vol. 4738, pp. 630–641. Springer, Heidelberg (2007). https://doi.org/10.1007/978-3-540-74889-2_55

13. Porteous, J., Cavazza, M., Charles, F.: Applying planning to interactive storytelling: narrative control using state constraints. ACM Trans. Intell. Syst. Technol. (TIST) 1(2), 1–21 (2010)

14. Robertson, J., Young, R.M.: The general mediation engine. In: Tenth Artificial Intelligence and Interactive Digital Entertainment Conference (2014)

15. Ryan, J.O., Summerville, A., Mateas, M., Wardrip-Fruin, N.: Toward characters who observe, tell, misremember, and lie. In: Eleventh Artificial Intelligence and Interactive Digital Entertainment Conference (2015)

16. Ryan, M.L.: Possible Worlds, Artificial Intelligence, and Narrative Theory. Indiana University Press (1991)

17. Thomas, J.M., Young, R.M.: Annie: automated generation of adaptive learner guidance for fun serious games. IEEE Trans. Learn. Technol. 3(4), 329–343 (2010)

18. Ware, S.G., Young, R.M.: Glaive: a state-space narrative planner supporting intentionality and conflict. In: Tenth Artificial Intelligence and Interactive Digital Entertainment Conference (2014)

19. Ware, S.G., Young, R.M.: Intentionality and conflict in the best laid plans interactive narrative virtual environment. IEEE Trans. Comput. Intell. AI Games 8(4), 402–411 (2015)

20. Young, R.M.: Notes on the use of plan structures in the creation of interactive plot. In: AAAI Fall Symposium on Narrative Intelligence, pp. 164–167 (1999)

21. Young, R.M., Riedl, M.O., Branly, M., Jhala, A., Martin, R., Saretto, C.: An architecture for integrating plan-based behavior generation with interactive game environments. J. Game Dev. 1(1), 1–29 (2004)

22. Young, R.M., Ware, S.G., Cassell, B.A., Robertson, J.: Plans and planning in narrative generation: a review of plan-based approaches to the generation of story, discourse and interactivity in narratives. Sprache und Datenverarbeitung, Spec. Issue Formal Comput. Models Narrative 37(1–2), 41–64 (2013)

# A Systematic Analysis of User Experience Dimensions for Interactive Digital Narratives

Ashwathy T. Revi$^{(\boxtimes)}$ ⓘ, David E. Millardⓘ, and Stuart E. Middletonⓘ

University of Southampton, Southampton, UK
atr1n17@soton.ac.uk

**Abstract.** Providing intelligent feedback to aid authoring has been proposed as a way to speed up authoring, give the author more control, and to enable the authoring of more complex interactive narratives. However, there is little research investigating what concrete feedback items would be useful for interactive digital narrative (IDN) creators. In this paper, we discuss potentially useful feedback items in relation to authoring goals and concerns. We perform a systematic literature review to make a list of concrete feedback items of interest related to the most emphasised concern of authoring - the effect of the interactive narrative on the user. We identify 47 User Experience (UX) dimensions in the IDN literature that could serve as useful feedback items, covering 8 categories - Agency, Cognition, Immersion, Affect, Drama, Rewards, Motivation and Dissonance. This list combines and untangles how different IDN researchers have interpreted and expressed interest in the complex idea of UX in the past decade and gives us insight into what concrete aspects of UX might be useful to estimate via automated feedback.

**Keywords:** Intelligent feedback · Co-creation · User experience · Interactive narratives · Authoring goals · Mixed creation

## 1 Introduction

Authoring in Interactive Digital Narratives (IDN) is very challenging. Creators often have to compromise on either the interactive complexity or the quality of the IDN artefact created [31,32]. Most efforts at increasing interactivity, by relying on emergent narratives for example [32], do so at the expense of authorial control and/or quality. Subsequent efforts, like drama managers [33] try to retain complexity and improve quality by introducing new architectures and more sophisticated technology [34]. While some authoring tools support debugging and visualization of the underlying structure [35], as complexity increases these become hard to fully comprehend. A mixed initiative approach has been proposed as a way to overcome this issue of dissociative authoring [29] by giving the author feedback on the potential experiences possible within their work,

University of Southampton.

referred to as Narrative Analytics in [28] and Intelligent Narrative Feedback in [29]. Similarly, Artificial Intelligence (AI) and Natural Language Processing (NLP) open up a lot of opportunities for generating intelligent feedback; for example, sentiment networks [38], emotional arcs [51]. By using this feedback to inform authoring, the author could make use of the affordances offered by a complex system while retaining visibility and control, and by extension, quality.

But what exactly is the feedback required by authors? Due to IDN's interdisciplinary and relatively novel nature, collecting these by finding and interviewing a representative set of IDN creators would be challenging. In this paper we have therefore taken an alternative path, and present a systematic review of IDN literature, focusing on the goals and concerns of authors in order to identify an appropriate set of feedback items. Many papers talk about authoring goals, including expressing a specific intent [29], maximizing affordances of IDN [41] and creating a certain effect in the user [30,41]. However, the most emphasised goal is a good User Experience (UX). Importance of UX is also reflected in how IDN creators often use UX evaluation to measure their success [34].

Therefore, in this paper we focus on identifying the UX dimensions of IDN, with the idea that this could then form the basis of useful automated feedback to authors. The paper is structured as follows: Sect. 2 discusses related work and background, Sect. 3 outlines the methodology used for the systematic review, Sect. 4 presents the results, Sect. 5 discusses findings and potential applications, and Sect. 6 outlines future work and conclusions.

## 2  Related Work

Previous work has identified some high level categories of useful feedback items for authors. But these deal either with specific problems, for example structural analysis to identify dead ends or short experiences [28], or are not comprehensive in that they focus on specific aspects such as emotional experience [29]. Visualisation is an important element of mixed creation, for example [39] focuses on low level visualization of interaction design as progression maps. Similarly, [37] discusses automatic structural analysis using graph theory, and [26] suggests some low level computational metrics that show correlation with user experience dimensions. We are interested in higher level insights. For example, [40] talks about a similar idea of collecting parameters and then figuring out how to map them to corresponding cognitive processes but limits the scope of their discussion to two feedback items - suspense and surprise.

UX is a very broad area. Audience Studies is a whole field devoted to studying and developing theories surrounding audience's reception of media including IDN [54], and there are conceptualizations of UX (like those presented in [6] and [48]) which describe the process of experience or the relationship between design and experience. However, these do not easily extend to evaluation frameworks or feedback. A number of evaluation frameworks of UX have been proposed for IDN that could form this basis. For example, [42] consolidates Murray's high level interpretation of UX (as Immersion, Agency and Transformation [41]) with

Roth's framework [43], to get twelve concrete UX dimensions. Whereas [44] uses GEQ [45], NEQ [46], and NTQ [47] to create a specialised UX questionnaire. These are overlapping, but non-identical frameworks. Concepts like affect, curiosity, suspense and identification from [42] are closely related to the emotional engagement dimension in NEQ but are not quite the same. NEQ includes a narrative understanding dimension which is not talked about in [42]. Roth and Koenitz [42] notes how immersion is defined in different ways and settles on its broader high level definition, whereas in work by Kleinman et al. [44] immersion is simply the "capacity of the game contents to be believable".

There is clearly inconsistency and overlap in how UX is defined and understood by different researchers [30]. It is this that motivates our systematic literature review of papers talking about user experience in IDN.

## 3  Methodology

Our systematic literature review follows the established methodology set out in [57], this is formally five steps: outlining the research question, selecting keywords, selecting appropriate electronic resources, constructing a search method, and defining inclusion and exclusion criteria. The research question we are asking in the review is: *What concrete aspects of UX are of interest to IDN creators?*, and the following section outlines our approach to the other steps.

### 3.1  Constructing the Sample

Springer[1] was chosen as the electronic resource because it is a database that has good coverage of IDN specific research (for example, ICIDS proceedings). While other resources like CHI Play contain literature on HCI, they tend to be more focused on games. Since we are aiming for IDN focused literature we would have had to filter out a lot of papers. Only papers from the past ten years (2010–2020) were included in order to ensure that the UX dimensions identified were relevant to current approaches and technology. Saturation sampling was chosen as the search method since the potential set of matches was too large to exhaustively analyse. The following search phrase was built by listing commonly used keywords for UX and IDN, searching for the intersection and adjusting to reduce number of irrelevant results:

*((user OR player) NEAR/1 (evaluation OR experience OR experiences OR study OR studies OR engagement OR satisfaction OR enjoyment)) AND ("adventure game" OR "adventure games" OR "hypertext fiction" OR "emergent narrative" OR "emergent narratives" OR (interactive NEAR/2 (media OR cinema OR narrative OR narratives OR drama OR dramas OR fiction OR story OR stories OR storytelling) OR (game OR games) NEAR/1 (narrative OR narratives))*

Any paper having the above keywords is likely to talk about some aspect of user experience of IDN in some way. However, for practical reasons, we chose

---

[1] Springer Link - https://link.springer.com/.

the following inclusion and exclusion criteria to select papers that are likely to give us the most insight into which parameters are of interest:

1. *Does the paper focus sufficiently on narrativity and interactivity?* There are many types of IDN including Interactive Cinema, Mixed Reality, Storytelling Games and Documentaries and these were all included. Papers were excluded if they were discussing linear narratives, or did not put enough focus on narrativity. The framework proposed in [30] distinguishes narrative goals from system goals. Edutainment and games with a weak narrative component are examples of IDN applications that prioritize system goals over narrative goals. We wish to include only papers that focus primarily on narrative goals. For example, [58] is excluded because while it touches on narrative goals (affect, immersion), the primary focus is on learning.

2. *Is the paper about formalizing, measuring or evaluating user experience or some aspect of user experience of IDN or does it include some evaluation of it?* The kind of papers that are most likely to tell us which aspects of UX are of interest to IDN creators are those that include user experience studies or evaluation frameworks. Such papers also break down user experience into more concrete, measurable parameters. Papers that conduct computational evaluation instead of a user study also give us similar insights. Papers that theoretically formalize UX or discuss it in the context of IDN theory could help concretize UX and make the list more complete.

3. *Is the discussion on user experience in the paper detailed and concrete enough to provide relevant insight?* Some papers that discuss UX theoretically do so at a very high level [48–50] so including them is not useful for our purpose of concretizing it.

## 3.2   Coding Process

To enable saturation sampling, the results of the search were filtered and coded in batches of 20 papers. Each paper in the batch was compared to the criteria, and if it matched was reviewed, and coded as per the following process:

1. UX dimensions were interpreted based on how UX was structured or evaluated in each paper. This was sometimes explicit, for example [42], but sometimes it had to be interpreted from how the authors discussed UX, such as [1] where they evaluate UX in terms of felt and actual understanding, perceived interactivity, narrativity and dissonance.

2. Sometimes, the papers include a hierarchical representation of UX dimensions [42] but since we are interested in concrete concepts only leaf nodes (called *low level concepts* in this paper) are added to the codebook.

3. If any overlap between the low level concepts is encountered while merging to codebook, the conflicting low level concepts are deconstructed based on their definitions and separated out.

This process is continued until all the papers in the batch are processed. We then repeated the process for the next batch, until we encountered a batch with no new codes (saturation point). The number of papers included and new codes added per batch can be seen in Table 1.

**Table 1.** Systematic literature review - saturation sampling

| Batch number | Number of selected papers | Number of new codes |
|---|---|---|
| 0 (seed papers) | 4 | 28 |
| 1 | 10 | 13 |
| 2 | 6 | 4 |
| 3 | 6 | 2 |
| 4 | 5 | 0 |

### 3.3  Challenges, Nuances and Subjective Decisions

We are interested in subjective user experience. Properties completely intrinsic to either system or player are excluded (eg- details pertaining to interaction design like number of choices and extrinsic goals, motivation to start playing, player skills). Some properties, though subjective, are still so intrinsic or specific to either the user or the system that modelling them as intelligent feedback is unlikely to be either feasible or useful - eg Loss of self consciousness, or the desire to save some particular non player character (NPC). In such cases, if an underlying generalizable concept can be discerned based on why the author was interested in this, then it is this concept that is coded. For example loss of self consciousness may have been collected as an indicator of presence. Desire to save an NPC may be interesting because it indicates the degree of attachment or identification with that character. In order to scope and contain growth of the codebook, concepts that are specific to a certain kind of narrative layer (eg - video quality), type of IDN (eg - distance between locations) or multiplayer experiences (eg - social relatedness) and concepts collected for contextualization (eg reasons for quitting, suggestions for improvement) are also excluded.

The structure of UX is specified to different degrees in different papers. For example, it is very clear in [42] but vague in [3]. When the structure of UX is not clear in a paper, its interpretation and consequently the process of identifying the leaf nodes becomes more subjective. This impacts the decision regarding which concepts are concrete enough to be coded as low level. When a concept's concreteness is not clear from a paper, it is decided by considering the context and its description in other papers. This adds a level of subjectivity. Papers sometimes talk about UX concepts that are not central to the scope of the paper - in the background sections, follow up questions, when describing causal relationships to other concepts or in general discussion. Such mentions are often so brief that interpretation of meaning and concreteness would be too subjective, making merging them into the codebook difficult. So concepts that are not central to the framework or evaluation presented in the paper are excluded. This, again, becomes more subjective if the structure is unclear as discussed above. Coding for performed by the first author and the results were reviewed and discussed within the research team.

Splitting up old codes and revising the definitions are not seen as adding new concepts. When a code is split, the numbers are revised retrospectively. If enough information is not available to resolve an overlap between two concepts, the more concrete or well defined concept is kept and the other one is discarded. If overlap is minimal, both are kept. Concepts that are very similar are merged into a single low level concept and subtle differences are kept track of in the description.

# 4  Results

This process yielded 47 codes which can be placed under 8 categories as shown in Tables 2 and 3. The third column shows the number of papers in which the code was found. Note that the use of each concept in its original paper might vary slightly from the definitions given below. Sometimes only a subset of the code is mentioned. For example papers with an interest in just excitement or anxiousness, were counted as interested in game or at game affect type and/or affect intensity accordingly. Papers that don't mention the code but a higher level concept, for example, believability, were counted for all sub-codes based on its interpreted meaning. Papers where a code is mentioned very briefly or not as part of the central work were not counted. The last column shows the references as well as the sense in which concepts were originally used in those papers before they were split up or absorbed either fully or partly into the corresponding code. The following sections describe each category in more detail.

## 4.1  Agency

Six dimensions related to agency were identified: **Autonomy** or perceived freedom to do as the user wanted is related to the number and quality of options as well as navigational freedom. **Effectance** or perceived meaningfulness and impact of choices is related to being able to recognize when and how the story-world was causally affected by the player's actions through clear feedback. This is a requirement for **control** which means being able to intentionally bring about specific goals and outcomes. [5] is interested in the idea of persuasion or degree to which the player was persuaded to take a particular action. Conversely, [34] talks about the degree to which the player felt like he was being manipulated by the system. These concepts were coded as **manipulation**. [6] talks about **personalisation** or the extent to which the user feels that they experienced a story unique to their actions. This is related to the extent to which a user feels like they expressed their intention and extent to which they feel like the system understood this expression and has responded to it accordingly. Additionally **usability**, which refers to the user's experience with both the hardware and the software from a HCI perspective is also put under this category.

**Table 2.** Codebook: UX dimensions

| Category | Code | Num | References |
|---|---|---|---|
| Agency | Autonomy | 6 | Navigational freedom [12,13], availability of desired choices [17,27] autonomy [34,42] |
| | Effectance | 7 | Effectance [11,15,21,42] unnecessary choices [17] meaningful interaction [30], actions had no effect [27] |
| | Control | 4 | Flow [10,15] control [3,17] |
| | Manipulation | 3 | Likelihood of successful manipulation [5] autonomy [42] non limitation [34] |
| | Personalization | 1 | Personalization [6] |
| | Usability | 7 | Usability [3,11,17,19,26,42] effort to change story [19] |
| Cognition | Narrative Understanding | 9 | Epiphany [9], observed understanding [7] understanding theme, intent [1,12–14] narrative understanding [16,44] intelligibility [30] |
| | Game Understanding | 9 | Flow [6,10] clear feedback, goals [15] expectations [11,14,26] understanding how to interact [8,19] system intelligibility [30] |
| | Perceived Understanding | 4 | Epiphany [9] closure [30] perceived understanding [1,7] |
| | Logical Consistency | 11 | Epiphany [9] believability [3,7,11,14,26,42] visual communication [16] surprise, incongruency [40] immersion [44] coherence [34] inconsistencies [3,34] |
| | Ambiguity | 1 | Level of abstractness [30] |
| | Perceived Realism | 10 | Believability [7,26,42] character believability [3,11,14] intelligent response [15] perceived realism [16] presence, immersion, naturality [44] breaks - sense of strangeness [34] |
| | Challenge | 5 | Difficulty [6,10,15] was demanding [17] flow [10,42] |
| | Storification | 4 | Variation in experienced story [12] degree of storification [27] emergent narrative [24] narrative understanding, mental models [44] |
| Immersion | Presence | 7 | Sensory, imaginative immersion [10] presence [11,16,42,44] Loss of Self Consciousness [15] emotional, spacial immersion [21] |
| | Suspension of disbelief | 4 | Believability [7,26,42] role identification [14] |
| | Degree of focus | 10 | Absorption, attention, focus [8,15–17,44] flow [6,10,11,44], transformation of time [15], attraction [18], awareness of surroundings [19] |
| | Object of focus | 3 | Attraction towards [8,18] reference [20] |
| | Identification | 9 | Role adoption [11,26] cognitive/behavioral responses [15] emotional engagement [16] suspense [42] identification [14,16,34,42] perspective [20] like/dislike [4] |
| | Continuity | 7 | Flow [6,10,11,22], inconsistencies [3,34], breaks [34], relatedness [4] |
| | Aesthetics | 4 | Sensory immersion [10] pleasantness [11,17,26] |
| | Safety | 1 | Safety [6] |

**Table 3.** Codebook: UX dimensions contd

| Category | Code | Num | References |
|---|---|---|---|
| Affect | In game affect intensity | 17 | Suspense, tension, anxiety [7,10,12,21,25,26,42], Affect, emotional state [7,10,11,15,26,42], Enjoyment [7,11,22], Flow [10,44], emotional engagement/immersion [13,16,21,44], behavioural responses [15], Reception [16], closure [6], Curiosity [42], Pleasure [34], Surprise [3,42] |
| | In game affect type | 15 | Suspense [7,10,12,25,42] affect [7,10,11,15,24,42] enjoyment [7,11] flow [10,42,44] reception [16] closure [6] emotional state [18,26] curiosity [42] emotional engagement [44] pleasure [34] surprise [3] |
| | At game affect intensity | 5 | Annoyance [17], enjoyment [26,34,42] interest, fun [44] flow [42,44] |
| | At game affect type | 6 | Annoyance [17] affect-technical [24] enjoyment [26,34,42] flow [42,44] interest, fun [44] |
| Drama | Curiosity | 10 | Curiosity [3,7,11,13,14,17,22,26,42] temporal immersion [21] |
| | Closure | 2 | Narrative closure [6,30] |
| | Uncertainty | 13 | Epiphany [9], Suspense [7,10–12,26,40,42], imaginative/emotional immersion [10,21] curiosity [26,42] believability [11] predictability [3,17,40] Surprise [3,40] |
| | Expectation | 9 | Suspense [7,11,12,26,40] imaginative/ emotional immersion [10,21] expectation [14,40] surprise [3,40] |
| | Desired outcomes | 3 | Satisfaction with ending [17] dreaded/desirable outcomes [17,42] |
| | Novelty | 1 | Novelty [17] |
| | Variety | 2 | Variation in experienced story [12] variety [34] |
| | Themes | 4 | Theme [12,13] images [34] escalating climax [3] |
| Rewards | Eudaimonic appreciation | 4 | Eudaimonic appreciation [7,42] meaningfulness, take-away [14] pleasures of reflection [6] |
| | Sense of reward | 5 | Auteletic Experience, intrinsic rewards [15] feeling rewarded [3,6,17] curiosity [42] |
| | Learning | 1 | Cognitive responses [15] |
| | Interest | 2 | Increase of interest in the topic [14] edurability [17] |
| Motivation | To continue | 5 | Continuation desire [1,2,24,44] engagement [22] |
| | To replay | 5 | Desire to replay [10,12,17,23,24] |
| | To interact | 2 | Desire to explore/get involved [13] motivation to change story [19] |
| | Objectives | 1 | Objectives [24] |
| | Activities | 1 | Activities [24] |
| | Reinforcement | 2 | Catharsis [6] accomplishments [24] |
| Dissonance | Interactivity | 3 | Frequency choices [17] participation [21] interactivity [1] |
| | Narrativity | 1 | Perceived narrativity [1] |
| | Dissonance | 4 | Disruption [17,21] narrative play [23] separation of interactivity and narrativity [1] |

## 4.2  Cognition

Eight dimensions related to cognition were identified. **Logical consistency** is consistency of events and character behaviour as well as the themes and messages of the narrative. **Ambiguity** is the level of abstraction or clarity of the content. According to [30], narrative is said to be unambiguous when the content predisposes audience towards one and only one interpretation. **Degree of storification** is the extent to which a self-narrated story and mental models are created internally in the player. **Narrative understanding** is a measure of how much the user understands the story as intended by the author. **Game understanding** refers to how much the user understands game elements like clarity of goals, rules, boundaries and how to interact with and influence story. **Perceived understanding** is the degree to which users felt like they understood the narrative rather than their interpretation of it being conjecture. **Challenge** is a measure of how difficult users found the game and if they found that level of difficulty necessary, meaningful and enjoyable. **Perceived realism** is the game's closeness or resonance with reality judged on plausibility of events and character behaviour, perceived intelligence of system and characters and the degree to which the experience does not feel engineered.

## 4.3  Immersion

Eight dimensions of Immersion were identified. **Presence** is related to the degree to which the user feels like they have left the actual world and entered the story, the feeling of being in the mediated space with mediated people. **Suspension of disbelief** refers to the degree to which the player loses awareness of the medium through which the experience is transmitted. **Degree of focus** or absorption refers to the degree to which the user's abilities and attention is focused on the experience. Sometimes there is also interest in the **Object of Focus** - game, narrative or reality frame. **Identification** or connection refers to the perspective adopted by the user as well as affective disposition towards different story elements. It includes the degree to which users identify with the role and the story as well as the degree of attachment, empathy, and sympathy felt towards different characters. **Continuity** is the degree and duration of ongoing continuous involvement in the storyworld, merging action and awareness and the absence of breaks in the narrative caused by sudden changes in tone or the occurrence of abrupt, unconnected events. **Aesthetic pleasantness**, or the degree to which the user finds the setting and layout appealing, is also included in this category. Though not commonly discussed, [6] also talks about immersion in relation to the user's perceived **Safety** and how past a certain level of immersion, the user is at the risk of feeling unsafe.

## 4.4  Affect

While affect encompasses a vast range of experiences, we listed it in the codebook as in game and at game affect type and intensity. **Affect intensity** is the intensity of emotional arousal and engagement felt. **Affect type** refers to the type of affect. More than 40 types of affects were listed from all papers together (e.g. Exhilaration, Anger, Frustration, etc.). Listing them out as separate codes does not seem useful but an important distinction to make is between affect felt towards the application or the game itself versus the same emotions aroused by events in the narrative. This is similar to the idea of at-game and in-game frustration described in [52]. This is differentiated as **at-game** or **in-game** affect.

## 4.5   Drama

This category relates to traditional narratology and drama. **Curiosity** is defined here as the degree of interest in the story, progression and actionable possibilities, or simply, a desire to find out more. **Themes** refers to topics, images and tropes that the user identified in the experience. **Novelty** refers to perceived newness and innovation in different elements of the experience. **Variety** refers to number and diversity of choices, experiences and actions. **Closure** is the degree to which users felt like the experienced story was complete and that the relevance of all story elements was revealed [30]. Suspense and surprise were absorbed into other concepts including **uncertainty** or predictability of progression and system responses and **expectation** aroused by a situation or narrative prompt. Suspense also includes the code - **desired outcomes** which refers to the user's dreaded and desirable consequences as well as satisfaction with how the story progressed.

## 4.6   Rewards

Four dimension related to rewards were identified. **Eudaimonic appreciation** is a measure of perceived cognitive and emotional meaningfulness of the experience (in terms of deducing general life lessons, insights into the meaning of life or how much the source challenges perceptions and life stories of the user.) **Sense of accomplishment** is related to the degree to which the player found the experience intrinsically rewarding and considers his investment in it worthwhile. **Learning** is a measure of how much playing game improved skill, knowledge or intelligence and arousal of **interest** stands for the degree to which the experience created an interest in the topic or in IDN.

## 4.7   Motivation

Six dimensions related to motivation were identified - **Objectives** refers to intrinsic objectives that the user developed while playing. **Activities** refers to what types of actions (interface/solve/ sense/ socialize/experience story and characters/ explore/experiment/create/destroy) users planned to or wanted to perform. **Reinforcement** refers to types of rewards that kept them motivated (completion, advancement or achievement). This was included in this category rather than Rewards because they were interested in the reward in the context of continuation desire. The remaining dimensions - intensity of desire **to continue** playing, desire **to interact** and desire **to replay** are self explanatory.

### 4.8   Dissonance

The final category has only three codes. **Interactivity** refers to the user's perception and satisfaction of the degree of participation or interactivity. **Narrativity** refers to user's perception of the game's focus on narrative elements as compared to its game elements. **Dissonance** stands for the degree of perceived dissonance or harmony experienced between game and narrative elements.

## 5   Discussion

The main contribution of this paper is the codebook shown in Tables 2 and 3. While there have been many efforts to formalize and break down UX into simpler dimensions, they have resulted in many different interpretations - each concept being defined slightly differently in different papers and concepts overlapping each other to varying degrees in their many definitions. Our intention is not to promote what we believe UX should look like, or to claim that this is a definitive list of UX dimensions, rather the work presented here brings together and untangles those interpretations of UX expressed in the IDN literature, showing us ultimately what concrete dimensions of UX can be considered to be of interest to this specific community. The counts associated with each concept also gives us some insight into the relative interest and usefulness of modelling different dimensions of UX, although there will be other factors at play (for example, how commonly they are discussed in other communities, or the availability of instruments with which to measure them). The references column also tells us in what sense the interest was originally expressed.

Researchers are often interested only in specific aspects of UX but this table may be used in evaluation to give a broader and more complete understanding of UX for IDN, and to identify dimensions that are considered less frequently. For example, while effectance, autonomy and usability are widely evaluated, concepts like control, manipulation and personalization are given less attention, even though they might provide useful insights about the user's experience of agency. Other commonly used evaluation frameworks like [42] and [45] can be seen as focusing on a subset of the codes listed.

The main motivation for our list is so it can be used as a starting point for generating automated feedback for the author to assist authoring. For example, in game affect type and intensity are concepts that seem to be of interest to most IDN creators and there seems to be a good amount of literature on affect detection using NLP techniques(eg- [51,53]). The work presented in this paper can act as a starting point for such an investigation. Mapping these UX dimensions against a literature review of NLP techniques will give us insight into such possibilities. In the case of some of these concepts, like perceived realism and logical consistency, it is more straightforward to see what properties of the source cause the desired effects in the user. On the other hand, concepts like presence and degree of focus have complex causal relationships with system and content properties as well the other concepts and would be more difficult to model. Work in media psychology and audience studies like [54,55] and [56] discusses some of these concepts and the nature of their relationships with each other and the source more closely.

Authors usually want to create a certain pattern of effects on the user. For example, [42] talks about cyclical building up and relieving of curiosity. While it might be possible for the author to visualize, predict and create this effect when writing linear stories, it becomes hard to keep track of this when the space of potential stories grows. However, if curiosity, expectation, uncertainty and affective responses can be automatically modelled, then it should be possible to reflect this to the author for all the possible paths through their narrative, allowing them to more efficiently tailor the content and tune its effects on the user along all branches, resulting in better authorial control and user experience.

## 6   Conclusion

In this paper, we have examined what the IDN community considers to be the important UX dimensions for its users, readers and players. Our goal is to understand what automated feedback might be useful to IDN authors. To gather feedback items that will help the author we performed a systematic review of UX in the IDN literature. This process untangles the many overlapping interpretations of UX by different IDN researchers and yields a list of 47 feedback items covering 8 categories: Agency, Cognition, Immersion, Affect, Drama, Rewards, Motivation, and Dissonance. Our future work will investigate AI and NLP techniques that will help automatically estimate these. Integrating such feedback to an authoring environment would not only help detect problems but would also allow authors to closely tailor the experience for their users without massive-scale iterative playtesting. It could free them to write more complex narratives without losing sight of how each branch of those narratives impacts the user.

Authoring goals go beyond UX, and these could also be assisted by automation. For example, the desire to express a specific authorial intent calls for feedback at a lower level than UX. This is in part accomplished by visualizations such as those in Novella [35] and progression maps [39], but as complexity grows, more insightful views like sentiment networks, maps, timelines and dramatic arcs are also worth considering. Reviewing commonly applied narrative devices, formalisms, conventions and authoring practices might tell us which would be most useful. Similarly reviewing critical analyses of IDN works and IDN theory might show us what feedback items can help the author maximise the use of IDN affordances or train them in the art of IDN [36]. This might also mean feedback that helps them fluently use the authoring tool (e.g. system feedback [29]).

We hope that this research can become a foundation stone for these future mixed-initiative approaches. By focusing on the dimensions of UX specifically of interest to the IDN community we have shown the range of feedback that automation might usefully provide, as well as framing the existing work on UX as an evaluation method. Ultimately, providing IDN authors with automated feedback items should not only allow individual authors more control, but by enabling new complexity, it should also help IDN to mature as an art form.

# References

1. Bevensee, S.H., Dahlsgaard Boisen, K.A., Olsen, M.P., Schoenau-Fog, H., Bruni, L.E.: Project aporia – an exploration of narrative understanding of environmental storytelling in an open world scenario. In: Oyarzun, D., Peinado, F., Young, R.M., Elizalde, A., Méndez, G. (eds.) ICIDS 2012. LNCS, vol. 7648, pp. 96–101. Springer, Heidelberg (2012). https://doi.org/10.1007/978-3-642-34851-8_9

2. Bevensee, S.H., Dahlsgaard Boisen, K.A., Olsen, M.P., Schoenau-Fog, H., Bruni, L.E.: Aporia – exploring continuation desire in a game focused on environmental storytelling. In: Oyarzun, D., Peinado, F., Young, R.M., Elizalde, A., Méndez, G. (eds.) ICIDS 2012. LNCS, vol. 7648, pp. 42–47. Springer, Heidelberg (2012). https://doi.org/10.1007/978-3-642-34851-8_4

3. Seif El-Nasr, M., Milam, D., Maygoli, T.: Experiencing interactive narrative: a qualitative analysis of Façade. Entertain. Comput. 4(1), 39–52 (2013). https://doi.org/10.1016/j.entcom.2012.09.004

4. Vriesede, T., Nack, F.: StoryStream: unrestricted mobile exploration of city neighbourhoods enriched by the oral presentation of user-generated stories. In: Si, M., Thue, D., André, E., Lester, J.C., Tanenbaum, J., Zammitto, V. (eds.) ICIDS 2011. LNCS, vol. 7069, pp. 231–242. Springer, Heidelberg (2011). https://doi.org/10.1007/978-3-642-25289-1_25

5. Figueiredo, R., Paiva, A.: "I'm Sure I Made the Right Choice!" - towards an architecture to influence player's behaviors in interactive stories. In: Si, M., Thue, D., André, E., Lester, J.C., Tanenbaum, J., Zammitto, V. (eds.) ICIDS 2011. LNCS, vol. 7069, pp. 152–157. Springer, Heidelberg (2011). https://doi.org/10.1007/978-3-642-25289-1_16

6. Patrickson, B.: Multi-user interactive drama: a micro user drama in process. In: Si, M., Thue, D., André, E., Lester, J.C., Tanenbaum, J., Zammitto, V. (eds.) ICIDS 2011. LNCS, vol. 7069, pp. 199–206. Springer, Heidelberg (2011). https://doi.org/10.1007/978-3-642-25289-1_22

7. van Enschot, R., Boogaard, I., Koenitz, H., Roth, C.: The potential of interactive digital narratives. Agency and multiple perspectives in *Last Hijack Interactive*. In: Cardona-Rivera, R.E., Sullivan, A., Young, R.M. (eds.) ICIDS 2019. LNCS, vol. 11869, pp. 158–169. Springer, Cham (2019). https://doi.org/10.1007/978-3-030-33894-7_17

8. Socas-Guerra, V., González-González, C.S.: User attention in nonlinear narratives: a case of study. In: Cipolla-Ficarra, F., Veltman, K., Cipolla-Ficarra, M., Kratky, A. (eds.) CCGIDIS 2011. LNCS, pp. 104–111. Springer, Heidelberg (2012). https://doi.org/10.1007/978-3-642-33760-4_9

9. Di Pastena, A., Jansen, D., de Lint, B., Moss, A.: "The link out". In: Rouse, R., Koenitz, H., Haahr, M. (eds.) ICIDS 2018. LNCS, vol. 11318, pp. 206–216. Springer, Cham (2018). https://doi.org/10.1007/978-3-030-04028-4_21

10. Vayanou, M., Ioannidis, Y., Loumos, G., Kargas, A.: How to play storytelling games with masterpieces: from art galleries to hybrid board games. J. Comput. Educ. 6(1), 79–116 (2019). https://doi.org/10.1007/s40692-018-0124-y

11. Roth, C., Klimmt, C., Vermeulen, I.E., Vorderer, P.: The experience of interactive storytelling: comparing "Fahrenheit" with "Façade". In: Anacleto, J.C., Fels, S., Graham, N., Kapralos, B., Saif El-Nasr, M., Stanley, K. (eds.) ICEC 2011. LNCS, vol. 6972, pp. 13–21. Springer, Heidelberg (2011). https://doi.org/10.1007/978-3-642-24500-8_2

12. Schoenau-Fog, H., Bruni, L.E., Khalil, F.F., Faizi, J.: Authoring for engagement in plot-based interactive dramatic experiences for learning. In: Pan, Z., Cheok, A.D., Müller, W., Iurgel, I., Petta, P., Urban, B. (eds.) Transactions on Edutainment X. LNCS, vol. 7775, pp. 1–19. Springer, Heidelberg (2013). https://doi.org/10.1007/978-3-642-37919-2_1

13. Schoenau-Fog, H., Bruni, L.E., Khalil, F.F., Faizi, J.: First person victim: developing a 3D interactive dramatic experience. In: Aylett, R., Lim, M.Y., Louchart, S., Petta, P., Riedl, M. (eds.) ICIDS 2010. LNCS, vol. 6432, pp. 240–243. Springer, Heidelberg (2010). https://doi.org/10.1007/978-3-642-16638-9_32

14. Roth, C.: The 'Angstfabriek' experience: factoring fear into transformative interactive narrative design. In: Cardona-Rivera, R.E., Sullivan, A., Young, R.M. (eds.) ICIDS 2019. LNCS, vol. 11869, pp. 101–114. Springer, Cham (2019). https://doi.org/10.1007/978-3-030-33894-7_11

15. Moser, C., Fang, X.: Narrative control and player experience in role playing games: decision points and branching narrative feedback. In: Kurosu, M. (ed.) HCI 2014. LNCS, vol. 8512, pp. 622–633. Springer, Cham (2014). https://doi.org/10.1007/978-3-319-07227-2_59

16. Zagalo, N., Louchart, S., Soto-Sanfiel, M.T.: Users and evaluation of interactive storytelling. In: Aylett, R., Lim, M.Y., Louchart, S., Petta, P., Riedl, M. (eds.) ICIDS 2010. LNCS, vol. 6432, pp. 287–288. Springer, Heidelberg (2010). https://doi.org/10.1007/978-3-642-16638-9_44

17. Kolhoff, L., Nack, F.: How relevant is your choice? In: Cardona-Rivera, R.E., Sullivan, A., Young, R.M. (eds.) ICIDS 2019. LNCS, vol. 11869, pp. 73–85. Springer, Cham (2019). https://doi.org/10.1007/978-3-030-33894-7_9

18. Grinder-Hansen, A., Schoenau-Fog, H.: The elements of a narrative environment. In: Koenitz, H., Sezen, T.I., Ferri, G., Haahr, M., Sezen, D., Çatak, G. (eds.) ICIDS 2013. LNCS, vol. 8230, pp. 186–191. Springer, Cham (2013). https://doi.org/10.1007/978-3-319-02756-2_23

19. de Lima, E.S., Feijó, B., Barbosa, S., Furtado, A.L., Ciarlini, A., Pozzer, C.: Draw your own story: paper and pencil interactive storytelling. In: Anacleto, J.C., Fels, S., Graham, N., Kapralos, B., Saif El-Nasr, M., Stanley, K. (eds.) ICEC 2011. LNCS, vol. 6972, pp. 1–12. Springer, Heidelberg (2011). https://doi.org/10.1007/978-3-642-24500-8_1

20. Theune, M., Linssen, J., Alofs, T.: Acting, playing, or talking about the story: an annotation scheme for communication during interactive digital storytelling. In: Koenitz, H., Sezen, T.I., Ferri, G., Haahr, M., Sezen, D., Çatak, G. (eds.) ICIDS 2013. LNCS, vol. 8230, pp. 132–143. Springer, Cham (2013). https://doi.org/10.1007/978-3-319-02756-2_17

21. Vosmeer, M., Schouten, B.: Interactive cinema: engagement and interaction. In: Mitchell, A., Fernández-Vara, C., Thue, D. (eds.) ICIDS 2014. LNCS, vol. 8832, pp. 140–147. Springer, Cham (2014). https://doi.org/10.1007/978-3-319-12337-0_14

22. Soares De Lima, E., Feijý, B., Furtado, A.L.: Video-based interactive storytelling using real-time video compositing techniques (n.d.). https://doi.org/10.1007/s11042-017-4423-5

23. Mitchell, A., McGee, K.: Supporting rereadability through narrative play. In: Si, M., Thue, D., André, E., Lester, J.C., Tanenbaum, J., Zammitto, V. (eds.) ICIDS 2011. LNCS, vol. 7069, pp. 67–78. Springer, Heidelberg (2011). https://doi.org/10.1007/978-3-642-25289-1_8

24. Schoenau-Fog, H.: Hooked! – evaluating engagement as continuation desire in interactive narratives. In: Si, M., Thue, D., André, E., Lester, J.C., Tanenbaum, J., Zammitto, V. (eds.) ICIDS 2011. LNCS, vol. 7069, pp. 219–230. Springer, Heidelberg (2011). https://doi.org/10.1007/978-3-642-25289-1_24
25. Bída, M., Černý, M., Brom, C.: Towards automatic story clustering for interactive narrative authoring. In: Koenitz, H., Sezen, T.I., Ferri, G., Haahr, M., Sezen, D., Çatak, G. (eds.) ICIDS 2013. LNCS, vol. 8230, pp. 95–106. Springer, Cham (2013). https://doi.org/10.1007/978-3-319-02756-2_11
26. Szilas, N., Ilea, I.: Objective metrics for interactive narrative. In: Mitchell, A., Fernández-Vara, C., Thue, D. (eds.) ICIDS 2014. LNCS, vol. 8832, pp. 91–102. Springer, Cham (2014). https://doi.org/10.1007/978-3-319-12337-0_9
27. Hannesson, H.J., Reimann-Andersen, T., Burelli, P., Bruni, L.E.: Connecting the dots: quantifying the narrative experience in interactive media. In: Schoenau-Fog, H., Bruni, L.E., Louchart, S., Baceviciute, S. (eds.) ICIDS 2015. LNCS, vol. 9445, pp. 189–201. Springer, Cham (2015). https://doi.org/10.1007/978-3-319-27036-4_18
28. Millard, D.E., West-taylor, C., Howard, Y., Packer, H.: The Ideal ReaderBot: Machine Readers and Narrative Analytics (2018)
29. Suttie, N., Louchart, S., Aylett, R., Lim, T.: Theoretical considerations towards authoring emergent narrative. In: Koenitz, H., Sezen, T.I., Ferri, G., Haahr, M., Sezen, D., Çatak, G. (eds.) ICIDS 2013. LNCS, vol. 8230, pp. 205–216. Springer, Cham (2013). https://doi.org/10.1007/978-3-319-02756-2_25
30. Bruni, L.E., Baceviciute, S.: Narrative intelligibility and closure in interactive systems. In: Koenitz, H., Sezen, T.I., Ferri, G., Haahr, M., Sezen, D., Çatak, G. (eds.) ICIDS 2013. LNCS, vol. 8230, pp. 13–24. Springer, Cham (2013). https://doi.org/10.1007/978-3-319-02756-2_2
31. Bruckman, A.: The Combinatorics of Storytelling: Mystery Train Interactive (1990)
32. Aylett, R.: Emergent Narrative, Social Immersion and "Storification" (n.d.)
33. Roberts, D.L., Isbell, C.L.: Desiderata for Managers of Interactive Experiences: A Survey of Recent Advances in Drama Management (n.d.)
34. Utsch, M.N., Pappa, G.L., Chaimowicz, L., Prates, R.O.: A new non-deterministic drama manager for adaptive interactive storytelling. Entertain. Comput. **100364** (2020). https://doi.org/10.1016/j.entcom.2020.100364
35. Green, D.: Novella: an authoring tool for interactive storytelling in games. In: Rouse, R., Koenitz, H., Haahr, M. (eds.) ICIDS 2018. LNCS, vol. 11318, pp. 556–559. Springer, Cham (2018). https://doi.org/10.1007/978-3-030-04028-4_66
36. Koenitz, H., Dubbelman, T., Roth, C.: An educational program in interactive narrative design. In: Cardona-Rivera, R.E., Sullivan, A., Young, R.M. (eds.) ICIDS 2019. LNCS, vol. 11869, pp. 22–25. Springer, Cham (2019). https://doi.org/10.1007/978-3-030-33894-7_3
37. Partlan, N., et al.: Exploratory automated analysis of structural features of interactive narrative. In: Fourteenth Artificial Intelligence and Interactive Digital Entertainment Conference (2018). www.aaai.org
38. Labatut, V., Bost, X.: Extraction and analysis of fictional character networks: a survey. ACM Comput. Surv. **52**(5), 1–40 (2019). https://doi.org/10.1145/3344548
39. Carstensdottir, E., et al.: Progression Maps: Conceptualizing Narrative Structure for Interaction Design Support (n.d.). https://doi.org/10.1145/3313831.3376527
40. Bruni, L.E., Baceviciute, S., Arief, M.: Narrative cognition in interactive systems: suspense-surprise and the P300 ERP component. In: Mitchell, A., Fernández-Vara, C., Thue, D. (eds.) ICIDS 2014. LNCS, vol. 8832, pp. 164–175. Springer, Cham (2014). https://doi.org/10.1007/978-3-319-12337-0_17

41. Murray, J.: Hamlet on the Holodeck: The Future of Narrative in Cyberspace, 2001 edn. (1997)
42. Roth, C., Koenitz, H.: Evaluating the user experience of interactive digital narrative. In: Proceedings of the 1st International Workshop on Multimedia Alternate Realities, Co-Located with ACM Multimedia 2016, AltMM 2016, pp. 31–36 (2016). https://doi.org/10.1145/2983298.2983302
43. Vermeulen, I.E., Roth, C., Vorderer, P., Klimmt, C.: Measuring user responses to interactive stories: towards a standardized assessment tool. In: Aylett, R., Lim, M.Y., Louchart, S., Petta, P., Riedl, M. (eds.) ICIDS 2010. LNCS, vol. 6432, pp. 38–43. Springer, Heidelberg (2010). https://doi.org/10.1007/978-3-642-16638-9_7
44. Kleinman, E., Caro, K., Zhu, J.: From immersion to metagaming: understanding rewind mechanics in interactive storytelling. Entertain. Comput. **33**, 100322 (2020). https://doi.org/10.1016/j.entcom.2019.100322
45. Brockmyer, J.H., Fox, C.M., Curtiss, K.A., McBroom, E., Burkhart, K.M., Pidruzny, J.N.: The development of the game engagement questionnaire: a measure of engagement in video game-playing. J. Exp. Soc. Psychol. **45**(4), 624–634 (2009). https://doi.org/10.1016/j.jesp.2009.02.016
46. Busselle, R., Bilandzic, H.: Measuring narrative engagement. Media Psychol. **12**(4), 321–347 (2009). https://doi.org/10.1080/15213260903287259
47. Green, M.C., Brock, T.C.: The role of transportation in the persuasiveness of public narratives. J. Pers. Soc. Psychol. **79**(5), 701–721 (2000). https://doi.org/10.1037/0022-3514.79.5.701
48. Suovuo, T., Skult, N., Joelsson, T.N., Skult, P., Ravyse, W., Smed, J.: The game experience model (GEM). In: Bostan, B. (ed.) Game User Experience And Player-Centered Design. ISCEMT, pp. 183–205. Springer, Cham (2020). https://doi.org/10.1007/978-3-030-37643-7_8
49. Patrickson, B.: Multi-user interactive drama: the macro view - three structural layers. In: Si, M., Thue, D., André, E., Lester, J.C., Tanenbaum, J., Zammitto, V. (eds.) ICIDS 2011. LNCS, vol. 7069, pp. 317–321. Springer, Heidelberg (2011). https://doi.org/10.1007/978-3-642-25289-1_38
50. Cavazza, M., Young, R.M.: Introduction to interactive storytelling. In: Nakatsu, R., Rauterberg, M., Ciancarini, P. (eds.) Handbook of Digital Games and Entertainment Technologies, pp. 377–392. Springer, Singapore (2017). https://doi.org/10.1007/978-981-4560-50-4_55
51. Reagan, A.J., Mitchell, L., Kiley, D., Danforth, C.M., Dodds, P.S.: The emotional arcs of stories are dominated by six basic shapes. EPJ Data Sci. **5**(1) (2016). https://doi.org/10.1140/epjds/s13688-016-0093-1
52. Miller, M.K., Mandryk, R.L.: Differentiating in-game frustration from at-game frustration using touch pressure (2016). https://doi.org/10.1145/2992154.2992185
53. Alm, C.O., Roth, D., Sproat, R.: Emotions from text. In: Proceedings of the Conference on Human Language Technology and Empirical Methods in Natural Language Processing, HLT 2005, pp. 579–586 (2005). https://doi.org/10.3115/1220575.1220648
54. Green, M.C., Jenkins, K.M.: Interactive narratives: processes and outcomes in user-directed stories. J. Commun. **64**(3), 479–500 (2014). https://doi.org/10.1111/jcom.12093
55. Christy, K.R., Fox, J.: Transportability and presence as predictors of avatar identification within narrative video games. Cyberpsychol. Behav. Soc. Network. **19**(4), 283–287 (2016). https://doi.org/10.1089/cyber.2015.0474

56. Witmer, B.G., Singer, M.J.: Measuring presence in virtual environments: a presence questionnaire. Presence: Teleoperators Virtual Environ. **7**(3), 225–240 (1998). https://doi.org/10.1162/105474698565686
57. Kitchenham, B.: Procedures for Performing Systematic Reviews (2004)
58. Novak, E.: A critical review of digital storyline-enhanced learning. Educ. Technol. Res. Dev. **63**(3), 431–453 (2015). https://doi.org/10.1007/s11423-015-9372-y

# Digital Storytelling in a Museum Application Using the Web of Things

Mortaza Alinam[(✉)], Luca Ciotoli, Frosina Koceva, and Ilaria Torre[iD]

Department of Informatics, Bioengineering, Robotics and Systems Engineering,
University of Genoa, Genoa, Italy
{mortaza.alinam,luca.ciotoli,frosina.koceva}@edu.unige.it,
ilaria.torre@unige.it

**Abstract.** The traditional notion of museum has changed. Museums' mute character is transformed into storytellers that communicate experience to their audience. Innovative technologies enhance the interactivity of storytelling and enable the audience to experience learning and entertainment. In this paper, we present WoTEdu, an interactive storytelling project based on the Web of Things (WoT) paradigm. WoTEdu enhances the audience edutainment experience through interaction with museum artefacts.

**Keywords:** Digital storytelling · Edutainment · Human Computer Interaction (HCI) · Cultural heritage · Internet of Things

## 1 Introduction

Despite the complex relationship between ICT technologies, content to be shared, and visitors' experiences of cultural heritage environments [5], the use of new technologies offer great potential to this domain [17]. The cultural heritage domain is adopting new and different technologies [6] that provide the domain with novel models for experiencing and enjoying contents, preserving and promoting them [5], and offering easier access and a multi-perspective view of cultural heritage artefacts [18].

Museums play the role of intermediary between cultural heritage and visitors, and are often described as places and environments for *education* and *enjoyment* [10,24]. The European Union also encourages innovative uses of museums to support education through the cultural heritage resources [25].

Nowadays, museum are increasingly seen as places of *experience* and *communication*. Accordingly, museums are storytellers, that share stories and experiences with their audience [12].

Interactive storytelling makes museums a dynamic environment [15], which provides the audience with playful learning, active engagement and *edutainment experience* [22]. Storytelling, as a means to communicate experiences [9], can take advantage of different technologies such as virtual reality, mobile augmented reality, mixed reality, multi modality and liquid interfaces, with the aim to enhance the story (narration) and interactivity.

© Springer Nature Switzerland AG 2020
A.-G. Bosser et al. (Eds.): ICIDS 2020, LNCS 12497, pp. 75–82, 2020.
https://doi.org/10.1007/978-3-030-62516-0_6

The *Internet of Things (IoT)* is an extension of the Internet connectivity to physical objects and devices, i.e., *things*, in addition to human users. IoT supports the integration of different technologies, computing systems and services, making them networked [1]. The *Web of Things (WoT)* enables IoT objects and devices to be accessible via standard and well-supported Web technologies [21].

IoT has been used in museums and cultural heritage applications mostly to support localization, content delivery and guidance through artworks (e.g., [5,26]). There are also some projects where artworks and objects tell their story and are used to personalize the interaction with visitors (e.g., [14,27]). However, in these approaches the physical things do not interact directly with other things and do not have behaviours associated with them. They are mostly used to store localized information and tales about the artworks.

In this paper, we present WoTEdu, which is a WoT-enabled interactive storyteller in the Nautical Cultural Heritage domain. WoTEdu aims to enhance visitors' edutainment experience enabling them to interact with museum artefacts during their interactive storytelling experience. Other than supporting visitors' interaction with artefacts *(human-to-thing interaction)*, WoTEdu enables the dialogue between artefacts *(thing-to-thing interaction)* so to update each other's state which changes while visitors interact with them. This opens the way to research studies on artefact-focused storytelling [2,7,8,13].

The contribution of our paper is to propose a novel approach for interactive storytelling in the perspective of *artefact-focused storytelling*. This is intended as a pilot application for future investigation in terms of efficacy for edutainment and enhanced user experience using WoT technology.

The paper is structured as follows: Sect. 2 presents our pilot application and its architecture, Sect. 3 discusses the design choices with respect to the user experience in the application context of edutainment, Sect. 4 presents a case study and a scenario. Finally Sect. 5 concludes the paper.

## 2    WoTEdu Pilot Application

Nautical Heritage museums are repositories of numerous artefacts whose functionalities are sometimes not very clear for visitors (e.g., sailing instruments, sundials, astrolabes, etc.) and would require additional easy-to-understand information. These cultural heritage artefacts can be enriched in terms of educational objects [19] and interactive capabilities to enhance learning and entertainment experiences.

WoTEdu is a WoT-enabled interactive storyteller. Its high level architecture is displayed in Fig. 1. It includes:

- the Story and Interaction Managing System (SIM), which is in charge of managing the interaction logic and the storytelling flow,
- the WoT-enhanced real-world artefacts in the museum, equipped with sensors and communication capabilities that allow the interaction with other artefacts and with the user,

– the Interactive display, that is used for the digital storytelling and for some input tasks required to participants (e.g., selection on an interactive map, as shown in Fig. 3).

The figure includes also some examples of events that are triggered and that condition the flow of the stories. They are real events from outside of the museum or from inside, detected by sensors. The pilot application that we present in this paper engages participants in a collaborative edutainment activity where each participant embodies a character in the story.

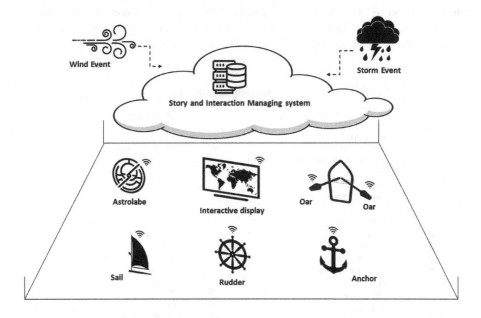

**Fig. 1.** High level WoTEdu architecture, which includes WoT-enhanced real-world artefacts, an interactive digital display and the SIM system.

WoTEdu enables each person to participate in the construction of narratives, to engage in active problem solving through interacting with the WoT-enhanced museum artefacts, and to reflect on narrative experiences [15].

## 3   WoTEdu Audience Experience

Audience experience enhancement is the guiding principle for WoTEdu design, aimed to support engagement and education [11].

Different dimensions of the user experience have to be considered in technology-enhanced storytelling for edutainment. We could not find in the literature one single model that perfectly fits the requirements of our application context. However, the combination of two models turned out to be useful to identify the relevant dimensions for WoTEdu design. We considered the 16 dimensions of a model for the evaluation of Educational Digital Storytelling Environments (EDSE) [20], based on the constructivist paradigm of learning, and 12 dimensions of user experience in Interactive Digital Narrative (IDN) [23], based on Entertainment Theory. Figure 2 identifies them as Education and Entertainment respectively. The two columns distinguish, among such dimensions, those which are mostly related with the Task and the Story (TSD dimensions) and those more dependent on participant's Personal Features (PFD dimensions). Due to page constraints, we can't provide more details on that.

Accessibility issues have also been considered with respect to such dimensions and in relation to both the physical artefacts and the digital component. Taking it into account for different disabilities makes the task very complex and it is still in progress in the project. Therefore it won't be dealt in this paper.

| WoTEdu Affordance | | |
|---|---|---|
| | TSD dimensions | PFD dimensions |
| Edutainment — Education | Collaborative Learning<br>Creativity and Innovation<br>Multiple Representations<br>Motivation<br>Gender Equality<br>Cognitive Effort<br>Feedback<br>Learner Control<br>Flexibility<br>Learner Activity<br>Sharply-Focused Goal Orientation<br>Experiential Value | Cultural Sensitivity<br>Value of Previous Knowledge<br>Knowledge Organization<br>Metacognition |
| Edutainment — Entertainment | Usability<br>Effectance<br>Autonomy<br>Presence<br>Suspense<br>Flow | Believability<br>Role-identification<br>Eudaimonic appreciation<br>Affect positive vs negative<br>Enjoyment |

Fig. 2. Dimensions for WoTEdu audience experience design, focused on Education and Entertainment goals and split in dimensions mostly dependent on the Task and Story (TSD) and dimensions that are more related to the user's Personal Features (PFD).

PFD dimensions are highly related to audiences' feelings and emotions (e.g. cultural sensitivity, believability, etc.), so their evaluation will mostly be performed through observation and interview with participants, while TSD features are mostly based on objective features of the task and the story. Usability evaluation will be particularly critical, especially with respect to the smart physical objects that show both traditional and enhanced digital behaviours [3,4].

# 4   Case Study

WoTEdu is a project designed through the collaboration of the Galata Sea Museum of Genoa, Italy. The interactive storytelling we designed addresses groups that can vary from three to eight persons (preferably, but not necessarily, young adults like the target of escape rooms [16]). The lower limit is due to the collaborative nature of the experience (e.g., a group of oarsmen in a galley) and the upper limit to the simultaneous interaction with the WoT-enabled artefacts.

The content of the stories is designed together with the manager and curators of the museum, who identified the topics of interest, concerning maritime-related science and history (sea exploration, cartography, maritime economics, etc.). Therefore, in order to enhance and promote this resource of heritage, WoTEdu tells stories that are inspired from different medieval navy stories (the exploration of America and various naval battles).

### Participants and Tasks

For the design of the case study, we considered a group of four people: one captain and three oarsmen. The tasks are split into two categories: specific and shared tasks. The *specific tasks* are specially assigned to participants during the WoT-Edu experience, while the *shared tasks* are the ones that can be accomplished by each participant, regardless his/her specific role. For example, when, during the narration, the anchor needs to be raised or an option has to be selected on the interactive map, each of the participants can fulfill the task depending on his/her position or availability).

### Scenario

The participants of the group engaged in this innovative museum experience of WoTEdu interactive storytelling perform the following steps:

- Participants select the adventure that they want to experience on the interactive map;
- WoTEdu starts telling the story and, in order to proceed with the narration, participants are engaged in different tasks.

Tasks are to be performed through direct interaction with museum artefacts. Besides user-artefact interaction, WoTEdu enables also artefact-artefact interaction, where the WoT-enhanced artefacts can access and update each other's state. Below is sketched the starting of the interaction (see Table 1), while Fig. 3 shows a portion of the interaction flow and related storytelling.

As shown in the figure, the WoT-enabled objects (the astrolabe, the anchor, the oars and the rudder) are displayed at the sides of the figure, while the central part of the figure sketches the digital storytelling and the task required from the participants. When a participant interacts with an object, the object makes some actions that depend on the interaction type, but that usually include telling and explaining about itself, sending feedback to the user and sending messages to other objects in order to make the story proceed.

**Table 1.** Digital storytelling and interaction flow user-artefact, artefact-artefact.

| | |
|---|---|
| *Choosing a story:* | The group chooses a story from the interactive map display, e.g., exploration, battle, trading, chasing, ... |
| *Forming a galley crew:* | Each participant takes a role in the crew e.g., captain, oarsmen, ... |
| *Positioning:* | The galley crew is engaged in the interaction with artefacts—astrolabe, rudder, oar—to get the position, start navigating, ... |

From the technical point of view, the WoT application that is being developed is based on the Mozilla WebThing platform and API[1] that provide an open source implementation of the newly released W3C standard for the Web of Things. For the prototype we use six Things represented by Arduino[2] boards and various sensors (rotary and gyroscope, which collect data generated by the interaction of the user with the things, e.g., the rudder and the oars).

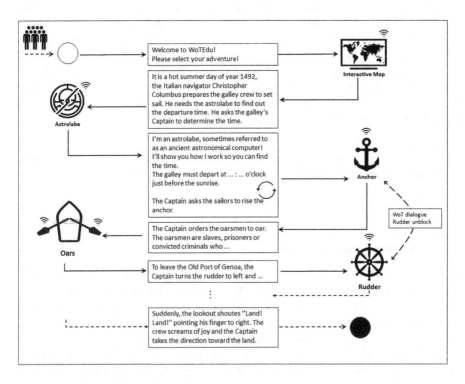

**Fig. 3.** Digital storytelling and interaction flow user-artefact, artefact-artefact.

---

[1] Mozilla webthing platform - https://iot.mozilla.org/docs/, Mozilla WoT API - https://iot.mozilla.org/wot/.

[2] Arduino - https://www.arduino.cc/.

## 5    Conclusions

In this paper we presented an innovative project, WoTEdu, that exploits the Web of Things paradigm to engage users in interactive storytelling with the aim to enhance the user experience with the museum content. The Web of Things enables the interaction with the museum artefacts that are equipped with sensors and communication capabilities. The artefacts dialogue with the users telling themselves, showing and explaining details about how they work and engaging users with physical interaction tasks. The artefacts dialogue also with other physical and digital objects, including the Story and Interaction Managing system which is in charge of handling the interaction logic and the storytelling flow. At the current stage of development, we implemented the messaging and storytelling infrastructure and we identified with the museum curators the museum artefacts that can be physically used and touched by visitors in order to be WoT-enabled.

The artefacts selection for WoTEdu and in general for this type of applications is crucial because, besides the educational value of the object, it is required that it has features and capabilities to allow physical/digital interaction human-to-thing and thing-to-thing.

The next step will be the full implementation of the pilot application in order to perform a formative and layered evaluation. The current evaluation of the design concept and principles using heuristic methods is promising.

**Acknowledgements.** The authors gratefully acknowledge the valuable contribution of Francesco Calcagno and Gabriele Taccioli to the development of the WoT prototype.

## References

1. Atzori, L., Iera, A., Morabito, G.: The internet of things: a survey. Comput. Netw. **54**(15), 2787–2805 (2010)
2. Benford, S., Hazzard, A., Xu, L.: The Carolan guitar: a thing that tells its own life story. Interactions **22**(3), 64–66 (2015)
3. Cena, F., Console, L., Matassa, A., Torre, I.: Principles to design smart physical objects as adaptive recommenders. IEEE Access **5**, 23532–23549 (2017)
4. Cena, F., Console, L., Matassa, A., Torre, I.: Multi-dimensional intelligence in smart physical objects. Inf. Syst. Front. **21**(2), 383–404 (2017). https://doi.org/10.1007/s10796-017-9758-y
5. Chianese, A., Piccialli, F., Jung, J.E.: The internet of cultural things: towards a smart cultural heritage. In: 2016 12th International Conference on Signal-Image Technology & Internet-Based Systems (SITIS), pp. 493–496. IEEE (2016)
6. Damala, A., Ruthven, I., Hornecker, E.: The MUSETECH model: a comprehensive evaluation framework for museum technology. J. Comput. Cultural Heritage (JOCCH) **12**(1), 1–22 (2019)
7. Darzentas, D., Flintham, M., Benford, S.: Object-focused mixed reality storytelling: technology-driven content creation and dissemination for engaging user experiences. In: Proceedings of the 22nd Pan-Hellenic Conference on Informatics, pp. 278–281 (2018)
8. Darzentas, D.P., Brown, M.A., Flintham, M., Benford, S.: The data driven lives of wargaming miniatures. In: Proceedings of the 33rd Annual ACM Conference on Human Factors in Computing Systems, pp. 2427–2436 (2015)

9. del Carmen Villaseñor Ferrer, M.: Building echoes: the role of storytelling in museums and galleries. University of London, London (2007)
10. Garcia-Cardona, S., Tian, F., Prakoonwit, S.: Tenochtitlan - an interactive virtual reality environment that encourages museum exhibit engagement. In: Tian, F., Gatzidis, C., El Rhalibi, A., Tang, W., Charles, F. (eds.) Edutainment 2017. LNCS, vol. 10345, pp. 20–28. Springer, Cham (2017). https://doi.org/10.1007/978-3-319-65849-0_3
11. Grant-Smith, D., Donnet, T., Macaulay, J., Chapman, R.: Principles and practices for enhanced visual design in virtual learning environments: do looks matter in student engagement? In: Student-Centered Virtual Learning Environments in Higher Education, pp. 103–133. IGI Global (2019)
12. Hooper-Greenhill, E.: Changing values in the art museum: rethinking communication and learning. Int. J. Heritage Stud. 6(1), 9–31 (2000)
13. Speed, C., Manohar, A.K.: Storytelling within an internet of things. In: Aylett, R., Lim, M.Y., Louchart, S., Petta, P., Riedl, M. (eds.) ICIDS 2010. LNCS, vol. 6432, pp. 295–296. Springer, Heidelberg (2010). https://doi.org/10.1007/978-3-642-16638-9_48
14. Marulli, F.: IoT to enhance understanding of cultural heritage: fedro authoring platform, artworks telling their fables. In: Atanasovski, V., Leon-Garcia, A. (eds.) FABULOUS 2015. LNICST, vol. 159, pp. 270–276. Springer, Cham (2015). https://doi.org/10.1007/978-3-319-27072-2_35
15. Mott, B.W., Callaway, C.B., Zettlemoyer, L.S., Lee, S.Y., Lester, J.C.: Towards narrative-centered learning environments. In: Proceedings of the 1999 AAAI Fall Symposium on Narrative Intelligence, pp. 78–82 (1999)
16. Nicholson, S.: Peeking behind the locked door: a survey of escape room facilities. Pozyskanoz (2015). http://scottnicholson.com/pubs/erfacwhite.pdf
17. Olaniyi, H., Sahuleka, K.: New methods in museums: telecommunications through immersive technologies. Electron. Bus. 18(1) (2019)
18. Ott, M., Pozzi, F.: Towards a new era for cultural heritage education: discussing the role of ICT. Comput. Hum. Behav. 27(4), 1365–1371 (2011)
19. Patel, M., Walczak, K., Giorgini, F., White, M.: A cultural heritage repository as source for learning materials. In: VAST, pp. 213–222 (2004)
20. Psomos, P., Kordaki, M.: A novel pedagogical evaluation model for educational digital storytelling environments. In: Proceedings of E-Learn, pp. 17–21 (2011)
21. Raggett, D.: The web of things: challenges and opportunities. Computer 48(5), 26–32 (2015)
22. Resnick, M.: Edutainment? No thanks. I prefer playful learning. Associazione Civita Report on Edutainment 14, 1–4 (2004)
23. Roth, C., Koenitz, H.: Evaluating the user experience of interactive digital narrative. In: International Workshop on Multimedia Alternate Realities, pp. 31–36 (2016)
24. Skyrda, M., Chuieva, K., Boiko, A., Stolyarov, B.: Role of museums in education and cultural tourism development: policy brief (2012)
25. Sonkoly, G., Vahtikari, T.: Innovation in Cultural Heritage: For an Integrated European research policy. European Commission, Publications Office (2018)
26. Spachos, P., Plataniotis, K.N.: BLE beacons for indoor positioning at an interactive IoT-based smart museum. IEEE Syst. J. (2020)
27. Vassilakis, C., Poulopoulos, V., Antoniou, A., Wallace, M., Lepouras, G., Nores, M.L.: ExhiSTORY: smart exhibits that tell their own stories. Future Gener. Comput. Syst. 81, 542–556 (2018)

# User Testing Persuasive Interactive Web Documentaries: An Empirical Study

Nicole Basaraba[1]([✉]) [iD], Owen Conlan[1], Jennifer Edmond[2], and Peter Arnds[2]

[1] ADAPT Centre, Trinity College Dublin, Dublin, Ireland
basarabn@tcd.ie
[2] School of Languages, Literatures and Cultural Studies, Trinity College Dublin, Dublin, Ireland

**Abstract.** Although iDocs are a newer genre of non-fiction IDNs, there are few studies reporting results on their impact and the user experience. A common goal of iDocs is to engage the pubic in social, economic and environmental issues. This investigation applied the iDoc genre to cultural heritage to create a prototype for user testing titled *Sentenced to Transportation: A Virtual Tour of Australia's Convict Past*. The user testing completed in this study analysed three key variables: the level of perceived agency based on the narrative structure, choices provided in the interface design, and ability to persuade further user participation. The results show that users can be persuaded through the narrative design to proceed non-linearly and to engage in further user participation post-interaction.

**Keywords:** iDoc · User testing · UX design · Cultural heritage · Virtual tour · Klynt

## 1 Introduction

The origin, definition, and scope of interactive documentaries (iDoc), which are also called web-docs, collab-docs, or participatory-docs [1], are more difficult to pinpoint in the literature than the other interactive digital narrative genres (IDN). In a general sense, iDocs are "any project that starts with an intention to document the 'real' and that uses digital interactive technology to realize this intention" [1]. The fluidity of this genre stems from the many terms used to describe different works, the common remediation of genre conventions from linear documentary film, and because iDocs are studied along with cinema, interaction, videogames, and video art [2]. The key genre requirements for iDocs are moving images, full-screen viewing, and audio content [2]. Many iDocs are distributed on the web, but they are also built on a variety of digital platforms including DVDs, mobiles, GPS devices and gallery installations [1]. Navigation impacts many design choices and iDoc creators need to continually innovate ways of marrying the interface with the narrative "and no individual work establishes a template for future i-docs" [3]. iDocs that replicate an existing structure or design, O'Flynn (2012) argues, are likely to fail because each project has different aims for the core experience and desired communicative effect [3]. For example, transmedia documentaries that rely on curation and collaboration of user-generated content are different than those where the

A.-G. Bosser et al. (Eds.): ICIDS 2020, LNCS 12497, pp. 83–91, 2020.
https://doi.org/10.1007/978-3-030-62516-0_7

design is based on highly structured and authored content systems [3]. An affordance of iDocs is that they can present multiple and contested points of view from a single author or from a community of authors and allow users to come to their own conclusions [1]. Documentary has the ability to enhance public knowledge, provide citizens with informational resources to aid decision-making, and they act as potential platforms for action and participation [4]. Since iDocs have the potential to persuade the public into civic action, selecting the right narrative structure and adapting it to the specific project requirements is crucial to achieve the desired impacts. The selection of one narrative structure over another has not been widely investigated and there are few studies reporting results of the user experience with iDocs. This study involved the development and user testing of an iDoc prototype titled *Sentenced to Transportation: A Virtual Tour of Australia's Convict Past*. This heritage-focused tourism iDoc, was tested with a group of users from the public to analyse three key variables: the level of perceived agency based on the selected narrative structure, the users' preferred content modalities, and ability to persuade further user participation. The results provide insight into the challenges for complex interface designs for IDNs and highlighted areas for further empirical testing for future iDocs and other video based IDNs.

## 2   User Testing Studies on Interactive Video and Documentaries

As the field of study in iDocs became more established, a number of iDocs were produced between 2009–2012, many of which became highly cited in scholarly literature, such as *Highrise* (2009), *Prison Valley* (2010), and *Welcome to Pine Point* (2011) [1]. One of the first projects to be called an iDoc, *Moss Landing* (1989), examined life in the small town of California through hyperlinked video clips that were accessed by the user via "hotspots" [5]. Other commonly cited examples of iDocs are *Gaza/Sderot* (2008), *Bear 71* (2012), *Hollow* (2013) and *Fort McMoney* (2013). To date, most iDoc research has been conducted as case study analysis [6–8] rather than user interaction studies. Overall, as Roth and Koenitz (2019) note, only a few studies have evaluated the effectiveness of IDNs [9].

Previous user-testing studies have been conducted with different fictional IDNs including the video game Façade [10]; *Turbulence*—a fictional hypernarrative interactive movie [11]; B4—an iDoc [12]; and the Netflix film *Black Mirror: Bandersnatch* [9, 13]. The study on the fictional computer-based interactive movie, *Turbulence*, had eight participants – limited to academics with backgrounds in cinema and video games – in an exploratory study of the phenomenological experience [11]. The *Turbulence* study showed that users were confused regarding who the protagonists were, what the conflict was, and approximately half made use of alternative plotline options [11]. *Turbulence* users had trouble identifying the hotspots (i.e., links) and said there were too few of them; they were split between whether the interaction increased or decreased their engagement; and they gained meaning through self-implication in the narrative [11]. This expert audience noted interface design issues and that the agency provided may not have been meaningful. Kolhoff and Nack's (2019) study on *Bandersnatch* involved 169 participants who thought they were given the right number of choices and had adequate control but were unhappy with the choice predictability and the consequences, and they complained about dead-ends [13]. Overall, 72% found watching *Bandersnatch* worthwhile despite the fact that only 45% of participants were satisfied with the ending they selected [13]. Participants stated that the novelty factor was more positive than the film itself and this increases pressure for future interactive films and iDocs to have a more intriguing, agency-driven and satisfying story [13]. These user studies highlighted issues with the interface design and an interest in the novelty of the genre.

The social functions of iDocs are well demonstrated in the example of *Fort McMoney* (2013)—a documentary game that addresses the economic and environmental impacts of Canada's oil sands industry in Fort McMurray, Alberta, to encourage collective debate and decision-making [4]. The documentary game presented audio-visual information, fostered debates through weekly forums, formed public opinion through various polls, and contributed to collective decision-making through weekly referenda [4]. Although *Fort McMoney* inspired participatory action, only 1,869 of the 300,000 players contributed to debates and iDoc studies show that it is typical to see a one per cent participation rule in digital projects [4]. Therefore, iDocs can be used to varying degrees of success to generate public participation.

## 3 Case Study: An iDoc for Australian Convict History

The UNESCO World Heritage Sites (WHSs) were chosen as the narrative topic for this practice-based research for a variety of reasons. Firstly, UNESCO sites are recognised as culturally significant to the world rather than a single culture, they allow for multiple perspectives to be represented in an IDN, and their designation involves a rigorous selection process based on a set of criteria. After applying additional researcher-determined selection criteria (e.g., English-language options), the 11 UNESCO Australian Convict Sites were selected including: Hyde Park Barracks, Cockatoo Island; Old Government

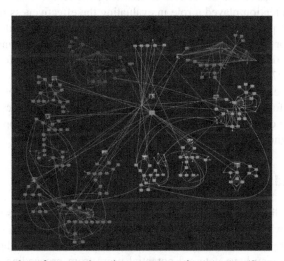

**Fig. 1.** Klynt screenshot of concentric action space narrative structure (Sentenced to Transportation, 2020).

House; Old Great North Road; Port Arthur Historic Site; Cascades Female Factory; Coal Mines Historic Site; Brickendon and Woolmers Estates; Darlington Probation Station; Fremantle Prison; and Kingston and Arthur's Vale Historic Area (KAVHA).

The objectives of developing an iDoc prototype on the Australian Convict Sites were to employ a specific emergent narrative structure to test its applicability as a suitable method for creating IDNs for cultural heritage topics and to gather qualitative and quantitative user feedback. User feedback was used to determine whether: (1) a narrative was communicated through the use of a Concentric Action Space narrative structure (see Fig. 1), (2) the desired level of agency was achieved, and (3) whether the user was inspired to take further action.

## 4   Methodology

The iDoc prototype incorporated multimodal content (audio, video, text, 3D images, paintings, etc.) and was built using Klynt software and the exported files were uploaded to the FTP of the hosting website (nicolebasaraba.com/Australian-convicts-prototype). A user survey was developed to collect qualitative and quantitative data, and it was approved by the Ethics Committee for Trinity College Dublin before being launched. The survey included author-driven questions to determine the effectiveness of the non-linear narrative structure, multimodal interface design and the iDoc's persuasiveness. System Usability Scale questions were included as a baseline for collecting quantitative data on testing a new system. Quantitative survey questions "assume a task-based philosophy" rather than user perception and interpretation of their experience with the system [14]. Scholars have noted a major conflict between artistic and HCI perspectives on user interaction because art is inherently subjective and HCI aims to be objective [14, 15]. For example, "a users' report of unpleasantness may be positive or even desirable, if the system author intends to use her stories to challenge the reader's belief system" [14]. Thus, authorial intention played a role in evaluating the effectiveness of the emergent narratives and the qualitative survey questions were posed as per the authorial objectives of the iDoc. Prior to launching, a pilot test was conducted, and minor adjustments were made to the iDoc and the survey. The experiment was live for a four-week period between January 27, 2020–February 20, 2020 and the data were collected using Qualtrics software. The iDoc was accessible via a web page after the user completed the informed research consent form. Once the users were finished exploring the iDoc, they could end the experience by clicking the "Take survey" button located on the top corner of each story node throughout the iDoc.

## 5   Results and Findings

Data from the landing web page with the informed consent form shows that 235 people visited the page while the survey was live, but 45 completed the whole survey. This suggests that there was enough interest in the iDoc to inspire click-throughs but that the consent form may have deterred potential users from proceeding with the study (considering there was a 21% response rate).

## 5.1 Navigation and Narrative Structure

The map menu was chosen in order to present users with a non-linear navigation that included different entry points into the narrative. Since the map was presented as the main menu, users evidently returned to it. Secondly, the "Stories" menu buttons (provided in a sticky footer menu) also provided another non-linear narrative navigation as they were curated protostories by common themes: Convict Life, Irish Stories, Indigenous Stories and Female Stories. Several questions regarding navigation were posed to understand how users made selections when presented with multiple options. The first WHS selected by most users to explore was Fremantle Prison (29%) followed by Hyde Park Barracks and KAVHA each with 13%. Users selected the site because they had prior knowledge of them, they were interested in the location and/or imagery presented, or reportedly made a random selection—although a few noted that their choice was driven by left-to-right default navigation (see Fig. 2). Since so many users selected Fremantle Prison (located on farthest left on the map), the left-to-right navigation may be less random than users reported since it is a natural phenomenological reaction in English to read left-to-right which translates into common website navigation as well. As for subsequent narrative navigation options, 75% of users selected a non-linear or alternative menu option.

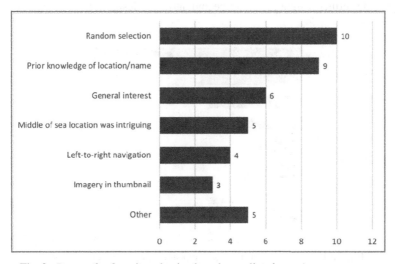

**Fig. 2.** Reason for first site selection based on collated users' text responses.

The respondents made equal use of the linear (forward and back) arrow navigation and the new narrative paths accessed by text-based buttons. Users returning to the map and text-based menus demonstrates that the majority (71%) engaged in a non-linear exploration of the narrative and used the alternative narratives paths provided. The more frequent use of the map menu and "Stories menus" indicates that website users may be more accustomed to the hierarchical tree-like web-based structure and may have been looking for a breadcrumb trail to indicate where they were in the narrative.

## 5.2 Multimodality Preferences

The main modalities respondents preferred were video (67%) and text (13%). Some nodes in the Fremantle Prison and KAVHA narrative paths offered users the option to learn about the content through video instead of the text content or voice-over. Video is conventionally the primary modality in iDocs so this may have also influenced respondents' preference for it and because Web 2.0 has resulted in the increased societal consumption of video content (e.g., YouTube). When asked which content modality they would like to see more of in the iDoc, more respondents than expected, 32% indicated that they would like more interaction buttons (see Fig. 3). However, the only control removed in terms of navigation was the ability to return to the first introductory node (i.e., homepage) since the aim was for users to select a new narrative path from the map menu. Users were provided with all the possible types of interactions offered through the Klynt software and were provided with more options than commonly seen in most iDocs, which offer less interactivity in order to maintain more authorial control over the narrative structure. This result also correlates with Knoller and Ben Arie's (2009) user experience survey, where users reported that there were too few "hotspots" (or hyperlinks) available [11] and reiterates that there are discrepancies between user reports and their experience. Thus, more qualitative methods of analysis on multimodal preferences could provide further insight for interface and narrative design for future studies.

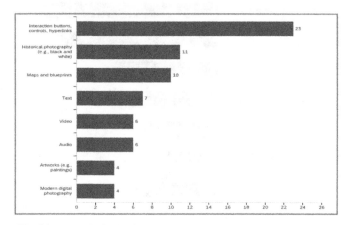

**Fig. 3.** Users' desire for increased appearance of content modalities.

## 5.3 Level of Choice and Dramatic Agency

The respondents provided some contradictory answers in terms of their level of perceived freedom to choose and desire for more interactivity choices. The results show a high level of choice was perceived as 76% of users reported having sufficient freedom to choose which content to interact with (see Fig. 4). On the other hand, only 17% felt that the choice they made impacted the content that was presented to them and 38% were unclear as to whether their choices had an impact (see Fig. 5). Both these questions were included as a measure against the credibility of what respondents reported in their answers. Considering the wording of Q13 was the negative inverse of Q11, if it was framed as a positive outcome, the curves in Figs. 4 and 5 would likely be more closely aligned. Overall, users were provided with agency but may have been unable to infer how their choices made an impact since they were (intentionally) not shown the entire scope of the narrative, which included 290 nodes of content.

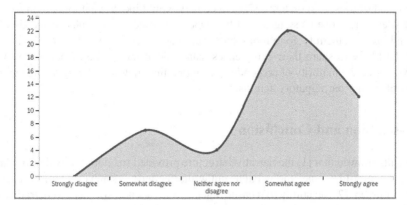

**Fig. 4.** User responses to Q11 – "I had sufficient freedom to choose content."

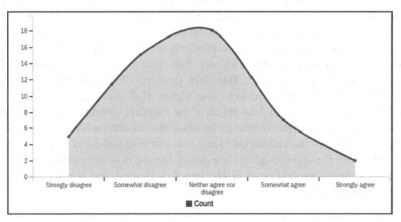

**Fig. 5.** User responses to Q13 – "I felt my choices had no consequences on what was presented to me".

### 5.4 Inspiring Post-interaction User Participation

In regard to inspiring participation, the survey results show that users would be willing to take various further actions after their experience with the iDoc. For example, 55% of respondents were likely to engage in a low level of participation by looking at one of the additional resources hyperlinked within the iDoc, such as novels, films, or external hyperlinks. As for a more-involved level of participation, the results showed that 54% of respondents indicated that they would likely visit one of the 11 Australian Convict Sites after viewing the iDoc. In response to the follow-up question of which site they would visit, 48% selected the site that they first chose from the map menu. This implies that more than half of respondents (52%) explored more than one WHS in the iDoc. Furthermore, 67% of respondents selected that they would physically visit more than one site and of those respondents 37% stated they would like to visit more than four of the 11 sites. These results suggest that the iDoc persuaded users to physically visit the sites and inspired them to go to more than one. In addition to this, 52% of respondents would be likely to share their experiences using social media. Thus, persuasion was achieved since the majority of respondents reported that they were likely to engage in a variety of further participatory actions.

## 6   Discussion and Conclusion

The results showed that (1) the narrative structure provided freedom for exploration and encouraged non-linear navigation but its unfamiliarity due to its newness to users caused some confusion; (2) the ability to measure agency was inconclusive due to contradictory participants' responses and the difficulty of measuring this academic concept through multiple choice survey questions with public users; and (3) users were inspired to visit one or more WHSs, view additional materials, and to share their travel experiences and the iDoc with their social networks. As a proof of concept, the iDoc prototype provided many navigation options and modalities (e.g., map, video, and images) for users to personalise their experience. Respondents felt they had the freedom to choose protostory paths and they expressed an awareness that more narrative existed behind the other options they did not select. Therefore, the iDoc allowed for multiple narrative paths and holds a high level of replay value. Future IDN user studies could use A/B testing to help examine exactly how much of the narrative structure users need see in order to understand its scope without giving up authorial control. A lab setting would also allow for user training/orientation to any new narrative system interactions prior to testing and time for additional qualitative data gathering post-interaction which could help inform future iDoc and other IDNs' interface designs and non-linear narrative structure developments.

## References

1. Aston, J., Gaudenzi, S.: Interactive documentary: setting the field. Stud. Documentary Film **6**(2), 125–139 (2012)
2. Almeida, A., Alvelos, H.: An interactive documentary manifesto. In: Aylett, R., Lim, M.Y., Louchart, S., Petta, P., Riedl, M. (eds.) ICIDS 2010. LNCS, vol. 6432, pp. 123–128. Springer, Heidelberg (2010). https://doi.org/10.1007/978-3-642-16638-9_16
3. O'Flynn, S.: Documentary's metamorphic form: webdoc, interactive, transmedia, participatory and beyond. Stud. Documentary Film **6**(2), 141–157 (2012)

4. Nash, K.: I-Docs and the documentary tradition: exploring questions of citizenship. In: Aston, J., Gaudenzi, S., Rose, M. (eds.) I-Docs: The Evolving Practices of Interactive Documentary. Wallflower Press, USA (2017)
5. Moss Landing. MIT Docubase (1989). https://docubase.mit.edu/project/moss-landing/
6. Aufderheide, P.: Interactive documentaries: navigation and design. J. Film Video **67**(3–4), 69–78 (2015)
7. Vázquez-Herrero, J., Negreira-Rey, M. C., Pereira-Fariña, X.: Interactive documentary contributions to the renewal of journalistic narratives: realities and challenges (2017)
8. Gifreu-Castells, A.: Mapping trends in interactive non-fiction through the lenses of interactive documentary. In: Mitchell, A., Fernández-Vara, C., Thue, D. (eds.) ICIDS 2014. LNCS, vol. 8832, pp. 156–163. Springer, Cham (2014). https://doi.org/10.1007/978-3-319-12337-0_16
9. Roth, C., Koenitz, H.: Bandersnatch, yea or nay? Reception and user experience of an interactive digital narrative video. In: Proceedings of TVX'2019: ACM International Conference on Interactive Experiences for TV and Online Video, 5–7 June 2019, Salford, United Kingdom. ACM, pp. 247–254 (2019)
10. Milam, D., Seif El-Nasr, M., Wakkary, R.: Looking at the interactive narrative experience through the eyes of the participants. In: Spierling, U., Szilas, N. (eds.) ICIDS 2008. LNCS, vol. 5334, pp. 96–107. Springer, Heidelberg (2008). https://doi.org/10.1007/978-3-540-89454-4_16
11. Knoller, N., Ben Arie, U.: Turbulence – a user study of a hypernarrative interactive movie. In: Iurgel, Ido A., Zagalo, N., Petta, P. (eds.) ICIDS 2009. LNCS, vol. 5915, pp. 44–49. Springer, Heidelberg (2009). https://doi.org/10.1007/978-3-642-10643-9_8
12. Gantier, S., Labour, M.: Empowerment and the I-Doc model user. Empowering Users Through Design, pp. 225–247. Springer, Cham (2015)
13. Kolhoff, L., Nack, F.: How relevant is your choice? In: Cardona-Rivera, Rogelio E., Sullivan, A., Young, R.Michael (eds.) ICIDS 2019. LNCS, vol. 11869, pp. 73–85. Springer, Cham (2019). https://doi.org/10.1007/978-3-030-33894-7_9
14. Zhu, J.: Towards a mixed evaluation approach for computational narrative systems. In: Proceedings from the International Conference on Computational Creativity (ICCC), vol. 12, pp. 150–154 (2012)
15. Höök, K., Sengers, P., Andersson, G.: Sense and sensibility: evaluation and interactive art. In: Proceedings of the SIGCHI Conference on Human Factors in Computing Systems, pp. 214–248 (2003)
16. Sauro, J., Lewis, J.R.: Quantifying the user experience: practical statistics for user research. Morgan Kaufmann (2016)

# Towards the Emergent Theatre: A Novel Approach for Creating Live Emergent Narratives Using Finite State Machines

Craig Paul Green$^{(\boxtimes)}$ ⓘ, Lars Erik Holmquist ⓘ, and Steve Gibson ⓘ

Northumbria University, Newcastle upon Tyne, UK
craig.p.green@northumbria.ac.uk,
www.northumbria.ac.uk

**Abstract.** In this project, we introduce finite state machines as a way to simultaneously connect an audience's input with performer output during a live performance. Our approach is novel in that we can redefine the traditional notion of an author, by dividing and balancing the responsibilities for creating and developing emergent narrative between three elements: the audience, finite state machines, and the performers. This also allows audience members a large degree of freedom to input into the system, as we can consider audience inaction as a form of productive action. We have developed the Data Generation Engine (DGE), software that generates data to be used by performers for creating and developing narrative and to provide audiences with opportunities to manipulate the DGE's data generation and distribution mechanisms. We argue that using this approach in a live theatre context allows a consistent narrative to emerge while giving the audience the freedom to engage in the narrative without disrupting the performance.

**Keywords:** Emergent narrative · Finite state machines · Immersion · Audience agency · Live theatre

## 1 Introduction

Emergent Narrative redefines the traditional author and is viewed as a solution to the fabled "Narrative Paradox" which "revolves around the conflict between pre-authored narrative structures - especially plot - and the freedom a VE offers a user in physical movement and interaction, integral to a feeling of physical presence and immersion" [14]. An Emergent Narrative requires little to no pre-authoring as narrative is developed bottom-up via interactions between lower level intelligent agents in a story space [3]. This means that these agents must be autonomous, intelligent, and emotional in-order to structure their part of the emerging narrative [13].

In our approach, we have developed the Data Generation Engine (DGE) which allows us to structure the emergent narrative process in a specific way. The high level structurally coherent and emotionally apt narrative is produced

© Springer Nature Switzerland AG 2020
A.-G. Bosser et al. (Eds.): ICIDS 2020, LNCS 12497, pp. 92–101, 2020.
https://doi.org/10.1007/978-3-030-62516-0_8

by improvisational performers, who build narratives based on interpretations of data generated by the DGE. Improvisational theatre is well suited for this as the mechanisms it employs for developing narrative are already well established and are suitable for emergent narrative [28]. The DGE is tasked with producing continuous streams of useful data, whilst providing the audience a way to input into its data generation and distribution process. One of the project objectives is to understand what the term 'useful' means in this context, and how data can be effectively communicated to performers. A unique aspect of our approach lies in the ability to adapt to audience engagement preferences, whilst balancing the responsibility of emergent narrative creation and development between the audience, DGE, and Performers. This is paradoxical, as there is tension between the audience's responsibilities for developing the narrative and their freedom to interact with the DGE at their leisure. Our approach tackles this issue by allowing audience inaction to be considered as a form of productive action. Audience actions are limited to manipulating the type of data produced and where it is distributed, but not the speed at which it is produced and distributed. A Similar approach provides audience members with opportunities for removing objects from a digital environment which causes changes in character behaviours [8]. This approach allows for a considerable amount of freedom for the audience to engage with the system, implementing real-time planning systems [30].

## 2   Related Work

Theatre and the performing arts have a long history of exploring the nature of interactivity and the boundaries between the audience and performers. When we consider the techniques commonly used by improvisational theatre (improv), we see complex systematic methodologies, engaging with audiences, performers and environments for dynamic problem-solving in real-time [15]. Improv "typically involves a troupe of actors that perform short scenes based on "games" that are selected for them. Games typically involved telling the actors rules for what they can/cannot do in a scene and a suggestion from the audience" [15]. Here, the performance is contextualised by a set of rules which are partially developed by the audience. The audience's agency consists of helping to create the data at specific moments in the performance. This comes at a cost, as performer-audience engagements can be clumsy, and it relies heavily on an audience's ability and desire to help create this data.

Augusto Boal's *Theatre of the Oppressed* [7] changes the dynamic of the audience by utilising interactivity as a means of creating social and political change. It "is a set of dramatic techniques whose purpose is to bring to light systemic exploitation and oppression within common situations, and to allow spectators to become actors" [9]. Modern performance artists have tackled audience agency since the 1970's when Marina Abramović began compelling her audiences to action. Often these actions would be reactive to Abramović's violence towards her own body [1]. The Artist group Blast Theory often merges technology and performance. In their work *A Machine To See You* [6], mobile phones are used in a location-based cinema experience. Phones are used to give instructions to audience members travelling around a city, performing tasks. These tasks include meeting up with characters played by actors and collecting items distributed around the city.

Gaming and digital interactive media have substantially advanced our understanding of audience interactivity and emergence. In this space, emergence is often reliant on the actions and explorations of the player (audience). Games such as *Minecraft* [19] and *The Sims* [18], give players the tools to create their own narrative space, with non-playable characters (NPCs) inhabiting this space. It is then down to the player to develop their own narratives. The Game *Dwarf Fortress* [2] extends this by procedurally generating a world with a backstory and in-depth character profiles, giving players more contextual information for the narrative building. The use of dilemma's in interactive narrative provide us with a way in which to process and define the parameters of a narrative [12]. We can see specific uses of this in games such as *The Walking Dead* [26]. In this game the player is often confronted with dilemma's in-order to progress through the story, leading to a variety of different endings. *Façade* [27] is a story-driven emergent narrative game that "integrates story level interaction (drama management), believable agents, and shallow natural language processing in the context of a first-person, graphical, real-time interactive drama" [17]. It follows a set story with the player taking on a specific role. The game tries to accurately simulate natural conversations between agents and the player to develop the plot.

In a research context, the development of believable story agents for interactive and emergent narrative is a key goal with multiple approaches which often utilise some sort of drama management system [23,24,29]. Drama managers are intelligent systems built to "observe the virtual world and to make changes to the virtual world or virtual characters in order to coerce the interactive player's experience to have certain features" [22]. *FearNot!* [5] powered by the FAtiMA agent architecture [10], is an emergent narrative system that is designed for anti-bullying education. It involved children taking the role of an invisible friend advising an NPC who is being bullied [4] FearNot! takes inspiration from Forum Theatre, one of the dramatic techniques of *Theatre of the Oppressed* [7] whereby a performer will act out a scene and then engage the audience in the planning of actions for the next scene [9].

The above examples all aim to connect audience and performers, creating connections that vary in complexity and approach. We take influence from these examples, but our system seeks to simplify the connection, attenuating the systems variety. This stops the performers from being overwhelmed by the input of the audience as this input is filtered through the DGE, creating information that is beneficial to the performance.

## 3 The Data Generation Engine

The Data Generation Engine (DGE) has been implemented in Unity, which is a cross-platform games development engine. The DGE consists of multiple finite state machines working in tandem to generate data. The finite state machines generate several sets of data that are given to individual onstage performers, each performer has specific data to use for their performance. We are also able to create global data sets for all performers to use. The DGE is specifically designed to allow audience members limited control over the mechanisms that determine type and destination of data being generated, but not the actual data itself. This creates a situation whereby the audience has to work with the DGE in-order to control the flow of data, rather than having control over individual data points.

Finite state machines are "mathematical abstractions used to design algorithms" [25], meaning a finite state machine's actions are predefined using a set of states and inputs. Video games often use finite state machines for their NPCs. First-person shooter games provide us with an example of this. When a player shoots at an NPC, the NPC might register that it is being shot at, state one. It might respond to this by finding cover, state two. Then it might fire back, state three. These are three possible states based on one possible stimulus. We refer to our finite state machines as agent's whose behaviours are defined by their current state, shown as green, red or gray spheres in Fig. 1. Agent states change when interacting with their environment, and so agent behaviours are intrinsically linked to the configuration of this environment. A data set is assigned to each agent that incrementally changes based on these interactions. We use this mechanism to allow audience members a way to indirectly manipulate the data used by performers, by allowing them a way in which to manipulate the agent's environment.

The agents have a complex interconnected relationship with their environment. Each second they are active, a set of data they carry is incrementally changing. The data consists of a negative number, a positive number, and an average between the two. The agents have four separate states: curious, hungry, dividing, and dead. Whilst curious, the agents will seek out the closest Objects of Interest to them. These are objects in the environment that change agent data when agents interact with them. Whilst the agents are in the curious state, a number representing their hunger level is incrementally changing every second. Once it reaches a threshold the agent will enter the hungry state, changing its behaviour to seek out a Food Source Object. Once it finds and interacts with a Food Source Object it returns to the curious state. The agents have a dividing number with a threshold, which also incrementally changes. When this threshold is reached, the agent divides, creating a new agent with new data. When an agent divides twice, it enters the dead state and deposits its data for performers. Agents change colour based on their data, to allow the audience an understanding of the data they carry.

The environment in which agents inhabit includes two types of interactable objects that can be modified by the audience. These are Objects of Interest and Food Source Objects. The Objects of Interest, shown as green or red capsules in Fig. 1, stay in specific locations around the environment and the Food Source Objects, shown as blue cubes in Fig. 1 are randomly placed. Objects of interest will attract agents when in the curious state. They are finite state machines and can be in two different states, visualised through the colour of the object. If an agent interacts with a green Object of Interest, the agent's positive data set will increase by one. If red, the agent's negative data set will increase by one. The audience can change the colour of Objects of Interest simply by interacting with them. When an agent has interacted with an Object of Interest, the object disappears and reappears after a random amount of time between three and eight seconds. Once it reappears it changes to the next colour. Doing this helps to ensure balanced data is generated when fully automated. It also provides a continual need for the audience to interact with the DGE if they wish to influence the performance. Agents are attracted to Food Source Objects when in the hungry state. These objects disappear when an agent interacts with them, reappearing at a random position in the environment after a few seconds. Food Source Objects help to move the agents around the environment, so agents don't get stuck interacting with a set number of Objects of Interest. They can also be modified by the audience. When an audience member interacts with a Food Source Object it will attract all agents within five Unity units (five metres).

Digital Representations of Performers, shown as a green and a red cylinder in Fig. 1, are non-interactive objects that are key to creating data specific to each onstage performer. Once an agent has finished its life cycle, it will stop all other activities to find and deposit its data at the nearest Digitally Represented Performer. These objects hold data which is accumulated from the agent data generation process. This data is then communicated to a corresponding actual onstage performer. We use the same colour coding as the Objects of Interest for these objects so that the audience can quickly assess the state of the data being communicated to the specific performers. In future work we intend to test methods in which audience members have more control over this mechanism, potentially allowing audience members to select specific agents when in the dead state and direct them to their desired performer.

## 4   The Audience

We consider the audience as an integral part of the emergent narrative process, whether they engage with the DGE or not. This is because the automated data generated by the DGE is designed to output balanced data that fluctuates within a certain range. So, we assume that any interactions from the audience will ultimately disrupt this balance. We presume that by default, a balanced data set will be most desirable for the performers and the audience. As this provides a neutral stage setting to be altered by the audience and provides small fluctuations in the data for performers, giving them more freedom in the way performers can interpret the data. This is a major factor when considering audience agency. Agency, as defined by Murray is "the satisfying power to take meaningful action and see the results of our decisions and choices" [20]. Murray argues that if we input into a system and the output does not correspond to the audience's expectations, agency is not extended [20]. Audience agency within our context

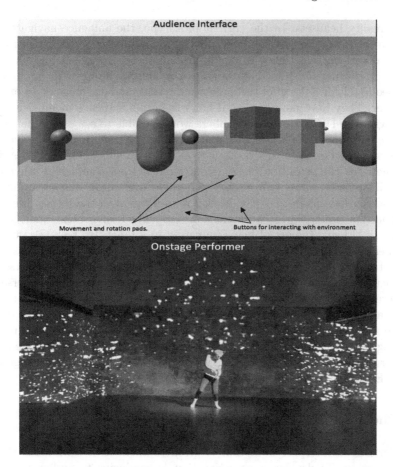

**Fig. 1.** Top: Prototype audience interface and view of digital environment. Bottom: View of performer onstage

is reliant on the audience's ability to understand the causal links between their actions when interacting with the DGE and the output of the onstage performance. So, being able to change the data generated beyond the threshold of the automated generation, creates explicit cues that can be causally linked back to audience actions within the DGE. Our system implements "Extra-Diegetic agency", meaning the audience is an external force on the narrative [16]. This has allowed us to implement a certain type of audience agency, whereby the audience must work with the DGE to gradually change the data, as defined in Sect. 3. By doing this, the performers can anticipate the type and frequency of data given to them, allowing them to tailor their performance more effectively than if the data had no discernible pattern.

Audiences can input into the DGE via a wide variety of computer hardware, including – personal computers, mobile phones, tablet computers, and virtual reality headsets. In the current prototype, the audience navigates this environment in the first-person viewpoint and can interact by tapping or clicking predefined buttons. They can walk around the environment and have 360 degrees of viewing freedom, but they are not able to jump or fly around the space see Fig. 1 for a detail of the audience interface and an image of an onstage performer. They have no avatar so if more than one audience member is interacting with the DGE, audience members won't be able to see each other in the virtual environment. This design decision is meant to help keep the audience members focused on agent interactions to enhance immersion. Murray describes immersion "as the sensation of being surrounded by a completely other reality, as different as water is from air, that takes over all of our attention, our whole perceptual apparatus" [20]. Mason refines this with the terms "Mechanical immersion" and "Narrative Immersion" [16]. The former being analogous to the idea of "Flow", the act of being immersed in a repetitive task [21], and the latter being "the transporting of one's consciousness to a story and events" [16]. Our system allows for a combination of the two, audiences can be immersed by the repetitive task of changing the digital environment to become immersed in an emerging narrative on stage. The audience is limited by the DGE's data generation and distribution mechanisms. Yet audience members have a large degree of freedom. They might want to be immersed by the onstage performance, or they might want to focus totally on the DGE, or a hybrid of the two. We might consider a group of audience members whereby one or more of them engage with the DGE whilst the others monitor changes in the performance.

## 5   The Performers

The Performers interpret data that is given to them as a continuous stream of information. To develop a narrative that is conducive to audience agency, a set of rules around data interpretation must be generally understood and be visually explicit so that the audience can relate performer actions to their actions. There is the possibility for data to be communicated in a large variety of ways, such as using on-stage sound, lights and video, shown in Fig. 1. We are currently able to consider any hardware which can be controlled by Musical Instrument Digital Interface (MIDI) as a communication method. Our prototype uses LightKey to control the onstage lights and the Gesture and Media System (GAMS) for directing robot lights to specific performers. LightKey is a piece of software that allows for MIDI controllable stage lighting, and the GAMS is a live motion tracking system that allows performers to manipulate stage equipment via movement and gestures [11]. This means we can automate tracking lights so that performers can understand to whom data belongs. The GAMS also provide a convenient way in which we can implement performer input into the DGE. This mechanism could allow performers to add new information into the system, such as introducing audience interactable props or changes in scenes etc.

The colour, position, brightness, and focus of the robot lights we are using for the prototype can be modified by the DGE. Performers might interpret changes to this light in a few different ways. They might consider the colour of their spotlight as a cue for how they should act towards other performers, and the brightness to mean how dominate they should be in the scene. They can also interpret these cues in a literal sense, for example, if a performer is acting out a scene where they are gambling, they might use the brightness of the light as a cue to say whether they are winning or not. These are basic examples, and we envisage that a multitude of different cues will be implemented to extend the available narrative information. It is important to understand and design these cues in a way that is conducive to the extending of audience agency. This leads to a difficult balancing act between the freedom for performers to interpret data and the audience's ability to causally link their input to performer actions. By running performer workshops, we will be able to gain insights into how to tackle this issue.

## 6  Conclusion

In this paper, we have presented a novel approach to creating Emergent Narrative within a live theatre context. We have established how this approach, using our Data generation Engine software, mediates interactivity between the audience and onstage performers and how it automates a data generation and distribution process. We have briefly detailed ways in which this data could be useful for performers creating and developing narrative and how we can communicate this data to performers when onstage. This is achieved by using generated data to modify onstage equipment such as lighting, sound, and video that is individualised per-performer. We redefine the relationship between audience and performers, as one whereby a combination of all parties involved in the performance are considered as joint authors. We have also established a way in which an audience can have a large degree of freedom to contribute to the emerging narrative at their leisure and still be an integral part of the entire performance. This is made possible by establishing a standardised data automation process, which creates data that typically fluctuates between a set of parameters. It is then possible to distinguish between audience interactions and automation, and so the choice to allow for automation or to interact is an integral one. We are currently in the final stages of prototyping and the next step is deployment. In this stage we will test the system with improvisational performers. This will be an iterative process, utilizing workshops to evaluate and improve the system based on performer feedback. This project is a step towards developing a system that can be tailored to many performance situations including improvisational dance and stand-up comedy, giving the audience a way to contribute positively in a manner that allows for the narrative to develop consistently and coherently.

**Acknowledgments.** The work is supported by Paper Dove Company Ltd. and the Intensive Industrial Innovation Programme European Regional Development fund.

# References

1. Abramovic, M.: Rhythm 0. Studio Morra, Naples, Performance Art (1974)
2. Adams, Z., Adams, T.: Dwarf Fortress. Bay 12 Games (2002)
3. Aylett, R.: Emergent narrative, social immersion and "storification". In: Proceedings of the 1st International Workshop on Narrative and Interactive Learning Environments, pp. 35–45 (2000)
4. Aylett, R.S., Louchart, S., Dias, J., Paiva, A., Vala, M.: FearNot! – an experiment in emergent narrative. In: Panayiotopoulos, T., Gratch, J., Aylett, R., Ballin, D., Olivier, P., Rist, T. (eds.) IVA 2005. LNCS (LNAI), vol. 3661, pp. 305–316. Springer, Heidelberg (2005). https://doi.org/10.1007/11550617_26
5. Aylett, R., Louchart, S., Dias, J., Paiva, A., Vala, M.: FearNot! VICTEC European project, eCircus European project (2007). https://sourceforge.net/projects/fearnot/
6. Blast Theory: A machine to see with (2010). https://www.blasttheory.co.uk/projects/a-machine-to-see-with/. Commission for 01 San Jose, Banff New Media Institute and Sundance New Frontier. premiered in San Jose, 16 Sept 2010
7. Boal, A.: Theatre of the Oppressed. Theatre Communications Group, New York (1985)
8. Cavazza, M., Charles, F., Mead, S.: Character-based interactive storytelling. IEEE Intell. Syst. **17**(4), 17–24 (2002)
9. Coudray, S.: The theatre of the oppressed. Online Article (2017). https://www.culturematters.org.uk/index.php/arts/theatre/item/2455-the-theatre-of-the-oppressed. Accessed 8 June 2020
10. Dias, J., Mascarenhas, S., Paiva, A.: FAtiMA modular: towards an agent architecture with a generic appraisal framework. In: Bosse, T., Broekens, J., Dias, J., van der Zwaan, J. (eds.) Emotion Modeling. LNCS (LNAI), vol. 8750, pp. 44–56. Springer, Cham (2014). https://doi.org/10.1007/978-3-319-12973-0_3
11. Gibson, S.: Opto-phono-kinesia (OPK): designing motion-based interaction for expert performers. In: Proceedings of the Twelfth International Conference on Tangible, Embedded, and Embodied Interaction, pp. 487–492. ACM (2018)
12. Harmon, S.: An expressive dilemma generation model for players and artificial agents. In: Proceedings of the 12th Conference on Artificial Intelligence and Interactive Digital Entertainment, pp. 176–182. AAAI Press (2016)
13. Kriegel, M., Aylett, R., Dias, J., Paiva, A.: An authoring tool for an emergent narrative storytelling system. In: AAAI Fall Symposium - Technical Report (2007)
14. Louchart, S., Aylett, R.: Solving the narrative paradox in VEs - lessons from RPGs. In: Rist, T., Aylett, R., Ballin, D., Rickel, J. (eds.) Intelligent Virtual Agents, vol. 2792, pp. 244–248. Springer, Berlin Heidelberg (2003). https://doi.org/10.1007/978-3-540-39396-2_41
15. Magerko, B., et al.: An empirical study of cognition and theatrical improvisation. In: Proceeding of the Seventh ACM Conference on Creativity and Cognition, pp. 117–126. ACM Press (2009)
16. Mason, S.: On games and links: extending the vocabulary of agency and immersion in interactive narratives. In: Koenitz, H., Sezen, T.I., Ferri, G., Haahr, M., Sezen, D., Catak, G. (eds.) ICIDS 2013. LNCS, vol. 8230, pp. 25–34. Springer, Cham (2013). https://doi.org/10.1007/978-3-319-02756-2_3
17. Mateas, M., Stern, A.: Integrating plot, character and natural language processing in the interactive drama façade. In: 1st International Conference on Technologies for Interactive Digital Storytelling and Entertainment (TIDSE 2003), Darmstadt, Germany. p. 13 (2003)

18. Maxis: The Sims. Electronic Arts (2000)

19. Mojang Studio: Minecraft. Sony Interactive Entertainment (2009)

20. Murray, J.: Hamlet on the Holodeck : The Future of Narrative in Cyberspace. Free Press, New York (1997)

21. Nakamura, J., Csikszentmihalyi, M.: Flow theory and research. In: The Oxford Handbook of Positive Psychology, 2nd edn., pp. 195–203. Oxford University Press (2002)

22. Riedl, M.: A comparison of interactive narrative system approaches using human improvisational actors. In: Proceedings of the Intelligent Narrative Technologies III Workshop on - INT3 2010, ACM International Conference Proceedings Series, pp. 1–8. ACM Press (2010)

23. Riedl, M., León, C.: Toward vignette-based story generation for drama management systems. In: Workshop on Integrating Technologies for Interactive Stories. 2nd International Conference on INtelligent TEchnologies for interactive enterTAINment (2008)

24. Riedl, M.O., Stern, A.: Believable agents and intelligent story adaptation for interactive storytelling. In: Göbel, S., Malkewitz, R., Iurgel, I. (eds.) TIDSE 2006. LNCS, vol. 4326, pp. 1–12. Springer, Heidelberg (2006). https://doi.org/10.1007/11944577_1

25. Shead, M.: Understanding state machines (2018). https://www.freecodecamp.org/news/state-machines-basics-of-computer-science-d42855debc66/. 6 June 2020

26. Skybound Games, Telltale Games: The Walking Dead. Telltale Games (2012)

27. Stern, A., Mateas, M.: Façade. Procedural Arts (2005)

28. Swartjes, I., Vromen, J.: Emergent story generation: lessons from improvisational theater. In: Intelligent Narrative Technologies: Papers from the AAAI Fall Symposium. AAAI Fall Symposium Series (2007)

29. Cardona-Rivera, R.E., Sullivan, A., Young, R.M. (eds.): ICIDS 2019. LNCS, vol. 11869. Springer, Cham (2019). https://doi.org/10.1007/978-3-030-33894-7

30. Young, R.: Notes on the use of plan structures in the creation of interactive plot, In: Programming and Applications with Xt (OPEN LOOK Edition, pp. 1053–1066. Prentice Hall (1999)

# A Novel Design Pipeline
# for Authoring Tools

Daniel Green[(⊠)], Charlie Hargood, and Fred Charles

Bournemouth University, Bournemouth, UK
{dgreen,chargood,fcharles}@bournemouth.ac.uk

**Abstract.** Interactive digital narrative research presents a diverse range
of authoring tools [1,4,8,12,14]. Although our field often publishes the
technology, it less often publishes a refined UX design pipeline for those
tools' authoring experience. This is despite the UX of these tools long
being identified as a key challenge [14] and UX design pipelines being
an active area of research in adjacent technologies such as the games
that sometimes deliver our stories [3,10,11]. We present a three-stage
design pipeline targeting the creation of interactive narrative authoring
tools that is informed by existing design pipelines that consider the user
and their experience at all stages. We then detail our own application
of this pipeline to the design of a new authoring tool, reporting on the
methodologies, analyses, and findings of each step.

**Keywords:** Interactive narrative · Authoring tools · User experience

## 1 Introduction

Without a well-designed user experience (UX), accessibility is reduced, and systems can become restricted to those with appropriate technical knowledge. This
is true for Interactive Digital Narrative (IDN) authoring tools as much as any
other software where poor UX can act as a gatekeeper preventing creatives from
using the medium [12]. In order to increase the usability of our authoring tools,
we must not only design our authoring tools around the underlying narrative
data models. We must also consider the authoring experience at all stages by
incorporating them into established design and development processes.

Existing publications in this space detail features of the technology and sometimes an overriding philosophy behind the design of the tool, such as the support
of specific patterns [12] or "language-based" principles [9]. However, detailed UX-
centric design pipelines, such as in other software or games [10], are rarer, despite
discussions in this space identifying key UX concerns with these tools for some
time [14]. It follows that there is a gap in this domain that might be addressed
by more research into refined UX design methodologies and pipelines.

In this paper, we present our own design pipeline for creation of IDN authoring tools informed by NNGroup's Product Design Cycle[1] and Hamm's *Wireframing Essentials* [6]. We then describe our own application of the pipeline for

---

[1] https://www.nngroup.com/articles/ux-research-cheat-sheet/.

© Springer Nature Switzerland AG 2020
A.-G. Bosser et al. (Eds.): ICIDS 2020, LNCS 12497, pp. 102–110, 2020.
https://doi.org/10.1007/978-3-030-62516-0_9

the design of an authoring tool that supports our *Novella 2* narrative model [5]. By using the design of our own tool as a case study we highlight what can be learned from the application of this pipeline and how wider authoring tool design might benefit from such a process.

## 2   The Pipeline

Our pipeline consists of three phases—*Research, Discover,* and *Refine.* The *Research* phase includes creation of a persona(s) to represent a typical user of the target audience, analysis of where in a pipeline the tool would best fit, and a Minimum Viable Product (MVP) listing of required features per user requirements and expected functionality. This ensures that the target audience is known, the software is positioned for practical use, and early requirements are identified. The *Discover* phase involves creation of candidate designs in the form of static, low-fidelity wireframes, and involvement of potential users in an exploratory participatory design process, both based on the previous phase's output. After this phase, there should be a final candidate design ready to progress. The *Refine* phase takes the final candidate design, and from it creates a high-fidelity, interactive wireframe. This is then refined further using a RITE philosophy [10, 11], ensuring that the final mockup has been tested with actual users to identify and fix any potential usability issues. These three phases are informed by industry-standard techniques, and after completion, will result in a refined mockup prototype that is suitable for use in development.

### 2.1   Research

**Persona Creation.** Personas typically evolve from insights into actual target users, but for our field, access to professionals is limited, so we instead surveyed relevant job postings and literature to build up a profile. 14 job postings from a range of leading video game studios were used as a representative sample of expected skills and requirements for the target audience of our authoring tool. Using NNGroup's persona guidelines[2], the tabulated skills and requirements were combined with information on the role of a Narrative Designer present in *The Game Narrative Toolbox* [7] to help build our final persona.

**Pipeline Analysis.** It is important for authoring tools development to not only know how, but *when* the tool will be used. For game narrative authoring tools, this is knowing where it fits within the game development pipeline. The point at which the narrative team are involved and their level of engagement with development differs not only between studios, but even between games of the same studio. We looked at the approaches existing game studios take to implementing narrative and considered upstream and downstream processes [7] to help frame the position in the pipeline, taking into account the intended function of our

---

[2] www.nngroup.com/articles/persona.

particular tool design. Combining these, we were able to build an understanding of where the tool would fit within a real game development pipeline.

**MVP.** For our prototype tool, the MVP was building a core list of constraints and requirements that consider the persona, pipeline position, satisfy the underlying narrative model functionality, and cater for expected tool functionality.

## 2.2  Discover

The *Discover* phase is about creating and iterating upon candidate designs based on the output of the *Research* phase, preparing them to be further developed in the *Refine* phase. Taking into account outputs of the *Research* phase, several candidate designs should now be drafted. In our case, we created two high-level design variations as static wireframes. We used an approach based on participatory design [13] allowing us to identify the first impressions formed by users and to uncover any faults or desires early on in the design process.

**Methodology.** The participant demographic was students of IDN who have any level of experience with existing authoring tools. Participants, in individual moderated sessions, were firstly shown an introduction document that covered the persona, a high-level vision of the tool, its required functionality based on the MVP, and a detailed description of the underlying model. Participants then used think-aloud protocol to sketch and annotate the way that they intuitively envisioned an interface supporting the descriptions they had just read. It was critical to our approach that the detailed description in the introduction contained no leading or suggestive phrasing to bias this process. These sketches were explored in an unstructured interview seeking to understand their motivation and to expand upon their ideas. Following this, they were shown our own candidate designs and engaged in discussion about their interpretation, as well as the advantages and disadvantages of each approach.

**Results and Discussion.** The experiment was run with three participants, all with previous experience in authoring IDN. In participants' own designs, all intuitively defaulted to graph-based systems with nodes connected with lines. Another trend between all participants was the use of an outliner panel on the left of the interface to show hierarchical relationships to the user. Property editing was implemented either as a popup window or a sliding panel, both being used to allow for non-intrusive editing in a way that did not permanently take up screen real-estate. All participants highlighted the importance in their approaches of using distinct shapes and colors to differentiate between elements of the model, with the intention being to aid quick identification.

Our first design was described as in intuitive and fluid due to the familiarity of the flowchart-like visuals. However, there was mixed feedback about how the design provides hierarchical context to the user. A suggested solution was the addition of an outliner, something that all participants had in their own designs.

Our second design was preferred by all participants. All participants spoke positively about the inclusion of an outliner due to its ability to provide an overview of the story and given context as to the current position when editing. The most discussed part of the design was the multilayer 'artboard' system which provides a window to see the contents of a node without explicitly traversing into it. This was praised for providing extra context and therefore a better understanding of the story at a given point without the need for further traversal.

Taking into account the feedback from participants, it was decided that the second candidate design was to be chosen, with feedback from participants being considered for inclusion in the design.

## 2.3   Refine

The final phase is *Refine* which involves taking the chosen candidate design and feedback from the *Discover* phase and information from the *Research* phase and using them to refine the prototype. As the chosen candidate design is an approach rather than a prototype, it first needs to be expanded upon, which involves enhancing its features and visual quality, transitioning into a high-fidelity mockup with interactivity. In our case, features were added inline with user feedback, constraints, and requirements outlined in previous phases. A notebook was created alongside the new prototype to have a clear understanding of what everything should do, which sometimes is unclear due to limited capability of prototypes. Examples within the prototype were also contextualized to reflect an actual game story rather than placeholder content. The methodology used in this process is based upon the philosophy of the RITE method [11], which positions itself as a discount usability test, and has extensive use in the games industry [10]. The goal is to produce a prototype with a refined user experience by detecting and fixing miscommunications and misunderstandings that participants encounter.

**Methodology.** The participant demographic was students of IDN who have any level of experience with existing authoring tools. Participants, in individual moderated sessions, were shown a document that covered a summary of the persona and an overview of the details about the tool. Following this, they were walked through three short videos from *Mass Effect*[3], which were simplified and recreated in the prototype. A total of 36 tasks were created based on mandatory functionality that users should be able to perform in the tool, mostly phased as 'show me how' or 'walk me through' due to limited interactivity of prototypes. Participants completed each task using the prototype and think-aloud protocol. This was semi-structured in that further questioning could take place based on how the participant responds. If participants require minimal assistance when completing a task (clarification of behavior, pointed in a broad direction) then the RITE spreadsheet is marked with **X** representing error as miscommunication of a feature. If they are unable to continue without assistance, a **Z** is marked, representing failure as a misunderstanding of a feature. If a mark is made, further questions were asked to identify the cause which aids generating solutions. For

---

[3] Mass Effect. BioWare, 2007.

| Task | Problem Description | P1 | P2 | P3 | P4 | P5 | P6 | P7 | Fix 1 | Fix 2 | Fix 3 |
|------|--------------------|----|----|----|----|----|----|----|-------|-------|-------|
| T4 | Couldn't figure out how to create a Frame. | | | X | | | | | Note 1 | | |
| T8 | Struggled to identify the nodes in the Canvas. | | X | | | | | | Note 2 | | |
| T6 | Thought that double clicking a node edited its label. | | X | X | | | | | Note 3 | | |
| T10 | Unable to navigate into a node in Artboard mode. | X | | | | | | | Note 4 | | |
| T13 | Unable to add Node Templates to the Canvas. | X | | | | | | | Note 5 | | |
| T13 | Unable to create Node Templates from the editor. | X | | | | | | | Note 6 | | |
| T17 | Unable to add links to nodes. | | X | Z | | | | | Note 7 | | |
| T28 | Scripts window contained scripts unclear. | X | X | X | | | | | Note 8 | | |
| T32 | Couldn't tell that colored variables relate to the outputs. | Z | | | - | | | | | | |
| T33 | Struggled with states in the Simulation Mode. | | X | X | | | | | Note 9 | Note 10 | Note 11 |

**Fig. 1.** RITE spreadsheet showing changes due to errors (**X**) and failures (**Z**). Columns P1–P7 are participants. **Note 1:** Added a Frame icon to the toolbar. **Note 2:** Added 'Main' Group to the Outliner. **Note 3:** Double clicking a node edits the label. **Note 4:** Replaced expand icon and darkened color. **Note 5:** Changed '+ Node Template' to 'Insert Node Template', moved buttons to right, darkened text. **Note 6:** Added labeled headers to lists in all Editor panels. **Note 7:** Connection panels animate a + button. **Note 8:** Added a label to the left of the script dropdown and hidden the help text in a popup. **Note 9:** Added an explicit save button and moved delete behavior into a popover no longer requiring applying states to delete them. **Note 10:** Renamed delete button to read 'Delete...'. **Note 11:** Renamed delete button to read 'Manage'.

each task, the participant's expected solution was compared with the intended solution of the design. Participant answers were rephrased and repeated back to them to resolve potential ambiguity, allow them to expand upon their answer, and to give time to take more accurate notes [2]. Tweaks and fixes were made to the prototype between participant sessions based on RITE spreadsheet entries, feedback from participants, and moderator observations. Logs and copies of the prototype were stored per participant to help track change over time.

**Results and Discussion.** Seven participants took part in the experiment. Each participant interacted with an *iPad Pro* acting as a real-time preview of the prototype, controlled by the moderator. Figure 1 shows the problems that participants P1–P7 encountered and changes made to mitigate them. If a cell is empty, the problem was not encountered by the participant. Shaded cells represent a corresponding change being used. A summary of key changes follows with a sample of the final refined interface shown in Fig. 2.

**Artboard Button.** In T10, P1 incorrectly assumed the icon button on Artboards was for closing and only clicked after guessing. The icon was updated to be less ambiguous and no others experienced troubles.

**Node Creation.** Creating nodes, tested in T3, was done via the Canvas' context menu. P3 suggested adding physical buttons, which was implemented by adding an array of icon buttons to the Toolbar. These buttons could be clicked on or dragged from into the Canvas, with their different interaction method being distinguished by dotted outlines. All following participants used the buttons over the context menu, and all correctly identified the drag-drop behavior.

**Frames.** Frames, tested in T4, were originally created using the Canvas' context menu and didn't take into account selections. P1 suggested autofitting to selection, which was added to the prototype and the task text updated accordingly. P3 required assistance with creation but no change was made as their thought process greatly increased complexity and was contradictory to established paradigms. P4 suggested adding a button for Frames to the toolbar, after which all participants used this button over the context menu.

**Adding Links.** Adding links to nodes could originally be done only through a context menu, and was tested in T17. P2 and P3 struggled with adding links. A fix was introduced to reveal a hidden '+' button on the node's connection panel upon hover. All following participants defaulted to the new hover functionality.

**Outliner.** The Outliner originally displayed nodes made by the user only. In T8, participants had to identify types of nodes in the Canvas, with P2 using the Outliner hierarchy to help them, but incorrectly identified some. To help distinguish between the types, a parent 'Main Group' was added to the Outliner. After adding this extra context, participants were able to identify all types without trouble, using the Outliner as a reference.

**Node Templates.** Creation and insertion of Node Templates was refined in tasks 13 and 14. The insert button, originally labeled '+ Node Template', was identified by P1 as creation. The label was changed to 'Insert Node Template' and a context menu alternative was added to the Canvas. After these changes, no participants had trouble inserting them. Creation was done in an editor window using a context menu on an item list. This was problematic for P1 as the purpose of the list was unclear. The solution involved adding labeled headers to all item

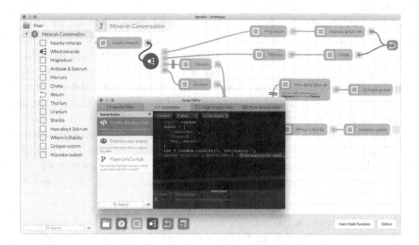

**Fig. 2.** A snapshot of the refined authoring tool design with an editor window open.

lists, and as a suggestion from P2, adding an explicit '+' button to the headers as an alternative to context menus. The labeled headers were then added to every list for all editor windows. After these changes, no participants had trouble creating elements, and most defaulted to the '+' buttons in the headers.

**Node Properties.** Editing of node properties, refined in T6, was originally done by double clicking a node to show a temporary floating window. P1 suggested that the popup should be detachable, remaining permanent unless closed. P2 and P3 instead expected double clicking to edit a node's label in-place, so the behavior was changed and opening properties was demoted to the context menu. Half of the remaining participants double clicked the node to edit its label, with the other half preferring to use the properties panel.

**Scripts.** All script editor panels have a collapsible error list, looked at in T23. P1 suggested that the clarity could be increased by adding a colored bar and icon to reinforce that it shows errors. After this change, all participants identified its function correctly. T28 looked at a node's custom scripts, which are edited in a dedicated window for that node. P1–P3 were unable to change which script was being edited without assistance. This was fixed by better labeling the dropdown used to select scripts, and by expanding upon yet counter-intuitively hiding the help text behind an info button. With these changes, all following participants read the help text and had no trouble selecting and assigning custom scripts.

**Simulator Variables.** The Simulation window highlights variables that impacts outputs or sibling triggers, and was tested in T32. P2 was unable to identify this relationship, but upon discussion they decided it was misinterpretation of colors. It was decided to not make changes until further occurrences, of which none happened, and as such this was treated as an outlier.

**Simulator Variable States.** T32 had participants complete a number of steps relating to variable state management in the Simulator window using a small desktop application that mimicked the states panel in the prototype. Initially, this was done with a single editable combobox and delete button, with deletion requiring assignment of a state first. P2 and P3 found the behaviors confusing. With their feedback, an explicit save button was added (although placebo, as it functioned identically to submitting in the combobox) and deleting was changed to show a popup to select what to delete rather than deleting the current state. All following participants were able to complete the tasks, even though the underlying functionality didn't change. However, P4 still hesitated with deleting, and after discussion, the delete button was suffixed with ellipsis to suggest further action. P5 and P6 hesitated less, so the label was changed one last time to read 'Manage'. This change appeared successful, as P7 did not hesitate at all, and the terminology used allows for further expansion of state management rather than only deleting.

**Recordings.** After P6, a Recordings feature was added to the Simulation window without disturbance of other features to allow capture and playback of story traversals to better support users in their testing and to reduce human error.

Its design largely copies that of variable states, which had already been greatly refined. Corresponding tasks to test this were also added. The RITE method is flexible enough to allow for modifications like this, as long as there is a followup to the changes. P7, who went through the new tasks, had no trouble explaining and operating the feature, and explicitly commented upon its similarity to variable states, saying that they found this intuitive as a result.

## 3   Conclusions

In this work we have identified a gap in existing authoring tool research concerning formal UX design pipelines. We present our own pipeline for authoring tool UX design and show through a case study of our own tool design how it has helped us to refined the UX. Following our design pipeline will cover identification of potential users and requirements of the tool, exploration and ideation of early designs, and refinement of the designs to be ready for implementation, at all stages considering the user. We demonstrate the potential of the pipeline by walking through our own application of it in the creation of our own authoring tool design. We were able to identify, report on, and fix usability problems that we otherwise would not have noticed, especially if creating the design without involving users. For example, the Scripts window in our tool is core to the model, but the RITE process demonstrated that users found the initial design confusing. Without this we may have mistakenly assumed that this was clear.

Our contributed design pipeline is composed of various user research methodologies that we believe are best suited to our needs, yet remain the most flexible for the design of other future authoring tools. However, as established earlier the specific methodologies used will depend on the context of the tool being developed. Our intent with this contribution is not to insist on a single UX design pipeline but rather to confirm their value to IDN authoring tools, and how one might be developed in a similar context.

## References

1. Bernstein, M.: Storyspace 1. In: Proceedings of the Thirteenth ACM Conference on Hypertext and Hypermedia, pp. 172–181. ACM (2002)
2. Bromley, S.: Interviewing players. In: Games User Research. Oxford University Press (2018)
3. Desurvire, H., El-Nasr, M.S.: Methods for game user research: studying player behavior to enhance game design. IEEE CG&A **33**(4), 82–87 (2013)
4. Green, D., Hargood, C., Charles, F.: Contemporary issues in interactive storytelling authoring systems. In: Rouse, R., Koenitz, H., Haahr, M. (eds.) ICIDS 2018. LNCS, vol. 11318, pp. 501–513. Springer, Cham (2018). https://doi.org/10.1007/978-3-030-04028-4_59
5. Green, D., Hargood, C., Charles, F.: Novella 2.0: a hypertextual architecture for interactive narrative in games. In: Proceedings of the 30th ACM Conference on Hypertext and Social Media, HT 2019. ACM (2019)
6. Hamm, M.J.: Wireframing Essentials. Packt Publishing Ltd., Birmingham (2014)

7. Heussner, T., Finley, T.K., Hepler, J.B., Lemay, A.: The Game Narrative Toolbox. CRC Press, Boca Raton (2015)
8. Koenitz, H.: Three questions concerning authoring tools. In: AIS, ICIDS (2017)
9. Martens, C., Iqbal, O.: Villanelle: an authoring tool for autonomous characters in interactive fiction. In: Cardona-Rivera, R.E., Sullivan, A., Young, R.M. (eds.) ICIDS 2019. LNCS, vol. 11869, pp. 290–303. Springer, Cham (2019). https://doi.org/10.1007/978-3-030-33894-7_29
10. Medlock, M.: The rapid iterative test and evaluation method (RITE). In: Games User Research. Oxford University Press (2018)
11. Medlock, M., Wixon, D., Terrano, M., Romero, R., Fulton, B.: Using the RITE method to improve products: a definition and a case study. UPA **51** (2002)
12. Millard, D.E., Hargood, C., Howard, Y., Packer, H.: The storyplaces authoring tool: pattern centric authoring. In: AIS, ICIDS (2017)
13. Muller, M., Kuhn, S.: Participatory Design. Commun. ACM **36**(6), 24–28 (1993)
14. Spierling, U., Szilas, N.: Authoring issues beyond tools. In: Iurgel, I.A., Zagalo, N., Petta, P. (eds.) ICIDS 2009. LNCS, vol. 5915, pp. 50–61. Springer, Heidelberg (2009). https://doi.org/10.1007/978-3-642-10643-9_9

# Toward a Block-Based Programming Approach to Interactive Storytelling for Upper Elementary Students

Andy Smith[1]([⊠]) [iD], Bradford Mott[1] [iD], Sandra Taylor[1], Aleata Hubbard-Cheuoua[2] [iD], James Minogue[1], Kevin Oliver[1] [iD], and Cathy Ringstaff[2] [iD]

[1] North Carolina State University, Raleigh 27695, NC, USA
{pmsmith4,bwmott,smtayl23,jminogu,kmoliver}@ncsu.edu
[2] WestEd, Redwood City 94063, CA, USA
{ahubbar,cringst}@wested.org

**Abstract.** Developing narrative and computational thinking skills is crucial for K-12 student learning. A growing number of K-12 teachers are utilizing digital storytelling, where students create short narratives around a topic, as a means of creating motivating problem-solving activities for a variety of domains, including history and science. At the same time, there is increasing awareness of the need to engage K-12 students in computational thinking, including elementary school students. Given the challenges that the syntax of text-based programming languages poses for even novice university-level learners, block-based programming languages have emerged as an effective tool for introducing computational thinking to elementary-level students. Leveraging the unique affordances of narrative and computational thinking offers significant potential for student learning; however, integrating them presents significant challenges. In this paper, we describe initial work toward solving this problem by introducing an approach to block-based programming for interactive storytelling to engage upper elementary students (ages 9 to 11) in computational thinking and narrative skill development. Leveraging design principles and best practices from prior research on elementary-grade block-based programming and digital storytelling, we propose a set of custom blocks enabling learners to create interactive narratives. We describe both the process used to derive the custom blocks, including their alignment with elements of interactive narrative and with specific computational thinking curricular goals, as well as lessons learned from students interacting with a prototype learning environment utilizing the block-based programming approach.

**Keywords:** Narrative-centered learning · Block-based programming · Digital storytelling

## 1 Introduction

Digital storytelling, which combines traditional storytelling with rich digital technologies, has emerged as an innovative approach for engaging students in deep, meaningful

© Springer Nature Switzerland AG 2020
A.-G. Bosser et al. (Eds.): ICIDS 2020, LNCS 12497, pp. 111–119, 2020.
https://doi.org/10.1007/978-3-030-62516-0_10

learning [1–3]. Digital storytelling enables the creation of effective and engaging learning experiences that support diverse individual needs [2] and creative exploration of scientific phenomena [4]. However, studies have shown that the success of digital storytelling activities can vary between individual students, and can be improved through interventions such as emotional priming [5], focusing the story creation on scene level details rather than macro story structure [6], and by having students enact their stories through a physical medium such as a puppet show [7].

As a process, creating, refining, and presenting a story reflects many computational thinking concepts. There is a growing recognition of the importance of enabling K-12 students to engage with and develop competence in computational thinking [8, 9]. However, teachers at the elementary levels often lack computer science or computational thinking training, raising the need for activities and tools that can help them integrate computational thinking into their classrooms. Building on Papert's [10] work on programmable environments for learning, creating rich block-based programming environments to support novices has seen success in bringing computational thinking to K–12 education [11]. Block-based programming environments remove many of the hurdles to programming activities, such as the need to learn the complex syntax of traditional programming languages. However, difficulties remain, especially in younger grade levels, leading to a growing body of research providing guidelines for creating age-appropriate learning environments to support computational thinking [12].

In this paper, we investigate how to engage upper elementary students in the creation of interactive narratives while simultaneously developing computational thinking practices. This paper describes our initial work in developing a narrative-centered learning environment for computationally-rich digital storytelling using custom blocks designed to facilitate age-appropriate block-based programming. The learning environment and custom blocks are described in detail, as well as results from a pilot study to evaluate the usability and effectiveness of the learning environment.

## 2 Related Work

Narrative offers an exceptionally promising tool for engaging students in computationally-rich problem solving. Narrative experiences are powerful, helping us connect with others and understand the world around us [13]. Narrative has a unique ability to serve as an effective means for communicating personal understandings of concepts, such as science phenomena, to others [14]. While prominent in elementary education, storytelling is often exercised in the context of language arts, and actualized with either pencil and paper or word processing programs. Digital storytelling seeks to augment the creativity and effectiveness of storytelling, while also expanding storytelling to other subjects [1]. While there are many variants, most digital storytelling activities revolve around students researching a topic, then creating a multimedia presentation of the story that is presented to their teacher and peers [1]. Digital storytelling activities have shown benefits to student learning and engagement [2], visual memory and writing skills [15], and 21st century skills such as problem solving, argumentation, and cooperation [16].

However, the benefits of digital storytelling are at least partially dependent on students' ability to construct narratives, increasing the importance of a well-designed story creation environment, especially for younger learners. One approach to mitigate these concerns has been to embed the story creation process into a more scaffolded context including block-based programming environments. In the La Playa environment, students from ages 9 to 11 use a modified version of Scratch [11] to create animated stories involving sprites, audio clips, and events triggered by user inputs [17]. Horn, AlSulaiman, and Koh [18] utilized a tangible, sticker-based block language to engage students in creating programs in the context of an interactive storybook. While many of the narratives created by these systems focus heavily on sprite manipulation and animation, this work extends these efforts by designing and investigating a block-based programming environment focused primarily on interactive stories by guiding students through the creation of interactive teleplays.

## 3  INFUSECS Narrative-Centered Learning Environment

To enable upper elementary students to create interactive digital stories, the INFUSECS narrative-centered learning environment was designed and developed. INFUSECS specifically focuses on the creation of interactive teleplays. Teleplays consist of several parts, including multiple scenes, multiple characters, dialog between characters, and narration. An additional feature of the environment is supporting audience participation to allow for interactivity in the teleplays. As students develop their teleplays, they can insert moments in the narrative where they would like to ask the audience a question, and change the story depending on how the audience responds.

For example, imagine a scenario where students are asked to create a narrative on how a shipwrecked crew is rescued from a remote island. A sample teleplay (shown in Fig. 1) would describe a set of characters and where on the island the characters were located. After some dialog discussing possible solutions to the crew's predicament, the audience might be asked if the crew should signal for help with a light source using Morse code, or use a siren to create noise to signal a passing ship. Based on the audience response, the narrative can branch and present the rest of the teleplay reflecting the audience's choice. Alternatively, the audience participation may only affect a smaller portion of the teleplay, such as allowing the audience to pick which message is sent.

This story creation process engages learners with several core computational thinking practices, as defined by the K-12 Computer Science Framework (www.k12 cs.org), including recognizing and defining computational problems, developing and using abstractions, creating computational artifacts, testing and refining computational artifacts, and collaborating around computing.

Teleplays are created in INFUSECS by leveraging Google's Blockly framework [19]. Blockly is an open source JavaScript library for building block-based programming editors. Compared to other block-based programming editors such as Scratch and Snap!, Blockly supports several features desirable for creating a block-based environment for elementary-grade students. First, Blockly allows for a customizable toolbox and block palette. This helps mitigate cognitive load issues by presenting students with only the blocks needed for a given scenario, rather than all the available blocks in the programming language. Second, Blockly facilitates the creation of custom blocks, allowing developers to redesign existing blocks to create the necessary functionality to support

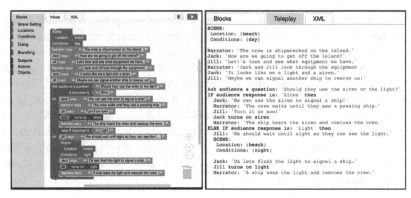

**Fig. 1.** Screenshots of a sample narrative displayed in INFUSECS'S block-based story tab and teleplay tab

digital storytelling. Blockly also allows for the generation of text-based representations of the blocks. While this feature of Blockly is normally used to generate text-based code equivalents of block-based programs, in INFUSECS this feature is used to generate script-like representations of the teleplays, visible at any time via a *Teleplay* tab at the top of the interface.

The INFUSECS learning environment and its custom blocks also leverage findings from previous work with block-based programming environments for upper elementary students [17, 20, 21]. These findings include leveraging visual affordances in the appearance of the blocks, prioritizing sequential programming over event-driven programming, enabling customization and editing rather than being fully generative, and limiting complicated syntax and vocabulary.

The set of custom blocks for INFUSECS was designed to support four main features of interactive narratives: describing a scene, character dialog (including narration), branching, and actions to be performed while performing the teleplay.

The *Scene* block, shown in Fig. 2a, allows students to set the location and conditions where the events in the narrative take place. Location and condition blocks are defined before the activity to fit with a motivating scenario framing a particular digital storytelling activity (e.g., how a shipwrecked crew survives on a remote island). This also allows INFUSECS to leverage Blockly's type-checking capabilities, and prevent students from attaching incompatible blocks to fields, a feature also afforded by the color-coding scheme of blocks.

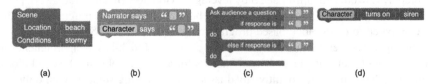

**Fig. 2.** Custom blocks used in the INFUSECS learning environment

The *Dialog* blocks, shown in Fig. 2b, are the core blocks of the storytelling system, as the majority of the content in the student-generated teleplays is dialog between characters or statements by the narrator. A line of dialog is generated through the combination of a *Character says* block and a *Text* block. The name property of the Character block is editable, and an additional *Narrator says* block is provided.

The *Ask audience* block, Fig. 2c, is designed to allow students to incorporate audience participation into their teleplays, while also providing them an opportunity to experiment with conditionals and flow control. The *Ask audience* block contains three properties that must be defined by learners. The first property is the question that will be asked to the audience, and then the two possible responses the audience should respond with to the question. Below each response, students can place the dialog and events that are specific to that branch of the narrative.

Finally, a set of *Action* blocks (example shown in Fig. 2d) were added to allow for denoting times when an action may be taken during the performance of the teleplay (i.e., stage directions). *Action* blocks consist of three separate blocks; a subject, an action, and an object. Subjects are the character in the story completing the action. Objects and actions are designed to be pre-populated based on the learning domain in which the storytelling activity is situated. For example, the scenario described in the sample story above is designed to be used as part of a science unit on electricity, thus the blocks included were aligned with items commonly found in science classrooms, and focused on actions like turning on and off a siren or light. These actions are color-coded to differentiate them from other blocks, and can be developed to correspond to items that can be used as props when students are presenting their final story to the class.

## 4   Pilot Study

To better understand how the INFUSECS learning environment supports digital story-telling and computational thinking in upper elementary classrooms, a pilot study was conducted at a K-8 school in the southeast United States. The primary goal of the study was to observe how pairs of students working together were able to use INFUSECS to create a story as well as to obtain feedback on the successful and unsuccessful aspects of the learning environment and how it could be improved.

Participants in the pilot study included 6 fourth grade students ages 9-10, consisting of 4 males and 2 females. The pilot study took place over approximately 60 min. The 6 students were grouped into pairs to work together. Students reported a range of previous experience with block-based coding environments, with 3 students reporting a familiarity of 6-7 out of 10, and 3 students reporting a familiarity of 1-3, with 1 being low familiarity and 10 being high familiarity.

Before using the INFUSECS learning environment, students were given a brief presentation on the learning environment and story development task, as well as a short video introducing a motivating scenario to act as the inciting event for their stories. The video presented how a team of scientists were shipwrecked on an island in the South Pacific after a powerful storm. Before the ship sank, the scientists were able to transport most of their equipment to shore. Students were then told that they would be creating stories about what the crew would do next and how they would get off the island.

Next, the students were given a brief tutorial on using INFUSECS and began working in dyads to plan their stories for a period of 5 min. A brief starter story was loaded into the environment, demonstrating a *Scene* block, a line of dialog from the narrator describing the shipwreck, and an *Ask audience* block to encourage students to include audience participation in their stories. Student pairs then used the learning environment for approximately 30 min to author their stories. Each group was paired with a member of the research team, who took notes on their observations, and were available to answer questions the students had about using the learning environment. After creating their stories, all six students gathered together as a group with a member of the research team for a brief 10 min focus group where they discussed their overall impressions of the learning activity and INFUSECS (Fig. 3).

**Fig. 3.** Students creating a story using the INFUSECS learning environment

All three groups showed an ability to use the learning environment to create short narratives in the allotted time. Each group was able to define the location and conditions of an initial scene, as well as generate dialog between characters. Overall, groups generated stories ranging from 9-12 blocks in length, consisting mostly of narration and dialog between characters. Two of the 3 groups utilized *Action* blocks, and 2 of the 3 groups incorporated a scene change into their narrative. Students also demonstrated a conceptual understanding of the structure of the teleplays, such as editing every occurrence of a character's name in the program and dialog when they decided to remove a character or modify the character's name.

All groups were able to manipulate the blocks to change the ordering of events, often reading back what they had developed aloud, or using the *Teleplay* tab to view their story before returning to the blocks to incorporate revisions. Students also were able to successfully edit and revise their stories, though there were some usability issues such as text blocks highlighting the entire text when clicked, which caused some dialog to be erased rather than edited as intended. Students were able to utilize the domain-specific *Action* blocks provided, though they struggled incorporating them coherently into their story, highlighting a need to further scaffold this content either beforehand, or during the revision process.

All 3 groups struggled to use the *Ask audience* block effectively. While in discussions with their partners, they exhibited some evidence of understanding how it worked, as well as a desire to utilize the block in their story, only one group was able to create a question with multiple responses, though one of the branches was not fully populated. During the focus group after the students finished using the learning environment, all students were generally positive about INFUSECS. Of interest, they noted that while typing was difficult, they found the process much easier than writing a story with pencil and paper or other tools. One student suggested allowing the recording of audio clips to reduce the typing burden. The main points of confusion expressed by the students were around the *Ask audience* block. Other suggestions for improvements included the addition of more scene locations and weather conditions, and more types of actions and objects for the domain-specific blocks. Additionally, the students requested improvements to the visualization of their teleplays, with suggestions ranging from an animated version of their blocks being generated, to a text version that would play out the blocks sequentially rather than showing the entire teleplay at once.

## 5  Discussion

Overall, the INFUSECS narrative-centered learning environment was successful in enabling students to create play-like narratives, while engaging students in computational thinking concepts such as abstractions, debugging/revising, order of execution, and conditionals. Though the narratives students developed were short, given more time with the learning environment, higher quality narratives could likely be produced. One set of issues observed by multiple members of the research team during the pilot study revolved around collaboration within the student dyads. Often it appeared that each student was attempting to tell a different story, leading to disagreement and distracting from the goal of the activity. While collaboration is an important practice in K-12 education, more scaffolding or structure is needed to ensure successful collaboration.

A promising potential improvement to the learning environment is to incorporate a longer and more structured planning phase in the activity. One student mentioned that their group was distracted changing character names at times, and that perhaps if they defined the story and characters in more detail before entering the block-based environment, they would have been more productive. While a planning phase could be conducted outside the environment using pencil and paper, incorporating it into the learning environment would enable desirable features such as generating dialog blocks prepopulated with character names to reduce typing, and initializing the workspace with parts of the narrative laid out from the planning phase.

The main point of student confusion related to the block-based programming interface was the *Ask audience* conditional block. Though students generally seemed to understand how the block worked conceptually, only one group was able to successfully utilize it. Potential improvements include providing examples of its usage to students beforehand, and having the block prepopulated with an example question and responses rather than being empty.

There are several limitations to these findings, most notably the small sample size and abbreviated time students had to use the learning environment. However, the system was successful at enabling the creation of narratives, and will be available for use by interested parties. [1] Additionally, the source code of the environment is provided for those that wish to modify and extend the set of blocks available in the learning environment.

## 6  Conclusions and Future Work

As the importance of engaging learners at all grade levels in computational thinking continues to grow, the need for novel and effective learning activities also increases. Digital storytelling is a natural fit for this need, and a potentially effective way of embedding computational thinking into existing subjects like science and language arts. Conversely, the structured format and intuitive interface of block-based programming can help overcome some of the difficulties students face when constructing stories, allowing them to better focus on communicating their ideas and experimenting with revising their final product.

To better enable digital storytelling in upper elementary classrooms, the INFUSECS narrative-centered learning environment was created leveraging the Blockly framework. A set of custom blocks was designed specifically to facilitate digital storytelling, while also engaging students with important computational thinking concepts. A pilot study was conducted with 6 fourth grade students along with a focus group to gather feedback from the students, demonstrating the usability of the system for students at this age level, and highlighting the promise of the learning environment for enabling the creation of interactive narratives. Overall, the feedback showed students preferred the block-based interface over traditional pencil and paper activities and indicated several areas for improvement.

Future iterations of the learning environment will focus on expanding the set of storytelling blocks available to students, as well as investigating integration of the generated narratives with visualization technologies. Additionally, the environment will be expanded to include a more robust story planning phase and interface to facilitate more structured and higher quality stories.

**Acknowledgments.** This research was supported by the National Science Foundation through grants DRL-1921495 and DRL-1921503. Any opinions, findings, and conclusions expressed in this material are those of the authors and do not necessarily reflect the views of the National Science Foundation.

## References

1. Robin, B.R.: Digital storytelling: a powerful technology tool for the 21st century classroom. Theory Into Pract. **47**, 220–228 (2008)

---

[1] http://projects.intellimedia.ncsu.edu/infusecs/

2. Smeda, N., Dakich, E., Sharda, N.: The effectiveness of digital storytelling in the classrooms: a comprehensive study. Smart Learn. Environ. **1**(1), 1–21 (2014). https://doi.org/10.1186/s40 561-014-0006-3

3. Yang, Y.T.C., Wu, W.C.I.: Digital storytelling for enhancing student academic achievement, critical thinking, and learning motivation: a year-long experimental study. Comput. Educ. **59**, 339–352 (2012)

4. Henriksen, D., Mishra, P., Fisser, P.: Infusing creativity and technology in 21st century education: a systemic view for change. Educ. Technol. Soc. **19**, 27–37 (2016)

5. Rao, N., Chu, S.L., Faris, R.W., Ospina, D.: The effects of interactive emotional priming on storytelling: an exploratory study. In: Cardona-Rivera, Rogelio E., Sullivan, A., Young, R.Michael (eds.) ICIDS 2019. LNCS, vol. 11869, pp. 395–404. Springer, Cham (2019). https://doi.org/10.1007/978-3-030-33894-7_42

6. Brown, S.A., Chu, S.L., Loustau, T.: Embodying cognitive processes in storytelling interfaces for children. In: Cardona-Rivera, Rogelio E., Sullivan, A., Young, R.Michael (eds.) ICIDS 2019. LNCS, vol. 11869, pp. 357–363. Springer, Cham (2019). https://doi.org/10.1007/978-3-030-33894-7_37

7. Chu, S.L., Quek, F., Tanenbaum, J.: Performative authoring: nurturing storytelling in children through imaginative enactment. In: Proceedings of the International Conference on Interactive Digital Storytelling, pp. 144–155 (2014)

8. Grover, S., Pea, R.: Computational thinking in K-12: a review of the state of the field. Educ. Res. **42**, 38–43 (2013)

9. Shute, V.J., Sun, C., Asbell-Clarke, J.: Demystifying computational thinking. Educ. Res. Rev. **22**, 142–158 (2017)

10. Papert, S.: Mindstorms: children, computers and powerful ideas. Basic Books, Inc. (1980)

11. Resnick, M., et al.: Scratch: programming for all. Commun. ACM **52**, 60–67 (2009)

12. Hill, C., Dwyer, H.A., Martinez, T., Harlow, D., Franklin, D.: Floors and flexibility: designing a programming environment for 4th-6th grade classrooms. In: Proceedings of the 46th ACM Technical Symposium on Computer Science Education (SIGCSE), pp. 546–551 (2015)

13. Bruner, J.: Acts of Meaning. Harvard University Press, Cambridge, MA (1990)

14. Avraamidou, L., Osborne, J.: The role of narrative in communicating science. Int. J. Sci. Educ. **31**, 1683–1707 (2009)

15. Sarica, H.Ç., Usluel, Y.K.: The effect of digital storytelling on visual memory and writing skills. Comput. Educ. **94**, 298–309 (2016)

16. Niemi, H., Multisilta, J.: Digital storytelling promoting twenty-first century skills and student engagement. Technol. Pedagog. Educ. **25**, 451–468 (2016)

17. Franklin, D., et al.: Using upper-elementary student performance to understand conceptual sequencing in a blocks-based curriculum. In: Proceedings of the Conference on Integrating Technology into Computer Science Education, ITiCSE, pp. 231–236 (2017)

18. Horn, M.S., AlSulaiman, S., Koh, J.: Translating roberto to omar: computational literacy, stickerbooks, and cultural forms. In: Proceedings of the 12th International Conference on Interaction Design and Children, pp. 120–127 (2013)

19. Fraser, N.: Google blockly-a visual programming editor. https://developers.google.com/blo ckly/

20. Dwyer, H., Hill, C., Hansen, A., Iveland, A., Franklin, D., Harlow, D.: Fourth grade students reading block-based programs: predictions, visual cues, and affordances. In: Proceedings of the 2015 ACM Conference on International Computing Education Research (ICER), pp. 111–120 (2015)

21. Weintrop, D., Hansen, A.K., Harlow, D.B., Franklin, D.: Starting from scratch: outcomes of early computer science learning experiences implications for what comes next. In: Proceedings of the 2018 ACM Conference on International Computing Education Research (ICER), pp. 142–150 (2018)

# Twine and DooM as Authoring Tools in Teaching IDN Design of LudoNarrative Dissonance

Jonathan Barbara$^{(\boxtimes)}$ (iD)

Saint Martin's Institute of Higher Education, Hamrun, Malta
jbarbara@stmartins.edu

**Abstract.** Teaching Interactive Digital Narratives (IDNs) to undergraduate students ought to be more than branching narratives and using popular authoring tools. Exposing them to challenges of IDNs and pushing them to address these issues can help students think beyond the conventional. Authoring tools may fail to provide functionality to support tackling such issues but coupling a popular branching narrative authoring tool such as Twine with a gameplay focused level editor such as one for DooM provides for interactive narratives that reflect upon one such challenge: LudoNarrative Dissonance. A team of three students' submission using such tools is described and its outcome discussed in terms of its relevance to the ICIDS community interested in teaching IDNs to undergraduate students.

**Keywords:** Authoring tools · LudoNarrative dissonance · Education

## 1 LudoNarrative Dissonance in IDNs

The "narrative paradox" and "ludonarrative dissonance" are two aspects that take center stage with interactive storytelling [1] where the narrative is not an excuse for the game mechanics but a critical element of the experience and likewise the interaction is not an "interactivisation" of a story [2, 3] but an equally important element. Conversely, the question of story vs. game is not about a perfect balance, but about creative decisions, and thus we might reframe ludonarrative dissonance as a conscious design choice, such as in games like *A Way Out* (Electronic Arts, 2018). It is this sense in which we will approach ludonarrative dissonance in this paper, an analysis of which was used to shed light on the different narrative interpretations one may have of IDNs [5]. *A Way Out* forces the dissonance onto the player resulting in a betrayal aesthetic where the inmate character's player is felt betrayed by the undercover cop's player [4]. This paper looks into how we can bring this dissonant element of IDN design by considering a case study involving teaching IDN to undergraduate students using a combination of available authoring tools. Koenitz and Eladhari identify five critical issues in the teaching of IDNs amongst which is the "daunting challenge" of compiling a list of IDN authoring systems with which to teach students the craft of IDNs [1]. In their review of IDN authoring tools, Green et al. mention challenges in accessing these systems in order to assess their features: be it unavailability or the limitations of free versions that were made use of [6]. In a larger

© Springer Nature Switzerland AG 2020
A.-G. Bosser et al. (Eds.): ICIDS 2020, LNCS 12497, pp. 120–124, 2020.
https://doi.org/10.1007/978-3-030-62516-0_11

analysis, Shibolet et al. identified a counter-problem: many such authoring tools are developed in separate efforts and are short-lived [7]. Koenitz and Eladhari are critical of the naïve use of *Twine* [1] just because it is accessible and popular as other tools may better serve a given project [1], and educating enthusiastic undergraduate students has its own particular requirements to be met if we are to sow interest into the field. In this particular case, *Twine*, with its mainly textual deliverables, falls short of our demand for design and implementation of ludonarrative dissonance. Looking at the top game engines on the market, *Unreal Engine* and *Unity*, neither supports interactive narrative authoring directly through built-in tools. However, both support plugins, such as the *Interactive Story Plugin*[2] (Unreal Engine, at a fee) or the Ink interactive fiction language[3] (Unity).

However, plugins are not an ideal solution, since they influence students' perceptions by creating a problematic hierarchy where the game engine is taken as the core element and the narrative through a plugin appears as an afterthought. Instead this paper takes inspiration from Jenkins' suggestion that every medium should make "its own unique contribution to the unfolding of the story"[4] and applies it to authoring tools. This paper argues that rather than be limited by the choice of a single authoring tool, one can complement the use of *Twine* with a an accessible, graphical, gameplay-centric development tool in order to provide final year undergraduate students with an interactive narrative design task that employs both narrative and gameplay choices and allows them to include their comparison in its design. The choice of game-authoring tool fell on *DooM* (id Software, 1993), due to its ability for modification through level editors developed to take advantage of its open source level format.

## 2  Implementation

The case study involves three students who were assigned a combined assignment for their Interactive Narrative Design and Level Design courses wherein *Twine* was used for the branching narratives and *DooM* for the level editing. The assignment required that the choices made in the branching narrative were to be repurposed into the gameplay and the potential for ludonarrative dissonance be addressed and highlighted. Students were on average 19 years old and varied from being avid *DooM* players to being interested more in films and *anime* than games.

Contextual preparation was carried out by having the students play in class the modular *DOOM Board Game* to give the students a tangible sense of level design and challenge setup. The students were then given a crash course on the basics of the original *DooM* level design using one of the freely available *DooM* level editors. The students then watched the first 60 min of the *DOOM* movie (Universal Pictures, 2005) until the scene when one of the space marines sends out a request for support.

The students were then tasked to develop an interactive narrative involving interleaved *Twine* and *DooM* episodes, in which the player forms part of the support team

---

[1] https://twinery.org.

[2] https://www.unrealengine.com/marketplace/en-US/product/interactive-story-plugin.

[3] https://assetstore.unity.com/packages/tools/integration/ink-unity-integration-60055.

[4] http://henryjenkins.org/blog/2007/03/transmedia_storytelling_101.html.

answering this call. *Twine* was to convey the narrative as well as allowing players to perform narrative choices while *DooM* would provide the gameplay and allow the player to confirm (or not) the narrative choices made.

## 2.1 Development Process

The students presented three distinct pathways at each decision point, with the branching narrative developed in *Twine* and the three paths in *DooM*. In the branching narrative the player was briefed and presented with a choice of weapon to train upon and the corresponding target monster for that weapon before leading them to the first *DooM* level. Here the level design focused around a single starting room with each of the three exits leading to one of the available weapons (See Fig. 1) but passing through the exit, a hidden switch would trigger the door closure blocking access to the other weapon choices. This goes against the *DooM* principle of 100% exploration but provides the player with the chance to live up to their narrative choice or to change their mind and make a different choice of weapon. Each of the three areas provided encounters with the monsters linked to the chosen weapon, as in the *Twine* narrative. Foreshadowing was implemented by providing a peek of the upcoming monsters beside the end of level switch, providing a link to the next chunk of *Twine* narrative.

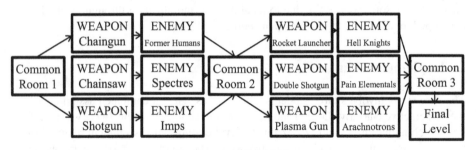

**Fig. 1.** *DooM* level design

Following completion of the level, the player returned to *Twine* and picked the matching exit screenshot. This allowed the students to compare the chosen path in the *Twine* narrative with the actual choice made within *DooM*. In case of mismatched choices being detected, the player was admonished and any difficulty in dealing with the monsters attributed to their choosing different to their training and warned not to do it again. Another *Twine+DooM* sequence takes the player through more training and harder monsters with foreshadowing of the final boss monsters being given without providing engagement, as with the limited firepower it would be fatal. Back in *Twine*, the pacing was kept up by not commenting on any mismatched choices but rather sending for the final briefing before the end of level boss monsters with training only being given on the weaker of the three boss monsters (Mancubus).

A final level, where the player meets the three boss monsters in sequence provided for gameplay closure. After the end of the game, narrative closure was provided in a final *Twine* segment leaving the player with a choice of influencing the marine's future in retirement, being transferred to other planets, or ending in a mental hospital. Closure was also provided should the player die during the game and not wish to continue playing. Figure 2 zooms in on the narrative choice implemented in *Twine* followed by the DooM gameplay thereafter followed by a briefing of the gameplay outcome based upon which exit was chosen. This would reflect upon their gameplay choice of weapon and enemy in comparison with their earlier narrative choice of training.

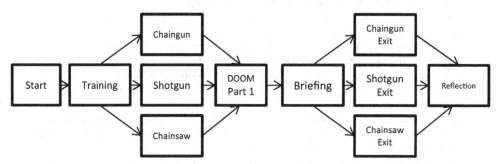

**Fig. 2.** *Twine* branching narrative interleaved with *DOOM* and post-game reflection

## 3    Discussion

In this study, a novel approach to teach undergraduate game design students in interactive narratives reframed ludonarrative dissonance as a potential conscious design choice. Use was made of two authoring tools: the *Twine* engine for the narrative choices and the *DooM* level editor for the gameplay choices. A transmedia-inspired approach was used to familiarise the students with the assignment scope using a board game and part of a movie, both written around the *DooM* gameworld. They were then tasked to create an intertwined *Twine* and *Doom* experience where the narrative choices made in Twine could be confirmed, or not, as gameplay choices in *DooM*.

The educational focus of the ICIDS community can benefit from experimental methodologies that may shed light on different approaches towards IDN Scholarship, especially when augmented with the students' critical analysis of their own work.

The ludonarrative dissonance afforded by this non-conventional collaboration of authoring tools provides a starting point towards incorporating ludonarrative dissonance into the design of the game. The choice of tools also complemented each other: *Twine*'s lack of inherent visuals is compensated by *DooM* 3D perspective graphics while its lack of narrative is compensated by *Twine*'s narrative engine.

Any inconsistency between the choices made in the narrative and through gameplay need to be pre-conceived and taken care of in the design. Thus training your students to be on the lookout for this will go a long way towards creating believable interactive narratives.

# References

1. Koenitz, H., Eladhari, M.P.: Challenges of IDN research and teaching. In: Cardona-Rivera, Rogelio E., Sullivan, A., Young, R.M. (eds.) ICIDS 2019. LNCS, vol. 11869, pp. 26–39. Springer, Cham (2019). https://doi.org/10.1007/978-3-030-33894-7_4
2. Koenitz, H.: Design approaches for interactive digital narrative. In: Schoenau-Fog, H., Bruni, L.E., Louchart, S., Baceviciute, S. (eds.) ICIDS 2015. LNCS, vol. 9445, pp. 50–57. Springer, Cham (2015). https://doi.org/10.1007/978-3-319-27036-4_5
3. Koenitz, H.: Towards a specific theory of interactive digital narrative. In: Interactive Digital Narrative, pp. 107–121. Routledge (2015)
4. Roth, C., van Nuenen, T., Koenitz, H.: Ludonarrative hermeneutics: *a way out* and the narrative paradox. In: Rouse, R., Koenitz, H., Haahr, M. (eds.) ICIDS 2018. LNCS, vol. 11318, pp. 93–106. Springer, Cham (2018). https://doi.org/10.1007/978-3-030-04028-4_7
5. Kubiński, P.: Play It Again, Stanley: Mise en Abyme and Playing with Convention and Narrative in The Stanley Parable (2017)
6. Green, D., Hargood, C., Charles, F.: Define "authoring tool": a survey of interactive narrative authoring tools. In: 11th International Conference for Interactive Digital Storytelling: ICIDS 2018, 5–8 December 2018, Dublin, Ireland (2018)
7. Shibolet, Y., Knoller, N., Koenitz, H.: A framework for classifying and describing authoring tools for interactive digital narrative. In: Rouse, R., Koenitz, H., Haahr, M. (eds.) ICIDS 2018. LNCS, vol. 11318, pp. 523–533. Springer, Cham (2018). https://doi.org/10.1007/978-3-030-04028-4_61

# A Comparison of Children's Narrative Expressions in Enactment and Writing

Niloofar Zarei[1]([✉]), Francis Quek[1], Sharon Lynn Chu[2], and Sarah Anne Brown[2]

[1] Texas A&M University, College Station, USA
{n.zarei.3001,quek}@tamu.edu
[2] University of Florida, Gainesville, USA
{slchu,sarah.brown}@ufl.edu

**Abstract.** This paper aims to explore how children use body-based enactment as a scaffold to compose written stories. We conducted a study where 17 children use a digital story authoring tool to enact and record stories as videos, then write the stories on paper while viewing their acting videos. We compared narrative structure and coherence in story enactment videos and writings and found that the structure of children's narratives in the enacted and written forms varies significantly in terms of the idea units count. Coherence is generally higher in the enactment as well, especially for younger children. Our results imply that while story enactment scaffolds children's imaginative narrative creation, further support in interactive authoring systems might be needed for them to translate their enacted story successfully into writing.

**Keywords:** Storytelling · Children · Design · Human-computer interaction · Narrative writing · Enactment · Pretend play

## 1 Introduction

Free-form pretend play activities are common ways for creative expression in children. Variations of such activities have been referred to in previous literature by terms such as *make-believe play* [8], *drama/dramatic play* [20] or *imaginative enactment* [5]. With minor differences, these terms tend to be used interchangeably for a broad range of embodied activities that involve the use of one's body and manipulation of physical objects to externalize thoughts [16]. Due to the extensive benefits and importance of pretend play for children, various approaches have been proposed in HCI research to nurture these activities [15,23], use them to support children with special needs and abilities [6], or apply them as a scaffold for learning [12]. The type of enactment in these systems range from use of tabletop toy setups [17], to puppet-based systems [1] to full-body enactment [4]. Many of these applications focus specifically on enacting stories because stories are a common mode of expression, reflection, and learning for children [10].

© Springer Nature Switzerland AG 2020
A.-G. Bosser et al. (Eds.): ICIDS 2020, LNCS 12497, pp. 125–130, 2020.
https://doi.org/10.1007/978-3-030-62516-0_12

In this paper, we investigate body-based enactment as a facilitator for children's story writing. Writing is a complex task and involves the mastery of several underlying skills [11]. Activities such as storyboarding [14] can scaffold children's learning process for writing and are sometimes referred to as *prewriting* activities. Therefore our approach can be described as using body-based enactment as a pre-writing activity for narrative writing. This approach has been explored in the past in the context of language arts classrooms [9]. However, there is limited knowledge with respect to the design of interactive technology to support children's narrative writing through enactment.

## 2    Background and Related Work

Previous work has extensively investigated the use of different drama types in the classroom to support young children's reading and writing. Regarding the strategies to include drama in classroom activities, Cremin et al. [7] investigate two methods of integration: the *genre-specific method* and the *seize-the-moment method* and found that the latter engages the children more and can result in a more complex story writing outcome. McNaughton [18] also investigated the benefits of drama versus group discussion for imaginative writing in a controlled experiment. They found that the children in the drama group wrote richer and longer stories. These examples and other similar works demonstrate that enactment can be a successful pre-writing activity.

Previous work has investigated children's thought processes and interaction changes when using an interactive storytelling system. Theune et al. [24] show that children's communication style during the activity changes over time with their attention. Brown et al. [2] investigate children's thinking process in a solo enactment-based storytelling activity and found that thinking in micro-steps rather than the macrostructure results in richer stories. The body of work on children-specific writing tools are limited, and most systems are designed for higher-level students or adults. For instance, intelligent tutoring systems such as the *Writing Pal* [22] and *ICICLE* [19] are examples of these works. Given the differences in the design of educational tools for children and adults, there is a need for research focused on designing tools to support children's writing activities.

## 3    Research Questions and Approach

In his book *Toward a Theory of Instruction* [3], Jerome Bruner theorizes that humans represent knowledge in three ways in the learning process: through actions (*Enactive* representations), through images or graphical summaries (*Iconic* representations), and through symbolic or logical systems such as language (*Symbolic* representations). Following this theory, we investigate the use of story enactment, an enactive representation of narrative, as a way to support the child to progress towards written expression, which is a symbolic representation of the narrative. Our research question is: *When using body-based enactment as a pre-writing strategy, is there a significant difference in the structure, coherence of children's imaginative narratives in the pre-writing and the final written outcome?*

## 4 Interactive Story Authoring System

Our story authoring system was designed to allow children to express stories through full-body enactment, record their story enactment as videos, and play them back as desired. Each story is created as a collection of scenes that are organized in a timeline view. Details like title, background, character, and object for the scene can be added to each scene. Once a scene has these details added and filled out, the child can act it out and record their video. The acting area is a 10 ft by 10 ft space with a green backdrop set up so that in the video recording, the child appears to be in the virtual story environment with the background of their choice appearing in the video. During the act, the child uses a generically-shaped prop representing the object interacted with within that scene. For example, a stick can represent a pickaxe. Once all the scenes in a story are recorded, the interface allows for playback of the scenes in the order they are organized as a continuous story. A more detailed description of the system can be found in [25].

We conducted a study using our enactment-based storytelling system with 17 children participants (13 males, 4 females) in the age range of 8–12. Each participant attended a 90-min study session, consisting of a 20-min practice and introductory story creation task, 45 min of story creation, enactment, and revision based on a one-sentence story starter prompt, and about 20 min of viewing their recorded story enactments and writing their story on paper.

## 5 Data Coding and Measures

The qualitative coding of our data was performed by two coders, who were not part of the study conceptualization or study conduct. For each data point (participant), we had a written version and an enacted version (in the form of a video) of the same story. Two coders extracted the structure in both formats of the stories and graded them for coherence. The agreement between the coders was established based on a 33% subset of the data. They had about 87% percent agreement on the structure codes, and a substantial agreement for the coherence grades with a Cohen's Kappa value of $\kappa = .695$. The rest of the data was divided between the coders so that each coder only received one format of a particular participant's story to code - to ensure that a coder will not induce structure and context from one format to another. The comparison of the structure and coherence was made a posteriori by the researchers.

Our coding method for story structures was adapted from the Purpose Hierarchy method by Grosz and Sidner [13]. *Structure Matching Scores* were calculated for each participant based on the level of matching between the story structures in the written and enacted formats. We analyzed the structure codes generated for each story's formats and divided ideas into two categories: common ideas and mismatching ideas. Common ideas are those that have been conveyed in both formats, and mismatching ideas are those present only in one of the formats. The ideas in each category were then counted and normalized by the total count of ideas present in both formats. This procedure resulted in two different scores for each format of a story to quantify the level of similarity between the structures: the number of ideas and the number of mismatched ideas.

Our coding method for the coherence of stories was adapted from the Narrative Coherence Coding Scheme by Reese et al. [21]. *Story Coherence Scores* were assigned by the coders based on an adapted version of the rubric in [21] that has three sub-measures: (1) Context (time and place), (2) Chronology (order of events), and (3) Theme (topic development). A total grade was also calculated by summing up these three scores.

## 6   Results

The results show a significant difference in terms of the number of ideas between the two formats of stories: $F(1, 16) = 12.688, p = 0.003$. The enacted version of the stories contained a significantly higher number of ideas ($M = 33.82$) compared to the written version of the stories ($M = 17.53$) over all participants. The percentage of mismatched ideas in the enacted format ($M = 0.49$) was significantly higher than the percentage of mismatched ideas in the writing ($M = 0.12$); $F(1, 16) = 30.128, p < 0.001$). These results suggest that the structure in the written and enacted stories are significantly different when comparing the number of ideas expressed in each format.

We did not observe any significant differences in coherence scores over the whole dataset. However, we observed that in participants who were 10 years old or younger (N = 13), the estimated marginal means of all the coherence sub-scores and the overall coherence grade were higher in the enactment format. This pattern was reversed for participants who were 11 or 12 years old (N = 3) - meaning they had higher estimated marginal means in the written stories. ANOVA tests on the coherence scores on the participant sample excluding the 11–12 year-olds showed a significant difference effect in theme sub-scores ($F(1, 13) = 5.692, P = 0.033$) as well as a marginally significant difference for the total coherence grade ($F(1, 13) = 4.339, p = 0.058$). The theme scores were significantly higher in the enacted stories (M = 1.79), and the total coherence grades were also higher in the enacted stories (M = 5.71).

## 7   Conclusion and Future Work

In this paper, we investigated children's use of body-based enactment as a way to support narrative writing. We aimed to understand how children's expression of the story changes when they act or write them. We found that there is a more complex level of imagination present in the enacted videos in terms of the structure, and they are generally graded higher in terms of coherence. Future work should explore interaction design in narrative authoring systems to support children in successfully translating enactive imagination into writing.

# References

1. Bai, Z., Blackwell, A.F., Coulouris, G.: Exploring expressive augmented reality: the fingar puppet system for social pretend play. In: Proceedings of the 33rd Annual ACM Conference on Human Factors in Computing Systems, pp. 1035–1044 (2015)
2. Brown, S.A., Chu, S.L., Loustau, T.: Embodying cognitive processes in storytelling interfaces for children. In: Cardona-Rivera, R.E., Sullivan, A., Young, R.M. (eds.) ICIDS 2019. LNCS, vol. 11869, pp. 357–363. Springer, Cham (2019). https://doi.org/10.1007/978-3-030-33894-7_37
3. Bruner, J.S., et al.: Toward a Theory of Instruction, vol. 59. Harvard University Press, Cambridge (1966)
4. Chu, S.L., Quek, F., Sridharamurthy, K.: Ready... action! a performative authoring system for children to create animated stories. In: Proceedings of the 11th Conference on Advances in Computer Entertainment Technology, pp. 1–4 (2014)
5. Chu, S.L., Quek, F., Tanenbaum, J.: *Performative Authoring*: nurturing storytelling in children through imaginative enactment. In: Koenitz, H., Sezen, T.I., Ferri, G., Haahr, M., Sezen, D., Catak, G. (eds.) ICIDS 2013. LNCS, vol. 8230, pp. 144–155. Springer, Cham (2013). https://doi.org/10.1007/978-3-319-02756-2_18
6. Chung, C.H., Chen, C.H.: Augmented reality based social stories training system for promoting the social skills of children with autism. In: Advances in Ergonomics Modeling, Usability & Special Populations, pp. 495–505. Springer (2017). https://doi.org/10.1007/978-3-319-41685-4_44
7. Cremin, T., Goouch, K., Blakemore, L., Goff, E., Macdonald, R.: Connecting drama and writing: seizing the moment to write. Res. Drama Educ. **11**(3), 273–291 (2006)
8. Dias, M., Harris, P.L.: The effect of make-believe play on deductive reasoning. Br. J. Dev. Psychol. **6**(3), 207–221 (1988)
9. Edmiston, B., Enciso, P., King, M.L.: Empowering readers and writers through drama: narrative theater. Lang. Arts **64**(2), 219–228 (1987)
10. Garzotto, F., Paolini, P., Sabiescu, A.: Interactive storytelling for children. In: Proceedings of the 9th International Conference on Interaction Design and Children, pp. 356–359 (2010)
11. Gerde, H.K., Bingham, G.E., Wasik, B.A.: Writing in early childhood classrooms: guidance for best practices. Early Child. Educ. J. **40**(6), 351–359 (2012)
12. Gros, B.: Digital games in education: the design of games-based learning environments. J. Res. Technol. Educ. **40**(1), 23–38 (2007)
13. Grosz, B.J., Sidner, C.L.: Attention, intentions, and the structure of discourse. Comput. Linguist. **12**(3), 175–204 (1986)
14. Harrington, S.L.: An author's storyboard technique as a prewriting strategy. Reading Teach. **48**(3), 283–286 (1994)
15. Hong, J., Ko, D., Lee, W.: Investigating the effect of digitally augmented toys on young children's social pretend play. Digital Creativity **30**(3), 161–176 (2019)
16. Howes, C., Matheson, C.C.: Sequences in the development of competent play with peers: social and social pretend play. Dev. Psychol. **28**(5), 961 (1992)
17. Mansor, E.I.: 'my world (s)' a tabletop environment to support fantasy play for kindergarten children. In: Proceedings of the 6th International Conference on Interaction Design and Children, pp. 193–196 (2007)
18. McNaughton, M.J.: Drama and children's writing: a study of the influence of drama on the imaginative writing of primary school children. Res. Drama Educ. **2**(1), 55–86 (1997)

19. Michaud, L.N., McCoy, K.F., Pennington, C.A.: An intelligent tutoring system for deaf learners of written English. In: Proceedings of the Fourth International ACM Conference on Assistive Technologies, pp. 92–100 (2000)
20. Peter, M.: Drama, narrative and early learning. Br. J. Special Educ. **30**(1), 21–27 (2003)
21. Reese, E., Haden, C.A., Baker-Ward, L., Bauer, P., Fivush, R., Ornstein, P.A.: Coherence of personal narratives across the lifespan: A multidimensional model and coding method. J. Cognit. Dev. **12**(4), 424–462 (2011)
22. Roscoe, R.D., Allen, L.K., Weston, J.L., Crossley, S.A., McNamara, D.S.: The writing pal intelligent tutoring system: usability testing and development. Comput. Compos. **34**, 39–59 (2014)
23. Ryokai, K., Raffle, H., Kowalski, R.: Storyfaces: pretend-play with ebooks to support social-emotional storytelling. In: Proceedings of the 11th International Conference on Interaction Design and Children, pp. 125–133 (2012)
24. Theune, M., Linssen, J., Alofs, T.: Acting, playing, or talking about the story: an annotation scheme for communication during interactive digital storytelling. In: Koenitz, H., Sezen, T.I., Ferri, G., Haahr, M., Sezen, D., Catak, G. (eds.) ICIDS 2013. LNCS, vol. 8230, pp. 132–143. Springer, Cham (2013). https://doi.org/10.1007/978-3-319-02756-2_17
25. Zarei, N., Chu, S.L., Quek, F., Rao, N., Brown, S.A.: Investigating the effects of self-avatars and story-relevant avatars on children's creative storytelling. In: Proceedings of the 2020 CHI Conference on Human Factors in Computing Systems, pp. 1–11 (2020)

# Interactive Narrative Theory

# GFI: A Formal Approach to Narrative Design and Game Research

Rogelio E. Cardona-Rivera[1,2(✉)], José P. Zagal[2], and Michael S. Debus[3]

[1] School of Computing, University of Utah, Salt Lake City, UT, USA
[2] The Entertainment Arts and Engineering Program, University of Utah, Salt Lake City, UT, USA
rogelio@eae.utah.edu, jose.zagal@utah.edu
[3] IT University of Copenhagen, Copenhagen, Denmark
msde@itu.dk

**Abstract.** We present the GFI framework (standing for Goals, Feedback, and Interpretation), inductively developed to address the MDA framework's shortcomings as a lens and tool for modeling games. GFI stands parallel to MDA as a formal approach that offers bridging the gap between narrative design, game development, story analysis, and game research. Through GFI, we analyze foundational narrative design problems and systematically peek through the game design space, in order to evidence its analytical and generative traction. We believe these discussions signal GFI's potential to elucidate the narrative design process, making it easier for researchers and practitioners to decompose, study, and design a broad class of game artifacts.

**Keywords:** Goals · Feedback · Interpretation · Narrative design · Games

## 1 Introduction

Narrative designers aim to better-integrate narrative and gameplay [26,44], but the role remains contested. They are not necessarily "writers" or "authors," but are responsible for aspects of each; to different degrees depending on genre [28]. Is *environmental storytelling* [33] part of the job? What about writing cut-scene screenplays? Should they contribute to game design documents? [30] How should they manage the relationship between a game's ludic and narrative elements? [63, 73,77] What knowledge should they possess? [74].

Thus, the scope and extent of a narrative designer's role remains unclear. This knowledge gap is critical: we cannot build a cohesive body of narrative design knowledge without knowing what its scope should be. As a consequence, we do not know how to best *support* narrative design. This paper articulates a framework of concepts we argue are central to this practice. To us, a narrative designer is concerned with elements beyond *Mechanics*, *Dynamics*, and *Aesthetics*, or MDA [47]—itself the dominant formal approach to game design and game research. We argue they *also* must be concerned with *Goals*, *Feedback*, and *Interpretation*, or GFI—our proposed formal approach to narrative design.

© Springer Nature Switzerland AG 2020
A.-G. Bosser et al. (Eds.): ICIDS 2020, LNCS 12497, pp. 133–148, 2020.
https://doi.org/10.1007/978-3-030-62516-0_13

## 2    Related Work

GFI is most similar (and complementary) to the MDA framework. MDA decomposes a game into three design components: (1) Mechanics, "the components of the game at the level of data representation and algorithms" that reflect the rules, (2) Dynamics, "the run-time behavior of the mechanics acting on player inputs and each others' outputs over time" that reflects the system, and (3) Aesthetics, "the desirable emotional responses evoked in the player, when she interacts with the game system" that reflect the "fun."

Current works that conceptually describe interactive narrative games are often interactive narrative-specific accounts of MDA. Aarseth's [2] Narrative Theory of Games is an (interactive narrative-specific) model of the Mechanics: it describes components of games across a narrative-theoretic ontology that includes the story world (space), events, and entities (objects and agents). Koenitz's [54] SPP framework is a model of the Dynamics: it describes the behavior of games relative to the player's interaction with a System (of potential stories), which triggers a Process (of interactive story-refinement) that concludes as a Product (the effected narrative). Punday [71] characterizes Involvement, Interruption, and Inevitability (III) as central to the emotional force that an interactive narrative game carries; III is a model of the Aesthetics. Because they focus on different components of MDA, these works by Aarseth, Koenitz, and Punday are complementary; between themselves and to our work. GFI fills in vocabulary necessary to describe phenomena relevant to all—but crucial to interactive narrative—games, whose elements we posit are central to narrative design.

Game design schemas (and MDA in particular) conflict with narrative design ones [36, for example]: "...by separating narrative and game modes as distinct phenomena, integrated use has been thwarted...a siloing of game development roles, and ultimately, functions within a game" [26, p.33]. Designing games like this leads to the *narrative wrapper* [26]: narrative that "wraps around the gameplay to make it transportable and attractive," ultimately "unattached and disposable" [23]. We briefly discuss *how* MDA falls short of describing elements relevant to narrative design, propose GFI as a framework for describing those elements, and evidence GFI's analytical utility through several case examples.

## 3    GFI

GFI complements MDA. In MDA, *Mechanics* describe how players can act, not why they would want to. In GFI, *Goals* (Sect. 3.1) models player motivations and intentions, which are key for (ludic [38] and) narrative engagement [9,65]. Further, MDA's *Dynamics* describe what system behavior results from player inputs, not how to elicit inputs that are supported by the system. These inputs are determined by the tight-coupling of players to the perceivable features of their environments [61]. In GFI, *Feedback* (Sect. 3.2) models these features, critical to structuring the player's activity. Finally, MDA's *Aesthetics* describe what players feel, not what leads to it. Evoked emotions arise from what players think about, which presupposes an *Interpretation* (Sect. 3.3) of their experience [21].

## 3.1  Goals

**Goals** are conditions players are expected to meet to succeed at a game. They are widely thought of as structurally key to games [79], and have two broad senses (*player-defined* [12] ones are out of scope). *Ludological goals* are codified and recognized in-game [25]. *Narrative goals* are player-interpretations of ludological ones [19]. We discuss their ludological sense next; the narrative sense is in Sect. 3.3.

There are two kinds of ludological goals. All games have *ultimate goals* that determine their end conditions [84]. There are at least three (Table 1): *Win* a game (of *Chess*), *Finish* a game (of *Super Mario Bros.* [27, *SMB*]), or *Prolong* the act of playing (*e.g.* by surviving in *DayZ* [50]).

**Table 1.** Ultimate goals: conditions that determine a game's end [84].

| Ultimate | Description ("Games with this ultimate goal...") |
|---|---|
| *Win* | Effect an evaluation when a predefined state is reached |
| *Finish* | Effect *no* evaluation when a predefined state is reached |
| *Prolong* | Conclude against the designer or player's intent |

Achieving a game's ultimate goal requires satisfying the *proximate* [78] or *imperative* [25] goal, that it necessarily decomposes into, whose accomplishment entails the ultimate's. These *imperative goals* more-concretely require the player to effect a particular game state of affairs codified in the game itself [25]. There are at least 10 types (Table 2): *Choose, Configure, Create, Find, Obtain, Optimize, Reach, Remove, Solve,* and *Synchronize*. An imperative links game elements such as space, time, and entities [24]. Each one has a logical dual: its *prevention*.

**Table 2.** Imperative goals: conditions necessary to achieve a game's ultimate goal [25].

| Imperative | Description ("This imperative requires players to...") |
|---|---|
| *Choose* | Select one element from a finite set of elements |
| *Configure* | Manipulate elements such that they are in a "correct" state |
| *Create* | Bring an element into existence that was not before |
| *Find* | Locate a particular element |
| *Obtain* | Bring a particular element under control |
| *Optimize* | Accumulate a requested amount of a particular element |
| *Reach* | Navigate to a particular location |
| *Remove* | Eliminate an element from existence that existed before |
| *Solve* | Select one "correct" element from an infinite set of elements |
| *Synchronize* | Bring one or more elements into spatial/temporal unity |

Imperatives may infinitely decompose into more-specific others, creating a *Ludological Goal Hierarchy* [19]. The hierarchy's base maps onto a moment in gameplay. Figure 1 illustrates this idea: to *Finish SMB*, one must *Remove* (the agent depicted as) Bowser. To do so, one must *Reach* the axe. To do so, (in Fig. 1's state) one might want to *Prevent* (spatiotemporally) *Synchronizing* with the fireball. To do so, one might need to *Reach* the platform. And so on.

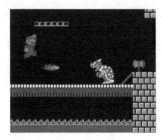

**Fig. 1.** *Finish SMB* requires *Remove*-Bowser via the more-specific imperative *Reach*-Axe, closer to the needed gameplay.

**Fig. 2.** The *Denotational Feedback* at the end of *SMB* elicits one interpretation of its ultimate goal: "Save the princess."

Analytically identifying a game's full hierarchy is challenging, since it must encompass all ludological goals a player may face in all possible playthroughs. However, ludological goals (and their hierarchy) are under the direct control of a designer who specifies what conditions "count" to satisfy the ludological goals. Next, we discuss how careful construction of feedback is required such that goals are *communicated* to the player in order to motivate their activity.

### 3.2 Feedback

**Feedback** is the designed multi-modal stimuli intended to convey perceptual information about the game's structural elements: its underlying ends (goals) and the available means to achieve them (mechanics). This may include things such as graphics, music, sound, text, and more.

Crafting feedback is arguably a narrative designer's most critical responsibility, and is what makes the practice of narrative design relevant to all but the most abstract games, including ones that do not necessarily place a primacy on narrative. (Narrative designer) Dansky [23] argues that people only think of *explicitly denoted* narrative elements as *the* game's narrative. However:

> There's also implicit narrative built into every game through the choice of setting, items, character design [...]   Or, [...] think about the archetypal tool you get in *Minecraft*. It's a pickaxe. It's not a tricorder. It's not a Black and Decker multi-tool. It's a pickaxe, and through its very pickaxe-ness - low tech, implied manual labor, etc. - it tells part of the story of the

world it exists in. [...] As soon as you decide what a game asset is, you're implying the narrative that allows it to exist and function. [23]

One way to conceptually model feedback is per a typology (Table 3) imported from linguistics [20], which parallels Genette's [39] tripartite model of narrative: the story, the discourse, and the narration.

**Table 3.** Typology of feedback available for narrative design.

| Feedback | Examples ("Feedback of this type includes...") |
|---|---|
| *Phonological* | Textual symbols, lines, shapes, haptics, sounds, lights, colors |
| *Lexical* | Words, images, vibration patterns, voices, music notes, sound effects |
| *Grammatical* | Texts, image sequences, camera shots, dialogue, music |
| *Denotational* | Description, exposition, narration, characterization |

*Phonological feedback* is at the level of narration: the sounds, signs, and haptics that can be structured to convey meaning. *Lexical feedback* is at a higher-level of meaning within narration: a language inventory of the smallest units of meaning. In *SMB*, phonological colors contribute to Fig. 1's depiction of the axe, which is lexical. *Grammatical feedback* is at the level of discourse: stimuli structured according to a corresponding syntax. Adherence to that syntax facilitates story sensemaking [18] and licenses inferences about underlying meaning. In *SMB*, image sequences are structured from left-to-right, which Grammatically suggests that the player progresses by going right-ward, potentially giving a clue on how to defeat Bowser for players who have never faced him before. Finally, *denotational feedback* is at the level of story: it includes stimuli that communicates the plot's event structure, and it most-closely matches the discussed sense of "explicit narrative." Figure 2 depicts exposition that is denotational: it signals to the player that their gameplay has concluded.

The content of Fig. 2's feedback reinforces a particular interpretation of the player's activity. This interpretation and the process that gives rise to it is the last element of GFI, which we discuss next.

### 3.3   Interpretation

**Interpretation** is both: (a) the situated *process* of deriving meaning from enaction [76], and (b) the *outcome* of that process. When discussing interpretation in games, what is usually meant is the outcome of the player's game experience. We typically want to answer: what is *the* narrative of a game?

Is it the space of *potential* narratives [54] the system affords? What of games *about* story creation [56]? In describing the interpretations of a game, we want to move away from false dichotomies like *ludology v. narratology* [32,35] toward a more nuanced understanding of how these mutually inform and constrain each other. For narrative design, we propose that it is important to shift the discussion

**Fig. 3.** The parallel goal hierarchies of *SMB* [19]. The suggested readings are: *To Finish SMB* means to "Save the Princess" (Toadstool); to *Remove-Bowser* means "Defeat Bowser"; and to *Reach-Axe* means "Destroy the Bridge with an Axe."

from the *outcome* of a player's interpretation, to the *process* that gives rise to the outcome. This process is what crystallizes the defining function of **narrative design**: structuring feedback relative to mechanics and goals aimed at guiding a player's *existing* interpretation of the game's narrative into a *preferred* interpretation. In this definition, the narrative designer (or whomever they represent) is who prefers the interpretation. Further, "structuring" is broad: narrative design *may* encompass changes to mechanics and goals, so long as these are intended to effect changes to the interpretation that players may derive.

The interpretation *outcome* is what defines a **narrative goal**: the meaning derived from a ludological goal (Sect. 3.1) as experienced in a game. The feedback in Fig. 2 scaffolds the player's interpretation of their accomplishment: the player's *quest* – a prominent element in primarily-narrative games [46] – is over. Thus, one way to narratively make sense of *To Finish* is as "Save the Princess."

Because narrative goals are interpretations of ludological ones, they both entail the **Parallel Goal Hierarchies** (Fig. 3). The *Ludological* side reflects the sub-ordinate goals needed to *satisfy* super-ordinate goals; *i.e.* the "how." In tandem, the *Narrative* side reflects the super-ordinate goals needed to *motivate* the sub-ordinate goals; *i.e.* the "why." The ludological side is best read top-down (you finish *SMB by* removing Bowser) whereas the narrative side is best read bottom-up (you defeat Bowser *for the purpose of* saving the Princess).

The hierarchies and their mapping is relative to the individual, and depends on both the game and its surrounding context. For instance, our interpretation of *SMB*'s *To Finish* as "Save the princess" is plausible due to its (discussed) quest-like nature *but also due* to the game's packaging, which asks: "Do you have what it takes to save the Mushroom Princess?" (Fig. 4).

**Fig. 4.** *SMB*'s packaging asks: "Do you have what it takes to save the Mushroom Princess?," which supports interpreting *SMB*'s ultimate goal as "Save the Princess."

However, interpretations can be fragile. For instance, nothing indicates that the player is in fact "destroying the bridge with an axe:" the corresponding animation is of such low framerate that a player may walk away with an alternate interpretation (*e.g.* the bridge retracted). Further, *is* the object at the location to reach even an axe? Its feedback suggests that via a *prototypical* [57] appearance, but the authors disagree: the third author sees it as a lever. In both cases it is the task of narrative designers to match feedback for a ludological goal to narrow the players' potential (existing) interpretation down towards the designer's intended (preferred) interpretation (conversely, a game designer might need to craft a ludological goal that aligns with the narrative designer's intended feedback).

Dena [26] offers one way to conceptually model interpretation: the *Sequence Method* [58], which is an established method for television (TV) series narrative design. This method models the player's interpretation as a *reader-response process* [51], driven by unanswered-questions, with an (eventual) *outcome* of answers, possibly inciting curiosity [26, p.43]:

> [The Sequence Method] divides the experience into a series of questions for the audience [...] the overall question introduced at the beginning and answered near the end, and [...] multiple short-term questions to keep driving the audience's interest. "[when] answered, the [TV] series is forced to either introduce new central questions or end." [58, *op. cit.*]

This method has been endorsed by several narrative designers within the games industry. Bryant and Giglio [15], who have designed for both movies and games, argue that the method is useful to structure objectives for level design. Further, Bernstein [10], who has designed for movies, games, and television, argues that this method works better than the 3-Act Structure [34] *because* it is objective-driven ("What's going to happen *next*?") and fits well within gameplay loops.

# 4   GFI as a Lens

GFI groups three analytical, separate, causally-linked, and perspective-dependent lenses (Fig. 5). Through them, we straightforwardly unpack several thorny narrative design issues that are potentially challenging to analyze with MDA alone; these analyses lend support to the utility of GFI.

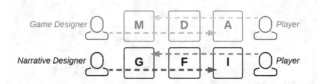

**Fig. 5.** Goals (like mechanics) are closer to the designer perspective. Interpretation (like aesthetics) is closer to the player. Feedback (like dynamics) bridges between these.

## 4.1   Ludonarrative Dissonance and Other Forms of Incoherence

(Game designer) Hocking coined the term *ludonarrative dissonance* in describing playing *Bioshock* [37]: "[it suffers from] a powerful dissonance between what it is about as a game, and what it is about as a story" [45, p. 256] The term has since been widely adopted, critiqued [80], and reformulated [8,81]. In view of GFI, it manifests via a mismatch between the ludological and narrative goal hierarchies.

For example, games with the ultimate goal *To Prolong* often suffer from a certain amount of incoherence when they also include a "campaign" or "story mode" with an overarching conclusive narrative goal. The incoherence arises because there is no clear narrative goal that makes sense of the ultimate one. In *Destiny* [5], once players achieve the narrative goal of "Defeat Atheon" (the final boss of the games' raid), they return to the gameworld where nothing has changed and the raid remains available to complete. Even once all of the game's most significant narrative goals have been achieved (*e.g.* side-quests and secondary missions), the player should still continue *To Prolong* their play. The lack of an "infinite narrative" (that aligns with *To Prolong*) poses a challenge if we want to see games without this fundamental incoherence, and perhaps directly motivates the use of procedural narrative generation [62].

There is also often dissonance/incoherence in games with multiple endings. *Nier: Automata* [68] has 26 different endings and (although many are optional) the player is required to successively complete the first 5 in order to witness all of the scripted narrative [52]. This creates dissonance: the game "indicate[s] to the player that an ending has been reached, only to enable continued play afterward, while coding the post-end portion of the game not as something extraneous, repeated, or additional, but an actual part of the game" [6].

Each time the player feels like they've *finished*, they learn that its narrative counterpart has not been fully realized: "[the game] continually deprives the player of a sense of narrative closure" [52] with successive playthroughs requiring a re-interpretation of the games ultimate narrative goal as new elements are introduced. For example, "reaching the B ending is a matter of following the same core narrative events from the perspective of the 9 S instead of 2B, with only small narrative additions and gameplay alterations" [52].

## 4.2 Edge-Cases of the Parallel Hierarchy

What if the Parallel Goal Hierarchies are imperfectly mapped? We consider two cases: there is a ludological goal with no evident narrative goal and *vice-versa*.

When a ludological goal has no evident narrative goal, the player has no interpretation and thus no way to know the ludological goal exists. The only way for this ludological goal to be achieved is for the player to meet it by chance. There are at least two contexts in which this happens regularly.

The first is via cheat codes and the second is through meta-reward structures such as secret trophies or achievements [42]. From the player's perspective, these ludological goals are met, but the player had no way of anticipating them from anything communicated via the game. Consequently, the player has no way to make sense of what happens other than appealing to conventions of the medium ("PS4 games have trophies" or "Konami games often have the Konami code").

Conversely, when a narrative goal has no evident ludological one, a player has no way of achieving said goal in the game. This can lead to player frustration, confusion, or disappointment ("The game asks that I do this thing, but it's impossible!"). This might be the result of a mistake or flaw in the game's implementation. Perhaps a player is told to activate a light switch, but it doesn't work due to a software bug [60]. Sometimes, it might be the result of purposeful design. (Narrative designer) Ramanan describes a scene in *Before I Forget* [1], a game that "takes place in the soft pastel-colored home of Sunita, a woman with early onset dementia" [83] in which players were reasonably confused:

> "[Players can't find] the bathroom, and [...] every door [they] open turns up in the same place, no matter which... [Players] were trying to see a system and a logic when dementia doesn't have any." *Ramanan as cited by Webber* [83].

## 4.3 Localization, Remakes, and Sequels

*Localization*, when a game is modified in order to be sold in a new market [66], is different from translation because:

> ...localizing a video game may involve making technically or culturally motivated changes that go beyond its textual structure, such as modifying the game code to accommodate the graphical discrepancies between source language and target languages [...] or even adjusting the game's marketing strategies. [22]

Thus, localization often results in transcreation: departing from the original source to an extent such that the target is significantly different [66].

In view of GFI, localization requires transforming a game's Narrative Goal Hierarchy to preserve the relationships between narrative goals and their ludological counterparts. When done poorly, the intended meaning of the player's activity can become opaque. Czech's [22] study of the Polish game market demonstrates how the narrative goal of "obtaining a killing spree" – *Removing* (defeating) a certain number of opposing players while *Preventing* your own *Removal* (defeat) – can become disassociated from its ludological goal, due to poor localization: it reads as obtaining "a series of victims" or "a series of donations."

*Osu! Tatakae! Ouendan!* [48, Ouendan] is a rhythm-action game first released in Japan, later localized by the same developer into *Elite Beat Agents* [49, EBA] for the North American (NA) market. The developer aimed to provide an experience comparable to Ouendan for NA audiences [59]. Interestingly,

> ...the localization team was not afraid to modify many of the aspects of Ouendan that were not part of the core gameplay. The result is a game with new characters and stories, [and] a new soundtrack – [...] one of the most relevant components in a rhythm game. Nevertheless, the Japanese game and the localized version feel strikingly similar, as the gameplay is virtually unchanged. [...] [EBA] retained the concept, mechanics and general atmosphere of [Ouendan], but involved a complete overhaul of both the textual and audiovisual elements [59].

GFI explains how Ouendan and EBA are *ludologically* the same but *narratively* different: localization effectively replaced the narrative goal hierarchy, but mapped it onto the same ludological one.

## 5   GFI as a Tool

In addition to its analytical traction, GFI *also* has generative traction to help us design games. Figure 6 illustrates a game-centered *interaction framework* [4]; it charts how GFI fills in gaps in the MDA model that must be filled to account for narrative design-related phenomena. In it, the (game) System contains the Ludological Goals that must be achieved for players to succeed at the game. These are presented to the player via Feedback that the Player observes and interprets. Intepretation yields the player's mentalization of Narrative Goals that motivate which tasks they end up pursuing, which forms part of their Aesthetic experience. Players attempt to carry out those tasks by articulating them through the game's afforded Mechanics, which result in run-time Dynamics that perform an update on the underlying game's System.

Under this framework, we propose that (1) *interpretation* is what should be considered as the end result that guides narrative design refinement, and (2) *goals* (with corresponding *mechanics*) and *feedback* are what should be refined to effect change in that interpretation. How to do so is beyond our scope; we briefly chart design challenges around player *expectations* [65] that GFI helps us grapple with.

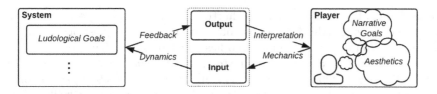

**Fig. 6.** An interaction framework for games that identifies how GFI fills in conceptual gaps in MDA that must be filled to account for narrative design.

### 5.1 Setting Up and Satisfying Player Expectations

Games are communicative acts [17]. In them, players/audiences expect designers/authors to "cooperate," as in dialogue [41]: speakers are tacitly expected by hearers to be as detailed as they *need* to be, truthful, on-topic, and clear [40]. Authors rely on or flaunt these expectations for communicative effect. For example, a seemingly random element of a story may have its purpose revealed later in the discourse (*e.g. Chekhov's Gun* [72]) or may lead audiences astray (the *Red Herring* [82]). The Parallel Goal Hierarchies give us the language to describe how designers can *also* setup and manipulate player expectations. Succinctly, players might be offered feedback to scaffold certain narrative goal interpretations, creating expectations about gameplay via the ludological goals they motivate, which in turn may be satisfied or subverted.

At the edge of a particular waterfall within *The Elder Scrolls V: Skyrim* [11, *Skyrim*], players are prompted with feedback that sets up a player's expectation: an audio cue with associated textual overlay that reads "Bard's Leap Summit Discovered." Given the prompt's timing (expectation of relevance) and content (expectation of detail), one rational interpretation is "Jump off the waterfall," with the implied (and dangerous) ludological goal *Reach*-Base of waterfall.

The interpretation emerges because in *Skyrim* that kind of overlay appears whenever a player enters a significant place (*e.g.* a city). Only if the player acts to satisfy the implied ludological goal (*i.e.* by jumping off the waterfall), does the player land safely in a pool, encounter a ghostly bard who describes their unsuccessful dive, and get an in-game skill-boost. That the player cannot encounter the ghost by simply exploring the base of the waterfall suggests a designer's *intentional* structuring of the feedback to elicit the narrative goal.

This is related to *narrative affordances* [16], action opportunities that players imagine will continue their unfolding story. In GFI, this is tantamount to eliciting and *satisfying* a player's expectations by way of a narrative goal that motivates a ludological one, the latter then recognized (possibly rewarded) by the game.

### 5.2 Subverting and Shifting Player Expectations

In contrast, the story of *Spec Ops: The Line* (*SpecOps*, [29]) diverges from the conventional hero story. It leads U.S. Army Captain Walker – the player-controlled protagonist – into taking ethically fraught actions [53]. As it unfolds, the player's interpretation of the ludological goals is shifted: expectations of the medium [14] ("You're a hero, so hurting enemies is the right thing to do") and of the genre [3] (third-person shooter) are narratively questioned and then *subverted* ("You're a war criminal who has just harmed civilians").

This is possible because actions in stories can be *functionally polyvalent* [31]: in *SpecOps*, "Soldier harms enemies" narratively *functions* [69,70] as "heroism" in the player's initial interpretation and is shifted to function as "villainy" via feedback that reinforces an *anti-hero* [75] interpretation.

Similarly, Brenda Romero (née Brathwaite), leveraged multiple interpretations in her boardgame *Train* [13] via the use of purposefully ambiguous mechanics and game elements. In *Train*, players are tasked with efficiently loading and delivering boxcars with yellow meeples to a terminal station only to learn the name of the destination towards the end: Auschwitz. Many players"realize" the intended meaning of the game's narrative goal, and then subversively act against the game's lugolodical goals: "Some of these players would derail the cars, while others would create virtual 'Denmarks' to give refuge to the tokens" [13].

# 6   Conclusions

GFI supports systematic design iteration: anticipating how changes to the game's structure will manifest in effects on players. By traversing GFI's three levels of abstraction, we expect designers can better conceptualize games, which might help "control for undesired outcomes, and tune for desired behavior" [47].

Throughout this paper, we decomposed games writ large, including ones that are not necessarily narratively-centered. This speaks to a fundamental claim that GFI buys into: all games afford to be interpreted *as* stories. This is vacuously true because we are narratively intelligent [43] and as Aarseth [2] has stated: people can narrativise anything. *Tetris* [67] is sufficiently representational [7] to afford discussing as symbolizing American life [64] or bodies in a grave [55].

However, the *point* of articulating GFI is to suggest that, while all games "tell" stories, some stories are more *intended* than others. (Game designer) Bateman [7] argues that everything that is representational – *i.e.* all feedback – contributes to the narrative. Thus, a game's potential for narrativization is proportional to the degree it communicates non-abstract information. The story in *SMB* is interpretatively simpler than that of *Skyrim*, but they are *both* stories nonetheless by virtue of being communicated via non-abstract feedback (*i.e.* phonological, lexical, grammatical, and denotational information). Thus, to elicit *intended* stories instead of alternate player-narrativizations, designers should center on manipulating the game's feedback. Our future work will explore *how*.

By formally understanding game design, we are better able to analytically describe particular game experiences, systematically investigate and predict causal determinants of those experiences, and better articulate the relevance of these research efforts to game design practice. GFI helps make sense of *how* game experiences are intrinsically narrative ones; we use it to reject the long-standing "antagonistic" relationship between story and gameplay as a false dichotomy.

GFI bridges narrative and game design and development, interactive digital narrative studies, and game research. In this paper, we use it to articulate what the activity of narrative design *is* and to explain phenomena that emerge from this design activity. We have presented GFI as a framework of modellable components, and have also presented models for each component; Goals are modeled with our Ultimate/Imperatives typology from prior work [25,84], Feedback is modeled with a typology imported from linguistics summarized in Table 3, and Interpretation is modeled via the question-answering focused Sequence Method [58]. We expect GFI to clarify and strengthen the iterative processes of developers, scholars, and researchers alike, facilitating the decomposition, study, and design of a broad class of game-based narrative experiences.

# References

1. 3-Fold Games: Before I Forget. 3-Fold Games (2017). Video game published for the Microsoft Windows and macOS platforms
2. Aarseth, E.: A narrative theory of games. In: Proceedings of the 6th International Conference on the Foundations of Digital Games, pp. 129–133. ACM, New York (2012)
3. Abell, C.: Genre, Interpretation and Evaluation. In: Proceedings of the 136th Meeting of the Aristotelian Society, vol. CXV, pp. 25–40 (2015)
4. Abowd, G.D.: Formal aspects of human-computer interaction. Ph.D. thesis, University of Oxford (1991)
5. Activision: Destiny. Bungie, Santa Monica, California (2014). Video game published for various platforms
6. Backe, H.J.: Consecutive endings and the aesthetic potential of cognitive dissonance. In: Proceedings of the 2018 Conference of the Digital Games Research Association: Extended Abstracts (2018)
7. Bateman, C.: Fiction Denial and the Liberation of Games [limited edition working paper], University of Bolton, Bolton (2013)
8. Bateman, C.: No-one plays alone. Trans. Digit. Games Res. Assoc. **3**(2), 5–36 (2017)
9. Bates, J., et al.: The role of emotion in believable agents. Commun. ACM **37**(7), 122–125 (1994)
10. Bernstein, J.: Reimagining story structure: moving beyond three acts in narrative design (2013). presented at the Game Developers Conference. https://www.gdcvault.com/play/1019675/Reimagining-Story-Structure-Moving-Beyond. Accessed 20 July 2020
11. Bethesda Game Studios: The Elder Scrolls V: Skyrim. Bethesda Softworks (2011). Video game published for the Microsoft Windows platform
12. Björk, S., Holopainen, J.: Patterns in Game Design. Charles River Media, Hingham (2005)
13. Brathwaite, B., Sharp, J.: The mechanic is the message: a post mortem in progress. In: Schrier, K., Gibson, D. (eds.) Ethics and Game Design: Teaching Values through Play, pp. 311–329. Information Science Reference, Hershey (2010)
14. Brice, M.: Death of the player (2013). http://www.mattiebrice.com/death-of-the-player/. Accessed 04 Apr 2019
15. Bryant, R.D., Giglio, K.: Slay the Dragon: Writing Great Video Games. Michael Wiese Productions (2015)
16. Cardona-Rivera, R.E.: A model of interactive narrative affordances. Ph.D. thesis, North Carolina State University (2019)

17. Cardona-Rivera, R.E., Young, R.M.: Games as conversation. In: Proceedings of the 3rd Workshop on Games and NLP at the 10th AAAI Conference on Artificial Intelligence and Interactive Digital Entertainment, pp. 2–8 (2014)
18. Cardona-Rivera, R.E., Young, R.M.: Desiderata for a computational model of human online narrative sensemaking. In: the Working Notes of the 2019 AAAI Spring Symposium on Story-enabled Intelligence (2019)
19. Cardona-Rivera, R.E., Zagal, J.P., Debus, M.S.: Narrative goals in games: a novel nexus of story and gameplay. In: Proceedings of the 15th International Conference on the Foundations of Digital Games (2020)
20. Cohn, N.: Your brain on comics: a cognitive model of visual narrative comprehension. Topics Cogn. Sci. (2019). https://doi.org/10.1111/tops.12421
21. Currie, G.: Arts and Minds. Oxford University Press, Oxford (2004)
22. Czech, D., et al.: Challenges in video game localization: an integrated perspective. Explor.: J. Lang. Lit. **1**, 3–25 (2013)
23. Dansky, R.: Screw narrative wrappers (2014). https://www.gamasutra.com/blogs/RichardDansky/20140623/219615/Screw_Narrative_Wrappers.php. Accessed 02 Mar 2020
24. Debus, M.S.: Unifying game ontology: a faceted classification of game elements. Ph.D. thesis, IT University of Copenhagen, Denmark (2019)
25. Debus, M.S., Zagal, J.P., Cardona-Rivera, R.E.: A typology of imperative game goals. Game Stud. **20**(3) (2020, forthcoming)
26. Dena, C.: Finding a way: techniques to avoid schema tension in narrative design. Trans. Digit. Games Res. Assoc. **3**(1), 35 (2017)
27. Nintendo Creative Department: Super Mario Bros. Nintendo, Tokyo, Japan (1985). Video game published for the Nintendo Entertainment System
28. Despain, W.: Writing for Video Game Genres: From FPS to RPG. CRC Press, Boca Raton (2009)
29. YAGER Development: Spec Ops: The Line. 2K Games, Novato, California (2005). Video game published for various platforms
30. Dille, F., Platten, J.Z.: The Ultimate Guide to Video Game Writing and Design. Lone Eagle Publishing Company, Los Angeles (2007)
31. Doležel, L.: Occidental Poetics: Tradition and Progress. University of Nebraska Press, Lincoln (1990)
32. Eskelinen, M.: The gaming situation. Game Stud. **1**(1), 68 (2001)
33. Fernández-Vara, C.: Game spaces speak volumes: indexical storytelling. In: Proceedings of the 2011 Digital Games Research Conference: Think Design Play. DiGRA (2011)
34. Syd Field: Screenplay: The Foundations of Screenwriting. Revised Ed. Bantam Dell (2005)
35. Frasca, G.: Ludologists love stories, too: notes from a debate that never took place. In: DiGRA Conference (2003)
36. Freytag, G.: Freytag's Technique of the Drama, An Exposition of Dramatic Composition and Art. Scott, Foresman and Company, Chicago (1896). Trans. by Elias J. MacEwan from the German original Die Technik des Dramas (1863)
37. Irrational Games: Bioshock. 2K Games, Novato, California (2007). Video game published for various platforms
38. Gaver, W.: Designing for homo ludens. I3 Mag. **12**(June), 2–6 (2002)
39. Genette, G.: Narrative Discourse: An Essay in Method. Cornell University Press, Ithaca (1980)
40. Grice, H.P.: Logic and conversation. In: Syntax and Semantics 3: Speech Acts, pp. 41–58. Elsevier (1975)

41. Grice, H.P.: Meaning. Philos. Rev. **66**(3), 377–388 (1957)
42. Hamari, J., Eranti, V.: Framework for designing and evaluating game achievements. In: Proceedings of the 2011 Conference of the Digital Games Research Association (2011)
43. Herman, D.: Storytelling and the Sciences of Mind. MIT Press, Cambridge (2013)
44. Heussner, T., Finley, T.K., Hepler, J.B., Lemay, A.: The Game Narrative Toolbox. Routledge, Abingdon (2015)
45. Hocking, C.: Ludonarrative dissonance in bioshock: the problem of what the game is about. Well Played **1**, 255–260 (2009)
46. Howard, J.: Quests: Design, Theory, and History in Games and Narratives. AK Peters/CRC Press, Wellesley (2008)
47. Hunicke, R., LeBlanc, M., Zubek, R.: MDA: a formal approach to game design and game research. In: Proceedings of the Workshop on Challenges in Game AI at the 19th National Conference on Artificial Intelligence (2004)
48. iNiS: Osu! Tatakae! Ouendan. Nintendo (2005). Video game published for the Nintendo DS platform
49. iNiS: Elite Beat Agents. Nintendo (2006). Video game published for the Nintendo DS platform
50. Bohemia Interactive: DayZ. Bohemia Interactive, Prague, Czech Republic (2018). Video game published for the Windows platform
51. Iser, W.: Interaction between text and reader. In: Suleiman, S.R., Crosman, I. (eds.) The Reader in the Text, pp. 106–119. Princeton University Press, Princeton (1980)
52. Jacevic, M.: "This. Cannot. Continue."-Ludoethical Tension in NieR: Automata. In: Philosophy of Computer Games Conference 2017 (2018)
53. Jørgensen, K.: The positive discomfort of spec ops: the line. Game Stud. **16**(2) (2016)
54. Koenitz, H.: Towards a theoretical framework for interactive digital narrative. In: Aylett, R., Lim, M.Y., Louchart, S., Petta, P., Riedl, M. (eds.) ICIDS 2010. LNCS, vol. 6432, pp. 176–185. Springer, Heidelberg (2010). https://doi.org/10.1007/978-3-642-16638-9_22
55. Koster, R.: A Theory of Fun for Game Design. O'Reilly Media Inc., Sebastopol (2013)
56. Kreminski, M.: Creativity support for story construction play experiences. In: Proceedings of the 15th AAAI Conference on Artificial Intelligence and Interactive Digital Entertainment, pp. 210–212 (2019)
57. Lakoff, G.: Cognitive models and prototype theory. In: Margolis, E., Laurence, S. (eds.) Concepts: Core Readings, pp. 391–421. MIT Press, Cambridge (1999)
58. Landau, N.: The TV Showrunner's Roadmap: 21 Navigational Tips for Screenwriters to Create and Sustain a Hit TV Series. CRC Press, Boco Raton (2013)
59. Lepre, O.: Divided by language, united by gameplay: an example of ludological game localization. In: Mangiron, C., Orero, P., Minako, O. (eds.) Fun for all: Translation and accessibility practices in video games, pp. 111–128. Peter Lang Bern, Bern (2014)
60. Lewis, C., Whitehead, J., Wardrip-Fruin, N.: What went wrong: a taxonomy of video game bugs. In: Proceedings of the Fifth International Conference on the Foundations of Digital Games, pp. 108–115 (2010)
61. Linderoth, J.: Beyond the digital divide: an ecological approach to gameplay. Trans. Digit. Games Res. Assoc. **1**(1), 17 (2013)
62. Martens, C., Cardona-Rivera, R.E.: Procedural narrative generation. Presented at the Game Developers Conference (2017). https://www.gdcvault.com/play/1024143/Procedural-Narrative. Accessed 20 July 2020

63. Mitchell, A., McGee, K.: Reading again for the first time: a model of rereading in interactive stories. In: Oyarzun, D., Peinado, F., Young, R.M., Elizalde, A., Méndez, G. (eds.) ICIDS 2012. LNCS, vol. 7648, pp. 202–213. Springer, Heidelberg (2012). https://doi.org/10.1007/978-3-642-34851-8_20

64. Murray, J.H.: Hamlet on the Holodeck: The Future of Narrative in Cyberspace. MIT Press, Cambridge (2017)

65. Murray, J.H.: Why Paris needs hector and Lancelot needs mordred: using traditional narrative roles and functions for dramatic compression in interactive narrative. In: Si, M., Thue, D., André, E., Lester, J.C., Tanenbaum, J., Zammitto, V. (eds.) ICIDS 2011. LNCS, vol. 7069, pp. 13–24. Springer, Heidelberg (2011). https://doi.org/10.1007/978-3-642-25289-1_2

66. O'Hagan, M., Mangiron, C.: Game Localization. John Benjamins Publishing Company, Amsterdam/Philadelphia (2013)

67. Pajitnov, A., Pokhilko, V.: Tetris. Independent (1984). Video game published for the Commodore 64 and the IBM PC

68. PlatinumGames: Nier: Automata. Square Enix (2017). Video game published for the Microsoft Windows, PlayStaion4, and XBox One platforms

69. Prince, G.: A Dictionary of Narratology, Revised edn. University of Nebraska Press, Lincoln (2003)

70. Propp, V.: Morphology of the Folktale. University of Texas Press, Austin (1968)

71. Punday, D.: Involvement, interruption, and inevitability: melancholy as an aesthetic principle in game narratives. SubStance **33**(3), 80–107 (2004)

72. Rayfield, D.: Anton Chekhov: A Life. Northwestern University Press, Evanston (2000)

73. Reed, A.A.: Changeful tales: design-driven approaches toward more expressive storygames. Ph.D. thesis, University of California Santa Cruz, Santa Cruz, CA, USA (2017)

74. Roth, C., Koenitz, H.: Towards creating a body of evidence-based interactive digital narrative design knowledge: approaches and challenges. In: Proceedings of the 2nd International Workshop on Multimedia Alternate Realities at the 10th ACM Multimedia Systems Conference, pp. 19–24 (2017)

75. Shafer, D.M., Raney, A.A.: Exploring how we enjoy antihero narratives. J. Commun. **62**(6), 1028–1046 (2012)

76. Shapiro, L.: Embodied Cognition. Routledge, New York (2019)

77. Skolnick, E.: Video Game Storytelling: What Every Developer Needs to Know About Narrative Techniques. Watson-Guptill Publications, New York (2014)

78. Smith, H., et al.: Plans and purposes how videogame goals shape player behaviour. Ph.D. thesis, IT University of Copenhagen (2006)

79. Stenros, J.: The game definition game: a review. Games Cult. **12**(6), 499–520 (2017)

80. Summerley, R.K., et al.: Ludic dysnarrativa: how can fictional inconsistency in games be reduced? Ph.D. thesis, University of the Arts London and Falmouth University (2017)

81. Tocci, J.: "You are dead. Continue?": conflicts and complements in game rules and fiction. Eludamos. J. Comput. Game Cult. **2**(2), 187–201 (2008)

82. Turco, L.: The Book of Literary Terms: The Genres of Fiction, Drama, Nonfiction. Literary criticism, and Scholarship. UPNE (1999)

83. Webber, J.E.: Why the best video games lie to you (2019). https://onezero.medium.com/why-the-best-video-games-lie-to-you-67ae22f1412f. Accessed 02 Mar 2020

84. Zagal, J.P., Debus, M.S., Cardona-Rivera, R.E.: On the ultimate goals of games: Winning, finishing, and prolonging. In: Proceedings of the 13th International Philosophy of Computer Games Conference (2019)

# Weird and Wonderful: How Experimental Film Narratives Can Inform Interactive Digital Narratives

Chris Hales[✉]

RISEBA University, Durbes iela 4, Rīga 1007, Latvia
chris.hales.interactive@gmail.com

**Abstract.** An analysis is made of historical experimental films in order to determine if alternative models and techniques of narration are in use that may inform current and future creators of interactive digital narratives (IDN). An overview of experimental film leads to five case studies chosen as being of most relevance to narrative: these discuss works by Deren, Greenaway, Frampton, Markopoulos and Rybczyński. All these works predate the establishment of digital and interactive technology. Characteristics of verticality and repetition, spiral structures, 'interlexia' transitions, voice-over disjunction, trance narratives, multiscreen and multilayering, and the use of equations and set theory to determine the form of the film, are shown to be of potential interest to IDN.

**Keywords:** Experimental film · Interactive narrative · Narrative structure

## 1 Introduction

All too often interactive digital narratives (IDN) take their inspiration and structure from Aristotle, Campbell, and other historically accepted formats devoted to generating satisfying narrative experiences. Whether novel, film or other format, such conventional approaches to storytelling can rarely do without characters, plot, settings, events and more often than not closure. There is, however, a form of filmmaking that occupies a certain niche—but is immensely popular with its devotees—and seeks new "ways of seeing" [1, p. 1] that question the traditional dramatic conventions, summarised thus by filmmaker Malcolm le Grice [2, p. 146]: "this fundamental search for cinematic forms which do not conform to a linear narrative structure and resolution is the main characteristic differentiating experimental film from mainstream cinema...".

This paper aims to explore experimental film in order to extend the research [3, 4] into alternatives to the near ubiquity of the classic story structures and to identify techniques and approaches that might usefully inform future creation in IDN. It seems to have been a neglected area of analysis, presumably because the field is diverse and many of its most vocal proponents were non-narrative and anti-illusionist in outlook and made films that annoy and provoke to the point of frustration. The enquiry starts with a short review of the experimental film by way of its various categorisations—it should be noted that

© Springer Nature Switzerland AG 2020
A.-G. Bosser et al. (Eds.): ICIDS 2020, LNCS 12497, pp. 149–163, 2020.
https://doi.org/10.1007/978-3-030-62516-0_14

nuanced alternative nomenclatures such as 'avant-garde cinema' are also in use but the chosen term here is 'experimental film'. It is a field of practice that has not been ignored by the establishment film theorists and Bordwell and Thompson [5] devote several pages to it, making it clear that there is substantial crossover between the experimental and mainstream cinema: an example is Chris Marker's *La Jetée* (1966) which was reworked into the Hollywood film *12 Monkeys* in 1995. The experimental films discussed here are made outside of mainstream systems of production and are not as well known as those feature films known as 'independent' or 'art house' (which would include, for example, much of the work of Godard, or Resnais' *L'Année Dernière à Marienbad*) or so-called 'puzzle films' [6] that reject classical storytelling techniques and replace them with complex and jumbled up narrative structures. Experimental films tend to be created by one individual with minimal funding and limited screening opportunities, the films are shorter than feature length and seldom utilise traditional dramaturgy. Utilising filmstock was the only option until the medium of videotape emerged in the late 1960s: this in its turn led to video installations and prototypic audience involvement that can be observed in 'expanded' film projects [7, 8]. Expanded cinema, however, lies outside the scope of this paper. Similarly, there is no specific discussion of experimental animation.

Film theorist Bordwell [9], building on Burch [10], examines several unconventional films through the lens of 'parametric narrative', explaining that in certain cases syuzhet and fabula shift in importance such that stylistic parameters completely dominate. The concept of parametric narrative has potential, yet Bordwell's parameters are only concerned with application of style and traditional film technique. For example, the only truly experimental film that Bordwell discusses is Michael Snow's *Wavelength* (1967), a 45-minute-long tracking shot through the length of a room in which the scant 'plot' is subordinated to the systematic development of certain cinematic parameters—focal length, light, colour, and sound (rising sinewave tones).

There are two common strategies employed by experimental filmmakers: firstly subversion, to explore alternative forms of film by all possible means in a way which might be playful, or radical and even destructive. The desire to subvert was applied to gaming by Mortensen and Jørgensen [11, ch. 7] and by Galloway [12] who classified 'countergaming' practices based on characteristics originally proposed to contrast orthodox cinema with the techniques of the avant-garde. A second strategy, practice-based and more constructive, is the exploration of more appropriate filmic forms to express a particular narrative vision by means of novel visual and structural devices.

## 2    Forms of the Experimental Film

The usual approach to classifying experimental film is to differentiate the forms of representation and technique. Bordwell and Thompson [5] propose just the two categories of abstract form and associational form (exemplified by 'poetic film'), whereas media artist Peter Weibel [13] refers to approaches based on materiality, multiple screens and narratives, time and space, sound, expanded cinema, and found footage. With the addition of the structural film and the artist's film (which usually involves an artist making a performance or action in front of the camera, and will not be pursued here) these categorisations adequately cover the major types of experimental film.

The abstract film form developed in the early 1920s and remains a staple of the experimental film canon to this day—digital techniques suit the genre perfectly. Despite its popularity abstract film is, essentially, a narrative-free concept that can be considered to be of limited value to creators of IDN, although it is worthy of note that Casey Reas [14] has used machine learning software trained on scans of vegetation to generate frames that are then manipulated in speed and rhythm to create sequences resembling the work of Stan Brakhage. Brakhage, a renowned film abstractionist, enriched his films with symbolist imagery and occasional representational fragments of narrative (*Dog Star Man* provides glimpses of a man ascending a wooded hillside with his dog) but his works were never intended as experiments in narrative other than by the subjective process of narrative logic imposed by the viewer's reading of the film. Filmmaker Hollis Frampton [15, p. 144] hints at this process by postulating the following which is somewhat prescient of today's 'emergent narrative':

BRAKHAGE'S THEOREM: For any finite series of shots ["film"] whatsoever there exists in real time a rational narrative, such that every term in the series, together with its position, duration, partition, and reference, shall be perfectly and entirely accounted for'.

Bordwell and Thompson's second category, the associational poetic form, can range from artistic expression to documentary and occurs commonly in various forms of IDN. The basic poetic film possesses both structure and narrative with content chosen and filmed (often with unusual camerawork or choice of shot) to illustrate specific themes and moods. A sub-genre of poetic film named the 'city symphony' includes Vertov's *Man With a Movie Camera* (1929) which inspired Lev Manovich's interest in database logic as an associational form [16, 17] and his subsequent experiments with *Soft Cinema* [18]. *Man with a Movie Camera* has undergone a shot-by-shot analysis of its style and structure in order to determine characteristics that could feed into the creation of new immersive interactive versions of 'city symphonies' [19]. Perry Bard used a similar template to permit web viewers to upload semantically matching shots, thus building up a crowd-sourced contemporary database that could be manipulated by custom software to create daily remakes of Vertov's original [20].

Although database generation of poetic narrative is no longer novel, a less well-known aspect of the poetic film worthy of further analysis is 'verticality', elaborated (in discussion) by filmmaker Maya Deren [21] thus:

The distinction of poetry is its construction (what I mean by "a poetic structure"), and the poetic construct arises from the fact, if you will, that it is a "vertical" investigation of a situation, in that it probes the ramifications of the moment, and is concerned with its qualities and its depth, so that you have poetry concerned, in a sense, not with what is occurring but with what it feels like or what it means. . . . Now it may also include action, but its attack is what I would call the "vertical" attack and this may be a little clearer if you will contrast it to what I would call the "horizontal" attack of drama.

Deren's legendary experimental film *Meshes of the Afternoon* (1943) and its treatment of verticality will be examined in more detail as a case study later in this text.

Moving on to Weibel's 'materiality' category of experimental film this is a self-referential conceit that foregrounds the celluloid or videotape itself, or the technology of its representation. One might extrapolate this to contemporary interest in the 'glitch' film, but narrative is not under investigation in these films. The same applies generally to found footage films, although certain filmmakers such as Martin Arnold and Ken Jacobs aim to reinterpret the narrative intention of the original material.

Weibel also distinguishes certain films which experiment with sound: this might take the form of noise aesthetics; converting visual imagery to sound via the film's optical soundtrack; sound-image disjunction, exemplified by Hollis Frampton's *Nostalgia* (1971); and a false unity of sound and image. The latter technique, combined with the use of voice-over as a neutral narrator, is notable in the early works of Peter Greenaway, whereas John Smith uses voice-over as a character in the first person to humorously challenge the viewer's understanding of films such as *The Girl Chewing Gum* (1976) and *The Black Tower* (1987). These creative strategies that examine the ways in which the language of voice-over shapes perception may have relevance now that research is being carried out into the role of voice-over in cinematic VR [22].

Multi-perspective narration and multiple screens form another category of experimental film put forward by Weibel, which has proliferated in recent times due to the affordances of video projection and inexpensive flatscreen monitors. Youngblood [23] picked up on the potential of superimposition/overlay in the late 1980s (with specific reference to Stan Brakhage) and in 2002 Manovich [24] considered multiscreen narration as a variation of Eisenstein's 'spatial montage' and suggested that spatial narrative in film has much potential for investigation. The importance here lies not on the mere juxtaposition or overlay of sequences but the way in which this conveys narrative. Two films of Zbigniew Rybczyński will be examined in detail later.

Structural cinema is one of the most unique categories of experimental film, which was influential according to Kluszczyński [25, p. 470] "in anticipation of and contributing conceptually to interactive, multi-media cyberculture art and interactive cinema". The term is broad [26] but the aspect most relevant to this paper is the analytical calculation and logic of a film's montage according to a set of rules—which might include parameters such as shot length and visual content—mapped out as 'scores'. Peter Greenaway's *Vertical Features Remake* will be examined in more detail below.

## 3    Case Studies of Specific Films and Filmmakers

The above overview reveals that only certain types of experimental film may usefully inform digital storytelling. Five case studies follow, all of which pre-date the digital age, each chosen to reflect a particular narrative issue. The choice offered is somewhat subjective but based on filmmakers who clearly pursue narratological concerns; are well established in the experimental canon; their works have been analysed in the literature (often by the filmmakers themselves); and their concerns are usually expressed through more than one film.

### 3.1  Structure and Sound: Peter Greenaway's Early Films

The 1978 film *Vertical Features Remake* by Peter Greenaway, a filmmaker discussed by Manovich [16, 17] and influential upon Jennings [3], includes schematic visualitions of its own audiovisual arrangements as part of the story. In his early films Greenaway [27] used structures such as the alphabet, mathematical equations and number series into which he could pin his stories—much of the skill being in developing the most appropriate narratives for the chosen scheme. In *Vertical Features Remake* a database of exterior shots of vertical items has been created which is not only revealed to the viewer but is the subject of the film itself: this demystification of the database mechanism is not uncommon in digital narratives, and as suggested by Paul can act as "a means of revealing meta-narratives" [28, p. 100]. *Vertical Features Remake* is a self-referential and potentially never-ending meta-narrative on the subject of the structuring of thematically filmed content and the generation of its soundtrack.

Two diagrams shown in *Vertical Features Remake* are transposed here from the artistic painted form they are portrayed in the film (see Fig. 1). *Vertical Features Remake* alternates four times between narrated sections using found footage to depict a fictional filmmaker whose lost film (consisting of neutral shots of vertical landscape features) is remade by researchers based on imprecise and incomplete documentation; and the reconstructed sections themselves which follow mathematical structuring for both audio (spoken and musical) and visual aspects. The film is organised as follows:

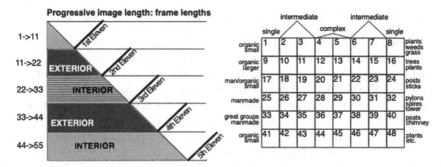

**Fig. 1.** Graphical translations of two schemas that appear in *Vertical Features Remake* as hand-drawn sketches. Many other such drawings appear in the film. Left: scene durations increase a frame at a time whilst alternating between groupings of eleven interior and exterior shots of vertical features. Right: Greenaway's sketch of how specific film content might be ordered.

**narrative–remake#1–narrative–remake#2–narrative–remake#3–narrative–remake#4**

Each remake is based on newly acquired information or the discrediting of earlier sources, and a complex story unfolds of how the lost film is to be constructed and which outcome if any is closest to the original. A humorous puzzle-solving narrative therefore emerges based on the quest to understand and hone the 'remake algorithm' which controls not only the visual content of the scenes but a spoken voice-over, music, and the rhythm and structure of the montage. There is no suggestion of closure (i.e. that the ideal remake has been found) and the remaking process could occur indefinitely if a computational interpretation was created with contemporary viewers acting as researchers to crack the filmmaker's algorithmic code.

Many of Greenaway's early films were based on the same conceit: a repetitive juxtaposition between two distinct elements, namely a complex story read by a narrator and seemingly unrelated documentary-style footage or stills. In *Vertical Features Remake* the two elements are necessarily distinct; *Dear Phone* (1976) consists of public phone box imagery alternating with story sections illustrated as a scribbled letter or script; in *Water Wrackets* (1975) the voice-over is continuous and recounts a bloody feud whilst random peaceful scenes of a tumbling stream are portrayed. In these early films actors are not used (*The Falls* is an exception [29, Ch. 4]) and the scripted narrative transforms non-fictional film content into a fictional story world.

Greenaway's use of a neutral voice to fictionally reinterpret the on-screen visuals lends itself to reinterpretation using current technology. A sequence of pre-filmed and/or audience-contributed shots relating to a chosen theme could be examined by image recognition and presented in real time accompanied by a synthetically-spoken voice-over. The filmmaker's role would become that of a machine learning 'trainer' who would customise the image recognition with datasets chosen so that the spoken narration is inspired by, but not directly representational of, the imagery portrayed on screen. The potential of this 'emergent machine gaze' can be observed in various digital artworks ranging from *The Giver of Names* [30] to *CKRBT* [31].

### 3.2  *Zorns Lemma* (1970) and "A Pentagram for Conjuring the Narrative"

Hollis Frampton's film *Zorns Lemma* is named after, and structured around, a mathematical equation. Its complex labyrinthine structure presents montage as a computational function and audiovisual narrative construction as a system of thought. Enns [32] provides a mathematical interpretation of *Zorns Lemma* that shows the film to be a cinematic/poetic instantiation of Zermelo's Axiom of Choice. Frampton, who wrote extensively and understood the FORTRAN programming language, colourfully defined a story as being "a stable pattern of energy through which an infinity of personages may pass, ourselves included" [15, p. 147]. His essay "A Pentagram for Conjuring the Narrative" [15, pp. 140–148] interprets the work of well-known storytellers as mathematical formulae—which, presumably, represent his stable patterns of energy.

*Zorns Lemma* relates to set theory and Frampton's set is the alphabet. The film's key forty-minute section is silent and every shot lasts just one second, based on constant repetition of alphabetic sequence, giving an overwhelming flow of visual information for the viewer to process. This key section, which is preceded by a voice-over reading from a schoolbook, commences with a repeating series of shots of the letters of the alphabet. Letters are then replaced by set after set of alphabetically arranged static shots of words, represented by street signage filmed in New York (for example the first three occurrences of 'B' are baby, back and bag). These in turn are gradually replaced by unrelated moving images (flames, waves, painting a wall, etc.) until a lengthy voice-overed shot of a couple walking into the distance concludes the film.

The visual style and rhythm of the film is reminiscent of Bill Seaman's *Ex.Mech* (1991, converted to CD-ROM in 1994) [33], an interactive work that permits users to select a video sequence to represent each part of a grammatically correct sentence and then to play back the self-composed composition. The usefulness of set theory is acknowledged in Seaman's writing [34] and set theory language is invoked by Raymond Queneau in *Exercises in Style* [35] although it is seldom discussed in the IDN literature. Despite the visual portrayal of New York, set theory itself is undoubtedly the self-referential subject of the narrative of *Zorns Lemma*. It is described by interactive film pioneer Grahame Weinbren [36, p. 70] as a "paradigm of a film that manifests its database foundation, indeed which corrals its meaning from the database it rests on. Its cinematic architecture provides its meaning". Gidal [26, p. 67] reports Frampton declaring "some people play that part of the film as a game. Some audiences were playing it so much they were waiting to see which would go out next and what would replace it and so forth. And when finally the 'c' does substitute in the last cycle of the film, there have been cheers". This seems to confirm that the process of representing the sets and subsets of visual content is the main intention behind *Zorns Lemma*, which could thus be considered a meta-narrative upon set theory itself. Interactivity could be added and the visual theme easily changed in the case of, say, a live cinematic event for a group audience using smartphone apps to actively contribute to and manipulate the themed sets of video content, not necessarily as a code-cracking game but as a narrative experience in its own right which need not necessitate closure.

Mathematical equations are a recurrent theme for Frampton, who also included them in his prose writing. Each of seven short fictional stories published in 1978 under the title *Mind Over Matter* [15, pp. 307–320] starts with an establishing paragraph urging the reader to imagine a particular situation; the second paragraph introduces a mathematical equation and what it represents; then follows the main story content; followed by an italicised coda that refers back to the mathematics. The haphazard and associative nature of these short stories is somewhat reminiscent of current usage of neural network AI to generate film scripts such as that for *Sunspring* [37]. In terms of mathematical equations explicitly used to generate digital narratives, an example would be Ian Flitman's *Hackney Girl* [38] which was inspired by the three Lorenz Attractor equations that are used to generate slight variations around a basic pattern.

### 3.3   Maya Deren's *Meshes of the Afternoon* (1943) and Trance Narratives

Adams Sitney [39, Ch. 1] provides a detailed description of *Meshes of the Afternoon* whose overall structure could be described as an intricately expanding spiral through states of mind based on repetition with increasing pace and variation upon elements of the film's initial sequence. Deren's poetic 'verticality', as described earlier in this paper, is mapped alongside the spiral structure in Fig. 2. Events involving a mirror-faced figure on a driveway outside the protagonist's house help make it clear when the spiral has taken a full turn. The ending of the film (the protagonist's death) suggests either the dream is continuing or the imagination achieved sufficient intensity to actually kill her: in fact the spiralling might easily have been continued without closure as 'incompletion' has been identified as an additional theme in Deren's work [40]. Deren [41] describes the narrative intention of *Meshes of the Afternoon* as:

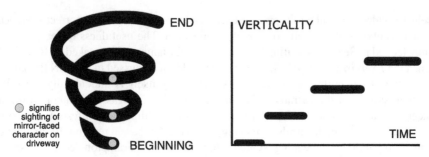

**Fig. 2.** The spiral structure of *Meshes of The Afternoon* and its narrative verticality graph. At each turn of the spiral the duration of that particular turn increases, as does its level of verticality (i.e. an elaboration and reinterpretation of the qualities and depth of the initial sequence).

. . . the interior experiences of an individual. It does not record an event which could be witnessed by other persons. Rather, it reproduces the way in which the sub-conscious of an individual will develop, interpret and elaborate an apparently simple and casual incident into a critical emotional experience.

Adams Sitney places *Meshes* into an entire genre of 'psycho-dramatic trance' narrative, including other films by Deren such as *At Land* (1944), and those of other filmmakers. These deal with weird and visionary experiences: a protagonist wanders through natural and architectural environments towards a psychological climax, expressed through rapid dislocated narratives and the portrayal of surreal experiences.

*Meshes* has a distinctive visual style that has been frequently pastiched in college film projects and pop music videos. With a new visual style and story outline it should be possible to move beyond mere pastiche: a reinterpretation of the trance narrative through contemporary practice might be to record a variety of expressive shots related to events and objects in a trance narrative spiral and to create a responsive viewing experience using bio-sensors. For example the 'meditation' parameter of Neurosky's *Mindwave* EEG headset could be used to push the viewer further along the spiral of the trance narrative: meditation values would be mapped to narrative verticality. A dramatic closure similar to that of *Meshes* could represent a possible endpoint of the experience, as could a return to the beginning of spiral due to a lack of trance/relaxation. Alternatively, closure could be dispensed with altogether to reflect Deren's interest in incompletion, the experience spiralling around the 'twisty little passages' of the mind. Venturing a step further the story need not be conveyed filmically but could be enacted by an interactor within a VR environment in the manner of the *VRWandlung/Metamorphosis* installation [42] in which the user has freedom to explore Gregor Samsa's room for a fixed time whilst narrative events unfold. A possible 'MeshesVR' could be designed to cut between multiple exploratory locations (doorway, bedroom, sitting room, staircase, driveway etc.) and items (mirror, key, knife) that appear in the original *Meshes*, carefully structured as a spiral of verticality under the influence of data from an EEG headset which would also be worn.

### 3.4 Gregory Markopoulos' "New Narrative Film Form" (1963)

In 1963 Markopoulos, a contemporary of Deren in the American avant-garde known for his poetic film works, wrote a tantalising journal article [43] entitled *Towards a New Narrative Film Form*, explaining that his proposed system:

> involves the use of short film phrases which evoke thought-images. Each film phrase is composed of certain select frames that are similar to the harmonic units found in musical composition. The film phrases establish ulterior relationships among themselves; in classic montage technique there is a constant reference to the continuing shot: in my abstract system there is a complex of differing frames being repeated.

Unfortunately for scholars of narrative this description is cursory with no detail or diagrams, but rhythmic flashes, superimpositions and complex cross-fades can be observed to be an important aspect of Markopoulos' films of this period. For Markopoulos these film phrases serve to implant thoughts, associations and, above all, emotions relevant to the more expository sections. Adams Sitney includes Markopoulos' early film *Swain* (1950) in his trance film categorisation and Deren's concept of verticality seems highly appropriate for the 'new narrative film form' in the sense that the flashes and transitions are devices that deepen the narrative in their own right: a simplistic attempt to represent a sample film (no particular film) is shown as Fig. 3.

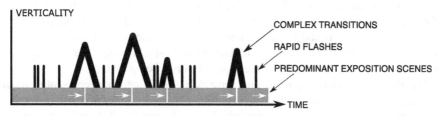

**Fig. 3.** A possible visualisation of Markopoulos' new narrative film form. Predominant exposition scenes on which the overall narrative is underpinned are interspersed with rapid flashes that insert single pulses of verticality. Complex transitions (potentially composed of both flashes and superimposition) increase the verticality depending on the duration of the transition.

At the extreme it can be difficult to differentiate between flashes, superimpositions and the predominant exposition, as the film becomes a unified whole made up of multicoloured fragments distributed over time, resonating against one another in the viewer's memory. The rapid flashes might usefully be considered as microlexia and the transitions as interlexia (or internodes) that provide an equal, but different contribution to the digital narrative as do the lexia themselves. These interlexia could find application in IDN: for example, when a user makes a choice on a Twine page, rather than a perfunctory cut or crossfade between two nodes, the transition itself could contribute creatively to the narrative using multilayered words and poetic phrases. Using an authoring software that would permit it, video, audio and still imagery could be blended to create evocative interlexial associations.

Markopoulos sometimes used both in-camera editing and in-camera superimposition for his transitions which could be considered a sort of real-time technique—and with contemporary digital technology, rhythmically pulsing multiple layers of pre-recorded material could be interactively blended and controlled by a performer (using specialist VJing software or custom coding) and this could be intercut with live camera material (or vice versa). Nevertheless, audience participation rather than passive viewing was a stated goal of Markopoulos. With a hint towards a more active viewer, Markopoulos claims that his new form "gradually convinces the spectator not only to see and to hear, but to participate in what is being created on the screen, on both the narrative and introspective levels ... a whole new scale of values is exposed, creating a rich potential narrative form in the motion picture" [43, pp. 11–12]. Markopoulos' desire for participation could be realised by a system that gathers personal data from a user (such as uploaded images, answers to a questionnaire, video from a webcam) and deploys it amongst previously prepared material in the form of creative personalised flashes and transitions inserted between the expository nodes of a multisequential narrative. The approach of incorporating user data is tried and tested and has been demonstrated in *You Who?* [44] and earlier online projects such as *Tackfilm* [45], *The Wilderness Downtown* [46] and *Just a Reflektor* [47].

### 3.5   Zbig Rybczyński's *Nowa Książka/New Book* (1976) and *Tango* (1981)

Kluszczyński [48] emphasises how Zbigniew Rybczyński's films made a significant contribution to delinearisation of the cinema and influenced early projects in multimedia. Rybczyński pushed the limits of 35 mm film creation to construct new visual languages to convey stories that would be "more realistic than pseudo-realistic film plots" [49]. The films *New Book* and *Tango* use multiscreen and multilayering to create the most appropriate visual representation for the types of stories being told.

*New Book* divides the screen into nine separately-filmed segments representing fixed locations in a town, such as a café or street corner. The modest story of a man traversing the town to purchase a new book becomes a portrait of the town itself. Activities take place simultaneously in all screen segments and characters/events move from one segment to another maintaining the synchronisation of the whole: this requires an active viewer to follow a particular character across all nine screens and/or to surveille a particular location. *Tango* is a layered and deconstructed portrayal of narrative, which was inspired by Rybczyński scraping away layers of wallpaper in his apartment and imagining its various previous inhabitants. Rather than a representation of simultaneity by division into adjacent segments, all characters inhabit the same time and space, but as separate entities as the result of a highly complex and time-consuming manual technique. There are 22 looped sequences of characters, each engaging in a typical activity: as time goes by the number of people simultaneously present in the frame (a fixed shot of a room) grows until, when all are present, the screen gradually empties and returns to its opening state. It is important to understand that the characters spatially interweave around each other and are not simply presented on discrete layers. Manovich [17] describes the result as ontological montage: ontologically incompatible elements placed together within the same time and space.

Multiform narratives are well known in digital storytelling, and Rybczyński's solutions (made without digital equipment) could inform the design of interactive equivalents. The multiform aspect is expressed visually and quite explicitly in the screen design and content rather than being a metaphorical construct. Thus Rybczyński's work is really only applicable to 2D visual content windows in formats such as digital video or WebP. Attaching algorithmic behaviour to each window or layer opens up possibilities for new combinations generated by internal rules and user interaction.

The format of surveilling multiple locations appeared in early video-based computer games, but it is noticeable that only one segment/window could be playing at a time, revealing the technical challenge in playing multiple video or animation streams simultaneously. In *Night Trap* [50] only one camera location (out of eight) could be viewed at a time; *Voyeur* [51] situated the player opposite a family home, making real-time decisions about which of the many windows to surveille. Outside of media art installations there are relatively few IDN examples of visual representation using multiple moving image windows due to the combined demand on the computer processor (decoding the video codecs) and hard drive transfer speed (delivering data from multiple files simultaneously). This restriction eases as the technology improves: the puzzle game *Framed* [52] illustrates a recent example in which the user must find a strategy to enable the protagonist to escape from a comic book page. The multilayered approach of *Tango* presents additional technical challenges because the moving image files need to be superimposed, rather than juxtaposed, in real time, so there is an additional overhead to process transparency, keying or masking.

## 4  Summary and Discussion

Themes that emerge are those of playfulness, participation, and incompletion expressed as repeating structures that do not demand closure. Both Greenaway and Frampton have made structural films in which their databases and procedural rules are quite explicitly revealed—in fact they themselves become the subject of the story which is a meta-narrative about the structuring of thematically filmed content. This invites the audience to participate in the film's construction or decoding, a process which technology could enhance with genuine interactivity. Frampton derives his rules from mathematical equations and uses set theory whereas Greenaway invents idiosyncratic algorithms: both approaches could be analysed computationally and realised as procedurally generated interpretations. Greenaway's technique with scripted voice-over (used also in Frampton's *Nostalgia*) acts as a tool to turn creative documentaries into works of fiction. The use of disjunction between what is spoken and what appears on screen might influence a present day project using text-to-speech and machine learning trained to make narrative sense out of an emergent machine gaze.

Deren and Markopoulos both take a poetic approach that concerns itself with internal thoughts and emotions. Deren's concept of the vertical "attack" of poetic narrative is equally applicable to the flashes and transitions of Markopoulos' new narrative form: these transitions act as 'interlexia' which transcend the usual function of a page/scene change and contribute impressionistic content in their own right. Deren's 'vertical' approach to narrative seems generalisable to the works of other filmmakers and with today's technology the axis of verticality of a spiral-structured trance narrative could be mapped to data from, for example, a brain-computer interface.

Rybczyński's films offer practical suggestions as to how appropriate multiform stories can be portrayed on screen in novel ways. They raise the issue as to whether the IDN field would benefit from analysing in more detail the important contribution of the visual style and design of the screen representation (output) of an IDN. Hence, for example, Koenitz' models of IDN systems [53] could be extended to include a layer relating to the role of the chosen method of audiovisual representation.

The arrival of 'new media' in the late 1980s was met with a mixed reception in the experimental film community: some filmmakers carried on as before or were openly hostile to emerging digital technologies whereas others embraced and investigated the new possibilities. In the latter category Chris Marker created a hyperlinked CDROM in 1997 entitled *Immemory*; Ken Jacobs [54] experimented with 3D; Peter Greenaway commissioned the 92 interactive *Tulse Luper Journey* games and explored transmedia [55]; Malcolm Le Grice prototyped database narrative in 1995 [56] and investigated audiovisual performances and the computer game [57]; Pat O'Neill collaborated with the *Labyrinth Project* [58]. Amongst those who emerged native to this 'new media', few seem to have explicitly acknowledged direct influence from experimental film. Luc Courchesne, known for his branching narrative 'portrait' installations and 360° *Panoscope*, specified Brakhage, Snow and Frampton as influences [59]. Chris Hales exhibited several interactive works inspired by the multiform films of Rybczyński [60]. In 1997 Kluszczyński [48, p. 139] reminded the emerging digital practitioners of the importance of experimental films in "disturbing the narrative order, undermining the domination of storytelling over the remaining elements of film structure and releasing the image, restoring and granting its autonomy". Experimental filmmakers, to a certain extent, became transformed into 'media artists' by the digital revolution.

## 5   Concluding Remarks

An overview of pre-1990s experimental film reveals it to be a very diverse and style-dominated field and only a few film types investigate issues of narrative structure and narrative technique. Future research could include experimental animation, expanded formats such as installations, contemporary video art, and a deeper analysis of the use of sound. The paper makes clear that experimental films have already contributed to IDN in the early days of database narratives and rhizomatic hyperlinking but it is felt that useful new knowledge is presented here in regard of:

- The spiral structures and vertical approach of trance narratives.
- Flashes, as microlexia, and transitions as interlexia, which contribute 'verticality'.
- Structures alternating narrative exposition with algorithmically generated 'remakes'.
- Meta-narratives in which database and algorithm are explicit and integrated to story.
- Mathematical equations and set theory as manipulators of story content.
- Use of voice-over to create either a disjunction or false unity of sound and image.
- The potential of emergent machine gaze as a basis for narrative experiences.
- Multiscreen and multilayering as visual forms to express multiform narratives.

– The contribution that the screen representation can make to expressing an IDN.

Practical outputs that might benefit from the knowledge presented here will probably themselves be experimental. The bibliography presented should provide a solid starting point to examine in more depth the world of experimental film. In regard of the films themselves, most can be accessed online and the author's parting advice would be: watch these weird and wonderful films and judge for yourselves.

# References

1. Rees, A.L.: A History of Experimental Film and Video. BFI, London (1999)
2. Le Grice, M.: A non-linear tradition–experimental film and digital cinema. In: Konopatzki, B., Krönung, A., Traub, I. (eds.). Catalogue of the 43rd International Short Film Festival, pp. 145–150. International Kurzfilmtage, Oberhausen (1997)
3. Jennings, P.: Narrative structures for new media. Leonardo **29**, 345–350 (1996)
4. Koenitz, H., Di Pastena, A., Jansen, D., de Lint, B., Moss, A.: The myth of 'universal' narrative models. In: Rouse, R., Koenitz, H., Haahr, M. (eds.) ICIDS 2018. LNCS, vol. 11318, pp. 107–120. Springer, Cham (2018). https://doi.org/10.1007/978-3-030-04028-4_8
5. Bordwell, D., Thompson, K.: Film Art: An Introduction, 10th edn. McGraw-Hill, New York (2013)
6. Buckland, W.: Puzzle Films: Complex Storytelling in Contemporary Cinema. Wiley-Blackwell, Chichester (2009)
7. Kelomees, R.: Constructing narratives in interactive documentaries. In: Kelomees, R., Hales, C. (eds.) Expanding Practices in Audiovisual Narrative, pp. 59–103. Cambridge Scholars Publishing, Newcastle (2014)
8. Hatfield, J.: Expanded cinema and narrative. Millen. Film J. **39**(40), 50–65 (2003)
9. Bordwell, D.: Narration in the Fiction Film. University of Wisconsin Press, Madison (1985)
10. Burch, N.: Theory of Film Practice. Princeton University Press, Princeton (1981)
11. Mortensen, T., Jørgensen, K.: The Paradox of Transgression in Games. Routledge, London (2020)
12. Galloway, A.: Gaming, Essays on Algorithmic Culture. University of Minnesota Press, Minneapolis (2006)
13. Weibel, P.: Narrative theory: multiple projection and multiple narration (past and future). In: Rieser, M., Zapp, A. (eds.) New Screen Media: Cinema/Art/Narrative, pp. 42–53. BFI, London (2002)
14. Reas, C.: Earthly Delights (2019). https://reas.com/earthly_1. Accessed 27 Aug 2020
15. Frampton, H.: On the Camera Arts and Consecutive Matters. MIT Press, Boston (2015)
16. Manovich, L.: Database as Symbolic Form. Convergence **5**(2), 80–99 (1999)
17. Manovich, L.: The Language of New Media. MIT Press, Cambridge (2001)
18. Kratky, A.: Lev manovich: soft cinema. In: Shaw, J., Weibel, P. (eds.) Future Cinema, the Cinematic Imaginary after Film, pp. 60–361. MIT Press, Cambridge (2003)
19. Alifragkis, S., Penz, F.: Dziga vertov's man with a movie camera: thoughts on the computation of style and narrative structure. Archit. Cult. **3**(1), 33–55 (2015)
20. Bard, P.: Man with a movie camera: the global remake. Public Art Dialogue **5**(2), 132–140 (2015)
21. Maas, W.: Poetry and the film: a symposium. Film Cult. **29**, 55–63 (1963)
22. Vosmeer, M., Roth, C., Koenitz, H.: Who are you? Voice-over perspective in surround video. In: Nunes, N., Oakley, I., Nisi, V. (eds.) ICIDS 2017. LNCS, vol. 10690, pp. 221–232. Springer, Cham (2017). https://doi.org/10.1007/978-3-319-71027-3_18

23. Youngblood, G.: Cinema and the code. Leonardo Suppl. Issue **2**, 27–30 (1989)
24. Manovich, L.: Spatial computerisation and film language (adapted from the language of new media). In: Rieser, M., Zapp, A. (eds.) New Screen Media: Cinema/Art/Narrative, pp. 64–76. BFI, London (2002)
25. Kluszczyński, R.: Re-writing the history of media art: from personal cinema to artistic collaboration. Leonardo **40**, 469–474 (2007)
26. Gidal, P.: Structural Film Anthology. BFI, London (1976)
27. Greenaway, P., Gras, V., Gras, M.: Peter Greenaway: Interviews. University Press of Mississippi, Jackson (2000)
28. Paul, C.: The database as system and cultural form: anatomies of cultural narratives. In: Vesna, V. (ed.) Database Aesthetics: Art in the Age of Information Overflow, pp. 95–109. University of Minnesota Press, Minneapolis (2007)
29. Willoquet-Maricondi, P., Alemany-Galway, M.: Peter Greenaway's Postmodern/Poststructuralist Cinema. Scarecrow Press, Lanham (2008)
30. Rokeby, D.: The Giver of Names (1990). http://www.davidrokeby.com/gon.html. Accessed 27 Aug 2020
31. Thompson, N.: CKRBT (2019). http://nyethompson.net/works/the-seeker-ckrbt.html. Accessed 27 Aug 2020
32. Enns, C.: Frampton's demon: a mathematical interpretation of Hollis Frampton's Zorns Lemma. Leonardo **49**(2), 156–161 (2016)
33. Seaman, W.: Ex.Mech, Artintact 1 CD-ROM (1994). In: Sommer, A. (ed.) The Complete Artintact DVD-ROM edition. Hatje Cantz, Stuttgart (2002)
34. Seaman, W.: Recombinant poetics and related database aesthetics. In: Vesna, V. (ed.) Database Aesthetics: Art in the Age of Information Overflow, pp. 121–141. University of Minnesota Press, Minneapolis (2007)
35. Queneau, R.: Exercices de Style. Gallimard, Paris (1982)
36. Weinbren, G.: Ocean, database, recut. In: Vesna, V. (ed.) Database Aesthetics: Art in the Age of Information Overflow, pp. 61–85. University of Minnesota Press, Minneapolis (2007)
37. Newitz, A.: Movie written by algorithm turns out to be hilarious and intense. Ars Technica, 6 September 2016. https://arstechnica.com/gaming/2016/06/an-ai-wrote-this-movie-and-its-strangely-moving/. Accessed 27 Aug 2020
38. Landow, G.: Hypertext 3.0: Critical Theory and New Media in an Era of Globalization. Johns Hopkins University Press, Baltimore (2006)
39. Sitney, P.: Adams: Visionary Film: The American Avant-Garde 1943–2000, 3rd edn. Oxford University Press, New York (2002)
40. Keller, S.: Maya Deren: Incomplete Control. Columbia University Press, New York (2015)
41. Deren, M.: Notes, essays, letters. Film Cult. **39**, 1 (1965)
42. Johnson, M.: VRWandlung (2018). http://files.cargocollective.com/c305679/VRWandlung-Press-Kit.pdf. Accessed 27 Aug 2020
43. Markopolous, G.: Towards a new narrative film form. Film Cult. **31**, 11–12 (1963)
44. Hales, C.: You Who? In: Holloway-Attaway, L., O'Dwyer, N. (eds.). Non-human Narratives Art Exhibition Catalogue, pp. 37–38. ICIDS (2018)
45. Tackfilm website (2010). https://tackfilm.se/. Accessed 27 Aug 2020
46. The Wilderness Downtown website (2011). http://www.thewildernessdowntown.com/. Accessed 27 Aug 2020
47. Just a Reflektor website (2015). https://www.justareflektor.com/. Accessed 27 Aug 2020
48. Kluszczyński, R.: (Audio) visual labyrinths. non-linear discourses in linear media. In: Konopatzki, B., Krönung, A., Traub, I. (eds.). Catalogue of the 43rd International Short Film Festival, pp. 138–144. International Kurzfilmtage, Oberhausen (1997)
49. Malinowski, T.: Friday to Saturday - a film about Zbig Rybczyński. Flying Brick Films, London (1991)

50. Digital Pictures: Night Trap. Digital Pictures (1992)
51. Philips POV: Voyeur. Philips Interactive (1993)
52. Love Shack: Framed. Noodlecake Studios Inc. (2015)
53. Koenitz, H.: Towards a specific theory of interactive narrative. In: Koenitz, H., Ferri, G., Haahr, M., Sezen, D., Sezen, T.I. (eds.) Interactive Digital Narrative: History, Theory, and Practice, pp. 91–105. Routledge, New York (2015)
54. Turvey, M.: Ken Jacobs digital revelationist. October **137**, 107–124 (2011)
55. The Tulse Luper Journey. http://www.tulseluperjourney.com. Accessed 27 Aug 2020
56. Le Grice, M.: The chronos project. Vertigo **1**(5), 21–25 (1995)
57. Le Grice, M.: Kismet, protagony and the zap splat syndrome. Millen. Film J. **28**, 6–12 (1995)
58. Kinder, M.: Tracing the Decay of Fiction: Encounters with a Film by Pat O'Neill. In: Shaw, J., Weibel, P. (eds.) Future Cinema, the Cinematic Imaginary after Film, pp. 356–357. MIT Press, Cambridge (2003)
59. Courchesne, L.: The construction of experience: turning spectators into visitors. In: Rieser, M., Zapp, A. (eds.) New Screen Media: Cinema/Art/Narrative, pp. 256–267. BFI, London (2002)
60. Hales, C.: Practical experimentation with parallel video streams. In: Hagebölling, H. (ed.) Interactive Dramaturgies, pp. 159–166. Springer, Berlin (2004)

# "How Do I Restart This Thing?" Repeat Experience and Resistance to Closure in Rewind Storygames

Alex Mitchell[(⊠)] [iD] and Liting Kway

National University of Singapore, Singapore, Singapore
alexm@nus.edu.sg, litingk@u.nus.edu

**Abstract.** Interactive stories are a kaleidoscopic form that both encourages and rewards repeat experience, allowing players to try out different variations of a story or see the story from different perspectives. This may be one reason for the increasing use of rewind game mechanics, where players are required to repeatedly play a storygame before eventually reaching some form of conclusion. While this seems to be playing to the strengths of the medium, what is not clear is how rewind structures can be explained by current models of repeat experience in interactive stories. Through a close reading of the storygame *Elsinore*, we explore the impact of rewind game mechanics on repeat play, in terms of the player's ability both to determine when the end has been reached, and to subsequently replay beyond closure. Our observations suggest that rewind mechanics may frustrate, rather than support, closure and repeat experience of storygames, and may require a revision of current theories of rereading and repeat experience.

**Keywords:** Replay · Rewind mechanics · Rereading · Replay · Storygames

## 1 Introduction

One of the defining characteristics of interactive stories is the ability for players to go back and try out different variations of the story. The ability to make choices and see the outcome of those choices both encourages and rewards repeat play, allowing players to either see the way that those choices changed the course of the story, or see the same story from a different perspective. Murray refers to this as kaleidoscopic form [1, 2].

There have been an increasing number of story-based games released in recent years that focus specifically on the need for players to repeat events multiple times to progress through the game and reach some form of an ending. Games such as *Save the Date* [3], *The Stanley Parable* [4], *Doki Doki Literature Club* [5], *Bandersnatch* [6] and *Nier: Automata* [7] are structured such that the player needs to repeatedly go back to move forward, utilizing what Kleinman et al. [8–10] refer to as a "rewind" game mechanic. This is not a new phenomenon, with interactive fictions such as *Spider and Web* [11] and classic video games such as *The Legend of Zelda: Majora's Mask* [12] incorporating time loops and the need to repeatedly replay the same or similar sequences, often with the

© Springer Nature Switzerland AG 2020
A.-G. Bosser et al. (Eds.): ICIDS 2020, LNCS 12497, pp. 164–177, 2020.
https://doi.org/10.1007/978-3-030-62516-0_15

eventual objective of "breaking out" of the loop. Even classic interactive stories without an explicit time loop narrative, such as *afternoon, a story* [13], tend to encourage repeat experience, either to make sense of what is happening in the story, or to come to some other sense of closure or completion [14].

This pattern of requiring the player to engage in repeated play with the goal of eventually reaching some conclusion raises interesting questions about the nature of repeat experience and endings. If a storygame is explicitly designed to encourage or even *require* replay, how then does a player know when they have really reached the ending? If an ending is eventually reached, why would the player go back and replay the storygame beyond the ending? And what would the player be doing if they did go back and replay at that point? If replaying is an inherent feature of interactive stories, the answers to these questions can help us to better understand both "rewind" storygames, and interactive stories in general.

To explore these questions, we conducted a close reading of *Elsinore* [15], an adaptation of Shakespeare's *Hamlet* [16] in which you play as Ophelia caught in a time loop as she repeatedly attempts to avert the tragic events of the original play. As the player goes through multiple repetitions of the timeline, a number of additional goals become evident, eventually focusing on the need for Ophelia to break out of the time loop and reach some form of ending. However, as we will discuss, the focus on a rewind mechanic makes it unclear both when the game actually comes to an end, and what it would mean to replay the game beyond this ending.

The works we are considering are what Reed refers to as *storygames*, "a playable system, with units of narrative, where the understanding of both, and the relationship between them, is required for a satisfying traversal" [17]. We use the term *player* to indicate the entity engaging with the storygame, and *play* for the activity the player is engaging in. At times we may refer to *reading* and *rereading*, after Mitchell [18, 19], to indicate the player is focused more on the narrative units than the playable system.

## 2 Why Do People Reexperience Stories?

The question of why people go back and reexperience stories has been explored in detail [20–26]. In the context of non-interactive stories, Calinescu [27] identified three types of rereading: partial rereading, simple rereading and reflective rereading. Focusing on interactive stories, there have long been debates as to whether people reread for variation or for closure [28–33]. Moving beyond this, Murray [2] argues that while people reread for variation, they are ultimately looking for some form of closure. Mitchell [18, 19] expands on this position, adapting Calinescu's categories to interactive stories. According to Mitchell, people initially reread interactive stories from a goal-directed perspective, similar to Calinescu's partial rereading. After reaching this goal, they shift to the equivalent of simple or reflective rereading. This requires a change in what the player is doing as they experience the storygame. What is not clear is what it means to engage in simple [34] or reflective rereading [35, 36] in an interactive story.

Kleinman [9, 10] has explored the notion of "rewind mechanics", the idea that the player needs to go back, either to a specific (restricted rewind) or any (unrestricted rewind) earlier moment in the same traversal, or to go back to the beginning of a narrative after a traversal (external rewind). This framework was later expanded to define rewind more broadly as "a narrative progression mechanic that allows the player to return to a previous point in either narrative and/or game-play." This mechanic "requires [the player] to rewind in order to progress the game narrative" [8]. There has also been work to explore how storygames that incorporate rewind mechanics potentially undermine the notion of rereading by breaking player expectations that a play session will be self-contained [37, 38], as can be seen in a game such as *Save the Date*.

## 3    Research Problem

Much work has been done to understand what it means to reexperience a storygame, and how this is different from rereading non-interactive stories. This work tends to focus on storygames where there is some form of "ending" beyond which the work can mechanically no longer progress. Whatever the player may feel in terms of reaching closure, the work is at an end. At this point, the reader can choose whether or not to go back and replay, either to complete their understanding (partial rereading), or to engage in simple or reflective rereading. The reader can also choose to stop playing.

What is not clear is how players respond to works that explicitly require replay [39], something that Mitchell [37] argues undermines expectations for rereading. Although Mitchell claims this forced replay, and the related cross-sessional play, is defamiliarizing [40], Kleinman et al. [8–10] suggest it is, in fact, an increasingly common approach. Regardless, this type of work foregrounds the problematic nature of "endings" in interactive stories. For these works, the "end" often triggers a rewind, with the actual end coming after a longer traversal resulting from one or more rewinds. In addition, as the player has already been repeatedly encountering the game as part of the rewind, it isn't clear what it would mean to "reread" this type of storygame.

This leads to the questions that we are exploring in this paper. If the ending of the work is indeterminate, what then would it mean to reexperience such a work, not in the sense of the enforced "rewinds" required by the work's mechanics, but in the sense that Mitchell [19] considers? When do these games end? How would a player replay these games? And how does this relate to Mitchell's model of rereading in interactive stories?

## 4    Method

To begin to explore these questions, we conducted a close reading of the storygame *Elsinore* [15], an adaptation of Shakespeare's *Hamlet* [16]. Structured as a point-and-click adventure game, the gameplay in *Elsinore* focuses on having the player character, Ophelia, talk to non-player characters (NPCs) as a means of collecting and using information referred to as "Hearsay", which is tracked in Ophelia's "Journal". Using information opens up "Leads", which represent narrative threads that can be pursued to completion, at which point they are "sealed" (marked with a wax seal in the Journal). Talking to NPCs can also change what the NPC and/or Ophelia believe and what goals NPCs are currently pursuing, and can reveal potential future events, which are displayed in a "Timeline". An underlying temporal predicate logic system determines which events will take place in the current timeline [41]. Repeat play in the form of a "rewind" is required to progress in the game, with total playing time in the range of 15–20 h, involving 20 or more rewinds, needed before some form of ending is reached.

Close reading is an approach adapted to the study of games by Bizzocchi and Tanenbaum [42] in which the researcher takes on a specific "naive player" perspective, and repeatedly plays a game so as to gain a deeper understanding of the structural features of the work. To aid the process, they recommend that the researcher adopt a particular set of "analytical lenses" to allow for a focus on specific features related to the investigation. For our close readings, we focused on the following questions: Have I reached the end? If so, how do I restart? And what am I doing when playing, both before and after restarting? Both authors played the game, discussed the play experience, and extracted the insights described in this paper. To facilitate a coherent description of play and acknowledge that our findings do not necessarily reflect those of all players, we frame our findings in terms of the first author's experience. To help make this apparent to the reader, all descriptions of gameplay are presented in the first person.

In the discussion of our close reading below, we consider a *traversal* to be an encounter that a player has with a storygame from a beginning to an end, as defined by Montfort [43]. A *beginning* is a point at which there is no stored state differentiating the storygame from its original state when first installed, and an *end* is a point at which there is no further action that the player can take without somehow, either implicitly or explicitly, resetting the storygame to its original state. These are deliberately mechanical definitions that do not refer to the player's perception of the beginning or ending.

Regarding the player's perception of an ending, which we refer to as *closure*, we distinguish between *narrative closure* and *system closure*. We consider narrative closure to be "the phenomenological feeling of finality that is generated when all the questions saliently posed by the narrative are answered" [44]. Following Mitchell et al. [36] we consider system closure to be equivalent to Murray's electronic closure, which "occurs when a work's structure, though not its plot, is understood" [2]. As discussed in [36], it is possible for a player to reach either narrative closure, system closure, or both, without necessarily having reached the end of a work. Conversely, a player may reach the end of a work without having reached one or both forms of closure.

A *replay* involves completing a traversal then playing from the beginning, whereas a *rewind* (following [10]) involves either going back to an earlier point within the narrative or gameplay, or going back to a "false beginning" where some stored state remains that represents non-zero progress. Note that simply returning to an earlier point within the same traversal, for example by loading a save point, is not a rewind. For this to be a "rewind mechanic" in Kleinman's [8] sense, the game must maintain some state to track the fact that the rewind occurred, otherwise there is no way that the player can be prevented from moving forward without having succeeded at the rewind mechanic.

## 5 Forced Rewinds and Cross-Sessional Puzzle Solving

The traditional idea of an "ending" is almost immediately overturned in *Elsinore*, with the use of the rewind mechanic and the need to repeatedly revisit the main timeline introduced early in the game. The game requires rewinding to progress, shifting the focus from a single traversal to an extended traversal stretching over repeated rewinds.

Following a brief "prologue" which introduces the player to the core game mechanics, setting and characters, the first evening arrives, and Ophelia sleeps. During the night she has a nightmare, presented as a series of images, in which the events of the original Shakespeare play are shown. When Ophelia wakes on Thursday morning, she realizes the events of the dream have not yet happened. This introduces the initial goal of the game: prevent the original events of the play from occurring. However, it quickly became evident that there were other goals that I needed to work towards.

As the events of the play unfold, a cloaked figure approaches Ophelia on Saturday, and abruptly kills her. I was shown a black screen containing an illustration of a river, the text "I feel my body growing cold", and a button labelled "Try again". Pressing this button takes Ophelia back to her bed, where she wakes on Thursday morning. Here I quickly realized I was repeating the same events, with Ophelia inevitably and repeatedly killed by the mysterious assailant. Using Kleinman et al.'s terminology [8], this is a designer-controlled rewind, as the player cannot initiate it on their own. In fact, the player's goal is to *prevent* the rewind, as it hinders progress. There is also zero scope for the player to determine where to rewind to, as the rewind always resets to Thursday.

What is happening here is very much like games such as *Save the Date*: the player is presented with an obstacle that requires repeated rewinds to overcome. Stopping the mysterious assailant involves a shift to cross-sessional puzzle solving [37]. Once the player determines that Brit, lady-in-waiting to Queen Gertrude, may be the assailant, Ophelia must convince the captain of the guards to arrest Brit. This involves befriending Brit, after which she confesses and kills Ophelia. When the timeline restarts, it is possible to use the information gained from the confession to have Brit captured before she kills Ophelia again. Once Brit is captured, the playwright Peter Quince appears and declares that this "thread" of the story has been "snipped", and that Ophelia will no longer be in danger from Brit. However, it emerges that Ophelia needs to stop Fortinbras invading Denmark, which also requires puzzle-solving across sessions.

The game provides a number of tools to help with this repeated rewinding. After the first rewind, a "fast forward" mechanism is unlocked, letting you accelerate time in a form of dramatic compression [45]. Following the second rewind, a "restart" mechanism is added, allowing you to abandon the current timeline and jump back to Thursday morning, while retaining any information Ophelia has acquired. This additional means of rewind introduces player-controlled initiation, but the scope is still not in the player's control. It is also important to note that there is no manual "save game" mechanism, so the player is also unable to checkpoint specific game state.

Both the Brit and Fortinbras cross-sessional puzzles require information, in the form of Hearsay, from one timeline to be carried over to the next and focus on removing obstacles that terminate the timeline prematurely. In working to solve these puzzles, it became clear to me that there is a reason Ophelia needs to survive to Sunday morning, and my focus shifted from the intermediate goal of prolonging Ophelia's life, to the larger goal of trying to find a book, called the "Hand of Dionysus" or the "Book of Fate", which is causing the time loop. Through Quince, I discovered that the book is in the hands of Lady Simona, who will be at the Inn in the town outside Elsinore Castle on Sunday morning. Now, the motivation for solving the cross-sessional puzzles becomes to get this book and break out of the time loop.

At this point, my notion of the "end" of the storygame, and some sense of closure, was linked both to my understanding of the playable system – how to manipulate the various characters through the use of "hearsay" – and my understanding of the narrative – that Ophelia had been trapped in a time loop as the result of the Book of Fates. Once I had the book, I assumed that I would be able to break out of the loop and bring the game to an end, simultaneously reaching both narrative and system closure.

This was reinforced by what happens when Ophelia receives the book from Simona. She tells Ophelia that the book once belonged to Quince, and he has been using it to torment her. She also explains that once you use the Book of Fates "the clock on Elsinore advances forever", suggesting that there would be no turning back. At the same time, she cautioned that "a perfect world is a notion held only by fools and children". I wasn't sure what she meant, but I was looking for closure, and saw this as the most logical route to ending the game and resolving the story threads. However, after receiving the Book, Ophelia wakes on Thursday, with the Book on her table. Ophelia's reaction mirrored mine: "I thought that might have been the end of all this. But it wasn't."

## 6  Repeated Resistance to Closure

Although it seemed that solving the cross-sessional puzzles would bring the game to an end, *Elsinore* repeatedly resists attempts at both reaching an ending and achieving either narrative or system closure. It was not just the narrative twist related to Quince's role in the time loop that provided resistance to closure. The rewind mechanic, by allowing for several different ways the player could try to end the game, was also encouraging the player to defer closure and continue to engage with the time loop.

I had assumed that once I received the book, the loop would be broken, time would move inexorably forward as Simona had warned, and the game would come to an end. Instead, it turned out that Ophelia needs to decide *which* timeline will be the "permanent" future for the people living in Elsinore Castle. The Book lists 11 different "Fates", each represented by a page in the Book. When you select a page, you are presented with a choice to "abandon current timeline and revisit the event that cemented this fate". For Fates that you have not yet experienced to completion, there is no such option. Rather than taking me out of the time loop, acquiring the Book had instead given me the choice to end the loop, but also the temptation to stay until I find the "best" ending.

Soon after acquiring the Book, Ophelia has an encounter with the Ghost that heightens the tension between ending the game or continuing. The Ghost repeats Simona's warning that there is "no perfect world to be found" and suggests the way to overcome Quince is to use my power to choose which Fate to finalize. Here an additional option arose, as Ophelia suggested she could burn the Book. The Ghost cautioned against this, as although this would remove Quince's powers it would also trap everyone in the loop together with Quince. It did, however, open up a new option: rather than choose one of the less-than-perfect endings, I could instead end the game by remaining in the loop.

This suggests that the player, rather than reaching closure, is encouraged to continue to engage in something equivalent to Mitchell's [18, 19] partial rereading, exploring variations until the player decides either they have found the least bad Fate and will finalize it, or they will abandon any hope of ever leaving the loop and burn the Book.

Interestingly, partial rereading usually involves repeat play in search of closure *after* reaching the ending of the work, whereas here it is happening *before* the player has reached an ending, but while the player is repeatedly reexperiencing the timeline.

Given the Ghost's insistence that there was no best ending, and not seeing any obvious way to burn the Book, I chose the ending that most closely resembled the original Shakespeare play, which was actually the outcome I had been working so hard to avoid through the many time loops. This felt like a defeat, but at the same time it brought the promise of closure. However, the game makes you doubt even this decision, once again resisting closure. After selecting a Fate, each character tells Ophelia how they feel about the ending and why it is not the best ending. After all have spoken, the Ghost reminds Ophelia that if this is her choice, then she should stick with it. You are then given 2 options: "Choose This Fate" and "Restart Time". This is your first chance to turn back. If you select "Restart Time", Ophelia wakes on Thursday morning, back in the loop. If, however, you select "Choose This Fate", you are shown a second warning: "This will be inscribed as the true fate of Elsinore Castle, ending you from your endless loop. There will be no turning back." The two options are "Choose This Ending" or "Not Yet". The game was repeatedly resisting my attempts to end the game, but I chose to go on. After a short animation showing Ophelia drowning in the river the credits roll, followed by a still image from the animation and the words "FIN". The game then exits.

## 7   The End Is not the End: Resisting Both Ending and Closure

Here I assumed that I had finally reached the end. Reopening the game, the main screen had changed: whereas previously it had shown a scene in a graveyard with Elsinore Castle in the distance, now it showed the final scene from the Fate I had chosen. Where the first menu option has previously been "Continue Game", now it showed "Return to Elsinore". While my choice of a Fate had clearly had an impact, it seemed I was being given the chance to return to the game, presumably to continue from where I had left off. There was no "Restart" option on the main screen, and looking at the "Options" screen showed that while there was an option to "Erase all data", again there was no "Restart" option, nor was there any option such as "New game plus" as can be found in other games. At this point I was uncertain whether I had actually completed the game, or how I could go about replaying the game, other than choosing to "Erase all data".

This, combined with my memory of both Simona's warning that the fate I chose would be permanent and the Ghost's admonition to choose carefully, made me curious as to what would happen if I chose to "Return to Elsinore". Going back into the game after selecting a Fate leads to a conversation with the Ghost where he tries to convince Ophelia not to return. In addition, the Ghost warns Ophelia that if she does choose to return, any Fate that has previously been chosen will be removed from the Book.

Whereas previously I felt I had completed the game, now I felt that closure had been suspended, perhaps indefinitely. I didn't want to go back, as I thought I had understood both the story and the playable system, but now that sense of closure was confounded as it seemed I hadn't really finished the game. There was a tension between my feeling that the game was complete and the fact that mechanically nothing was stopping me from resuming, as opposed to restarting, the game. In fact, there was no clear way to restart the game. At the narrative level, there was a similar tension between Simona's statement that time would inevitably move forward and the assertion by the Ghost that Ophelia should not return on the one hand, and the possibility that Ophelia could return but at the cost of sacrificing her earlier choice of Fate on the other. In terms of both the playable system and the narrative units, I was no longer certain I had reached closure, or even the mechanical end of the game. The game seemed to be asking *me* to decide when to stop playing. In terms of Mitchell's [18, 19] model of rereading, I was unclear whether, if I went back into the game, I would be engaged in some form of rereading, or still engaged in my "first" reading, despite having reached (and lost) closure.

## 8  Playing for Closure Versus Playing for *Completion*

It is worth reflecting on how the game ended up like this. At the time I had gained access to the Book of Fates, I was playing version 1.4 of *Elsinore*. In earlier versions, the final choice when you select a Fate included additional text, in bold, stating: "Your save progress will be deleted". On launching the game after the end credits, rather than "Return to Elsinore", you would see the original "Start Prologue" option. Entering the game, you had to replay from the Prologue, with none of the Hearsay or Leads you had accumulated in your previous traversal, and without the Fast Forward or Restart tools.

Fans reacted strongly to this. Many reviews and comments in the Steam forum were similar to the following: "As it stands, the thought of starting anew without being able to go to a specific save game means I may not replay Elsinore, or if I do it won't be for a while due to time constraints" [46]. Players had been expecting there would be some way to reenter the game and work towards completing all the Fates, without having to replay the cross-sessional puzzles and accumulate the Hearsay that would enable the various Leads to be completed and the Fates unlocked.

The developers responded by releasing version 1.4, which implemented the ending system described above. The release announcement posted in Steam stated: "we knew that we wanted to capture the feeling that no matter what fate Ophelia chose for Elsinore, it was the final choice she would make. We believed most players would want to put down the game at that point and move on... It's clear that our original structure wasn't hitting our thematic goals for a large number of players" [47]. The developers had felt players would be wanting closure, whereas players were aiming for completion.

Interestingly, even in the original design you could in fact play through all the "endings" to the point where they appear in the Book of Fates, as long as you didn't select the final "Choose this ending" option. In addition, the game clearly warns players before the save file is deleted. Despite this, some players were unhappy with the finality of the original design. Instead, they wanted to be able to play all of the endings through to the credits, without putting in the effort of replaying from the start. This is what the updated version allows, if you ignore the Ghost's warning and return to Elsinore.

It is also important to note that in the updated version, there are in fact 2 mutually exclusive "final" endings: "burn the Book" and "Exeunt All". Choosing to burn the Book, by clicking on the candle that appears beside the Book after Ophelia mentions this option, renders all the Fates inaccessible, but does not actually end the game. After this point, all the player can do is repeatedly cycle through the time loop, having trapped

Ophelia and Quince in the loop forever. The only way to end the game is to quit. The other ending requires the player to finalize all the Fates in the Book, then wait for Quince to talk to Ophelia and offer her the ability to remove everyone from the "stage".

These various ways of ending the game all build upon the initial use of the rewind mechanic, which emphasizes repeat play and exploration of variations. Choosing any of the Fates requires the player to decide to stop playing, even though mechanically they could continue. This is putting the choice in the hands of the player, asking the player to consciously decide to "put down the game… and move on", as the developers initially envisioned, rather than enforcing this by deleting the save data. The "burn the Book" ending similarly requires the player to decide to stop playing, but provides some sense of narrative closure in terms of Ophelia's defeat of Quince and the explicit removal of all other endings. Finally, the "Exeunt all" ending is perhaps an implicit critique of the players who demanded the ability to complete all endings – in the final animation before the credits role, Ophelia joins Quince in his role as playwright and tormentor, treating the world as a stage and all the people within as mere puppets.

## 9  Replaying as Both Supporting and Resisting Rereading

Having explored the ways *Elsinore* first requires repeated rewinds, then resists closure, and finally pushes the responsibility for ending the game to the player, we will now look at what it means to replay *Elsinore* from the start. Before version 1.4, this was forced on the player after choosing a particular Fate, as the save data was erased. For players of version 1.4 or later, the only way to replay from the beginning is to go into the "Options" screen and choose "Erase all data" – there is no explicit "Restart" option.

The first thing that became obvious when playing through the "Prologue" for a second time was how much I relied on the "fast forward" mechanism. Without it, I was forced to slow down and pay attention to the dialogue. This encouraged me to take time to renew my knowledge of the characters and appreciate the writing. In terms of Mitchell's [18, 19] model, this could be seen as a form of simple rereading: reading again to recapture the feeling of the first experience. Interestingly, I was also paying attention to characters I knew had ulterior motives, such as Quince. I was looking closely for hints that he was more than he seemed and trying to figure out how I had missed this on my first traversal. This bears similarities to reflective rereading.

However, once the "fast-forward" and "restart" functions were unlocked, I shifted to a more goal-oriented form of play, often focusing on a specific Lead that I wanted to explore and then complete. I found I had an uneven recollection of specific events that sometimes made this difficult, as I had forgotten which Hearsay could be used to trigger which events. I could recall major plot points, such as Hamlet killing King Claudius, Brit being a spy for Denmark, and Irma attempting to poison Hamlet, but not the details of how I had discovered and then triggered these events during my first traversal. This suggests that to some extent I was now engaged in partial rereading.

At the same time, I realized that knowledge from my previous playthrough was actually hindering my replay experience. First-time players of *Elsinore* can be assumed to have no prior knowledge of the storygame. Even if they have read or watched *Hamlet* in other media, which may give them some insight into the characters and overall plot, they would not know how the playable system works, or which Hearsay Ophelia needs to collect and make use of to progress. As such, the player and Ophelia learn new information about both the narrative units and the playable system at the same time. However, in a replay of *Elsinore,* the player has knowledge that Ophelia does not possess. This disconnect came to interfere with my attempts to progress in the game.

For example, in the cross-sessional puzzle involving the mysterious assailant, Ophelia must figure out who is repeatedly killing her and prevent this from happening. As I already knew the identity of the spy, I tried to optimize my play such that I would only encounter the spy once and then complete the Lead in as few time loops as possible. However, this became an obstacle as Ophelia did not yet have the knowledge of who the spy was. By taking actions based on that knowledge I was actually preventing Ophelia from gaining the Hearsay she needed. No matter how hard I tried to avoid the spy, the rewind mechanic and the design of the cross-sessional puzzle ensured that Ophelia must die repeatedly before the puzzle can been solved. Even when I became aware of this problem, my prior knowledge continued to disrupt my replay. Once I realized that I needed to obtain the missing Hearsay, I was mechanically working through the puzzles and trying to gather the Hearsay as quickly as possible. I was no longer paying attention to the story, instead focusing almost exclusively on the playable system.

At this point, I forced myself to let go of any expectations I had from my first traversal, including narrative and system knowledge. By allowing myself to repeat the core mechanic of sharing information with characters, letting the narrative run its course, and having Ophelia die again and again as if I didn't know anything, I was able to develop a fresh, albeit not new, understanding of the story and the playable system. This was accompanied, at times, by enjoyment at encountering Leads that I had not previously seen or finished. For example, I discovered a new Lead involving Guildenstern and Rosencrantz, whom I had ignored on my first traversal.

Eventually I felt that I had reached a similar state as when I was playing *Elsinore* the first time around. I had completed the cross-sessional puzzles, accumulated a sizeable amount of Hearsay, and reacquainted myself with the relationship between the Hearsay and the ways they could be used to influence the story. This enabled me to engage in more exploratory play, trying out different possibilities and working to unlock different Fates. At this point, when I was no longer forced to rewind but had not yet finalized any Fates, I was engaged in what could be called *kaleidoscopic* play. By breaking free of the cross-sessional puzzles but deliberately avoiding triggering an ending, I was able to make use of the rewind mechanic to play with both the narrative units and the playable system, exploring variations and the ways my choices impacted the direction and shape of the story until I decided I had played enough, and I simply stopped playing.

## 10   Discussion: Rethinking Rereading in Rewind Storygames

The experience described above suggests that the structure of Elsinore's rewind mechanics, which explicitly represents information in the form of Hearsay and uses conversation as a means to gather Hearsay and overcome barriers to progress, supports a specific pattern of play. When the player and Ophelia have the same level of understanding of the story and playable system the player is able to focus on both, but once the player has completed the storygame and tries to replay, the mismatch between the player's and Ophelia's knowledge interferes with the rewind mechanic, making rereading, in the sense that Mitchell [18, 19] discusses, somewhat problematic. It is only when the replay is treated as if it is a first playthrough that play can progress smoothly. This form of replay as if playing for the first time is not accounted for in Mitchell's model.

To understand what is happening, we can examine Mitchell's model in more detail. Mitchell proposes that only after reaching closure will a reader consider what they are doing to be "rereading", equivalent to Calinescu's [27] simple or reflective rereading. At that point, what the reader is doing *changes* while their understanding of the storygame remains *invariant*. To support this type of rereading, Mitchell suggests storygames need to provide mechanics that can adapt to what the reader is doing when rereading beyond closure. In *Elsinore*, the core mechanic of gathering and using Hearsay to overcome obstacles by altering NPC goals and triggering events in the timeline strongly encourages goal-oriented play during an initial traversal, both before and after the cross-sessional puzzles are solved.

Initially the player is working to understand the playable system and the narrative units, and the core mechanic directly supports this. Once the player has overcome the cross-sessional puzzles and acquired the Book of Fates, they can shift to a more exploratory type of play, similar to Calinescu's reflective rereading. This is possible because the gameplay loop can adjust to this new type of play. The initial barrier of Brit killing Ophelia is literally gone, as Quince has "snipped" that narrative thread. Although the Fortinbras threat is still present, since Ophelia has the information about his hiding place, the player can quickly forestall the invasion in each loop and explore the various possible Fates. While the core mechanic is unchanged, the larger gameplay loop shifted from a forced rewind to overcome the cross-sessional puzzles, to a more exploratory use of the rewind mechanic and Hearsay to develop Leads and unlock new Fates, allowing the player to gain a deeper understanding of the storygame. We refer to this type of reflective rereading without replaying as *kaleidoscopic* play, after Murray's [2] notion of interactive stories as a kaleidoscopic medium.

Interestingly, this variation on reflective rereading is happening *after* the player has (at least temporarily) reached both narrative and system closure, but *before* the player has ended the game and started a true replay from the beginning. There is a difference here between engaging in reflective rereading while holding off on mechanically ending the game, and attempting to replay from the actual beginning. As we have seen, the structure of the core mechanic and the accompanying rewind mechanic becomes problematic on a true replay, as at this point the player has reached closure, and is trying to shift to either simple or reflective rereading. However, without a set of Hearsay that matches the player's knowledge of the story, the player eventually has to switch back to the original, goal-oriented form of play. The resetting of the game state has locked the larger gameplay loop back to its original form, making it difficult for the player to play beyond closure. This mismatch between how the player is trying to play the game, and what the mechanics actually support, frustrates the attempt at simple or reflective rereading. It is also not clear whether this is equivalent to partial rereading, as the player may already have both narrative and system closure – what they are lacking is the Hearsay required by the game mechanics to allow them to act on that closure.

This suggests that a rewind storygame such as *Elsinore,* which is explicitly designed to *require* repeat play, actually *frustrates* any attempt to replay the game from the start, as it forces replay to be the same as the original approach to playing. Storygames that aim to support replay beyond closure perhaps need to be designed to acknowledge what Mitchell suggests, which is that rereading is not, in fact, reading *again,* but reading in a *new way.* It also suggests that Mitchell's model of rereading needs to be extended to incorporate other forms of repeat experience, such as replaying as if playing for the first time and the kaleidoscopic play that arises from repeated resistance to closure.

## 11   Conclusion

In this paper we have explored how *Elsinore,* a storygame that makes use of a rewind mechanic that requires repeat play to progress, actively resists closure both by encouraging the player to engage in kaleidoscopic play, and by refusing to bring the game to an end, pushing the responsibility for ending the game from the system to the player. In addition, the very mechanics that require repeat play in the first traversal, in fact tend to frustrate and problematize attempts to reset the game and then replay from the start, requiring the player to replay as if they were playing for the first time until they reach the point where they can once again engage in kaleidoscopic play. These types of repeat experience are not fully explained by existing models of rereading in interactive stories.

These observations raise a number of questions regarding repeat experience of storygames. One immediate issue is whether designing for replay of the type encouraged by rewind mechanics actually hinders the type of rereading beyond closure as described by Mitchell [18, 19]. Beyond this, the type of kaleidoscopic play that *Elsinore* encourages once the cross-sessional puzzles are resolved suggests a need to extend Mitchell's model of rereading so as to better accommodate "the different kinds of closure a kaleidoscopic medium can offer" [2]. These are all areas for future exploration.

It is also important to note that our observations are based on close readings, and therefore reflect the experience of specific players with a specific storygame. Future work should make use of empirical studies of players to better understand to what extent these observations can be generalized, both to other players, and to other storygames.

**Acknowledgments.** This research is funded in part under the Singapore Ministry of Education Academic Research Fund Tier 1 grant FY2018-FRC2-003, "Understanding Repeat Engagement with Dynamically Changing Computational Media".

## References

1. Murray, J.H.: Research into interactive digital narrative: a kaleidoscopic view. In: Rouse, R., Koenitz, H., Haahr, M. (eds.) ICIDS 2018. LNCS, vol. 11318, pp. 3–17. Springer, Cham (2018). https://doi.org/10.1007/978-3-030-04028-4_1
2. Murray, J.H.: Hamlet on the Holodeck: The Future of Narrative in Cyberspace. The MIT Press, Cambridge (1998)
3. Paper Dino Software: Save the Date [PC computer game] (2013)
4. Galactic Cafe: The Stanley Parable [Computer Game] (2013)

5. Team Salvato: Doki Doki Literature Club! [Computer Game] (2017)
6. Netflix: Bandersnatch [interactive film] (2018)
7. Taro, Y.: Nier: Automata [Playstation 4 game] (2017)
8. Kleinman, E., Carstensdottir, E., El-Nasr, M.S.: Going forward by going back: re-defining rewind mechanics in narrative games. In: Proceedings of the 13th International Conference on the Foundations of Digital Games, pp. 32:1–32:6. ACM, New York (2018)
9. Kleinman, E., Fox, V., Zhu, J.: Rough draft: towards a framework for metagaming mechanics of rewinding in interactive storytelling. In: Nack, F., Gordon, A.S. (eds.) ICIDS 2016. LNCS, vol. 10045, pp. 363–374. Springer, Cham (2016). https://doi.org/10.1007/978-3-319-48279-8_32
10. Kleinman, E., Caro, K., Zhu, J.: From immersion to metagaming: Understanding rewind mechanics in interactive storytelling. Entertain. Comput. **33**, 100322 (2020)
11. Plotkin, A.: Spider and Web [Inform 6 game] (1998)
12. Imamura, T.: The Legend of Zelda: Majora's Mask [Nintendo 64, GameCube, Wii, Wii U game] (2000)
13. Joyce, M.: Afternoon, a Story. Eastgate Systems Inc. (1990)
14. Douglas, J.Y.: "How do I stop this thing?": closure and indeterminacy in interactive narratives. In: Landow, G. (ed.) Hyper/Text/Theory, pp. 159–188. Johns Hopkins University Press, Baltimore (1994)
15. Golden Glitch Studios: Elsinore [Computer Game] (2019)
16. Shakespeare, W.: The Tragedy of Hamlet, Prince of Denmark. Folger Shakespeare Library, Washington (1879)
17. Reed, A.: Changeful Tales: Design-Driven Approaches Toward More Expressive Storygames (2017)
18. Mitchell, A.: Reading Again for the First Time: Rereading for Closure in Interactive Stories (2012)
19. Mitchell, A., McGee, K.: Reading again for the first time: a model of rereading in interactive stories. In: Oyarzun, D., Peinado, F., Young, R.M., Elizalde, A., Méndez, G. (eds.) ICIDS 2012. LNCS, vol. 7648, pp. 202–213. Springer, Heidelberg (2012). https://doi.org/10.1007/978-3-642-34851-8_20
20. Galef, D.: Observations on rereading. In: Galef, D. (ed.) Second Thoughts: a Focus on Rereading, pp. 17–33. Wayne State University Press (1998)
21. Leitch, T.M.: For (against) a theory of rereading. Mod. Fict. Stud. **33**, 491–508 (1987)
22. Brewer, W.F.: The Nature of narrative suspense and the problem of rereading. In: Vorderer, P., Wulff, H.J., Friedrichsen, M. (eds.) Suspense: Conceptualizations, Theoretical Analyses, and Empirical Explorations, pp. 107–126. Routledge (1996)
23. Gardner, D.L.: Rereading as a mechanism of defamiliarization in Proust. Poet. Today **37**, 55–105 (2016)
24. Bentley, F., Murray, J.: Understanding video rewatching experiences. In: Proceedings of the ACM International Conference on Interactive Experiences for TV and Online Video, pp. 69–75 (2016)
25. O'Brien, E.: Enjoy it again: repeat experiences are less repetitive than people think. J. Pers. Soc. Psychol. **116**, 519–540 (2019)
26. Joyce, M.: Nonce upon some times: rereading hypertext fiction. MFS Mod. Fict. Stud. **43**, 579–597 (1997)
27. Calinescu, M.: Rereading. Yale University Press (1993)
28. Ciccoricco, D.: Repetition and Recombination: Reading Network Fiction: a Thesis Submitted in Fulfillment of the Requirements for the Degree of Doctor of Philosophy in English in the University of Canterbury (2005)
29. Bernstein, M.: Patterns of hypertext. In: Proceedings of Hypertext 1998, pp. 21–29. ACM Press (1998)

30. Bernstein, M.: On hypertext narrative. In: Proceedings of Hypertext 1909, pp. 5–14. ACM Press (2009)

31. Bernstein, M., Joyce, M., Levine, D.: Contours of constructive hypertexts. In: Proceedings of Hypertext 1992, pp. 161–170. ACM (1992)

32. Douglas, J.Y.: The End of Books - or Books Without End? Reading Interactive Narratives. University of Michigan Press (2001)

33. Harpold, T.: Links and their vicissitudes: essays on hypertext (1994)

34. Mitchell, A.: Rereading as echo: a close (re)reading of Emily Short's "a family supper". Issue Art J. **2**, 121–129 (2013)

35. Mitchell, A.: Reflective rereading and the SimCity effect in interactive stories. In: Schoenau-Fog, H., Bruni, L.E., Louchart, S., Baceviciute, S. (eds.) ICIDS 2015. LNCS, vol. 9445, pp. 27–39. Springer, Cham (2015). https://doi.org/10.1007/978-3-319-27036-4_3

36. Mitchell, A., Kway, L., Lee, B.J.: Storygameness: understanding repeat experience and the desire for closure in storygames. In: DiGRA 2020 - Proceedings of the 2020 DiGRA International Conference (2020)

37. Mitchell, A.: Antimimetic rereading and defamiliarization in Save the Date. In: DiGRA 2018 - Proceedings of the 2018 DiGRA International Conference, Turin (2018)

38. Mitchell, A., Kway, L., Neo, T., Sim, Y.T.: A preliminary categorization of techniques for creating poetic gameplay. Game Stud. **20** (2020). http://gamestudies.org/2002/articles/mitchell_kway_neo_sim

39. Mitchell, A.: Encouraging and rewarding repeat play of storygames. In: Dillon, R. (ed.) The Digital Gaming Handbook. CRC Press, Taylor and Francis (2020)

40. Shklovsky, V.: Art as technique. In: Russian Formalist Criticism: Four Essays, pp. 3–24, University of Nebraska Press, Lincoln/London (1965)

41. Zook, A.E., et al.: Playable experiences at AIIDE 2016. In: Twelfth Artificial Intelligence and Interactive Digital Entertainment Conference (2016)

42. Bizzocchi, J., Tanenbaum, T.J.: Well read: applying close reading techniques to gameplay experiences. In: Davidson, D. (ed.) Well played 3.0, pp. 262–290. ETC Press (2011)

43. Montfort, N.: Twisty Little Passages An Approach to Interactive Fiction. MIT Press, Cambridge (2003)

44. Carroll, N.: Narrative closure. Philos. Stud. **135**, 1–15 (2007)

45. Murray, J.H.: Why Paris needs Hector and Lancelot needs Mordred: using traditional narrative roles and functions for dramatic compression in interactive narrative. In: Si, M., Thue, D., André, E., Lester, J.C., Tanenbaum, J., Zammitto, V. (eds.) ICIDS 2011. LNCS, vol. 7069, pp. 13–24. Springer, Heidelberg (2011). https://doi.org/10.1007/978-3-642-25289-1_2

46. Hasselfrau, M.: The One Flaw. https://steamcommunity.com/app/512890/discussions/0/1639792569843722791/

47. Golden Glitch Studios: New Ending Structure Update! https://steamcommunity.com/games/512890/announcements/detail/466060812612004150

# The Case for Invisibility: Understanding and Improving Agency in Black Mirror's Bandersnatch and Other Interactive Digital Narrative Works

Anna Marie Rezk$^{(\boxtimes)}$ and Mads Haahr

School of Computer Science and Statistics, Trinity College Dublin, Dublin, Ireland
{rezka,haahrm}@tcd.ie

**Abstract.** With the launch and popularity of *Bandersnatch* (2018), interactive storytelling reached a mass audience in a different way to earlier works. However, as a narrative experience, *Bandersnatch* belongs to a particular class of Interactive Digital Narratives (IDNs): highly restrictive, nonlinear, branching structure films that offer limited agency and, in many ways, have less to offer than more sophisticated IDNs. While the simple format is appealing to new audiences, there is clearly scope for improvement. In this paper, *Bandersnatch* is examined as a representative of its format in an attempt to identify alternative design choices for improved agency, as well as assessing the choices' suitability for the format. The methodology for the analysis is Hartmut Koenitz's SPP model as well as its extension, the hermeneutic strip, which is applied to understand and assess the experienced agency. The final reflection on alternative design recommendations for *Bandersnatch* type works demonstrates that, by implementing features of invisible agency, the overall feeling of control of the player could be improved without losing narrative momentum. The improvements could be achieved by maintaining state of the behavioural tendencies (e.g., risk-taking behaviour) of the audience in their decision-making process and screening plotlines or endings that match their assessed tendencies.

**Keywords:** Interactive digital narrative · IDN · Interactive narrative design · Agency · Narrative momentum · Invisible agency · SPP model · Bandersnatch

## 1 Introduction

In December 2018, the online streaming platform Netflix published its first interactive production aimed at adults with *Black Mirror's Bandersnatch* film. The film offers its viewers the choice between two options during many key scenes, mimicking the structure of a Choose Your Own Adventure (CYOA) book. Some choices lead to dead ends, with the protagonist saying, "I should try again," similar to the video game trope of "Game Over," where the player has to respawn.

The popularity of *Bandersnatch* has brought interactive stories to a large audience; however, the format of this genre is subject to severe limitations in terms of agency. After

© Springer Nature Switzerland AG 2020
A.-G. Bosser et al. (Eds.): ICIDS 2020, LNCS 12497, pp. 178–189, 2020.
https://doi.org/10.1007/978-3-030-62516-0_16

the success of *Bandersnatch*, Netflix is planning to produce more interactive titles aimed at a mature audience, such as *Unbreakable Kimmy Schmidt: Kimmy vs. the Reverend* (2020) [1]. Moreover, production companies like CrtlMovie are dedicated to creating interactive films such as *Late Shift* (2016) [2]. It is evident that interactive films are on the rise, and therefore a discussion on how the format could be improved is important, timely and constructive.

The objective of this paper is to identify ways in which audience agency in *Bandersnatch*-like titles can be increased without jeopardizing narrative momentum. Because of its prominence and typicality, *Bandersnatch* is chosen as a representative of its subgenre of interactive film. Our methodology is to analyse *Bandersnatch* with regards to agency or (as audiences might perceive it) the "free will" it gives to its players in their choices, though these two concepts will not be used synonymously in this paper. Laura M. Ahearn had warned that by using them interchangeably in the realm of interactive narrative, one ignores the importance of necessary constraints imposed on the audience to drive the story forward [3, p. 46].

Therefore, it must be considered that increased agency through increased interaction may lead to a decrease in the narrative momentum. If the audience is in charge of the story, they might get stuck at certain plot points, thereby not allowing the story to unfold or develop in any meaningful way. These risks have to be taken into consideration when suggesting ways to increase interaction in storytelling.

## 2 Methodology

For this paper, Hartmut Koenitz's analytical framework, the SPP mode, will be used to analyse *Bandersnatch* (Fig. 1).

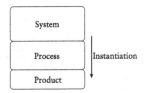

**Fig. 1.** Koenitz's SPP model [4]

In this figure, *system* is used to describe the interactive program itself, including both the software and hardware required for the interactive experience. The *process* is the user's interaction with the system, which ultimately results in a *product*, a singular storyline based on the user's input, which would be different if the user's input were to change. The product is therefore an instantiated narrative [4, pp. 97–98].

As part of the model, Koenitz introduces three additional terms: *Protostory*, *narrative design*, and *narrative vectors*. Protostory is the space of potential narratives, "containing the necessary ingredients for any given walkthrough." It stands for both the code and the interactive interface of the system, and thereby captures the "artistic intent that enables a participatory process of instantiation resulting in the realisation of potential narratives

[...] The term narrative design describes the structure within a protostory that describes a flexible presentation of a narrative" [4, p. 99]. In other words, the narrative design deals with the sequencing of elements and their connection in the narrations. A substructure of narrative design are the narrative vectors, as they provide specific directions for the story. They have to be understood as substructures that work in connection with the preceding and following parts of any narrative. Their purpose, as Koenitz states, is "to convey important aspects to the interactor, to prevent an interactor from getting lost and to aid authors in retaining a level of control" [4, p. 100]. A narrative vector could, for instance, be a sudden event in the plot that shapes the development of the story and can be compared to plot points in linear narratives (Fig. 2).

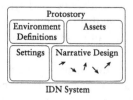

**Fig. 2.** The SPP model and its associated terminology for the analysis of IDNs [4]

One thing that is not covered by Koenitz's SPP model is the idea of agency. However, in a paper by Christian Roth, Tom van Nuenen and Koenitz himself, an extension to the model was introduced, namely the hermeneutic strip or double-hermeneutic circle [5]. This strip aims at illustrating the player's narrative meaning-making process. It reviews both the interpretation of the system overall, i.e., the players' reflection on what the system may allow and which freedoms or agency they have, but it also considers players' interpretations of already instantiated narratives (Fig. 3).

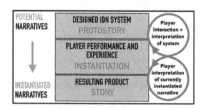

**Fig. 3.** The additional extension by the double-hermeneutic circle offers a methodological toolkit for the analysis of experienced agency [5]

It is important to understand that this extension to the model bears in mind that a player's behaviour and interaction with a system is shaped by previous experiences made in the interactive narrative. In short, past and present events influence a user's future behaviour. As this extension will help evaluate agency from a user's perspective at predefined points of the story, these key points must be identified first [5, p. 99].

For this paper, we will use Koenitz's framework and its extension to analyse *Bandersnatch*. By examining the protostory, all assets of the pieces, as well as all components that make up any storyline and the interface will be laid out. Going into more detail, the narrative design will define the segmentation of different scenes and the choices that connect them. By thoroughly analysing the narrative vectors, the level of control of the producers will be understood, as these plot points are the orientation points that hinder the audience/players from getting lost and losing the narrative momentum. The extension to Koenitz's SPP model will help evaluate the agency in each of these pieces from a user's perspective at predefined points. Therefore, all pieces analysed in this paper will be examined at key points with the hermeneutic strip, in an attempt to provide a clearer idea about their levels of experienced agency. It is important to add that the authors of this extension used it in the context of a quantitative analysis of players' reactions based on Let's Play videos found online, where they examined reactions at a predefined key scene. In this paper, we base our analysis on the range of *possible* reactions rather than a study of *actual* reactions.

## 3  Bandersnatch

*Black Mirror's Bandersnatch* (2018) was marketed as the first interactive narrative aimed at a mature audience on the streaming platform Netflix. Similar to other *Black Mirror* episodes, *Bandersnatch's* plot has a critical and introspective view on technology. One major difference between this and other *Black Mirror* episodes was that the critical view was on the technology used by the *audience* rather than by the characters in the story. In the case of *Bandersnatch*, the technology was the interactive experience itself, which was referred to in the plot of the film. This is done via one of the overarching themes of the film, which is agency or, as it is called in the film, "control." According to Roth and Koenitz, in *Bandersnatch*, these are both "explored in parallel – in the diegetic world and the interactive narrative experience" [6, p. 249]. The parallelism for control can, for instance, be seen in the protagonist, Stefan, losing his mind and even asking which outside force is controlling him in one of the plotlines, as he feels that he is becoming someone's (the viewer's) puppet.

### 3.1  Bandersnatch: System, Process and Product

*Bandersnatch* is an interactive film that allows its audience to choose between two possible paths at certain predefined choice points. When a choice point becomes active, the viewer has about ten seconds to choose one of two options, and if no choice is made, the system defaults to one of them. This feature allows what Roth and Koenitz called "passive consumption" [6, p. 249]. The structure of the narrative resembles that of a Gauntlet as defined by Sam Kabo Ashwell [7], because the overall thread is close to linear with some dead ends, backtracking and re-joining branches.

Analysing *Bandersnatch* using Koenitz's framework, where the system is the combination of software and hardware, the hardware is the viewer's device which is compatible with the interactive film. The interactive film can be viewed on multiple devices, such as smart TVs, mobile devices, laptops, and game consoles. Part of the system is also the interface, which is explained at the start of the film, followed by a question asking whether the viewer has understood it. This is the first instance in which the viewer interacts with the interface by choosing between two options presented as textual prompts. A horizontal line represents the remaining time to make a choice, the length of which decreases with time and disappears entirely after ten seconds. The virtual assets of the film are contained in the system as well. In this case these are the scenes and displayed choices as well as the program that outputs narratives according to the viewer's input. The system maintains state, as previous user inputs can be influential further down the line.

In *Bandersnatch*, the process is created by the user's actions as well as the opportunities provided by the system, i.e., the two options at each choice point. *Bandersnatch*'s Gauntlet structure has multiple dead ends, which prompt the audience to go back and make a different decision at a previous choice point, ultimately resulting in audiences sharing a very similar, or even near-identical, viewing experience, as even when official endings are reached, the system asks the viewers if they want to go back in order to explore different paths. In short, the longer the viewers choose to interact with the work, the more plotlines they unlock, ultimately resulting in having watched all of them. Therefore, the instantiated product here seems to be at odds with Koenitz's idea that "very different narrative products can originate from the same system – any concrete product represents only one particular instantiation" [4, p. 98], because the *Bandersnatch's* structure defeats the concept of a single walkthrough covering only one storyline. However, a major difference between the viewer's walkthroughs might always be found in the sequence in which they see the events or different storylines unveil.

### 3.2   Bandersnatch: Protostory, Narrative Design and Narrative Vectors

For the protostory in *Bandersnatch*, the content can be defined as scenes. The interface, as previously introduced, consists of the two textual options and the visual timer. The code is what allows the right scenes to be displayed in accordance with the viewer's input. Another part of the protostory is the interface of Netflix, which allows viewers to fast forward or backward ten seconds, pause, change the language or add/remove subtitles. It is important to note that in *Bandersnatch* viewers can only fast forward up until the next choice point, where a decision must be made.

Due to the Gauntlet structure of *Bandersnatch*, the narrative design is quite straightforward, and the overall thread is close to linear. For *Bandersnatch* the design can be segmented into bundles of scenes. There is flexibility between the bundles but not within them, meaning they can be added to the story in a flexible manner, for instance when the viewer reaches the end of one storyline and chooses to explore another.

The narrative vectors are mainly the scenes that are revisited after respawning from a dead end – but also the respawn function itself, as the new information – namely that the previously chosen option led to a dead end, helps the viewers figure out which way they are meant to go if they wanted to explore the story further without impacting the narrative momentum. It can be argued that the narrative vectors in Bandersnatch work in a way that facilitates the consumption of the majority, if not all, storylines that exist.

## 3.3  Bandersnatch: Double-Hermeneutic Circle and Agency

In order to understand the agency in *Bandersnatch*, we must first choose key scenes to analyse with the double-hermeneutic circle approach described by Roth et al. [5, p. 99]. Due to *Bandersnatch*'s non-linear structure, it makes sense first to investigate a scene that all players would encounter. For this purpose, we will consider the scene in which Mohan offers Stefan a job. Up to this point, players will have had two inconsequential decisions, namely the one where they decide which cereal Stefan should have for breakfast, and the one where Stefan chooses which song to listen to on his way to Tuckersoft. The job offer is therefore the third decision point in the film and presents a stark contrast to the previous two decision points, because the presented options of either accepting or declining a job offer seem like they would result in very different storylines.

When analysing *Bandersnatch's* upper hermeneutic circle, it can be argued that this decision point suggests that there will be two very distinct branches in the narrative structure from this point moving forward. Looking at the bottom hermeneutic circle, users at this point might be unsure whether or not their input can have plot-altering impacts due to the lack of immediate impact seen from previous choices, thereby doubting their agency altogether. Although the choice is being presented as highly consequential in comparison to the previous ones, the audiences cannot know for sure if it will end up being consequential. It can be argued that a novice IDN audience might expect two major branching storylines from here onwards, whereas a seasoned audience could be more aware of potential production constraints resulting in one of the options being a false choice.

Interestingly, if the option of accepting the job offer is chosen, the game reaches a dead end and allows users to go back to the same decision point. The second time around, however, the upper hermeneutic circle becomes different in the sense that while the dead-end option prompted a scene that would otherwise not have been accessed, the only real option for the user is to decline the job offer in order to allow the plot to move forward. In this case, players learn from their mistake due to the repetitive nature that allows for something equivalent to a respawn, and they get to choose the option they are actually meant to choose.

Another interesting scene is the decision point at which Stefan can either destroy his computer or throw tea over it. In this case, it does not seem like the audience has any say in what is about to happen; in short, it seems like all sense of agency is lost. As it is Stefan's goal to create a successful computer game, both options appear at odds with it and therefore the viewers are arguably unable to identify with either of the choices given; however they end up surrendering to the limitations of the presented options in order to drive the film forward. The experience constitutes a violation of the narrative contract through the removal of agency, as both presented options would sabotage the protagonist's goals.

It is only after this decision point passes that Stefan refuses to destroy his computer in a plot twist where he realizes that he is being controlled by an outside force. Of course, the first-time audience cannot know that Stefan will end up refusing to obey their commands, as all previous inputs – even if insignificant – resulted in respective outputs by Stefan, who is the character the player gets to control.

The audience is confronted with an almost identical scene in one of the endings, showing a frustrated grown-up Pearl who is trying to program an interactive film for Netflix but faces errors. Again, the player has to choose between either pouring tea over the computer or destroying it. If looking at the upper hermeneutic circle, where players reflect on what they might be able to do, but also by looking at the bottom hermeneutic circle, where the instantiated narrative is interpreted, players might be tricked into believing that this too is just an instance in which the character will end up ignoring the command given. However, Pearl actually ends up destroying her computer or throwing tea over it – depending on which option is chosen.

To sum up the degree of agency given to the audience in *Bandersnatch*, at most decision points two options are presented to the audience. In a few instances, only one option is given, for example in a flashback where Stefan's mother asks him if he was coming with her. Here the only option is "No," nodding to the idea that things in the past cannot be changed. As previously explored, sometimes the two options provided are essentially the same, as in the scenes where Stefan or Pearl want to destroy their computers.

Bearing in mind that agency is defined by Murray as "the power to take meaningful action and see the results of our own choices" [8, p. 159], the logic behind the outcomes of the audience's input is debatable. For instance, Stefan's choice of password to input to open his father's safe results in several entirely different scenes, which seems quite extreme, as the only difference in action is a different input of password. The right combination is never established; instead the audience is taken to a storyline that resonates with their chosen password combination. In this fashion, what Stefan finds "inside the safe" is determined by the audience's expectations, as Emily Short explains [9]. It can be argued that this design choice was made to encourage the audience to unlock the storylines behind the remaining password options as each of them transports Stefan to very different storylines that refer back to the chosen password.

Other choices seem to unleash a butterfly effect, as they cause a series of events to happen – all of which are entirely out of control of the audience. The most obvious example is when Stefan accepts the job offer and the film immediately fast forwards to a scene months later where the game's poor rating is revealed. Therefore, it cannot be said that all consequences of the user's input seem meaningful or logical, as in the *Bandersnatch* universe small changes in a user input sometimes can result in very different storylines. In a research questionnaire on *Bandersnatch* conducted by Lobke Kolhoff and Frank Nack with a sample group of 169 participants who had seen the

| | SA | A | NA | D | SD |
|---|---|---|---|---|---|
| Content frequency choices | 20% | 47% | 20% | 11% | 4% |
| In control experience | 21% | 33% | 24% | 15% | 7% |
| Desirable consequences | 5% | 26% | 46% | 20% | 4% |
| Foreseeable consequences | 5% | 14% | 33% | 36% | 11% |
| No choice while preferred | 14% | 30% | 27% | 20% | 9% |
| Unnecessary choices | 17% | 24% | 22% | 28% | 8% |

**Fig. 4.** Kolhoff and Nack's questionnaire results on agency in Bandersnatch (SA = strongly agree; A = agree; NA = neither agree nor disagree; D = disagree; SD = strongly disagree) [10]

film, 69% have said they disagree, or neither agree nor disagree with the claim that consequences in *Bandersnatch* are foreseeable [10, p. 82] (Fig. 4).

# 4  Reflection on Replayability, Narrative Momentum and Agency

After having analysed *Bandersnatch* with Koenitz's SPP model and its extension, this section will evaluate its replayability, narrative momentum, as well as agency.

As established, *Bandersnatch* is structured around a main narrative thread. The interface allows viewers to jump back to their previous choices and alter them, and even once an official ending has been reached, the film prompts its audience to decide if they want to go back and explore an alternative storyline that had not been unlocked yet. In this way, we could say *Bandersnatch* trades per-title replayability for per-scene replayability, as it seems to encourage the viewer to watch (close to) all scenes in one session.

In *Bandersnatch*, the narrative momentum is not influenced by the player's input, as choices have to be made within ten seconds during which the controllable character is shown to be reluctant about what to do next. If the player does not make a decision within the allotted time, the film defaults to one of the options.

When taking a deeper look at *Bandersnatch*, the interaction is facilitated by two textual prompts that lead to different actions of the protagonist and thereby change the plot. However, as previously discussed, there is a decision point at which Stefan refuses to follow through what he is being ordered to do by the audience and breaks the fourth wall by confronting the force that he thinks is controlling him – an act that according to Roth and Koenitz also breaks the viewer's identification with Stefan and encourages a reflection on agency [6, p. 249]. In this twist of events, the plot develops in a direction that is independent of the user's input, and what follows are streams of unexpected events, one of which involves Stefan killing his father. This is a significant act that is out of the audience's control in some storylines, while in other playthroughs the player gets to choose to either kill the father or back off during the same scene. Close to one of the endings, the audience can see Stefan proudly talking about his video game to his psychologist Dr Haynes and saying that he had finally finished it by reducing the amount of agency given to the player: "Now they only have the illusion of free will, but really I decide the ending." This quote by Stefan seems to go hand in hand with the structure of the interactive film, as multiple different paths can lead the audience to the same ending and some paths seem rather forced, like the one where Stefan unexpectedly kills his father.

Furthermore, the gravity of some of the decisions that the audience can make in *Bandersnatch* is not held to the same level throughout the film, as some choices can be entirely ignored by the system and manoeuvred around to have the same output as the option that was not chosen, such as when Stefan decides against taking LSD but his tea is spiked anyway. Other decision points offer two very similar options that would result in the same consequence but bring it about differently, which goes against the notion of agency and thereby further limits the perception of it. As Sercan Şengün explains, "Forcing a choice and constraining the alternatives or presenting inconsistent alternatives may thwart instead of support the feeling of freedom" [11, p. 184]. Some decision points let the player make rather trivial decisions while others can become a matter of life and death. However, the trivial decisions can bring about unforeseen consequences in a butterfly effect or by immersing the audience into the parallel realities that this interactive film is trying to fabricate. This theme could arguably be the work reflecting on the chaotic nature of the universe, highlighting that much of the experience of control in life is really an illusion at worst, or at best precarious and subject to a highly unpredictable universe.

### 4.1    Improved Design Recommendation for Bandersnatch and Its Format

The objective of this paper is to identify promising design recommendations that would allow for increased agency and more than just the illusion of it in *Bandersnatch*, as an example for a nonlinear, highly restrictive, branching structure film. In this section, respective ideas will be presented and discussed.

The issues raised with *Bandersnatch*'s agency revolve around the limits due to the binary choices, as well as further restrictions at several decision points that force the interactor to go a certain way. Additionally, some consequences to the audience's input seem arbitrary – a critique that could be understood and discarded as a stylistic or thematic choice but which, however, should still be addressed in the development of an improved model.

Considering the number of characters on behalf of whom the player can make choices, *Bandersnatch* briefly allows the players to make one choice on behalf of Pearl instead of Stefan. This is done after a time jump, therefore eliminating any conflicts of interests between her and Stefan. While exploring the possibility of having multiple characters to control in *Bandersnatch* might be interesting in theory, this would require many additional scenes and plotlines that would have to be cleanly intertwined.

Furthermore, it seems that *Bandersnatch* might have tiptoed around the idea of adding one quick time event in the scene where Stefan starts fighting his psychologist and then his father, as the player can choose between two options that would make him perform different attacks. Provided the devices compatible with the film allowed it, this scene could be redesigned or even elaborated by allowing the more impactful attack only if the player acted faster or succeeded at inputting a specific key-combination shown on screen. In *Bandersnatch,* both attacks trigger the same follow-up scene. However, implementing quick time events – even if they would have to be highly restrictive for this format – can be an interesting feature in interactive film, especially if they lead to different succeeding scenarios.

When looking back at Murray's definition of agency being "the satisfying power to take meaningful action and see the results of our decisions and choices" [8, p. 159], we can conclude that every narrative choice is made "consciously and visibly and the outcome is instantly associated with it" [11, p. 180] as Şengün states. This is where a different and rarely explored kind of agency, the so-called "invisible agency," becomes interesting. In this form of agency, the user is not prompted to make apparent choices, like the binary textual ones in *Bandersnatch*. Instead, the system employs an obscured method to read the player's intentions. This form of agency was used in the 2001 video game *Silent Hill 2*, in which the game assessed the players' psychological states based on their tendencies and behaviours while playing by maintaining state and then ultimately unlocked the different endings accordingly. [11, pp. 181–83] In short, as Şengün explains, "the choices the player makes are actually projected tendencies and they accumulate results in the long run" [11, p. 183–184].

In *Bandersnatch*, invisible agency could be implemented by assessing the intentions of the audience based on which of the options they choose. However, according to Şengün it is not advisable to base the assessment on criteria such as ethics and morality, as options offered might either be on opposite sides of a spectrum and therefore not subtle enough, or they may be too similar and result in a moral dilemma that in turn creates a challenge in assessing the player's intentions.

Bearing this in mind, one criterion to base the evaluation on would be the willingness to take risks or be self-destructive, as this can be clearly identified at various decision points. Examples would be the decision point at which Stefan is offered to take LSD or the choice of whether or not Stefan should destroy the computer if the alternative was to only hit the desk instead. By coming up with a measuring unit for the behavioural pattern that is to be assessed and maintaining state and ultimately displaying later scenes that are meaningful consequences to the audience's intentions, *Bandersnatch* would no longer seem arbitrary in the causality of its events, but instead the limited agency of the interactive film format would be increased, as meaningful results for the audience's input would be observed.

This design strategy would require an overall restructuring of the film's scenes in order to respond well to the user's input. It can be entirely up to the designers at which point the evaluated intentions and risk-taking behaviour of the audience would bear consequences, but the least invasive alteration would probably occur if these consequences are displayed in the final fifth of the film. The consequences could be shown in the actions that occur in the unlocked scenes, but they could also influence the presented options at decision points in said scenes.

By using this form of obscured agency to create a more meaningful chain of causality, the sense of agency can ultimately be enhanced, however the oblivious audience would not notice it. Being oblivious is necessary as players who are aware that the title has invisible agency likely to try to manipulate the film into a certain direction once they know that their behaviour is being evaluated. In doing so, the unlocked ending would no longer reflect a psychological profiling of them. Therefore, it adds to the level of enjoyment not to be aware of the invisible agency when playing through the interactive film for the first time. Once the players are aware of this additional layer of agency, they might become more likely to replay the film in order to manipulate it, and this may in turn improve the per-title replayability of *Bandersnatch*.

In order to facilitate a well-functioning form of invisible agency, the juxtaposed options at each decision point should not be obvious choices on opposite sides of a spectrum, as this would take away any possible challenge for the aware audience. By evaluating the risk-taking behaviour in percentages rather than with the polar question of yes/no at each decision point, the assessment can be conducted in a more precise and sophisticated manner. These percentages can then be accumulated to calculate the right outcome just before it is to be screened.

Another point worth exploring is the differences in format, duration and pacing. *Silent Hill 2* is an over eight-hour long gaming experience in which the user's behaviour determines the possible endings, while *Bandersnatch* is a significantly shorter interactive film of about one and a half to two and a half hours in length. However, *Bandersnatch* asks its audience to make concrete choices, therefore, though being fast paced in comparison, it has the tools to assess certain characteristics in its audience more efficiently without its overall duration becoming a threat to the accuracy of the assessment.

Ultimately, the narrative momentum as previously discussed cannot be influenced in *Bandersnatch*'s format as the audience has to make a decision within a defined amount of time even if the features of invisible agency were to be added.

## 5  Conclusion

It is evident that only increasing the number of instances during which the player can interact with a system does not necessarily increase the player's agency. Instead, the instances during which interaction is offered must be designed in a fashion that would allow for meaningful outcomes that give the player the feeling of being in control of or responsible for the narrative.

For a nonlinear, highly restrictive, branching structure film, like *Bandersnatch*, agency can be improved without jeopardizing the narrative momentum and without requiring an unreasonably high increase in production costs. As established, employing invisible agency to evaluate any given condition of the player, such as risk-taking behaviour or tendencies towards pre-defined psychological states, can contribute to offering more meaningful generated narratives that reflect the player's intentions better.

While in the past, the concept of invisible agency has been scarcely used, implementing it in interactive films like *Bandersnatch* would contribute to creating a more meaningful sequence of events in the instantiated narratives in accordance with the audience's input and thereby the overall felt agency or "free will" would be increased. Provided that the audiences of interactive films can be assumed generally to be aiming for a certain narrative outcome, adding the layer of invisible agency would offer an additional challenge for players – especially if they are replaying the entire film or are aware of the invisible agency feature – as they would try to manoeuvre the choices carefully to get their desired result. In combination with this challenge, this solution could prove itself promising in navigating the fine line between narrative and game successfully and invisibly.

## References

1. Vice Magazine: Netflix Is Going to Make a Lot More Weird, Interactive Movies Likes 'Bandersnatch'. https://www.vice.com/en_us/article/7xnq3a/netflix-more-interactive-movies-like-bandersnatch-rom-coms-todd-yellin-interview-vgtrn. Accessed 23 June 2020
2. CrtlMovie. https://www.ctrlmovie.com. Accessed 20 May 2020
3. Harrell, D.F., Zhu, J.: Agency play: dimensions of agency for interactive narrative design. In: AAAI Spring Symposium: Intelligent Narrative Technologies II, Stanford, pp 44–52 (2009)
4. Koenitz, H.: Towards a specific theory of interactive digital narrative. In: Koenitz, H., Ferri, G., Haahr, M., Sezen, D., Sezen, T.İ. (eds.) Interactive Digital Narrative, pp. 96–101. Routledge, New York (2015)

5. Roth, C., van Nuenen, T., Koenitz, H.: Ludonarrative hermeneutics: *a way out* and the narrative paradox. In: Rouse, R., Koenitz, H., Haahr, M. (eds.) ICIDS 2018. LNCS, vol. 11318, pp. 93–106. Springer, Cham (2018). https://doi.org/10.1007/978-3-030-04028-4_7
6. Roth, C., Koenitz, H.: Bandersnatch, yea or nay? Reception and user experience of an interactive digital narrative video. In: Proceedings of the 2019 ACM International Conference on Interactive Experiences for TV and Online Video, pp. 247–254. Association for Computing Machinery, New York (2019)
7. These Heterogenous Tasks: Standard Patterns in Choice-Based Games. https://heterogenous tasks.wordpress.com/2015/01/26/standard-patterns-in-choice-based-games/. Accessed 23 June 2020
8. Murray, J.H.: Hamlet on Holodeck: The Future of Narrative in Cyberspace, 2nd edn. MIT Press, Cambridge/London (2017)
9. Emily Short's Interactive Storytelling: Bandersnatch (Netflix). https://emshort.blog/2019/02/19/39189/. Accessed 20 June 2020
10. Kohlhoff, L., Nack, F.: How relevant is your choice?: user engagement and perceived agency in interactive digital narratives on video streaming platforms. In: Cardona-Rivera, R.E., Sullivan, A., Young, R.M. (eds.) Interactive Storytelling: 12th International Conference on Interactive Digital Storytelling, ICIDS 2019, Little Cottonwood Canyon, UT, USA, November 19–22, 2019, Proceedings, pp. 73–85. Springer, Cham (2019)
11. Şengün, S.: Silent hill 2 and the curious case of invisible agency. In: Koenitz, H., Sezen, T.I., Ferri, G., Haahr, M., Sezen, D., Çatak, G. (eds.) ICIDS 2013. LNCS, vol. 8230, pp. 180–185. Springer, Cham (2013). https://doi.org/10.1007/978-3-319-02756-2_22

# Dramatic Narrative Logics: Integrating Drama into Storygames with Operational Logics

Kenneth Tan[1,2](✉) 📵 and Alex Mitchell[1] 📵

[1] National University of Singapore, Singapore, Singapore
kennethetan@u.nus.edu, alexm@nus.edu.sg
[2] Nanyang Polytechnic, Singapore, Singapore
kenneth_tan@nyp.edu.sg

**Abstract.** Many videogames seek to be story-driven, incorporating story elements such as a hero-driven plotline, dramatic conflict and story structure in order to increase player immersion and engagement. Storygames have been discussed by theorists such as Buckles, Murray and Reed. However, the issue of the integration of dramatic devices with the playable system and operational logics in interactive narratives has not been adequately explored. Through close readings of two storygames, *Disco Elysium* and *Her Story*, this paper aims to investigate how narrative logics can be integrated into storygames in the context of Aristotelian drama, and how dramatic narrative units integrate operationally with the playable system. It also proposes a type of storygame, the dramatic storygame, where the playable system is closely tied with the processing and production of dramatic narrative units.

**Keywords:** Storygames · Aristotelian drama · Operational logics

## 1 Introduction

The term "computer storygame" was first coined by Buckles [1] in her dissertation on the computer text game *Adventure* [2]. She regards *Adventure* as the first true piece of interactive fiction, "in which the reader, for the first time, takes part in writing the story as s(he) reads it". Buckles also describes the close relationship between play, games, literature and storytelling traditions in forming the term "storygame", suggesting that works like *Adventure* can be considered "literature as a game", due to both their literary and game-like elements. She asserts that "if the main goal is for the reader to decipher some veiled meaning or to figure out the answer to a question or puzzle posed by the work, its basic character is game-like" [1]. Wardrip-Fruin also argues that storygames can be a form of "playable media" which may have no tangible quantifiable outcomes, such as Mateas and Stern's interactive drama project, *Façade* [3, 4]. It is the fundamental process of discovery and play that fascinates the player in a storygame.

Reed extends the definition of the storygame one step further by suggesting that storygames require a "playable system with units of narrative, where the understanding of both, and the relationship between them, is required for a satisfying traversal", and

© Springer Nature Switzerland AG 2020
A.-G. Bosser et al. (Eds.): ICIDS 2020, LNCS 12497, pp. 190–202, 2020.
https://doi.org/10.1007/978-3-030-62516-0_17

"a satisfying traversal of a storygame is a rewarding experience in part because of the shared and linked pleasures of narrative immersion and ludic accomplishment" [5]. Reed hints that for a satisfying traversal to occur, successful operational logics, which are "fundamental abstract operations – with effective interpretations available to both authors and players – that determine the state evolution of the system and underwrite the gameplay", are required [3]. These operational logics "weav[e] together the layers of abstraction in a storygame system, its external surface, and its internal processes" [5].

This paper explores Reed's concept of a "satisfying traversal" in the context of drama and proposes a theory of "dramatic narrative logics" that involves a three-step process – expressive input, narrative logics and the dramatic narrative unit.

## 2 Related Work

Reed posits that storygames are playable systems which allow the user "to input commands that change the state of an underlying simulation". Media, of which games are a subset, are also playable as pointed out by Wardrip-Fruin, and can be a "toy" from which we can create unique experiences [3].

Wardrip-Fruin proposes that the "surface" of the system (what the player sees and interacts with) is an abstracted interface where data and processes interact. Expressive processes occur between the interplay of the internal processes of the system and the player's experience [6]. According to Reed, an "expressive process is one through which an author's intention can be seen", allowing players to express themselves via distinctive intentions in a storygame. A storygame with expressive input implies a large enough set of possible interactions that "the player might feel ownership, discovery, or surprise as they consider possible ways of interacting with the system" [5].

Reed also argues that "ludic mechanisms and narrative content, and the way they interrelate, are both required for a successful traversal" [5]. Ludic mechanisms can come in different forms, one of which is Hunicke et al.'s MDA (Mechanics, Dynamics, Aesthetics) model. By moving between MDA's three levels of abstraction, we can conceptualize the dynamic behaviour of game systems. [7].

Mateas and Wardrip-Fruin present operational logics as a way of thinking about ludic mechanisms from the system's point of view. They are "fundamental abstract operations—with effective interpretations available to both authors and players—that determine the state evolution of the system and underwrite the gameplay", and "provide 'deep cores' that bind together issues ranging from the platform to reception level for specific representational domains" [8]. Narrative logics are postulated by Reed as "the subset of player affordances connected to story" and "are the subset of operational logics connected to how narrative actions are processed, and how narrative output that seems connected to those actions is produced." Reed believes that identifying narrative logics helps us to understand how the story responds to the player's actions [5].

In exploring storygames in the context of drama, Aristotle's classic, *Poetics*, is fundamental as it establishes dramatic theory based on Greek tragedies, which are forms of mimetic arts [9]. Aristotle sees tragedy as a superior form of mimetic representation, composed of plot, structure, character, style, thought, spectacle and lyric poetry. Aristotle's key dramatic devices include *Katharsis*, which maximizes the audience's pleasurable experience of emotion, *Peripeteia*, a change of direction in the course of events and *Anagnorisis*, a change from ignorance to knowledge or discovery. He considers *Anagnorisis* leading to *Peripeteia* to be a mark of superior tragedy. [9].

## 3    Research Question

Past research has suggested various approaches and frameworks to consider how game mechanics affect gameplay and the player experience. MDA provides multiple taxonomies to define aesthetics, but these aesthetics may be too broad and do not necessarily achieve structural and pervasive synthesis with dramatic narrative. Operational logics and its corresponding sub-logics, on the other hand, propose how to consider a system's aesthetics via a computational perspective, including game state presentation and game play experience, but does not necessarily take into consideration expressive input.

Reed asserts that narrative logics are key to communicating narrative to the player, and states that an understanding of both the playable system and its "units of narrative" (or narrative units), as well as the relationship between them, is required for a "satisfying traversal" in a storygame to occur. There are different ways in which a "satisfying traversal" can transpire, such as the "burst of insight" which occurs when "the player understands what story action will have the ludic consequence they desire" [5]. A detailed investigation of what makes the traversal feel satisfying in the context of drama, specifically Aristotelian drama, has not been carried out. In this study, we consider narrative units to be equivalent to George Landow's definition of lexia as "blocks of text", which can also include "visual information, sound, animation, and other forms of data" [10]. Narrative units may not necessarily be dramatic. In this study, we term narrative units which utilize key Aristotelian dramatic devices such as *Katharsis, Peripeteia* and *Anagnorisis* as "dramatic narrative units".

The research questions for this study are: How do narrative logics work in the context of Aristotelian drama? And how do these dramatic narrative units integrate operationally with the playable system?

## 4    Methodology

Tanenbaum and Bizzocchi developed a close reading technique for games, outlining the construction of analytical lenses, the performance of an imagined naïve reader and the construction of performative player stereotypes [11]. The approach does not, nor do we, attempt to claim that insights gained from close readings are either immediately or directly generalizable. Instead, they provide a deep, experiential understanding of particular cases of gameplay, as a first step towards further investigations.

Tanenbaum's approach will be used to analyze two games, namely *Disco Elysium* [12] and *Her Story* [13]. These particular games are selected as they display traits whereby dramatic agency and dramatic events are closely tied to the playable system, and display signs of satisfying traversal between narrative units and the playable system via an expressive process from the beginning to the end of the game. In *Disco Elysium*, the player's expressive input occurs via the player's decisions in shaping the main character's persona and stats, which continually impact the game's narrative output. *Her Story* is a murder-mystery storygame in which the narrative units are expressively explored by the player via a search engine database within a fictional police station.

Tanenbaum proposed the use of "analytical lens" to create "constrained close readings" of storygames [14]. The analytical lens used in this research would be focused on (i) how the game's playable system affords the player to create expressive input, (ii) how this expressive input is processed by the narrative logics, and (iii) how the processed expressive input produces narrative units. Focused questions include: Do I feel that the playable system is tied to agency and the narrative units occurring in the story? Are these narrative units dramatic according to Aristotle's key devices such as *Katharsis, Peripeteia* and *Anagnorisis*? Why or why not? What are my experiences, emotions and attitude towards the game with regards to the story choices I am making, and are they connected to dramatic narrative units and the playable system? What are the operational logics in the game, and how are they connected to these dramatic narrative units?

## 5    Case Study: *Disco Elysium*

In *Disco Elysium*, the player takes on the role of a cop who loses his memory after partying and drinking while investigating a lynching case by a group of union members in Revachol, a city beset by poverty, corruption and crime in the world of Elysium. The game is presented from an isometric perspective, and the player character (PC) explores the world adventure game-style, interacting with objects and people, and initiating branching dialogue with both non-player characters (NPCs) and with his own thoughts.

### 5.1    Expressive Input in *Disco Elysium*

The primary way the player engages in expressive input in *Disco Elysium* is by a constant process of formation of a unique character persona, decided via two aspects. The first aspect is decided by point allocation into four broad primary abilities: Intellect, Psyche, Physique and Motorics. Intellect influences your capacity to reason, Psyche is about the power to influence yourself and others, Physique is how well your body is built, and Motorics is how well you can move your body. When the game begins, the player can either pick one of three character archetypes: Thinker, Sensitive, or Physical, or enable further customization by creating their own character. Choosing one of the archetypes pre-determines the point allocation of the player's primary abilities. If the player chooses to create their own character, they can manually distribute these points.

I created a character of the sensitive archetype, since I wanted to play an emotional, "touchy feely" kind of character. The primary abilities associated with this character were Psyche and Physique, for Psyche the skills include Volition, Empathy, Authority, Esprit de Corps and Suggestion; for Physique the skills include Endurance, Pain Threshold, Physical Instrument, Electrochemistry, Shivers and Half-Light.

### 5.2    Narrative Logics in *Disco Elysium*

After establishing my PC's base skills, I discovered these expressive decisions constantly affected the narrative logics. Throughout the game, the PC's skills are personified. The

PC has internal branching-dialogue conversations with his skills, and these skills advise, comment and converse with the PC concerning the current situation and potential courses of action. The skills may even argue with one another.

Different types of skill checks are conducted throughout the game to access unique conversations with the PC's skills. For example, in the beginning of the game, the PC was sleeping and having a conversation with his limbic system and brain. My brain continually asked me if I wanted to wake up. I chose to keep on sleeping, but my brain eventually indicated that I experienced a physical sensation, and my body wanted to wake up. At this point, the game indicated there was a successful Volition skill check of medium difficulty. The Volition skill is associated with morale and keeping oneself together. Hovering the cursor over the text "Volition [Medium: Success]" indicated that I needed a score of 10 to pass the check, and I had 11. The system was conducting and processing automatic skill checks as I was playing the game. The game utilized my decisions during skill point allocations to silently conduct algorithmic checks. Corresponding dialogue was displayed that was unique to my character. In this case, Volition says, "You can take it, you're a Champion!" I term such a skill check an "automatic dialogue skill check" since the system processes the check for you without your knowledge and only informs you of success or failure along with the skill's dialogue.

Two other ways *Disco Elysium* used expressive input with narrative logics are via "white" and "red skill checks". Shortly after retrieving the keys from my pocket, I noticed my tie hanging from the fan overhead. In a white or red skill check, a pair of six-sided dice is "rolled" by the game, and other special bonuses or penalties are taken into consideration as part of the check. In this scenario, if I chose to grab the tie, I would have a 28% chance of success with a Savoir Faire white skill check with medium difficulty. Savoir Faire assesses flamboyance and panache. However, I noticed that I could pull on the fan to stop it from spinning, and when I did so the game granted me a +3 bonus to my check, giving me a revised 72% probability of retrieving the tie without failure and possible consequences. If a white skill check fails, that option is locked but can be re-attempted if the player allocates a skill point upon levelling up the associated skill, or if the player completes a special action connected with the particular skill check. For example, obtaining an ammonia ampoule and using it can enable a second attempt at a white Endurance skill check when approaching the corpse of a hanged man later in the game. The player may "level up" when sufficient experience points are gained from exploration or completing tasks.

Expressive input in *Disco Elysium* is also intertwined with branching dialogue choices and their associated skill checks. After getting dressed and exiting my hotel room, I encountered a beautiful blonde, Klassje, having a cigarette break in the corridor. I initiated a dialogue with Klassje, and she insisted I was a police officer. At this point, the game presented me with three choices, two of which demonstrated my uncertainty about who I was, and the last choice offering me the opportunity to assert myself authoritatively as a police officer ("Goddamn right I'm a policeman"), which I chose.

Subsequently, I was given the dialogue option of telling Klassje that I wanted her "physically". The subsequent red skill check of challenging difficulty for the Suggestion skill had a +1 bonus due to my previous authoritative dialogue choice. The red check was particularly pertinent as it could only be attempted once without any retries, rendering it "irreversible", so the stakes for success were higher. Since my Suggestion skill level was quite high at 5, I had a 72% chance of charming Klassje with the +1 bonus. Here I realized that my expressive input could also be considered to include my dialogue choices, since my probability of charming Klassje would have been lower had I not asserted myself authoritatively as a policeman.

In Day 3 of my *Disco Elysium* playthrough, I encountered a conditional algorithm during map exploration. The game interface presented a red bubble when I was walking near the church in West Revachol with a seagull flying overhead. A dialogue with the Endurance skill ensued, and Endurance reminded me of the seagull, whose story was one of "endurance" and "adaptation". I was presented with four dialogue options and chose "Whatever it takes to survive. I AM THE SEAGULL!" to align myself with the physical part of my persona. I was rewarded with a bonus of one health and one morale point. However, just a minute previous to the event, I had taken meds to restore 2 health and morale points each. I did not want to waste my meds, so I reloaded the game to maximize the benefits of my correct dialogue choice. However, when I reloaded the game, the red bubble did not appear. I later discovered that my lowered health affected a hidden conditional Endurance skill check that was occurring in the game's processing. There was an interplay between my expressive input decisions (choosing a fully fit and healed character) and the narrative logics of the game (the fact that the number of health points influenced conditional skill checks was hidden from the player, and only expressed with perhaps a minimum number of health points and endurance). In this way, the game presented unique narratives to me based on my expressive input. I term such an event an "automatic environmental skill check", since it only occurs via exploration in the game's environment. I also noted that had the situation been more "irreversible" (e.g. if I had saved my game a long time ago, making it hard to return to the save point), I would probably not have reloaded the game and I would have been frustrated instead from my selection of the "I AM THE SEAGULL!" dialogue option.

I also discovered that the persona I was forming via expressive input was preventing me from accessing certain routes in the game, and instead was directing me towards particular narratives. When I was attempting to reach Evrart Claire, the Union leader who was responsible for the strikes in Revachol and connected with the union members behind the lynching, the path to his office was blocked by Measurehead, a rascist goon in the service of the Union. After I finished listening to Measurehead talk about his "advanced race theory", I had the option of attempting to bypass Measurehead by either subscribing to his "advanced race theory" via a Conceptualization white skill check with medium difficulty, or by a Physical Instrument white skill check with formidable difficulty. The Physical Instrument skill is a reflection of the PC's physical prowess.

There was also an automatic dialogue skill check of medium difficulty for Half Light (the skill related to letting your body take control and threaten others), who suggested that I should rip into Measurehead with a punch and catch him off guard. Right after, an automatic dialogue skill check of easy difficulty occurred for Suggestion, who reminded me that I was a sensitive person, and that I should communicate (instead of using violence). The probability of successfully knocking out Measurehead was low at 28% with formidable difficulty, while that of Conceptualization was higher. In fact, there was a −1 penalty to the Physical Instrument roll since Suggestion is against the idea. Overall, I felt it would have been easier to choose the Conceptualization option and subscribe to Measurehead's theory. Here, my selected skillsets were almost dictating my choices at a crucial story situation, and my sense of player agency felt directed.

## 5.3 Dramatic Narrative Units in *Disco Elysium*

From the above discussion, it is clear that the actions I was taking in the form of expressive input were impacting the narrative, and to make sense of this I needed to pay attention to both the narrative logics and the resulting narrative units. It is now worth considering whether, and in what way, these narrative units can be considered dramatic.

*Katharsis (Emotion).* After the initial conversation with Klassje, where she rejected me and went off into her room, I attempted to open her door, which was locked. I then attempted to knock but there was no answer. An automatic dialogue skill check at easy difficulty was conducted by Inland Empire, and "a tremendous loneliness comes over you. Everybody in the world is doing something without you." Four dialogue options appeared, all reflecting the PC's sense of loneliness and despair: "I'm so alone", "Why are you doing this? Don't do this to me…", "Beauty, don't abandon me in all this ugliness!", and "Swallow the emotion." I felt Katharsis (Aristotle's dramatic device which functions to maximize the pleasurable experience of emotion) in the form of a sense of pity for the PC at this point, since he was rejected and ignored by Klassje. I might not have encountered this dramatic narrative unit had I allocated my skill points differently.

An automatic dialogue skill check at medium difficulty then resulted in Half Light's advice that "you should punch a fucking hole in it [the door]." My expressive input decision resulted in a Kathartic moment of anger, since I wanted to punch a "fucking hole" in the door. The immediate follow-up dialogue choices were also representative of Katharsis, since I had the options of shouting "Fucking whore!", punching the door, or suppressing the urge. These were all narrative units associated with Katharsis and resulting from the aggressive and vengeful persona I had created. Because Half Light's skill check was of medium difficulty, I noted that Half Light's advice was a less encountered event and was likely associated with my expressive decisions.

*Peripeteia (Reversal of Fortune), Anagnorisis (Discovery or Recognition).* While playing *Disco Elysium*, I experienced more dramatic tension around white checks or red checks as they potentially resulted in elation or relief (in the case of success from the probability roll) and disappointment or even anger (in the case of failure from the probability roll). White checks can be a source of dramatic tension when there is a low probability of success, since levelling up a low skill doesn't guarantee a significantly higher chance of success in subsequent checks. Often, in the case of the red check, I was more accepting of a failed outcome if there was a low probability, since it was irreversible. One might argue that the red check would have higher tension since it was irreversible, but white checks were tense too, since upon a level-up you could invest the point in any of the equally relevant 23 skills. Thus, the results from the white and red skill checks were also dramatic narrative units, since the probability of success or failure depended on my expressive input.

When I got down to investigating the lynched man, I found him hanging on a tree at the back of the hotel where I was staying. The perpetrators' tracks appeared in the hardened mud in front of the tree, and there was an option to make a white Visual Calculus check to assess the number and type of perpetrators via their footprints. I had a low Visual Calculus skill of 1 due to my low Intellect primary ability, and the probability of success was only 17%. However, I unexpectedly lucked out, and was able to analyze the tracks. Since I succeeded despite a low probability of success, I naturally felt the follow-up narrative unit was dramatic since it evoked Karthasis, Peripeteia (reversal of fortune) and Anagnorisis (discovery or recognition). Karthasis and Peripeteia was evoked first as I felt elated having "lucked out", and Anagnorisis was evoked next from the narrative information I gained from the discovery of new clues in the case. However, if I had high Visual Calculus and a high probability of success, I would have interpreted the follow-up narrative unit(s) as that of Anagnorisis only, since I would have expected success from the probability roll. This demonstrates how the combination of expressive input (my choice of the PC's abilities) and the narrative logics (the various ability checks) led the resulting narrative units to be perceived as dramatic.

# 6   Case Study: *Her Story*

In *Her Story*, there does not seem to be an embodied playable character at the start of the game; the player directly investigates the murder of Hannah's husband by searching the police database for short clips of the principal suspect's (Hannah's) video interviews with an off-screen detective interviewer. Hannah's interviews are transcribed, and the player takes note of key words relevant to the investigation. The player undergoes an iterative process of inputting these words into a search database to pull out relevant videos in order to find new leads to continue the investigation.

## 6.1   Expressive Input in *Her Story*

In *Her Story*, I was presented with a 90 s style Windows interface, and a search window with the opening search term "murder" already entered. Clicking on the search button opened up four initial videos. Unwatched videos had a yellow eye icon at the top left corner of their thumbnails. I could tag the videos with a description to help me remember what the video was about, and also add what I deemed to be the more important videos to my database session by clicking on "Add to Session".

I engaged in expressive input in *Her Story* via a combination of logical, creative and organizational approaches to solve the case. In playing the game, I was inclined to develop a notetaking approach that was unique to me. I decided to do this because I found the in-game tagging function difficult to access and the in-game organization tools inadequate. Since the videos are transcribed, I initially made a mental note of key words of Hannah's interview, but as the plot became more complicated, I created an Excel sheet for the videos to track my investigative journey. I used column headings such as "description", "notes", "clothes" (used to note the clothes that Eve or Hannah wore during the video, "person" (when I felt I was sure the character in the interview was Eve or Hannah"), and "keyword" (for the keyword I used to search for this particular video). I even created a date/time column for the video so I could have information on when exactly the interview took place. In all, I created a total of 230 rows of notes.

In the process of recording, questioning and analyzing clues from the game story in an iterative fashion, I also tried to address story gaps previously unclear to me in earlier rows of the spreadsheet. For example, after watching a video interview, I noted in row 26 of my notes (around 10% of my playthrough): "Curious about the tattoo - when Hannah wore a short blue T-shirt, she had a tattoo. According to the sleeve length, Hannah's tattoo should be visible in this video, but it is not. Therefore, they may be two different people." After hypothesizing that there were two interviewees in the videos, one of whom is Hannah and the other Eve, and that they were twins, I began to question which of the interviewees in each video was Hannah or Eve. In most of the interviews, the tattoo was not visible, so it was difficult to ascertain their identity.

I noted that expressive input in *Her Story* included the order in which I selected the videos based on key words that I deemed important, as well as the tagging of clips and the adding of clips via the "Add to Session" function. I had given up tagging using the game's tagging function about halfway into the game, because I had already typed down the key word that led me to each video in my spreadsheet. I considered my Excel sheet as part of my expressive input as it replaced the tagging and "Add to Session" function in the game interface. As I played the game, I also tended to systematically watch all the available video entries presented by the search before accessing videos with other key words. I felt that the order in which I accessed the videos was an important part of my expressive input. After watching each video entry, I could track the percentage of videos I had uncovered from the entire database via the database checker application in the desktop interface of the game. By the time I activated the game's end sequence, I had watched approximately 70% of the videos.

I felt that my biggest contribution in terms of expressive input was creating "My Story" out of "*Her Story*". My deductions and hypotheses as to what transpired were unique to me based on my analysis of the clues I watched and the order in which I watched them, which could have been different for another player.

## 6.2   Narrative Logics in *Her Story*

Since my investigation of Simon's murder was restricted by the fact that I could only access the first five videos in each search, I felt manipulated by the game's narrative logics which, in my view, had an aspect of ludonarrative dissonance [15], as a proper police database in the police station would not restrict your search query to five videos.

After fulfilling the game's end-game condition, I scrolled through my query history and noted that 21 queries had more than 5 entries. Of these, key words such as "Simon" (61 occurrences), "Hannah" (19 occurrences), "baby" (17 occurrences), and "pregnant" (10 occurrences), seemed to suggest videos that could provide information pertinent to the solution. I was presented with a realistic search engine and realistic-looking video interviews of the murder suspect(s), but the results of my expressive input, reflected in the search results, were restricted. After further reflection, I realized that this was probably necessary to prevent me from obtaining too many crucial clues and to prevent me from obtaining the most critical piece of information – why Hannah and Eve collaborated to lie to the police. I had obtained details of Simon's murder almost at the beginning of the playthrough, and I felt that the other key clues of the investigation included the discovery that there were two interviewees in the videos, that they were twins, that Hannah fumbled in one of the video interviews and mentioned Eve, and that both of them were probably pregnant with Simon's children.

I rationalized that restricting the search results to five videos kept certain aspects of the story open and ambiguous. In my playthrough, I had not figured out a way to invalidate Hannah's alibi that she was in Glasgow during Simon's murder, even though it was apparent to me that Hannah and Eve had agreed to collaborate to create an alibi for Hannah. Additionally, there were moments in the videos where both Eve and Hannah expressed signs of pregnancy or admitted they were pregnant. But since there seemed to be only one child in the game (the player character, as I later discovered), I figured that I had missed out a piece of information which could confirm my conclusion.

### 6.3  Dramatic Narrative Units in *Her Story*

In *Her Story*, my expressive input can be seen as the use of the Excel sheet which led to the order and choice of search terms. The narrative units are represented via the short video clips, which are accessed by typing in the search term(s). I now explain how the expressive input and narrative logics worked to make these narrative units feel dramatic.

*Karthasis (Emotion).*  About 30% into my playthrough, I had learnt enough about Eve's tragic story to empathize with her. She had been stolen from her real parents by the midwife, and when Hannah and Eve were reunited, I felt a sense of elation as they seemed to find sisterly love and comfort in each other's company, even though it was a relationship they kept hidden from the world. When Hannah got married due to her pregnancy and there was no way Eve could follow Hannah, Eve began to descend into a lifestyle where she was trying to find love and an identity similar to what Hannah was experiencing. I felt a sense of sadness when Eve candidly described how she felt she didn't exist and was trying to get pregnant with strangers in order to find a piece of that connection she had with Hannah. She had to stop as one of the men she had sex with gave her an STD. As the previous video clips had portrayed Eve's harsh, vagrant life, which was only fulfilled by her relationship with Hannah, I pitied her and felt devastated by her self-destructive actions. The order in which I encountered these videos, as a result of my expressive input, contributed to a large extent to the dramatic impact.

*Anagnorisis (Discovery or Recognition).*  In most of the video clips, Hannah had been wearing a long-sleeved blouse or outfit, but upon watching more clips, I observed that she had a tattoo on her left arm when she was wearing a bright blue T-shirt. When I compared this to another video of her wearing a floral dress recorded slightly earlier, I realized it was very unlikely they were the same person, since a new tattoo would still be healing, and Hannah would have protected her skin. The other possibility was that it was a fake tattoo, but I recalled a video which implied the interviewee was born at the same time as Hannah, but that the midwife had told Hannah's mom that the interviewee was dead when she was a baby. I had forgotten this story until I saw the tattoos, inciting Anagnorisis since I had discovered an important piece of narrative information.

*Peripeteia (Reversal of Fortune).*  After analyzing the video interviews, I identified and noted which sister was being interviewed in each video. I empathized more with Eve than with Hannah, since Hannah abandoned Eve for Simon. Eve was also the one who was setting up all the opportunities with boys for her sister, but Hannah broke the rules the sisters had made by selfishly wanting Simon for herself and eventually getting herself pregnant. While Hannah was eventually married and being taken care of by her husband, Eve was still living in their parents' attic with no support, and eventually had to make ends meet as a singer in a bar. Simon met Eve in the bar and started fancying her, eventually asking her out. Eve felt that Simon was romantic, and this was the first time in her interviews in which a man seemed to treat her the way she wanted to be. I experienced Peripeteia as Eve's fortunes were finally reversed and something good had happened to her for the first time since the sisters lived together in their parents' attic.

## 7 Discussion

The case studies presented above suggest that expressive input, combined with narrative logics, can set up a situation where the player perceives these narrative units as dramatic, using Aristotelian dramatic devices such as Katharsis (emotional experience), Peripeteia (reversal) and Anagnorisis (discovery). A "satisfying traversal" is thus achieved within the context of Aristotelian drama in the playable system. For example, in *Disco Elysium*, the player understands that their expressive input could be consistently rewarded with a dramatic experience from the game's automatic, white and red skill checks.

Reed postulates that playable systems with "easily enumerable inputs and little support for surprising, discovered actions" do not have expressive input. He cites "choose your own adventure" games which use branching narratives as examples [5]. However, the observations in these case studies suggest otherwise; authorial intent can perhaps be achieved in branching narratives using expressive input combined with narrative logics. For example, in my conversation with Klassje, I wanted to create a character with a strong yet sensitive persona. In my branching dialogue with Klassje, I was rewarded with a +1 bonus when potentially rolling a Suggestion red skill check, since I had previously chosen an authoritative dialogue option. Additionally, since my character had a high Suggestion skill, I had a high probability of succeeding the check and obtaining access to branching dialogue consistent with the persona I wanted to form.

A playable system has expressive input if the user can express their distinctive intentions through it [5]. This study suggests that playable systems can encourage out-of-game expressive input if equivalent in-game tools are perceived by the player to be inadequate. In the case of *Her Story*, the game interface provides in-game organizational tools to tag and save interview videos as the player attempts to chronologize and make sense of the numerous videos they view. However, the tags were perceived to be difficult to access and the clues required more detailed organization. Thus, I supplemented in-game tools with out-of-game tools such as spreadsheets to express myself more distinctly by achieving the best results. Out-of-game notetaking as a way of organizing clues and determining environmental orientation was also used by players of 80s fantasy gamebooks such as *The Warlock of Firetop Mountain* [16]. In *Her Story*, differing expressive input can influence the player's perception of the chronology and interpretation of the story and its characters. For example, if I had not seen Eve's videos which depicted her abandonment and emotional pain, I might not have pitied her. In fact, I might have seen her initially as a villain who impeded Hannah's happiness.

*Dramatic Storygames.* Findings suggest the importance of using dramatic narrative units with narrative logics to produce "dramatic narrative logics". Doing so may enhance the player's sense of ownership of the story, as the playable system processes these intentions and provides constant dramatic feedback in the form of dramatic narrative units. This further engages the player with the story since they recognize their expressive input produces dramatic outcomes.

In *Disco Elysium*, the four different ways expressive decisions from the player's skill point allocations can result in dramatic narrative units are: (i) an automatic dialogue skill check, (ii) an automatic environment skill check, (iii) a white skill check, and (iv) a red skill check. It is observed that the results from white and red skill checks can be dramatic narrative units themselves, since both Karthasis and Peripeteia can result from these checks e.g. the player's elation at passing a low probability skill check.

In *Her Story*, the player's expressive input comes from the selection of word queries and interview videos, which creates a pathway through which the player uncovers the story, as well as the out-of-game organization of clues. The player's sense of ownership is thus a result of an integrated system between dramatic narrative units, the playable system and the narrative logics.

# 8   Conclusion

This study proposes a definition of the "dramatic storygame" which integrates Aristotelian dramatic devices into the narrative logics of the playable system. This suggests that "dramatic narrative logics" are achieved when there is connectedness between (i) a playable system that allows expressive input, (ii) the processing of expressive input by narrative logics, and (iii) the resulting dramatic narrative units. For such storygames, this study proposes that they be considered "dramatic storygames".

Future work can involve deeper exploration of the factors influencing dramatic narrative logics, in particular how dramatic narrative logics influence and are influenced by agency. Murray believes the reader enjoys repeating the story from different perspectives [17–19], but agency may not necessarily be increased during replay from the perspective of a dramatic storygame. Douglas postulates that readers reread hypertext fiction not to experience variation but to seek closure [20]. In addition, an intense dramatic storygame which is more "irreversible" [21] can potentially encourage closure. These issues suggest that exploring the ways in which storygames can be considered "dramatic" can provide deeper insights into how players experience storygames.

# References

1. Buckles, M.A.: Interactive Fiction: The Computer Storygame Adventure (1985)
2. Crowther, W.W., Woods, D.: Colossal Cave Adventure (1976)
3. Wardrip-Fruin, N.: Playable media and text instruments. Dichtung Digital 1 (2005)
4. Mateas, M., Stern, A.: Façade. Procedural Arts (2005)

5. Reed, A.A.: Changeful Tales: Design-Driven Approaches Toward More Expressive Storygames (2017)
6. Wardrip-Fruin, N.: Expressive Processing: Digital Fictions, Computer Games, and Software Studies. MIT Press, Cambridge (2009)
7. Hunicke, R., Leblanc, M., Zubek, R.: MDA: a formal approach to game design and game research. In: Proceedings of the Challenges in Games AI Workshop, Nineteenth National Conference of Artificial Intelligence. AAAI Press, San Jose (2004)
8. Mateas, M., Wardrip-Fruin, N.: Defining operational logics. In: Proceedings of the 2009 DiGRA International Conference: Breaking New Ground: Innovation in Games, Play, Practice and Theory, DiGRA 2009, London, UK, 1–4 September 2009 (2009)
9. Aristotle: Poetics. Oxford University Press, Oxford (2013)
10. Landow, G.P.: Hypertext: the convergence of contemporary critical theory and technology. Johns Hopkins University Press, Baltimore (1992)
11. Tanenbaum, T.J., Bizzocchi, J.: Well read: applying close reading techniques to gameplay experiences. In: Davidson, D. (ed.) Well Played 3.0, pp. 262–290. ETC Press (2011)
12. ZA/UM: Disco Elysium. ZA/UM (2019)
13. Barlow, S.: Her Story (2015)
14. Tanenbaum, T.J.: Believability, adaptivity, and performativity: three lenses for the analysis of interactive storytelling (2008). http://summit.sfu.ca/item/8972
15. Hocking, C.: Ludonarrative dissonance in bioshock: the problem of what the game is about. https://www.clicknothing.com/click_nothing/2007/10/ludonarrative-d.html
16. Jackson, S., Livingstone, I.: The Warlock of Firetop Mountain. Puffin Books, New York (1984)
17. Murray, J.H.: Hamlet on the Holodeck: The Future of Narrative in Cyberspace. Free Press, New York (1997)
18. Murray, J.H.: From game-story to cyberdrama. In: Wardrip-Fruin, N., Harrigan, P. (eds.) First Person: New Media as Story, Performance, and Game, pp. 2–11. MIT Press, Cambridge (2004)
19. Murray, J.H.: Why Paris needs hector and Lancelot needs Mordred: using traditional narrative roles and functions for dramatic compression in interactive narrative. In: Si, M., Thue, D., André, E., Lester, J.C., Tanenbaum, J., Zammitto, V. (eds.) ICIDS 2011. LNCS, vol. 7069, pp. 13–24. Springer, Heidelberg (2011). https://doi.org/10.1007/978-3-642-25289-1_2
20. Douglas, J.Y.: The End of Books–or Books Without End? Reading Interactive Narratives. University of Michigan Press, Ann Arbor (2000). https://doi.org/10.3998/mpub.16751
21. Tan, K., Mitchell, A.: Choose your permanent adventure: towards a framework for irreversible storygames. In: Cardona-Rivera, R.E., Sullivan, A., Young, R.M. (eds.) ICIDS 2019. LNCS, vol. 11869, pp. 148–157. Springer, Cham (2019). https://doi.org/10.1007/978-3-030-33894-7_16

# When the Fourth Layer Meets the Fourth Wall: The Case for Critical Game Retellings

Steven Sych(⊠)

Concordia University, Montréal, QC, Canada
steven.sych@mail.mcgill.ca

**Abstract.** Game retellings are when a player tells of the significant moments arising from their experiences of a game. It has been suggested that retellings are a marker of a game's success, insofar as they are evidence that the game has produced something worth telling to others. This paper argues that a subset of retellings take a critical stance towards their 'own' game, surfacing failures and breakdowns and rendering them the objects of shared public scrutiny. These are self-reflexively critical retellings, and they present an underutilized tool for scholars and designers of interactive narrative.

**Keywords:** Retellings · Interactive narrative · Emergent narrative · Self-reflexivity

## 1 Introduction

Game retellings are when a player crafts a narrative or anecdote about their experiences of playing a video game. Such retellings can take a variety of shapes: from describing a moment from a game in a passing conversation, to sharing a humorous anecdote on Reddit [1, 2], to inventing details of quotidian life within your galactic empire [3]; players might even create news-style reports on a game's events [4], or end up crafting a narrative so compelling that it solicits critical commentary on the retelling itself [5, 6].

It is clear that, for both designers and academics, retellings present a unique opportunity. Retellings offer a glimpse into the experiences of the audience of games. Moreover, retellings provide this opportunity "in the wild," [3] thereby allowing theorists to approach what makes a good interactive narrative without preemptively importing theory and nonnative assumptions about the phenomenon.

Increasingly, the importance of retellings is being recognized. Mirjam Eladhari describes the retelling as a fourth textual layer [6], bringing it inside the framework of story construction itself. In a different vein but with a similar result, James Ryan's curatorial approach implies that anything that truly qualifies as emergent narrative is also a kind of retelling, since it is a result of an interactor's (or a system's own) act of

© Springer Nature Switzerland AG 2020
A.-G. Bosser et al. (Eds.): ICIDS 2020, LNCS 12497, pp. 203–211, 2020.
https://doi.org/10.1007/978-3-030-62516-0_18

curation [8]; for Ryan, all emergent narratives have therefore been 'retold' even if only on the level of a digital event log or to the authors themselves.[1]

Given their similar stance towards the importance of retellings, we should not be surprised to see that a similar claim is made by both Ryan and Eladhari regarding the relationship between retellings and the interactive narrative system's[2] *quality*. In Eladhari's words, the very existence of retellings implies that a game "has provided an experience that is significant or meaningful enough that it is worth telling someone else about" [6]. The system provides a meaningful experience, and the evidence is in the telling.

Eladhari goes further than Ryan on this point, arguing that—since retellings track narrative system quality— they could be useful as instruments of *critique*. By 'critique' here Eladhari means that retellings present a tool for assessing the depth, artistic quality, and originality of a narrative system. 'Critique' here implies analysis as well as assessment, and Eladhari calls for both a "blunt" [6] quantitative approach to retellings ('more retellings' being equated with 'better narrative system'), as well as a closer, detail-oriented analysis; while she does not expand much on what she means with the latter, similar work has since been started by Kreminski et al. [3].

I agree with Eladhari that retellings are a valuable resource for critique, but here—and as a way of following through with her call for a deeper analysis—I want to drive a wedge between narrative system *success* and the bare existence of retellings. In this paper, I make the case that a significant subset of retellings are themselves already critical of the narrative systems out of which they arise. These critical retellings focus on bizarre and uncanny outcomes of a narrative system; they mock, satirize, and ironically approach the machinations of their 'own' system. Sometimes, critical retellings actually lay bare the failures of their narrative system, taking its more bizarre outcomes as the object for satire and lifting these up for public display and shared scrutiny. My argument here will proceed stepwise through two sections:

1. In the first section, I present an account of critical retellings, describing them as anecdote-style game retellings that both refer to their own narrative systems reflexively and do so with a critical, ironic edge. Using two anecdotes from the game *Rimworld*, I argue that these examples work to ironically satirize and critique the results and mechanics of the game itself.
2. In the second section, I present a plausible alternative reading to my notion of critical retellings. Namely, I present the idea that the raw, uncanny, glitchy, *art brut*-like qualities of the outcomes of narrative systems are simply part of what it means for

---

[1] James Ryan identifies a failing of previous accounts of emergent narrative: previous thinking about the form assumed that the raw outputs of systems were themselves already narratives, with curation being relegated to an incidental term or ignored entirely. For Ryan, emergent narratives do not arise from systems alone, but rather in the meeting between systems and curators— be they AI or human, player or non-participating. For this reason, it seems fair to say that a retelling is a subset of what he means by curationist emergent narrative: retelling is curation with an additional, public-facing narrative layer.

[2] Here I borrow Eladhari's term (interactive narrative system) [6]. My main concern and body of evidence will however focus on games in particular. Games are 'popularized' communal objects that create the communities within which critical retellings circulate.

them to be 'well-made,' and that we cannot describe the retellings of these outcomes as properly critical. Against this idea, I argue that such retellings arise from the contribution of reteller reflexivity, which is all but anathema to the aesthetics of *art brut*.

In the end, I describe the critical retelling as a kind of immanent critique that is both compelling as a retelling and (simultaneously) self-reflexive analysis of a computational narrative system. These texts show how the less-than-desirable outcomes of a narrative system can be meaningfully and pleasurably redeemed through retellings themselves. I suggest further that scholars seeking to use retellings as an instrument of critique would do well to attend to the self-reflexive critiques and assessments already made public through retellings themselves, rather than taking those retellings to be merely a product of narrative systems.

## 2  An Account of the Critical in Retellings: Two Examples from *Rimworld*

Eladhari claims that retellings can act as an "instrument of critique" for interactive narrative systems [6]. By this she means both that the existence and quantity of retellings allow scholars and designers to assess whether a narrative system is 'well-made' or 'good,' and that retellings provide us with a dataset for deeper analyses. While Eladhari admits that there is a great deal of room for nuance here, the general claim is that retellings correlate with narrative system success. Against this, I want to contend here that there exists a subset of retellings that do not directly track the success of a narrative system insofar as they themselves are already engaged in the assessment and analysis of the narrative system out of which they arise. I call these *critical retellings*, and they are both retellings and a means of rendering a narrative system the object of shared public scrutiny. To explain what I have in mind here, I want to first look at two retellings from the colony building game *Rimworld*.

The first retelling I have in mind is told from the perspective of a prisoner of the player's colony [1]. With embellished dialogue, the reteller writes about how the prisoner is accosted by the player's "heavily-armoured interrogator":

> "You came into our town. Our peaceful fucking town. You—I had a wife. A wife and a kid. I had to watch them get turned into fucking mince-meat right infront [sic] of my eyes. I had to listen to their screams"

Despite this diatribe and the horrible events that preceded them, it is eventually revealed that the interrogator—the one who lost their entire family in the raid—is actually trying to recruit this prisoner to join their colony. The tone of the text is humorous, ironic, and in the end exhibits a degree of bathos. It laconically states, "Another failed recruitment attempt."

The second *Rimworld* retelling is told from the player's perspective and relates an anecdote involving a couple who visits the player's frigid polar colony [2]. While these guests arrive seeking rest and relaxation, both quickly succumb to hypothermia. A week later, the daughter of the two initial visitors as well as her husband arrive ("for some Rest & Relaxation," the reteller clarifies), and their stay results in a similar series of events.

The daughter of the initial pair is named Fanya, and the author writes that, after her own husband has died of hypothermia,

> "Fanya was in a similar situation to that of her mother. She was nearly dead from hypothermia and over 10 of her body parts had fallen off due to hypothermia, including her jaw and one ear. When she warmed up, I told her to leave. When she reached the edge of the map, I got a reputation bonus because Fanya exited healthy. '… Healthy'"

Again, we have a setup followed by humorous, ironic, and bathos-inflected ending. The title reads, "Honey. For this year's holiday, I want to go to that Ice Sheet colony where mum and dad died of hypothermia last week."

Both stories here are self-reflexively dealing with the mechanics of *Rimworld's* systems. The first story explicitly points to the prisoner recruitment mechanic in *Rimworld*, and anyone familiar with the game would know what the story is referring to; the second anecdote is related to *Rimworld's* system for having visitors and—more broadly—the storyteller system [9] in the game that tries to meaningfully set up events. One of the ways the storyteller operates is to introduce characters who have existing relationships. *Rimworld's* creator, Tynan Sylvester, has stated in an interview that,

> "We supply these labels, like say this is a person's sister, and suddenly everything has this new meaning […] It's pretty darn simple, just a matrix of numbers and labels, but they're so close to what we spend all our time thinking and telling stories about. A tonne of neuro-circuitry is just about finding connections in human relationships, and if you can spark that in the game, then people's brains just take over. There's this giant computer sitting there, trying to find connections and causal relationships and emotional inferences. You just have to get that motor running and all you need are a few simple labels, no more complicated than a children's book." [10]

While *Rimworld's* planets are large, the world ends up feeling rather intimate: it is full of family members, friends, lovers and enemies. The second retelling's reference to the game's (as it were) intimate labeling system, much like the reference to the prisoner recruitment system, would be quite familiar to players of *Rimworld*.

Both of these retellings, in other words, deal explicitly and self-reflexively with the game's systems, and both of them wink to a knowing audience. But they don't stop there: I contend that these retellings analyze and assess the outcomes of the narrative system in which they take place. They provide commentary on the game and its systems.

What is the content of this commentary? In the first story, players of *Rimworld* will recognize the ability to recruit prisoners as colonists— even when the prisoners have attacked, raided, and murdered members of the colony quite recently. In fact, dragging incapacitated raiders to prison and ordering colonists to chat endlessly with them is one of the best ways of getting recruits. But this first retelling analyzes this recruitment system's blind spots, exploring how it quite often leads to strange and immersion-breaking results—as when a colony member that has been significantly, personally harmed will obediently work to recruit those who harmed them. Similarly, in the second story, we again see a bizarre outcome of the game's systems (visitation and the intimate labelling of the storyteller). Again, this second retelling analyses how this system can lead to immersion-breaking results, as when a visitor ignores the grisly personal history of a given locale.

Both retellings lack emotional consistency or verisimilitude, and (crucially) the sardonic humour of the retelling comes to trade on precisely this. These retellings amplify the flaws in these systems for the sake of a pleasurable, *tellable* retelling: they lay out moments where these systems have produced bizarre, emotionally unbelievable, uncanny, and immersion-breaking situations. But instead of merely becoming frustrated with the systems, the players have taken to retelling as a way of publicly critiquing the narrative system through irony[3] and satire, winking at their audience who would have similar experiences with *Rimworld*: they have become critical retellers.

I read critical retellings as a kind of immanent critique, a way for authors to both present to their communities a compelling retelling and (simultaneously) publicly analyze, scrutinize—and even explicitly criticize the failings of—the narrative system that gave rise to it. Furthermore, at least in their most extreme cases (such as the two I describe above), critical retellings do not track narrative system quality. Instead, the stance of these retellings towards their respective narrative system is critical of that system, and this means that they can be compelling despite—even because of—their less than 'well-made' or 'good' story material.

Two caveats here before I move on: first, I am admittedly, dealing with *anecdotes* in these examples, and there are likely to be differences between these and story-length, narrative-focused or character-focused retellings. This should come as no surprise, since by their very definition critical retellings would tend to arise when a game has produced an output that would be more difficult to narrativize in a lengthy manner. Second, I am assuming that the readers of these retellings will have some direct experience with the game *Rimworld*, since both retellings are taking these common game mechanics (recruitment, visitation) explicitly as an object of reference.

These two limits are a site for further study. For now, suffice it to say that even a brief glance at the communities around *Rimworld* and other narrative-oriented colony-building games such as *Dwarf Fortress* [12] will make it clear that such humorous, ironic, and self-reflexive anecdotes are far from rare.[4] The question is how we read them, and the subsequent importance that is placed upon them.

## 3 Alternative Readings: Ryan's Computational *Art Brut*

Having a taciturn colonist obediently work to recruit a prisoner who just murdered their entire family, or having someone arrive for 'holiday' in the same unforgiving

---

[3] Part of why I see these retellings as explicitly critical is their use of irony. Irony, according to Linda Hutcheon, always has an 'edge' [11]: it's critical of something, and quite often the straight discourse that forms one half of its double-speak. Here the 'straight' discourse just is the narrative system.

[4] To list just two examples: the *Dwarf Fortress* retelling 'One Stands Alone' involves a character referencing the game's plummeting frame-rate [16], and the famous retelling 'Oilfurnace' ends with a bizarre, fourth wall breaking moment that references the *Dwarf Fortress* community mantra— *losing is fun* [14].

biome in which their parents have just died due to environmental conditions—these outcomes are on the verge of incoherence. But instead of simply being disappointed or frustrated with the system, the authors transform a narrative system limitation into an ironic, satirical success at the level of the retelling: the humour of these retellings trades on the bizarreness, the uncanny qualities, and the immersion-breaking character of the content which comes to be retold.

Nevertheless, there is an alternate reading of the above *Rimworld* anecdotes. More in line with Eladhari and Ryan's point that a retelling shows that a narrative system is well-made or has produced a 'good' outcome, one might argue that the two above anecdotes from Rimworld also fit this bill: one could claim that—as bizarre as these outcomes are—the very oddness might actually constitute part of what it means for such a narrative system to be successful.

James Ryan makes a similar point about the aesthetics of emergent narrative. He claims that, due to the computational genesis of emergent narratives, there are similarities between them and *art brut* ('outsider art') [8]. Jean Dubuffet, the 20th century painter who coined the French term, saw *art brut* as works arising from the raw expression of an artist's subjectivity rather than from the undermining adornments of training and convention. He writes,

> "By [art brut] we mean works executed by people free from artistic culture, in which mimicry, unlike what happens with intellectuals, has little or no part, so that these artists derive everything (subjects, materials, means of transposition, rhythms, ways of writing, etc.) from their own depths and not from the clichés of classical or fashionable art"[13, translation by author]

Similarly, for Ryan, *art brut* computational emergent narratives are those with "a sense of the crude, uncanny, alien, eccentric, deranged, marginalized, pure" [8]; they are works that that would not have been penned by a 'normal' human author working within the confines of institutional art and literature [8]. This gives them a bizarre, jarring, uncanny quality. And yet, though the works are bizarre, Ryan argues that this does not indicate the failings of a narrative system so much as it reveals the unique potential for pleasure afforded by the form. The raw and uncanny qualities of computational emergent narratives just *are* part of their appeal.

If Ryan is right about this, we might re-read what I have called critical retellings as narrative system successes, and then attempt to understand them along the same lines as we would understand any other retelling. The two *Rimworld* stories could then be read as the sharing of unique, if bizarre, details of interactions with a well-made narrative system. Indeed, the richer and more complex a narrative system is, the more significant this detail-comparing is likely to become; if the details are not only unique but uniquely odd, this might only increase the desire to publicly surface and compare such idiosyncrasies.

This alternative reading is plausible, but I do not believe it does justice to the *Rimworld* anecdotes cited above. First, I think it is at least reasonable to say that the narrative systems in these two *Rimworld* retellings have produced less than desirable outcomes. Such outcomes present a degree of incoherence within the game's own world, within its own history, or in relation to some basic laws of our own; through this incoherence, the very seams of the simulation itself are laid bare for all to see. Accordingly, both *Rimworld* stories present us with instances where, as a player, one might reasonably expect to become disappointed or frustrated with the system's results; likewise, both stories present us with outcomes where, as a designer, one can imagine looking at the narrative system's output as something in need of a fix. We can reasonably imagine a patch for *Rimworld* stating something like, 'Visitors will no longer attempt to take restful holidays where their immediate family members have recently died horrific deaths due to environmental conditions.'

Admittedly, this point is in no way conclusive. As stated earlier, part of the use of retellings is that they allow us to approach computational emergent narratives in a way that does not rely on the importation of theory. One cannot base an argument on what it is for a narrative system's outcome to be 'good' (coherent, immersive, representing our world, etc.) since this is to presuppose precisely what is at stake.

But beyond the outcomes of the narrative system appearing (internally or externally) incoherent or unsatisfying, I think we have another reason to read these examples as critical retellings as opposed to just 'successful' *art brut*. It boils down to the character of the retellings themselves, and in particular the clear self-reflexivity performed by the retellers. Given that a primary quality of *art brut* is its very lack of self-reflexivity—it is the art of prisoners, loners, the mentally ill, and other marginalized peoples, and by its very definition it lacks the self-reflexivity involved in imitation or reference or the palette of a shared history—then it is difficult to understand how such deeply self-reflexive *Rimworld* retellings could themselves be described in these terms. Put succinctly: the unique aesthetic of *art brut* arises from its somewhat naive relation to the act of creation, which is almost the precise opposite of what is at work in the *Rimworld* and *Dwarf Fortress* examples cited above.

A close look at the retellings themselves renders clear that these *Rimworld* anecdotes are profoundly self-reflexive—a quality of retellings that has remained under-theorized by scholars working in this area. This is why the concept of *art brut* or even glitch art [8] does not do justice to this aspect of these examples of retellings *as retellings*. To be fair to James Ryan, he is describing the aesthetics of the narrative system's output (and perhaps muddying the waters by relying on a retelling[5] in order to do so), while I am following Eladhari and taking retellings as a dataset to approach narrative systems and re-interpret that aesthetic understanding. Perhaps then we can simply say that the naive, '*art brut*' outputs of a narrative system may—in some cases and if they are '*brut*' enough—be taken up in a critical, self-reflexive, and ironic manner by retellers.

## 4   Conclusion: A Friction-Filled Partnership

Many of the above issues come down to a question of ontology, and an argument about the interplay of complex elements and forces that come to make a retelling what it is. Is a retelling primarily the product of a reteller, or primarily the product of a narrative system? It should be clear that this question poses a false dichotomy. The answer in any real instance is 'both.' In the words of Kreminski et al., we have a storytelling partnership

---

[5] Ryan's lengthy exploration of the aesthetics of emergent narrative as such relies on a specific retelling of the game *Dwarf Fortress* called 'Oilfurnace' [8, 14].

[15]. This text has made the case that sometimes this storytelling partnership can involve conflict—that friction *between* a system and a reteller is part of what allows these systems to support creativity—and that one manifestation of this friction is the critical retelling. Critical retellings as described above are game retellings that:

1. tend to be shorter and more anecdotal than 'narrative';
2. explicitly reference and reflect on the mechanics of the narrative system, or the nature of the narrative system itself;
3. speak directly to a knowing audience that would understand these same mechanics and their importance within the system;
4. retell with a critical edge that is performed through irony and satire;

For scholars following Eladhari and looking to use retellings to assess the depth, artistic quality, and originality of a narrative system, the assessments *already shared* by players in the form of critical retellings present an excellent starting point. I would implore scholars to attend to these moments of irony, self-reflexivity, and friction between retellers and the systems with which they partner.

## References

1. r/Talesfromrimworld - A story inspired by a recent raid, from a prisoner's perspective. https://www.reddit.com/r/Talesfromrimworld/comments/euoaum/a_story_insp ired_by_a_recent_raid_from_a/. Accessed 25 June 2020
2. r/Talesfromrimworld - 'Honey. For this year's holiday, I want to go to that Ice Sheet colony where mum and dad died of hypothermia last week. https://www.reddit.com/r/Talesfromrim world/comments/end89i/honey_for_this_years_holiday_i_want_to_go_to_that/. Accessed 25 June 2020
3. Kreminski, M., Samuel, B., Melcer, E., Wardrip-Fruin, N.: Evaluating AI-based games through retellings. In: Proceedings AIIDE (2019)
4. EVE News24: Breaking: Legacy Coalition/Imperium NIP Ending. http://evenews24.com/ 2020/06/21/breaking-legacy-coalition-imperium-nip-ending/. Accessed 25 June 2020
5. Burkinshaw, R.: Alice and Kev. https://aliceandkev.wordpress.com/. Accessed 25 June 2020
6. Eladhari, M.P.: Re-tellings: the fourth layer of narrative as an instrument for critique. In: Rouse, R., Koenitz, H., Haahr, M. (eds.) ICIDS 2018. LNCS, vol. 11318, pp. 65–78. Springer, Cham (2018). https://doi.org/10.1007/978-3-030-04028-4_5
7. Larsen, B.A., Bruni, L.E., Schoenau-Fog, H.: The story we cannot see: on how a retelling relates to its afterstory. In: Cardona-Rivera, R.E., Sullivan, A., Young, R.M. (eds.) ICIDS 2019. LNCS, vol. 11869, pp. 190–203. Springer, Cham (2019). https://doi.org/10.1007/978-3-030-33894-7_21
8. Ryan, J.: Curating Simulated Storyworlds. Ph.D. thesis. University of California, Santa Cruz (2018)
9. Wiki on AI Storytellers. https://rimworldwiki.com/wiki/AI_Storytellers. Accessed 25 June 2020
10. Wiltshire, A.: How RimWorld Generates Great Stories. Rock Paper Shotgun. https://www.roc kpapershotgun.com/2016/08/12/how-rimworld-generates-great-stories/. Accessed 25 June 2020
11. Hutcheon, L.: Irony's Edge: the Theory and Politics of Irony. Taylor and Francis, Hoboken (2013)

12. Adams, T.: Slaves to Armok: God of Blood Chapter II: Dwarf Fortress. https://www.bay12games.com/dwarves/ Bay 12 Games (2006)
13. Dubuffet, J.: L'art brut préferé aux arts culturels. Compagnie de l'art brut, Paris (1949)
14. Denee, T.: Oilfurnace (2015). https://www.timdenee.com/oilfurnace. Accessed 25 June 2020
15. Kreminski, M., Wardrip-Fruin, M.: Generative games as storytelling partners. In: Proceedings of the 14th International Conference on the Foundations of Digital Games, pp. 1–8 (2019)
16. Anonymous, One Stands Alone (2011). https://dfstories.com/one-stands-alone/. Accessed 25 June 2020

# What Might an Action do?
# Toward a Grounded View of Actions
# in Interactive Storytelling

David Thue[(✉)] [iD]

RISE Research Group, School of Information Technology, Carleton University,
Ottawa, ON, Canada
david.thue@carleton.ca

**Abstract.** Interaction is central to interactive narrative experiences,
but our understanding of player actions remains relatively shallow.
Recent works have widened our view of what an action might do, but
we still lack a way to identify, compare, and discover different kinds of
action that an interactive narrative's player might perform. In this work,
we present a way to model the interaction that occurs in an interactive
narrative process, offering a common ground upon which many kinds of
action can be distinguished, including kinds that might never have been
used. We demonstrate our method on *The Ice-Bound Concordance*, an
interactive narrative system that offers complex actions.

## 1 Introduction

The capacity for a player or audience to interact is a defining feature of Interactive Narrative media, but the common concept of a player *action* remains
relatively narrow. From the perspective of interactive narrative design [4], an
action is often viewed as a player's performance of a choice that they made,
where their choice can affect the immediate progression of their unfolding narrative experience. The popularity of this view is apparent from the widespread
use of directed graphs to summarize how a narrative experience might progress,
in both literature and practice. In such a graph, each node represents a segment
of narrative content, each directed edge represents a temporal ordering between
its connected nodes, and each outgoing edge from a node represents an action
that can progress the experience forward in time toward the target node. ...but
is this all that an action might do?

Prior analyses have demonstrated that various notions of player actions have
been used as parts of successful interactive narrative systems. These include *narrative rewinding* as discussed by Kleinman et al. [3] as well as *narrative sculpting*,
*social navigation*, *generation*, *storywrighting*, *negotiation*, and *administration*, as
discussed by Reed [9]. While these analyses offer useful examples of different
activities that players can engage in as part of a narrative experience, they do
not attempt to ground our understanding of what different kinds of action are
afforded by an interactive narrative system. We aim to do so in this work.

© Springer Nature Switzerland AG 2020
A.-G. Bosser et al. (Eds.): ICIDS 2020, LNCS 12497, pp. 212–220, 2020.
https://doi.org/10.1007/978-3-030-62516-0_19

Before proceeding, we must be careful to define "kind of action" – i.e., how should one recognize that two given actions are different kinds of action, in the way that we desire in this work? We derive our definition from the nature of one of the player activities that Reed discovered in his work: narrative sculpting [9]. Unlike the common notion of an action being something that changes the narrative world, narrative sculpting changes the structure of how any narrative experience can progress. In other words, narrative sculpting differs from the typical notion of a player action in that it changes a different aspect of the interactive narrative process [4]. Following this idea, we identify different *kinds of action* as those that change different aspects of an interactive narrative process.

Obtaining a grounded understanding of interactive narrative actions is important for three reasons. First, it can offer a new conceptual tool for interactive narrative design, empowering designers to carefully consider a variety of ways in which they could leverage interaction in their work. Second, it can offer a useful lens for interactive narrative analysis, allowing scholars to systematically catalog and categorize player actions in a more structured and nuanced way. Third, an initial grounded understanding can help researchers explore and discover new kinds of player actions, toward improving our shared knowledge over time. Our research challenge can thus be formulated as follows: We seek a way to model interaction in the context of Interactive Narrative that allows us to identify, compare, and discover different kinds of action that players might perform.

In this paper, we propose a new way to consider and understand player actions in an interactive narrative system. Compared to prior work, our method offers two key advantages. First, it is *flexible*. We have successfully reframed all of the notions of player actions that we mentioned above using a shared set of elements, though space limitations permit us to discuss only narrative sculpting in detail. This allows us to directly compare different kinds of actions on a common theoretical ground. Second, it is *generative*. Starting from a set of elements that model interaction in a "simple" interactive narrative system, the designer/analyst can recursively extend the model through a structured analysis. By the structure of this analysis (which we describe in Sect. 4), each new extension reveals a unique kind of action to consider. The set of possible models is infinite, but the extension process ends when the designer/analyst decides that no new extension is needed. As a result, exploring the set of possible models might allow a researcher to discover kinds of action that have never before been used. We suggest some potential candidates later on.

## 2 Related Work

In his recent dissertation [9], Reed explored the potential for action in the context of interactive narrative design. His analysis was informed by his knowledge and experience as an established creator of interactive narrative systems, and it was supported by an array of theoretical work spanning interactive narrative, narratology, and the study of both digital and analog games. Reed summarized his findings in terms of three modes of interactive narrative that differ from the common traversal of directed graphs: Sculptural Fiction, Social Simulation, and Collaborative Storygames. Sculptural Fiction gives a single player some actions that are typically reserved for a narrative designer, as they must pick and choose between elements of narrative content to *build* a directed graph (e.g., *The Ice-Bound Concordance* [10]). Social Simulation asks its player to learn to navigate a simulation of social behaviour across a cast of non-player characters (e.g., *Prom Week* [6]). Finally, Reed posited that players of Collaborative Storygames (e.g., *Dungeons & Dragons* [2]) tend to spend their time on four core activities: *generation* (creating new narrative content), *storywrighting* (assembling content in a coherent or satisfying way), *negotiation* (resolving conflicts between players), and *administration* (interpreting and carrying out rules). As an analysis of how players might act in interactive narratives, Reed's work succeeds in extracting several player activities that can help broaden our view. At the same time, it does little to help us understand or identify different kinds of action in relation to one another, or as part of a larger whole. We aim to remedy that in this work.

Carstensdottir [1] recently sought to model interaction in an Interactive Narrative context, defining both the Progression Model and Progression Maps as highly granular ways to represent any specific opportunity to progress through an interactive narrative experience. This work is complementary to what we present in this paper, as we have a different goal. While Carstensdottir sought to enable detailed analyses of how players understand and reason about the narrative world based on the observations that they perceive, we seek to enable new perspectives on the kinds of actions that players might be given to perform.

## 3   Defining an Interactive Process

Our approach relies on a particular notion of an interactive process. We define it first as a general construct and then explain it in the context of Interactive Narrative, yielding a match with Koenitz's definition of an *interactive narrative process* [4]. An *interactive process* is a collection of six data elements and three functions, as shown in Fig. 1. *Data* describes information and *functions* produce data when given other data as input. The data and functions are as follows:

- A **target object** identifies the object that can be changed by interacting in the process (e.g., a narrative world);
- a **set of actors** defines which players may act upon and/or observe the target object by participating in this process;
- an **initial state** defines how the target object should be at the start of any actor's experience;
- a **set of possible states** defines every way in which the target object might be (e.g., at different times in a narrative experience);
- a **set of possible observations** defines every observation that an actor might receive about the target object;
- a **set of possible actions** defines every action that an actor might perform to change the target object;

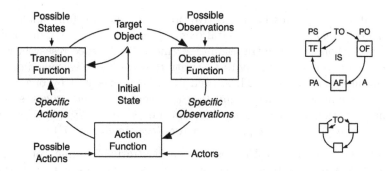

**Fig. 1.** Left: A diagram of an interactive process. Boxes show functions and arrows show the flow of data. Large arrows show the interactive loop. Italics show ephemeral elements for clarity. Right: Minified versions of the diagram that appear in later figures.

- an **observation function** determines what each actor should observe (given the set of possible observations) based on the target object's current state;
- an **action function** determines a possible action for each actor to perform based on the observation that each actor received (this represents the joint effect of all of the actors, who might or might not collaborate); and
- a **transition function** determines how a vector of all actor actions (one from each actor) should be used to transition the target object from its current state to a new state (given the set of possible states).

Koenitz stated that an interactive narrative process is defined and shaped by the actions that players perform and the opportunities that an interactive narrative system provides [4]. He further defined an interactive narrative system as a collection of all of the elements that can be used to produce interactive narrative experiences (including executable code, art assets, and the computing hardware in which they are situated) [4].

We propose that our definition of interactive process can serve well for modelling the interactive narrative process that Koenitz described, as choosing the target object to be a narrative's world yields a model that (i) provides opportunities to players via observations of the narrative world and (ii) gives them the ability to act to change it. We further propose that this model can also describe any interactive narrative process that considers a player action as something that progresses between nodes in a directed graph, which we discussed in Sect. 1. Specifically, when the target object is the story's narrative world, each node of the directed graph is a state of the narrative world, each outgoing edge is a possible player action, and each incoming edge describes how the narrative world transitions between states on the basis of a chosen action. The observation function allows the state to change in ways that the player might not observe.

**Function Execution.** Each function in an interactive process must be *executed*, meaning that a computer or one or more people must do some work to produce the function's output data. By considering execution in this flexible way, we ensure that we can represent interactive processes that are fully analog (e.g., *Dungeons & Dragons* [2]), fully digital (e.g., *Sheldon County* [11]), or combinations of both. Following the tradition of Artificial Intelligence research, we use the term *agent* to refer generally to an entity that can perceive some input and act to produce some output. Thus, each function is executed by one or more agents. For example, the action function is executed by the process's actors, while the transition and observation functions might be executed by a computer (e.g., in *Skyrim* [5]) or by the process's actors (e.g., in *Fiasco* [7]).

**An Interactive Narrative Process.** As an illustrative example, consider how an interactive narrative process (i.e., an interactive process with a narrative world as its target object) can be used to model the first Choose Your Own Adventure novel, *The Cave of Time* [8]. The target object is the narrative world of *The Cave of Time*, meaning the fictional place in which the story happens, along with every object and character in it. The set of actors includes only a single player. The initial state includes the player's character standing just outside a mysterious cave in a place called Snake Canyon. The set of possible states is defined by the 86 reachable sections of the book, each of which is a different state. Each section is reached by performing an action from the set of possible actions, which each direct the reader to turn to a particular page of the book. Each possible observation corresponds to the printed text (and sometimes a drawing) that appears in each section of the book. The observation function is executed by the player; they must manipulate the book in a way that allows them to perceive the contents of each section (e.g., by holding it open and upright). The player executes the action function at the end of each (non-terminal) section by choosing one of the printed actions to perform. Finally, the player also executes the transition function; given the current state (e.g., the fifth section) they turn pages to reach the section given by the action's text (e.g., "turn to page 46"), and thereby transition the narrative world to a new state.

Thinking generally, an interactive process is useful for modelling interaction because it represents a way for an actor to affect change – i.e., the process's target object can be changed by executing its action function (subject to the transition function). As we will see in Sect. 4, this capacity to represent acted change is what will allow us to consider different kinds of player actions in an interactive narrative process.

## 4   A Method for Modelling Interaction

We now propose a method for modelling interaction in an interactive narrative process, toward highlighting its capacity to identify and distinguish between different kinds of player actions.

At a high level, our method begins with a base model of an interactive narrative process (specifically, an interactive process from Sect. 3 with a narrative world as its target object) and then grows into a more complete model through a recursive sequence of steps. Each step examines one of the elements (data or function) of the interactive process and prompts the designer/analyst to answer a specific question: *Should (or can) any agent change that element?* If the answer is "no", then nothing further is done and another element of the process is examined in the next step (until no element remains unexamined). If the answer is "yes", then the model must grow, adding a *new* interactive process with a particular target object: the element for which the designer/analyst just answered "yes". The designer/analyst must define the elements of this new process (including which agents execute its functions), and then for each element ask *Should (or can) any agent change that element?* This is why the examination is recursive: with each answer of "yes", the model must grow again, creating a new interactive process with its own elements to examine. The model will be complete once every element of each of its processes have been examined, which will occur once the designer/analyst chooses to answer "no" for every remaining, unexamined element. The depth of detail included in each element's definition can be chosen to satisfy the designer/analyst's aims.

## 4.1   Modelling Interaction in the Ice-Bound Concordance

We demonstrate our method by modelling player interaction in *The Ice-Bound Concordance* [10]. This example is challenging because *Concordance*'s story contains multiple layers [9] as well as an example of sculptural fiction (recall Sect. 2). The outermost layer concerns the player's interaction with KRIS, a computational simulacrum of long-dead author Kristopher Holmquist. Each inner layer concerns Holmquist's incomplete account of the story of a unique group of people, where each group once inhabited different levels of a sinking polar research base. The player's task is to work with KRIS to complete each of the group's stories. This task is enabled via Reed's notion of sculptural fiction, wherein the player dynamically alters the structure of each inner story (including both themes and occurrences) until they reach a structure that they desire.

To address *Concordance*'s multi-layered nature, we begin with a base model comprised of several interactive narrative processes: one for the outer layer's story and one for each inner layer's story (Fig. 2). Each process's target object is set to the narrative world of its associated story, while the initial states, sets of possible states, and sets of possible observations are set based on the potential content of each story. The set of actors contains the player for every process, but the set of possible actions remains empty for every process except that of the outer layer's story. This is because the outer layer's narrative world is the only one upon which the player can directly act. All transition and observation functions are executed by the computer that runs *Concordance*, and the action functions are all executed by the player, though there is nothing to do in all but the outer layer's process. Keeping the player as an actor in the inner stories' processes is important because it models the player's ability to observe (by reading) the events of each inner story.

Having defined a base model for *Concordance*, we can now recursively examine its elements to (potentially) grow the model, asking whether or not each of them can be changed by any agent. The answer is "no" except for the transition function of each inner story's process. The answers for these elements are "yes"

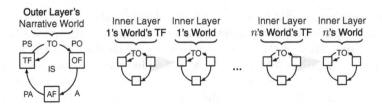

**Fig. 2.** Our complete model of *The Ice-Bound Concordance* [10]. See Fig. 1 for details.

because of the work that sculptural fiction entails – the player must be able to alter the structure of how a narrative experience can unfold, and this structure is precisely what each process's transition function represents. For each inner story process, the effect on the model is thus as follows. The model grows by the addition of one new interactive process whose target object is the transition function of the inner story's process. The remaining elements of each such process are defined by *Concordance*'s designers, and together they describe every possible story structure, how the player can observe and edit that structure, and what rules exist to shape how the editing proceeds (via the new process's transition function). To finish the analysis, we complete the recursive step, asking whether each of the elements in the newly created processes can be changed by the player. As every answer is "no", the examination ends and the model is complete.

The result is a model with $2n+1$ interactive processes, where $n$ is the number of inner stories that *Concordance* contains: one for the outer layer story, and two for each inner layer story (one that allows the player to observe the story, and another that allows the player to modify that story's structure; Fig. 2). This model confirms that Reed's notion of *narrative sculpting* is indeed a different kind of action from traversing an edge in a directed graph to affect a narrative world; instead of affecting the state of a narrative world, narrative sculpting affects the transition function that governs how a narrative world can proceed.

## 4.2   Limitations of the Method

Two of the notions of player actions that we noted in Sect. 1 posed a challenge for our model: *narrative rewinding* and *social navigation*.

**Narrative Rewinding.** As discussed by Kleinman et al. [3], narrative rewinding allows a player to revisit parts of the narrative world as though they were travelling back in time, providing opportunities to alter prior decisions and choose different actions. As Kleinman et al. show in their work, being able to rewind is different from the typical way that player actions traverse a directed graph. Typical traversals involve starting at one node and then visiting nodes that are progressively further (more nodes away) from the starting point. Meanwhile, directed graphs that allow rewinding must also contain edges that allow traversals that progress to nodes that are closer to the starting point.

In terms of our modelling method, narrative rewinding can be found in the base interactive narrative process that targets a narrative's world: by choosing particular actions via the action function, a player can cause the state of the world to change in a way that revisits a previously visited state. Although we can successfully identify narrative rewinding as an activity within one of our models, there are no two models that can distinguish between processes that allow or do not allow the narrative to be rewound. This highlights that our stated notion of what distinguishes between different "kinds of action" is only one of perhaps several dimensions along which actions can be usefully distinguished.

**Social Navigation.** Reed identified Social Games as a mode of interactive narrative that is distinct from navigating a directed graph to change a narrative world [9]. We refer to this notion of an action as *social navigation*, as the player must understand, reason about, and manipulate a simulated web of social relationships between a cast of non-player characters (NPCs; e.g., in *Prom Week* [6]). When we use our method to model interaction in a Social Game, the result is a model with two interactive processes: the base process targeting the narrative world, and a second process targeting the action function of the narrative world. This second process is created because each of the NPCs is an AI agent that can modify its own behaviour by changing the base process's action function. While the player of a Social Game generally cannot *directly* influence the behaviour of any NPC, they can *indirectly* influence such behaviours by acting in the narrative world. Our current modelling method does not distinguish between "changing the narrative world" and "changing the narrative world to affect how another actor changes the action function" as different kinds of action, but we hope to explore this as part of our future work.

## 5    Discussion and Future Work

In this work, we presented and demonstrated a new way to model how players can interact in an Interactive Narrative context. Contrary to prior work, our method can distinguish between various kinds of action on the basis of which aspects of an interactive narrative process they are able to change. This notion of how actions can differ represents a significant generalization from prior work, as it unifies several known kinds of action under a common representation and further supports the discovery of new kinds of action through the method we described. To imagine some of kinds of action that are potentially new, consider a connected set of three interactive processes: one is the base interactive narrative process, the second process targets an element of the first process, and the third process targets an element of the second process. With nine potential targets to choose from in each of the first and second processes, this leads to $81 + 9 + 1 = 91$ different kinds of action that such a model could allow. For example, a sneaky *Dungeons & Dragons* [2] player might creatively edit the Game Master's rule book before a game begins, thereby changing the set of possible states that are allowed during character creation and allowing them to create a character (as part of the story's initial state) that runs counter to the official rules.

We hope that the generative nature of our method will be used to explore this new space of possible actions, toward further diversifying the kinds of actions that players can perform in interactive narrative experiences.

## References

1. Carstensdottir, E.: Automated Structural Analysis of Interactive Narratives. Ph.D. thesis, Northeastern University (2020)
2. Gygax, G., Arneson, D.: Dungeons & Dragons. Tactical Studies Rules, Inc., United States (1974)
3. Kleinman, E., Caro, K., Zhu, J.: From immersion to metagaming: understanding rewind mechanics in interactive storytelling. Entertainment Comput. **33**, 100322 (2020). https://doi.org/10.1016/j.entcom.2019.100322
4. Koenitz, H.: Towards a theoretical framework for interactive digital narrative. In: Aylett, R., Lim, M.Y., Louchart, S., Petta, P., Riedl, M. (eds.) Interactive Storytelling, pp. 176–185. Springer, Berlin, Heidelberg (2010)
5. Bethesda Game Studios: Skyrim. www.elderscrolls.com/skyrim (2011)
6. McCoy, J., Treanor, M., Samuel, B., Reed, A., Mateas, M., Wardrip-Fruin, N.: Prom week: designing past the game/story dilemma. In: Proceedings of the 8th International Conference on the Foundations of Digital Games (FDG 2013). Chania, Crete, Greece (2013)
7. Morningstar, J.: Fiasco. Bully Pulpit Games (2009)
8. Packard, E.: Choose Your Own Adventure: The Cave of Time. Crossroads Press (1979)
9. Reed, A.: Changeful Tales: Design-Driven Approaches Toward More Expressive Storygames. Ph.D. thesis, UC Santa Cruz (2017)
10. Reed, A., Garbe, J., Apostol, N.: The Ice-Bound Concordance. www.ice-bound.com (2013)
11. Ryan, J.: Sheldon County. www.jamesryan.world/projects#/sheldon-county/ (2018)

# Towards Gestural Specificity in Interactive Digital Literary Narratives

Serge Bouchardon[✉]

Université de technologie de Compiègne, Compiègne, France
serge.bouchardon@utc.fr

## 1 The Gesture of Manipulation in Digital Literature

In the domain of digital or electronic literature[1], interactive works have already existed for several decades. In an *interactive* creation, manipulations by the readers are often required so that they can move through the work (for instance in hypertextual narratives). Such manipulations, in these interactive digital creations, are not radically new and there are many examples of literary works which require physical interventions on the part of the reader; for example in Raymond Queneau's *Cent mille milliards de poèmes* the reader must construct sonnets from a number of individually printed lines of poetry. Espen Aarseth proposes the term "ergodic literature" to describe this kind of works, arguing that "in ergodic literature, *nontrivial effort* is required to allow the reader to traverse the text" (Aarseth 1997: 1). Yet while some print works do require that the reader provides some physical input, what is somewhat new in interactive digital works is the fact that it is the text itself, and not only the physical medium, which acquires a dimension of manipulation. A digital text, as well as being a text provided for reading, can also afford an opportunity for manipulation. This dimension of the manipulation of the text, but also the whole range of semiotic forms (text, image, sound, video), opens a large field of possibilities in interactive digital creations. But to what extent can one speak of a gesturality specific to the Digital? We will focus on two interactive digital narratives among our own creations to try to answer this question.

## 2 Gesture and Meaning

Jeanneret (2000) claims that the simple act of turning the page of a book "does not suppose *a priori* any particular interpretation of the text." However, "in an interactive work clicking on a hyperword or on an icon is, in itself, an act of interpretation" (113). Jeanneret further suggests that the interactive gesture consists above all in "an interpretation realized through a gesture" (121). The distinction that Jeanneret proposes between turning a page and clicking on a hyperlink is not necessarily obvious and could be criticized. We can nevertheless point out that, in an interactive work, the gesture acquires a particular role, which fully contributes to the construction of meaning.

---

[1] "*The term refers to works with important literary aspects that take advantage of the capabilities and contexts provided by the stand-alone or networked computer*" (Electronic Literature Organization, http://www.eliterature.org/about). See also (Rettberg 2019).

© Springer Nature Switzerland AG 2020
A.-G. Bosser et al. (Eds.): ICIDS 2020, LNCS 12497, pp. 221–225, 2020.
https://doi.org/10.1007/978-3-030-62516-0_20

**Fig. 1.** DO IT: the Rock scene.

This is the case in the interactive narrative *DO IT*[2]. This digital creation offers four interactive experiences: adapt, rock, light up and forget. Each scene comes as an answer to contemporary injunctions: being flexible, dynamic and mobile, finding one's way, forgetting in order to move forward. These four scenes are integrated into an interactive narrative. It tells the story of someone who is struggling against the acceleration to time and the injunctions to move always forward, faster and faster. At each stage of the story, the gestures of the user contribute to the construction of meaning. For example, the character has to prove that he/she can be dynamic. The user can then shake the mobile phone - more or less strongly - to shake words and let other words appear – with a more or less negative meaning (see Fig. 1). In this example, we can see that the user's gestural manipulations can fully contribute to the construction of meaning.

## 3   Gesture and Figures of (Gestural) Manipulation

Numerous interactive works of digital literature, notably interactive narratives, do largely call upon what we may call *figures of manipulation*, meaning gestural manipulation (Bouchardon 2014). Since Antiquity, the figures have been a significant part of rhetoric, even though rhetoric should not be reduced to rhetorical figures. Figures are generally divided into four main categories: diction (e.g. alliteration), construction (e.g. chiasmus), meaning (tropes, e.g. metaphor) and thought (e.g. irony). The rhetorical figure is

---

[2] *DO IT* (2016) is an interactive app. freely available on: - Google Play: https://play.google.com/store/apps/details?id=com.tx.agir - App Store: https://appsto.re/cn/WDN8fb.i Video captures of the interactions: https://youtu.be/u6UOq-j_ZJ4.

traditionally defined as a "reasoned change of meaning or of language vis-a-vis the ordinary and simple manner of expressing oneself"[3]. Jean-Marie Klinkenberg (Klinkenberg 2000: 343) defines a rhetorical figure more precisely as "a *dispositif* consisting in the production of implicit meanings, so that the utterance is polyphonic". In interactive and multimedia writing, the polyphonic dimension of the figure also relies on the pluricodal nature of the content.

The *figures of manipulation*, meaning gestural manipulation (Bouchardon 2014), are rhetorical figures specific to interactive writing. It is a category on its own, along with figures of diction, construction, meaning and thought (Bouchardon 2012). Let us illustrate this point with *Loss of Grasp*[4], an online interactive narrative in ten different languages. In this creation, six scenes tell the story of a character who is losing grasp on his life. In the first scene, the reader unfolds the narrative by rolling over the sentences which appear on the screen. Each time a sentence is rolled over, a new sentence is displayed. But after a while, when the sentence "Everything escapes me" appears, the mouse cursor disappears. The reader can keep rolling over each sentence, but without the reference point of the mouse cursor. Through this "non-conventional media coupling" (Bouchardon 2014), the reader experiences loss of grasp with his/her gestures. The second scene stages the meeting of the character with his future wife, 20 years earlier. While the character "ask[s] questions to reveal her", the reader can discover the face of the woman by moving the mouse cursor. These movements leave trails of questions which progressively unveil her face. The questions themselves constitute the portrait of the woman. In the third scene, the character can't seem to understand a note left by his wife: "love poem or break up note?" The reader can experience this double meaning with gestures. If the reader moves the mouse cursor to the top, the text will unfold as a love poem; but if the cursor is moved to the bottom, the order of the lines is reversed and the text turns into a break up note. In the sixth and last scene, the character decides to take control again. A typing window is proposed to the reader, in which he/she can write. But whatever keys he/she types, the following text appears progressively: *I'm doing all I can to get a grip on my life again. I make choices. I control my emotions. The meaning of things. At last, I have a grasp...* Here again, the reader is confronted with a figure which relies on a gap between his/her expectations and the result of his/her manipulations on screen. Thus through his/her gestures and through various figures of manipulation – which could as a matter of fact appear as variations on a *figure of loss of grasp* – the reader experiences the character's *loss of grasp* in an interactive way.

## 4   Discussion

The examples analyzed above raise the question of the gesture and more largely of the engagement of the body in interactive digital literary narratives. Gestural manipulation is certainly inherent in writing and reading devices; however, the Digital results in a *passage to the limit* by introducing computation into the very principle of manipulation

---

[3] Quintilian, *De institutione oratoria*, IX, 1, 11–13.

[4] Bouchardon Serge and Volckaert Vincent (2010). *Loss of Grasp*, http://lossofgrasp.com. Video captures of the interactions: https://youtu.be/nd6_b158qOs. Video presentation: https://youtu.be/6JPUhILHIy0.

(Bachimont 2008). What can happen when the user makes the gesture of typing a letter on the keyboard? Another letter may be displayed instead, or the typed letter may leave the input field and fly away, or that gesture can generate a sound, run a query in a search engine, or even turn the computer off (all these examples are to be found in digital literature)... From this simple gesture, the realm of possibilities exceeds the anticipation inherent in the gesture. Because of the arbitrariness and opacity of computation, the Digital introduces a gap between the user's expectations based on his/her gestures and the realm of possibilities offered.

The Digital makes it possible to defamiliarize the gestural experience inherent to reading and writing, to make it *unfamiliar* and even *strange* again. Defamiliarization is of course the project of many avant-gardes and literary approaches (and more generally, art approaches). But one could argue that there are particularities to the digital mode of defamiliarization. In literature, defamiliarization concerns the linguistic aspect. In digital literature, defamiliarization concerns not only the linguistic dimension, but also the iconic and sound dimensions, as well as the gestural dimension. However, there is one difficulty: as Simanowski rightfully asks, "how can we identify the "unusual" in a realm of expression not yet old enough (and growing too fast) to have established the "common"?" (Simanowski 2010: 16). It is undoubtedly through the question of gesturality that the experience of defamiliarization can be made explicit, insofar as a repertoire of gestures has begun to stabilize with digital devices (PC and tactile devices). In interactive digital literature, the interactive gesture and the interactive gestural manipulation are defamiliarized thanks to the opacity of computation. In this sense, one could speak of a gesturality specific to the Digital, which is particularly well highlighted in interactive digital literary narratives.

The role played by computation, by digital programs and interfaces, must be taken into account to analyze gestural manipulations and to grasp their specificities. Hypothesizing that there is a gesturality specific to the Digital entails the necessity to sensitize and train users to the role of gesture in the construction of the meaning of a digital creation. It is indeed important to understand and analyze the semiotics and the rhetoric specific to these gestural manipulations when teaching digital literacy. Understanding gesturality through digital literary narratives should be part of digital literacy teaching.

## References

Aarseth, E.: Cybertext, Perspective on Ergodic Literature. John Hopkins University Press, Baltimore (1997)

Bachimont, B.: Formal signs and numerical computation: between intuitionism and formalism. critique of computational reason. In: Schramm, H., Schwarte, L., Lazardzig, J. (eds.) Theatrum Scientiarum: Instruments in Art and Science, pp. 362–382. Walter de Gruyter Verlag, Berlin (2008)

Bouchardon, S.: Figures of gestural manipulation in digital fictions. In: Bell, A., Ensslin, A., Rustad, H. (eds.) Analyzing Digital Fiction, pp. 159–175. Routledge, London (2014)

Bouchardon, S.: Digital Manipulability and Digital Literature, Electronic Book Review, August 2012 (2012). ISSN 1553 1139. http://electronicbookreview.com/essay/digital-manipulability-and-digital-literature/

Jeanneret, Y.: Y a-t-il vraiment des technologies de l'information? Editions universitaires du Septentrion, Paris (2000)

Klinkenberg, J.-M.: Précis de sémiotique générale. De Boeck, Brussels (2000)

Rettberg, S.: Electronic Literature. Polity Press, Oxford (2019)

Simanowski, R.: Reading digital literature. In: Simanowski, R., Schäfer, J., Gendolla, P. (eds.) Reading Moving Letters. Digital Literature in Research and Teaching. Transcript, Bielefeld (2010)

# Interactive Narrative Impact
# and Applications

# Capturing User Emotions in Interactive Stories: Comparing a Diegetic and a Non-diegetic Approach to Self-reporting Emotion

Sarah Anne Brown$^{(\boxtimes)}$ ⓘ, Cheryl Resch ⓘ, Vanessa Han ⓘ,
Srividya Vaishnavi Surampudi ⓘ, Pratyusha Karanam,
and Sharon Lynn Chu ⓘ

University of Florida, Gainesville, FL 32611, USA
sarah.brown@ufl.edu

**Abstract.** Capturing the player's emotions in an interactive story can serve many purposes, such as to understand player response to a story or to alter the story's path. The concept of diegesis defines the boundary between the story world and the real world, and has been used to explore different ways of conceptualizing user interface (UI) elements in interactive media. This paper explores methods of capturing players' emotions during an interactive story and the concept of diegesis. Specifically, we posit that whether emotion capture exists in a diegetic versus a non-diegetic space can affect its accuracy when capturing player emotion. We developed two interactive stories with two emotion capture methods, one using a diegetic approach, and the other using a non-diegetic approach. We conducted a study with 64 participants to compare the two emotion capture approaches. Our results show that a diegetic approach leads to a better story experience, but that a non-diegetic approach leads to the player's emotion being captured more accurately. We discuss the implications of the study results for integrating emotion capture in the design of interactive stories.

**Keywords:** Interactive storytelling · Emotion capture · Diegesis

## 1 Introduction

Interactive stories are imbued with unique properties that allow them to leverage the emotions of their audience [25]. The emotional impact of interactive stories has even been wielded as a means to change user behavior [1,3,7,15,26]. Thus, it is useful to capture players' emotions while they are playing interactive stories to be able to, for example, evaluate the effectiveness of the story for changing user behaviors, drive the path of a nonlinear narrative [16,21], or maintain a certain emotional experience intended by the author [10]. Typically, emotion capture approaches rely on either having players self-report their emotions [29] or use

ⓒ Springer Nature Switzerland AG 2020
A.-G. Bosser et al. (Eds.): ICIDS 2020, LNCS 12497, pp. 229–242, 2020.
https://doi.org/10.1007/978-3-030-62516-0_21

physiological methods [8, 16] or other computational methods (e.g., facial expression recognition). However, physiological sensing and computational approaches can be impractical in casual settings due to the additional equipment or constraints required [29]. In our work, we are interested in self-report approaches to the capture of player emotion.

The concept of *diegesis* can be understood as the division between the story world and the world we exist in [14, 20]. Prior research has explored the placement of user interface (UI) elements, such as in-game shop interfaces, in interactive media within the diegetic space [11, 17]. Thus, we propose two ways of capturing emotion in an interactive story using the self-report method, that of the diegetic and the non-diegetic. Interactive stories are experienced both in the diegetic and non-diegetic worlds. In the diegetic world, the player assumes their role as the player-character in the world of the story, while in the non-diegetic space, they exist in their own physical world or environment.

This idea is also supported by the definitions of player and character by Carter et al. [6], where the player is explained as a "persistent, socially performed identity", indicating her existence in the real world; and the character is explained as a "fictional identity within the narrative" or the story world. In other words, we embody the character we control in the world of the story, but still exist in our own identity in the real world outside of the story. The player may feel different emotions depending on whether she adopts the perspective of the embodied character, or her own perspective as an external person responding to the story. For example, a player may feel sad about a specific scenario conveyed by the story (e.g., if the scenario was applied to her own life), but as the character in the story, the player may think that the character should be happy about the scenario given the specific circumstances of the story, the character's described personality, values, history, etc.

In our research, we are interested to capture the emotions of players as they exist in the real world in response to them playing the interactive story. We conducted a study that investigated how well a diegetic self-report UI (henceforth shortened to DEC method for 'diegetic emotion capture') compared to a non-diegetic UI (henceforth shortened to NDEC method) can capture player emotion. We also investigated the differences in story experience between the two emotion capture methods proposed. Our results contribute to a new understanding of capturing emotion across the diegetic space in interactive stories, which to the best of the authors' knowledge has not been explored previously. The specific research questions for our study were:

**RQ1:** *Is there a significant difference between how accurately players self-report their emotions while engaged in an interactive story using a diegetic approach as opposed to a non-diegetic approach?*; and
**RQ2:** *How differently do players experience an interactive story when emotion is captured using a diegetic approach versus a non-diegetic approach?*

# 2 Background and Related Work

## 2.1 Emotion Capture in Interactive Storytelling

In his review, Zhao [30] delineated three primary ways in which emotion is captured for use in interactive stories, citing the research of Yannakakis and Togelius [29]: subjective (emotion is reported by the player), objective (emotion is captured through physiological means), and game-based (emotion is inferred through interaction). Similar to the subjective approach, we primarily explore the use of a selection made by the players themselves during the story.

In related literature on the capturing of emotion in video games, the focus has primarily been on objective, or physiological sensing [2,5,9], though some have explored the previously mentioned game-based approach [18]. Yannakakis and Togelius also comment on the issues of using physiological sensing, noting the hardware can be intrusive and not always practical for use [29]. A review of 15 articles investigating physiological sensing in video games brings to light certain limitations in the scope of emotion captured by prior research [5]. The kinds of emotions captured by these papers were primarily stress, anxiety, fear, and arousal. This is understandable, given that many of the games used as stimulus in these studies lacked a narrative and were more action-oriented (Tetris, Guitar Hero, racing games), or were games specifically designed to instigate high-arousal emotions (horror games). Though there is plenty of work investigating how the player's emotion may be used to influence the dynamic adaptation of interactive stories [8,10,16,21], there seems to be scarce literature investigating the capture of emotion *for* interactive stories (i.e., how players respond to the story). For instance, emotions in an interactive story meant to induce more subjective or complex emotions such as nostalgia, anticipation, or joy may be better captured through a subjective measure in which the player self-reports their emotion, than via physiological sensing.

## 2.2 Diegesis and Diegetic UI

An earlier definition of diegesis by Gérard Genette in 1969 defined diegesis as the "spatiotemporal universe" of the story [4]. This concept has long been applied to film theory to differentiate between the narrative and elements of the film which are "only available to the audience", such as the musical score or titles [19]. A simple way to understand diegesis in interactive stories is to picture it as the difference between the world of the story and the reality we exist in [20]. Indeed, diegesis defines the boundary between which the story world ends and the 'real' world begins [14]. In the study of interactive media, there has long been discussion of whether elements exist in the story world, or diegetic space; the real world, or non-diegetic space; or perhaps blur the lines between the two [13,14]. The idea of diegetic user interfaces has been increasingly explored, particularly with regards to video games [11,17,27]. A key consideration when it comes to diegetic and non-diegetic elements in this realm is that while diegetic elements serve better to engage the player in the story, non-diegetic elements provide useful, and often necessary information that aid in gameplay [11]. The focus thus far has been on the impact of diegetic UI on immersion, with current research indicating that removing non-diegetic elements increases the player's experienced immersion [11,17,27]. Elements that have been explored include in-game shop interfaces [17] and the heads-up display (or HUD, which can include displays for player life, score, and menu icons) [11,19]. With regards to the HUD, it has even been proposed that instead of removing the HUD entirely, due to the useful information it provides, it could be implemented through augmented reality to increase immersion for these typically non-diegetic features [27].

In a discussion of emotions with respect to diegesis, different conceptualizations of the player also become relevant. The definitions of player and player-character, such as those presented by Carter et al. [6], seem to indicate a separation of the two across diegetic space. The player is the individual in their own reality experiencing the interactive story or game, whereas the player-character is that same individual embodying a persona within the story world. It is unclear whether the player therefore exists solely in the non-diegetic space and the player-character in the diegetic space, or if the relationship suggests a blurring of the player between the two as the player navigates two realities at once. Character identification could be an influencing factor of this experience, which Van Looy defines as consisting of the degrees to which "the player desires to be more like their avatar", "the player sees their avatar as similar to themselves", and "the player feels as if they *are* the avatar when playing the game" [28]. Schneider et al.'s work suggests that the simple presence of a story in a game increases identification between the player and character [23]. It is important to consider that the player experiences the story both as themselves and as the player-character when designing subjective emotion capture methods, as the emotion reported may be influenced by the emotions of the player-character. The question is whether the distinct embodiments of experiencing emotions can be disentangled.

## 3    System Description

### 3.1    Interactive Story Designs

To investigate the effects of a diegetic approach to emotion capture as opposed to a non-diegetic approach and to answer our research questions listed in the Introduction, we designed two interactive stories. Our interactive stories were built through the online survey platform Qualtrics. The stories were both about a stressful semester and final exam of a college student, explored through vignettes drawn from some of the researchers' own experiences. The theme was chosen specifically for an audience of college students, given that we recruited participants from an undergraduate computer science course for our study. We chose to align the theme to the sample population to ensure that the stories written have a greater chance of resonating emotionally with our participants, and for participants to identify with the characters in these stories. The basic plot points the stories covered were:

1. It's the start of the semester and the character is enrolled in several courses.
2. The character looks up their professor's rating online and it looks bad.
3. As the semester goes on, the character is missing classes and assignments, causing worry for their grade.
4. The character goes to their professor's office hours.
5. The character is invited to go for a night out on the town.
6. A week later, the character ends up sick with the flu.
7. The character reaches out to classmates and starts a study group.
8. The final exam is soon, so the character starts pulling all-nighters to prepare.
9. On the day of the exam, the character's alarm does not go off.
10. The character makes it to the exam room and struggles with their laptop not being charged and phone going off while taking the exam.
11. The character finishes the exam, tired but hopeful for future semesters.

The two stories were made to be comparable in the sense that in either story, at any given scene, the same events and general reactions are covered. In one story, the main character's name was Taylor, and in the other, the name was Ash.

To serve as an example of how these stories were unique but still comparable for the purposes of the study, one chapter of Ash's story was: *Okay, so the plan is to go to the first class and pass judgement then. And, as it turned out, the professor actually seems pretty friendly and willing to work with students... But partway through the semester, a few weeks later, it dawns on me that I've been missing class left and right, not turning in assignments, not keeping up with the coursework. I'm starting to get anxious for my grade.*

For Taylor's story, the corresponding chapter was written as: *I'll pay really close attention to the first class and see what it's going to be like for myself. The professor doesn't actually seem that bad... As the semester goes on, I realize I've been missing a lot of classes, and forgetting to turn in assignments on time. There's an anxious pit in my stomach. Things aren't looking great...*

In both stories, we chose a gender neutral name and did not specify the characters' gender at any given point, to prevent gender bias from affecting character identification. The characters also did not have a visual avatar, but were only portrayed textually through descriptions of their thoughts and experiences. The stories used a text-based choose-your-own-adventure format, where each scene presented consisted of text describing the scene, and then four player options for how to proceed (see Fig. 1 for a mockup of both emotion capture approaches, as well as a screenshot of the interface). It should be noted, that while the story took on the appearance of a branching narrative from a player's perspective, every story choice in a given chapter led to the same following chapter.

## 3.2 Capturing Player Emotions In-Game

Given our focus on a self-report method, the emotion capture method took the form of choices the player would make themselves throughout the interactive

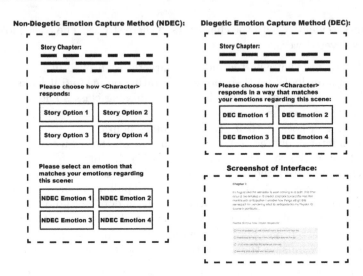

**Fig. 1.** A mockup of our interface, showing a story scene that implements the NDEC method (left), the DEC method (right), and a screenshot of our interface (below).

story. In both the DEC and NDEC, we made it clear to participants to make their choice according to their own emotions. Each story chapter page emphasized the following note: *"Note that by 'you', we mean you as in the person you are every day, existing in the world outside of this story"*. This note was adapted from the definition of the player found in Carter et al. [6].

We extracted the emotion options for the capture of player emotion while playing an interactive story from the Differential Emotions Scale (DES) [24]. This scale was selected for its variety of discrete emotions that suited our purpose of capturing emotion subjectively. However, we only considered 4 core emotions from the DES: enjoyment, sadness, anger, and surprise, that were presented as forced-choice options to the player. The reason for not providing all 10 emotions measured by the DES is that we administer the scale itself to capture baseline emotion (see Sect. 3.3), and answering the full scale for all 10 emotions *during* engagement in the story would become unwieldy. The emotion options question was also accompanied by a likert scale question, asking participants to rate how much the emotion option that they selected matched their emotions regarding the story scene, on a continuous scale of 1 (not at all) to 5 (a lot) (input through a slider that allowed for decimal values). We used this value later in our analysis to calculate the 'strength' of the player's indicated emotion. Depending on the emotion capture approach (diegetic or non-diegetic), the 4 focus DES emotions were conveyed as options differently. Visual outlines of how the emotions were presented in each approach can be found in Fig. 1, and are described below.

**In the DEC Method,** the emotion options are embedded in action options to allow the story to progress. Thus, we placed the emotion capture within the story context itself for our diegetic approach. For example, the 'Anger' emotion option embedded with a story option in the third chapter of the stories is: *"This is not my fault, the TA's won't accept my excuses!"* Here, players are choosing an option that both reflects their own emotions as they play through the story, while simultaneously choosing how the character responds to the story scene. By embedding emotions in story choices, a certain degree of subjectivity in how those emotions are perceived in the prose of the story choice arises. To validate that our emotion-embedded story choices reflected the correct emotions, we ran a pre-study with 7 participants. Participants were recruited via word-of-mouth, and included 5 females and 2 males, with 3 between the ages of 18–24 years old, 3 between 25–39, and 1 between 40–60 years old. Participants were asked to sort the 4 options for each story scene into categories representing each of the 4 emotion words. This took the form of essentially a place mat with a box for 'Happy', 'Sad', 'Anger', and 'Surprise', into which cut-outs of the prompts were sorted by set of 4 per story chapter. An emotion-embedded story prompt was judged as successfully reflecting the desired emotion if 70% of participants identified the emotion correctly. Twenty-eight of the 40 emotion prompts were identified accurately by 100% of the participants, 10 by 85.7%, and 2 by 71.4%. We proceeded with this set of emotion-embedded choices for the DEC method.

**In the NDEC Method,** the emotions are provided as separate choices from story options, thus existing outside of the story for the non-diegetic approach. The story options were written to be outlook-based, based on how the character looked toward their future, and not associated with any particular emotion. An example of one of the non-diegetic story choices is *"I think if I spend my energy wisely now and do good work during this all nighter, I'll be able to improve my grade."* Separately from their story choice, players would choose an emotion option from the emotion keywords of 'Enjoyment', 'Anger', 'Sadness', or 'Surprise' to indicate their own emotions.

### 3.3   Capturing Baseline Player Emotions

In order to measure how accurate either emotion capture method is, an appropriate baseline of the actual emotion experienced by the player is needed. Baseline emotion for the player and player-character was captured using the Differential Emotions Scale (or DES) [24]. The DES consists of 3 emotion keywords each for a total of 10 emotions. Given that our emotion capture methods only captured 4 core emotions (see Sect. 3.2), we administered the DES with only the 12 emotion keywords associated with those 4 emotions: Enjoyment, Anger, Surprise, and Sadness. Like the 'strength' value, the DES scale to capture the baseline emotion of the player was also provided on a continuous scale of 1 (not at all) to 5 (a lot), with a slider that allowed for decimal values.

   Baseline emotion was captured for both the player's and the player-character's emotion. On the questionnaires which administered baseline emotion, notes were used to explain the difference between the player's and the player-character's emotion, which were adapted from definitions of player and character found in Carter et al. [6]. For the interactive stories, we did not capture emotion baseline at every story chapter, instead choosing 3 which were evenly spaced to be representative of the story's beginning, middle, and end (Chaps. 2, 6, and 10). This was to prevent the study protocol from becoming cumbersome for participants.

# 4    Study Description

## 4.1    Study Design

The study used a within-subjects design, with 'emotion capture approach' as the single independent variable. Emotion capture approach had two levels: diegetic emotion capture (DEC) and non-diegetic emotion capture (NDEC). Thus, participants played through two different but comparable interactive stories, one of which utilized a DEC method, and the other, a NDEC method. The order of the two stories and the order of the two capture methods were both counterbalanced, for a total of 4 possible condition orders spread across the participant sample.

**RQ1 Measures.** For our first research question which investigates how well each emotion capture approach is able to capture players' emotions during the course of an interactive story, we operationalized 'player emotion' as either the player's emotion as an external user (*em-player*), or the player's emotion as the story character (*em-char*). For the former, we measured the extent to which emotions players indicated during the story (*em-dur*) match with emotions they indicated on the baseline DES scale answering as themselves (*em-base-player*). For the latter, we measured how much *em-dur* matches with emotions player indicated on the baseline DES scale answering as the player character (*em-base-char*).

**RQ2 Measures.** For our second research question, which investigates differences in story experience between the two emotion capture approaches, the following measures were taken: **overall experience** was assessed by administering the Game Experience Questionnaire (GEQ) [12] at the end of each story, with the items adapted slightly to accommodate an interactive story instead of a video game (that the questionnaire was initially designed to assess). The GEQ contains 7 subconstructs: competence, sensory and imaginative immersion, flow, tension/annoyance, challenge, negative affect, and positive affect. At the end of each story, we also measured **character identification**, with the scale from Van Looy et al. [28]. Only items for the avatar identification construct were used, as the other constructs (game identification and group identification) did not apply to an interactive story of the type used in the study. For three story chapters in either story, we also measured **relatedness to story event** via the following single question: *"How much can you relate to this event from your own experiences?"* This question was on a scale of 1 (not at all) to 5 (a lot).

We also included comparison questions after both stories had been played through. These questions asked participants to compare the DEC method and the NDEC method on different aspects. For each question, participants had to score each emotion capture approach on a scale of 1 (not at all) to 5 (extremely), followed by answering an open response question to explain their scores. The comparison questions were as follows: *How easy did you find... 1) it to make the decision of how Taylor/Ash would respond in either story?; 2) it to choose your emotion in either story?; and 3) each story in terms of your ability to go through the story feeling immersed and fully involved in the story as a whole?*

## 4.2 Participants and Protocol

We recruited our participants from an undergraduate computer science course through a participant pool system. Participants were provided with extra course credit in exchange for their participation in our study. We had a total of 64 participants, 50 male and 14 female. Participant ages ranged from 18 to 24 years (62 participants) and 25–39 years (2 participants). Demographics included 27 participants identifying as White, 15 as Hispanic or Latino, 3 as Black or African American, 17 as Asian or Pacific Islander, and 2 as other.

The study was conducted entirely online. Participants experienced our stories and questionnaires via the Qualtrics survey platform. Upon signing up for the study, they were provided with a link that automatically sorted them into one of our 4 study condition orders. The Qualtrics questionnaire guided the participants through the steps shown in Fig. 2. Our protocol for the individual stories is shown in the expanded portion of Fig. 2.

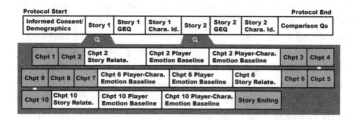

**Fig. 2.** A diagram of our study protocol

# 5 Data Analysis and Results

## 5.1 RQ1: Accuracy of Captured Player Emotion

We calculated the accuracy of the captured emotion to participants' emotions as the player (*em-player*) and to participants' emotions as the player-character (*em-char*) as the difference between the captured emotion's 'strength' and the average score of the keywords for that emotion on the baseline DES that participants filled at the end of 3 chapters. Accuracy scores for the 3 story chapters were averaged for each emotion capture approach to obtain a single accuracy score for *em-player* and a single score for *em-char*, for each study condition. Before averaging, we ensured that there were no significant differences among the 3 plot points for both *em-player* and *em-char*. Friedman tests were ran on the accuracy scores with plot point as independent variable for each condition. No significant differences were found, indicating that the plot points were comparable. Thus, the final accuracy score for *em-player* for each condition was calculated as *((chapter2(em-dur - em-base-player) + (chapter6(em-dur - em-base-player) + (chapter10(em-dur - em-base-player))/3*. The final accuracy score for *em-char* was calculated similarly, with *em-base-player* instead of *em-base-char*.

Much of our data was not normally-distributed as assessed via the Shapiro-Wilk test, so non-parametric tests were used to compare the study conditions. A Wilcoxon signed-rank test was ran on the final accuracy scores for *em-player* and *em-char* with emotion capture method as independent variable. A statistically significant difference between the 2 emotion capture methods was found for both *em-player* ($Z = -4.220$, $p = 0.000$) and *em-char* ($Z = -4.561$, $p = 0.000$). For *em-player*, the NDEC method had a lower mean ($M = 0.705$; $SD = 0.985$), indicating higher accuracy with respect to the player emotion, than the DEC method ($M = 1.442$; $SD = 0.961$). Note that smaller scores reflect greater accuracy. For *em-char*, the NDEC method showed the lower mean as well ($M = 0.318$; $SD = 1.068$), compared to the DEC method ($M = 1.238$; $SD = 0.930$).

## 5.2   RQ2: Story Experience

Friedman tests were conducted on story relatedness scores across the 3 plot points, separated by condition, to ensure that the plot points were comparable enough to be averaged together. No significant difference was found. We averaged story relatedness scores for the 3 plot points for our final analysis.

Wilcoxon signed-rank tests were conducted to compare the two approaches in terms of all aforementioned story experience measures. Only measures that showed significant differences between the two emotion capture methods are reported below. Significant differences between our two emotion capture methods were found for the **'negative affect'** subconstruct of the GEQ ($Z = -2.180$, $p = 0.029$); **ease of choosing action**, as measured by our first comparison question ($Z = -2.018$, $p = 0.044$); and **ease of feeling immersed**, as measured by our third comparison question ($Z = -2.428$, $p = 0.015$). For negative affect, the NDEC method had the higher mean ($M = 2.635$; $SD = 1.002$) than the DEC method ($M = 2.437$; $SD = 1.028$). For ease of choosing action, the DEC had the higher mean ($M = 3.453$; $SD = 1.208$), compared to the NDEC ($M = 3.047$; $SD = 1.174$). For ease of feeling immersed, the DEC had the higher mean ($M = 3.063$; $SD = 1.296$), compared to the NDEC ($M = 2.688$; $SD = 1.194$).

## 5.3   Comparison Questions

To analyze the open-ended responses from the questions asking participants to compare the DEC and the NDEC methods, the qualitative coding process as specified by Saldana [22] was followed. One coder did two cycles of coding on all the responses, first assigning descriptive codes, and then assigning categorical codes from the descriptive codes. Based on the categorical codes, the coder developed an initial coding scheme. Three other coders used the initial coding scheme to independently do 3 coding passes on the responses. Discussions were held among all the 4 coders after each coding pass. Amendments were done to the coding scheme during each discussion, and the coders used the revised scheme each time for their next coding pass. The final intercoder agreements established were 71.7% for comparison question 1, 82.4% for question 2, and 70.0% for question 3. An intercoder agreement level of 70% is typically deemed acceptable. The final coding scheme can be found in Table 1, with the percentage frequency of occurrence of each code. We note that in our coding, one participant response could contain multiple codes. The frequency percentages are shown organized into whether the response indicated a preference for the NDEC method, the DEC method, or the same for both methods.

**Table 1.** Our final coding scheme for the comparison question responses, broken down by approach preference. (no. of code occurrences/total no. of code occurrences, in %'s).

| Code | NDEC | DEC | Same |
|---|---|---|---|
| Difficulty of decoupling emotion from action | 1.46 | 6.34 | 0.00 |
| Difficulty of decoupling own emotion from chara.'s | 3.41 | 8.78 | 0.49 |
| Relation to stories/characters | 4.88 | 4.88 | 11.22 |
| Quality of story | 0.98 | 1.95 | 9.76 |
| Identification of own emotion | 0.49 | 4.39 | 0.98 |
| Degree of immersion | 0.00 | 2.93 | 0.49 |
| Relation to story options | 3.41 | 1.46 | 1.95 |
| Non-relevant/-decipherable | 5.37 | 9.76 | 14.63 |

## 6    Discussion

Our results showed that the NDEC method is significantly more accurate at capturing player emotion than the DEC (RQ1). We attribute this to the fact that while the NDEC method explicitly asks for player emotion via simple emotion words, the DEC method blurs the story world and the real world in terms of player emotions. Our other results however, indicate that this does not mean the NDEC method is inherently superior to the DEC method for emotion capture. In terms of story experience, we saw that the NDEC scored higher in terms of negative affect, and the DEC condition scored higher in terms of ease of choosing action and ease of feeling immersed. Additionally, in our qualitative responses, the category code 'Degree of immersion' in Table 1, only showed in responses where the DEC condition was rated higher (and thus, more preferred) than the NDEC. These results are in line with prior research (e.g., [11,17,27]) that showed diegetic UI elements result in higher immersion. Our work thus confirms that the same can be concluded for emotion capture in interactive stories.

However, our study results further showed that while playing through an interactive story, irrespective of emotion capture approach, participants more accurately report the emotions of the player-character than their own emotion. In both the DEC and the NDEC conditions, the accuracy scores calculated were smaller for the player-character than that of the player. This was unexpected, as the emotion capture methods explicitly requested the player's emotion, not the player-character's. This finding is supported by the large frequency of responses addressing the difficulty of participants to decouple their own emotion from character emotion. One example of such responses illustrating the decoupling difficulty is: *"It is natural to have an emotion to scenarios you are put into. It is not so easy to separate your own emotions from those of a character and think about how they might/should react"*. This finding suggests that capturing emotion via a self-report method within an interactive story can lead to a better capture of player-character emotion than the emotions of the player.

In summary thus, the implications of our study results for player emotion capture within the design of interactive stories are that approaches have to be found that integrate the accuracy of capture of non-diegetic UI without compromising the player's story experience. For example, one approach may be to make the prompt for the story choice directly address the player by breaking the fourth wall (e.g., 'What do **you** want to do?'). This may make the prompt to self report the player's own emotion as they exist in their own reality less jarring, and prevent a break in immersion, while maintaining the accuracy of the emotion capture method. Another approach may be to ensure that the player identifies fully with the player character prior to engagement in the interactive story. If it can be assumed that the player's emotions will be the same or very similar to the player character's, then using a diegetic UI to capture player emotion will be accurate. Such an approach may also help to resolve the problem that players tend to better convey their perceived player-character emotions (instead of their own emotions), irrespective of the type of UI used.

## 7   Conclusion

We conducted an investigation of two means of self-reporting emotion in interactive stories: a non-diegetic emotion capture (NDEC) method and a diegetic emotion capture (DEC) method. Our results showed while that the NDEC method resulted in higher accuracy to player emotion, the DEC provided a better story experience for participants. We also found that via either method, emotion capture using a self-report means was more accurate to player-character emotion than player emotion. We contribute an understanding of self-report emotion capture as a diegetic user interface element, backed by empirical evidence, and suggest that future work should seek hybrid methods, blurring the lines of diegesis to mitigate some of the effects observed. Limitations of our work include that our interactive stories were simple in nature and solely text-based, and the fact that our stories were designed specifically for a college student population. Additionally, as this was an online study, we had no way to ensure participants paid full attention while taking part in our study.

**Acknowledgements.** This research was supported by NSF Grant #1736225, *To Enact, To Tell, To Write: A Bridge to Expressive Writing through Digital Enactment.*

# References

1. Amresh, A., Sinha, M., Birr, R., Salla, R.: Interactive cause and effect comic-book storytelling for improving nutrition outcomes in children. In: Proceedings of the 5th International Conference on Digital Health 2015, pp. 9–14 (2015)
2. Bateman, C., Nacke, L.E.: The neurobiology of play. In: Proceedings of the International Academic Conference on the Future of Game Design and Technology, pp. 1–8 (2010)
3. Bratitsis, T.: A digital storytelling approach for fostering empathy towards autistic children: lessons learned. In: Proceedings of the 7th International Conference on Software Development and Technologies for Enhancing Accessibility and Fighting Info-exclusion, pp. 301–308 (2016)
4. Bunia, R.: Diegesis and representation: beyond the fictional world, on the margins of story and narrative. Poetics Today **31**(4), 679–720 (2010)
5. Callejas-Cuervo, M., Martínez-Tejada, L.A., Alarcón-Aldana, A.C.: Emotion recognition techniques using physiological signals and video games-systematic review. Rev. Fac. de Ingeniería **26**(46), 19–28 (2017)
6. Carter, M., Gibbs, M., Arnold, M.: Avatars, characters, players and users: multiple identities at/in play. In: Proceedings of the 24th Australian Computer-Human Interaction Conference, pp. 68–71 (2012)
7. Chauveau, L.A., Szilas, N., Luiu, A.L., Ehrler, F.: Dimensions of personalization in a narrative pedagogical simulation for alzheimer's caregivers. In: 2018 IEEE 6th International Conference on Serious Games and Applications for Health (SeGAH), pp. 1–8. IEEE (2018)
8. Gilroy, S., Porteous, J., Charles, F., Cavazza, M.: Exploring passive user interaction for adaptive narratives. In: Proceedings of the 2012 ACM International Conference on Intelligent User Interfaces, pp. 119–128 (2012)
9. Granato, M., Gadia, D., Maggiorini, D., Ripamonti, L.A.: Feature extraction and selection for real-time emotion recognition in video games players. In: 2018 14th International Conference on Signal-Image Technology & Internet-Based Systems (SITIS), pp. 717–724. IEEE (2018)
10. Hernandez, S.P., Bulitko, V., Hilaire, E.S.: Emotion-based interactive storytelling with artificial intelligence. In: Tenth Artificial Intelligence and Interactive Digital Entertainment Conference (2014)
11. Iacovides, I., Cox, A., Kennedy, R., Cairns, P., Jennett, C.: Removing the HUD: the impact of non-diegetic game elements and expertise on player involvement. In: Proceedings of the 2015 Annual Symposium on Computer-Human Interaction in Play, pp. 13–22 (2015)
12. IJsselsteijn, W.A., de Kort, Y.A., Poels, K.: The game experience questionnaire. Eindhoven: Technische Universiteit Eindhoven, pp. 3–9 (2013)

13. Jørgensen, K.: Between the game system and the fictional world: a study of computer game interfaces. Games Cult. **7**(2), 142–163 (2012)
14. Kleinman, E., Carstensdottir, E., Seif El-Nasr, M.: A model for analyzing diegesis in digital narrative games. In: Cardona-Rivera, R.E., Sullivan, A., Young, R.M. (eds.) ICIDS 2019. LNCS, vol. 11869, pp. 8–21. Springer, Cham (2019). https://doi.org/10.1007/978-3-030-33894-7_2
15. Melcer, E.F., et al.: Teaching responsible conduct of research through an interactive storytelling game. In: Extended Abstracts of the 2020 CHI Conference on Human Factors in Computing Systems, pp. 1–10 (2020)
16. Nogueira, P.A., Rodrigues, R., Oliveira, E., Nacke, L.E.: Guided emotional state regulation: understanding and shaping players' affective experiences in digital games. In: Ninth Artificial Intelligence and Interactive Digital Entertainment Conference (2013)
17. Ogier, H., Buchan, J.: Exploring the feasibility of diegetic in-game store user interfaces. In: Proceedings of the Australasian Computer Science Week Multiconference, pp. 1–10 (2017)
18. Pedersen, C., Togelius, J., Yannakakis, G.N.: Modeling player experience for content creation. IEEE Trans. Comput. Intell. AI Games **2**(1), 54–67 (2010)
19. Pfister, L., Ghellal, S.: Exploring the influence of non-diegetic and diegetic elements on the immersion of 2D games. In: Proceedings of the 30th Australian Conference on Computer-Human Interaction, pp. 490–494 (2018)
20. Prestopnik, N.R., Tang, J.: Points, stories, worlds, and diegesis: comparing player experiences in two citizen science games. Comput. Hum. Behav. **52**, 492–506 (2015)
21. Roberts, D.L., Narayanan, H., Isbell, C.L.: Learning to influence emotional responses for interactive storytelling. In: AAAI Spring Symposium: Intelligent Narrative Technologies II, pp. 95–102 (2009)
22. Saldaña, J.: The Coding Manual for Qualitative Researchers. Sage, California (2015)
23. Schneider, E.F., Lang, A., Shin, M., Bradley, S.D.: Death with a story: how story impacts emotional, motivational, and physiological responses to first-person shooter video games. Hum. Commun. Res. **30**(3), 361–375 (2004)
24. Shantz, C., et al.: Measuring Emotions in Infants and Children. Cambridge University Press, United Kingdom (1982)
25. Stapleton, C., Hughes, C.: Interactive imagination: tapping the emotions through interactive story for compelling simulations. IEEE Comput. Graph. Appl. **23**(5), 11–15 (2003)
26. Szilas, N., Richle, U., Boggini, T., Dumas, J.: Using highly interactive drama to help young people cope with traumatic situations. In: Aylett, R., Lim, M.Y., Louchart, S., Petta, P., Riedl, M. (eds.) ICIDS 2010. LNCS, vol. 6432, pp. 279–282. Springer, Heidelberg (2010). https://doi.org/10.1007/978-3-642-16638-9_42
27. Taylor, M.: Augmenting the HUD: a mixed methods analysis on the impact of extending the game UI beyond the screen (2017)
28. Van Looy, J., Courtois, C., De Vocht, M., De Marez, L.: Player identification in online games: validation of a scale for measuring identification in mmogs. Media Psychol. **15**(2), 197–221 (2012)
29. Yannakakis, G.N., Togelius, J.: Experience-driven procedural content generation. IEEE Trans. Affect. Comput. **2**(3), 147–161 (2011)
30. Zhao, H.: Emotion in interactive storytelling. In: FDG, pp. 183–189 (2013)

# Interpretive Play and the Player Psychology of Optimal Arousal Regulation

Matthew Higgins$^{(\boxtimes)}$ (iD) and Peter Howell (iD)

University of Portsmouth, Portsmouth, UK
{Matthew.Higgins,Peter.Howell}@port.ac.uk

**Abstract.** Building on previous discussions of interpretive play in story-focused digital games, a psychological foundation of narrative interpretation is proposed. First, how narrative information is synthesized with prior experiences and expectations into 'situation models' in long-term memory. Second, how pleasure is derived from increased arousal through engaging with novel, unfamiliar stimuli. This psychological foundation is then compared to contemporary approaches to narrative design, particularly in *Her Story* and *Dear Esther*. The relevance of the proposed cognitive psychological foundation is also considered in regard to digital games with no documented intentional use psychologically, primarily through an analysis of player behaviour and response in *Gone Home*. Results are comparable to the psychological model, particularly the prominent roles of recalling and forming expectations, and how player attention is often attracted to novel, unfamiliar, or unexpected stimuli. The ongoing aim of this work is to further investigate interpretive play in the context of digital games and continue to develop the cognitive psychological foundation. Future work shall also contextualise the research and findings though the development of commercial games.

**Keywords:** Interpretive play · Arousal regulation · Digital games · Narrative · Cognitive psychology · Schema

## 1 Introduction

The concept of *interpretive play* has been discussed previously in the context of digital games, with various perspectives on how the interpretation of a narrative specifically can be considered a form of play. Upton [1] argues that whilst story games possess a "vacuity of their moment-to-moment play", this is overshadowed by a "compensatory complexity" in the "interpretive play" spaces that they construct, broadly suggesting that the interpretation of narrative can be considered a form of play in itself. More recently, Bozdog and Galloway [2] adopt this perspective in an analysis of how *What Remains of Edith Finch* [3] supports interpretive play through slowness, ambiguity, narrative, and aesthetic aspirations.

Previous work has explored psychological foundations of interpretive play. For example, Boyd [4] pays particular attention to the evolutionary purpose of play as a form of practice and training and argues that engagement with art more broadly is a form of cognitive play.

© Springer Nature Switzerland AG 2020
A.-G. Bosser et al. (Eds.): ICIDS 2020, LNCS 12497, pp. 243–257, 2020.
https://doi.org/10.1007/978-3-030-62516-0_22

Further exploration of the psychology of interpretive play is warranted. A detailed psychological foundation will aid in discerning methods via which game designers can facilitate interpretation as a form of play in their games to enhance the player experience. This paper suggests that the cognitive processing of narrative stimuli may be considered a playful activity, particularly when sought out as a source of increased arousal and enjoyment. Two key psychological aspects are considered: first, the processing of narrative stimuli into mental models in long-term memory; second, the cognitive process through which pleasure is gained by reaching and maintaining an optimal state of arousal. A theoretical model of optimal arousal regulation in interpretive play is presented and applied to a discussion of contemporary approaches to storytelling in digital games, specifically in *Dear Esther* [5] and *Her Story* [6]. This discussion is then further contextualized in a thematic analysis of a stimulated recall study of players of *Gone Home* [7]. This analysis further demonstrates the applicability of the theoretical model in a digital game without the explicit psychologically inspired design intent that both *Dear Esther's* and *Her Story's* creators describe.

## 2   The Cognitive Psychology of Narrative Interpretation

Cognitive processing can be more broadly understood as the coordination and management of stimuli through working memory [8] which interfaces with long-term memory to organize and store information for subsequent retrieval. How stimuli are organized and stored in long-term memory and recalled by working memory is of particular relevance to narrative processing.

Schema theory proposes that long-term memory is an associative structure of clusters of familiar and relevant memories and knowledge specific to particular phenomena [9, 10]. This associative structure affords quicker processing of relevant concepts and the formation of expectations of potentially relevant stimuli.

Psychological studies of narrative demonstrate the use of schema when participants interpret and retell a narrative [11–13], with individual interpretations varying due to sociocultural differences between participants. Retellings of the 'War of the Ghosts' narrative in Bartlett's study for example, found that these interpretations aligned more with the participant's individual sociocultural backgrounds, with a Native American story structure being retold through a more typically English lens. Schemas differ between individuals and are influenced by various factors, including prior experience of the stimuli or situation, and sociocultural background. When playing games, it is likely that individuals have specific schema for different media, genres, or franchises, as outlined in Howell's [14, 15] discussion of ludic cognition and methods of disrupting recall of schemas in horror games (specifically, in the development of *Amnesia: A Machine for Pigs* [16]). Interpreting narrative involves the similar activation in long-term memory of relevant experiences and expectations of narrative (e.g. genre, medium, or common story structures) [17] which then help in forming understanding and expectations of the current narrative via working memory.

The understanding of a narrative, and any associated expectations, are considered to be stored in long-term memory in the form of situation models [18, 19], which can be understood in this context as narrative-dedicated schema. A situation model is a synthesis of the meaning inferred from the text (i.e. the game) and an individual's relevant schema in long-term memory. Situation models can contain a large amount of complex data, such as information regarding the speaker or narrator, character intentions, relationships, opinions, and emotions. Zwaan et al. [20] propose several categories of information that an individual's situation model may contain, described as five 'event indices': temporality, spatiality, protagonist, causality, and intentionality. Zwaan et al. argue that each of these indices are monitored and updated when any change, or discontinuity, occurs. For example, if a significant shift in time occurs, the temporality index of the situation model is replaced either with an existing, more relevant index or with a newly constructed index. Zwaan et al. suggest that effort of comprehension positively correlates with discontinuity and consequent updating of event indices.

Situation models may be updated via an incremental process, with new information being gradually implemented. Zacks et al. [21, 22] argue that if a situation changes entirely, such as between scenes in a film, or chapters in a book (which they term 'event boundaries'), then the existing model may instead be replaced by a prior model, or with a newly constructed situation model. This 'global updating' is also suggested to be involved in the prediction of future events, or if significant information is introduced that requires a large portion of a narrative, or multiple event indices, to be reconsidered – for example, a narrative twist. Further research on event boundaries also suggests that situation models are more regularly updated at event boundaries [23], at the start and end of events. This also suggests that individuals switch to relevant situation models depending on the current state of a narrative. For example, the many characters and storylines in *Detroit: Become Human* [24] that the player experiences will involve a situation model for events occurring in Connor's storyline and another for events occurring in Kara's. The player must switch between situation models as they switch between storylines in different chapters; as storylines merge later in the game, the player must also construct new situation models through combining relevant aspects of prior models.

## 3 The Pleasure of Narrative Interpretation

Various psychological theories discuss how humans can derive pleasure from cognitively engaging activities and suggest that individuals seek out novel, unfamiliar stimuli. There is a distinction between the pleasure experienced from this form of engagement as compared to pleasure experienced as a direct physiological response. For example, Oatley's taxonomy of emotional literary response [25] suggests responses from the 'external', where the reader 'confronts' the text to discern meaning (affect from assimilation and accommodation to schema), and 'internal', where the reader 'enters the world of the text' (affect through sympathy, empathy, or emotional memories triggered by the text). Csikszentmihalyi [26] makes a similar comparison between pleasure and 'enjoyment', the pleasure derived from more effortful activity, such as playing a game of tennis or reading a book. Oliver and Bartsch [27] similarly propose the distinction between 'enjoyment', being the immediate affective response to media, such as humour from comedy or fear from a thriller, and 'appreciation' as the cognitive response, associated with meaningful and thought-provoking media experiences. In the current discussion, interpretation as a means of deriving pleasure from a narrative aligns principally with 'appreciation' or Csikszentmihalyi's 'enjoyment'.

Focusing on the pleasure derived from cognition, the 'need for cognition' describes a tendency to engage in and enjoy thinking, with "a need to structure relevant situations in meaningful, integrated ways" and "a need to understand and make reasonable the experiential world" [28]. Furthermore, some individuals have a greater tendency to enjoy cognitive effort. For example, in a study in which participants identified as high or low in the Need for Cognition Scale completed either a simple or complex version of a number-circling task, "subjects categorized as high in need for cognition reported enjoying the complex task more than the simple task" [29, 30].

Psychological perspectives on curiosity further support the assertion that individuals actively seek out novel or unfamiliar stimuli. Optimal-arousal theories of curiosity suggest that individuals desire to achieve and maintain a particular state of pleasurable arousal and will therefore engage in 'exploratory behaviours' (i.e. curiosity) and seek out new information to achieve this optimal arousal [31, 32]. Physiological arousal in this context is how wide awake, alert, or excited someone is, which determines the level of attention directed towards a stimulus. This is not directly linked to pleasure, but rather dictates to what degree we are aware and engaged. Further research also suggests that individuals engage in exploratory, curiosity-driven behaviours to reduce displeasure found in experiences of uncertainty [33, 34], in which seeking and acquiring further information that reduces the uncertainty is consequently 'rewarded' with pleasure. This understanding of curiosity and resolving uncertainty is reflective of Costikyan's discussion of the necessity of uncertainty in games [35] and more specifically parallel's To et al.'s [36] elaboration of 'narrative anticipation' as 'curiosity about the complex or ambiguous' and the player's desire to fully understand a story and it's 'internal logic'. This is also similar to the concept of 'cognitive closure', which also describes a motivation to seek out information to resolve or reduce an ambiguous situation [37–39]. Theories of cognitive closure distinguish between individuals that are keen to seek out closure and resolve ambiguity, and those that seem to be more comfortable with an ambiguous situation and have no immediate desire to resolve ambiguity, suggesting a threshold between individuals' enjoyment of more or less cognitively effortful activities.

Berlyne's [40] perspective on the 'psychobiology' (i.e. the combined functionality of psychology and biology) of aesthetics more broadly considers arousal and its necessity to the experience of pleasure from engaging with aesthetic objects, such as art and media. While arousal is not directly linked to pleasure, heightened arousal can lead to both pleasure and displeasure (and in turn, aversion); the arousal allows individuals to direct attention towards a stimulus, prepares the body and mind for activity with a heightened awareness of the environment, and heightens preparedness to process more stimuli and information.

In aesthetics, Berlyne argues that arousal is provoked by discrepancies between the content of an individual's schema and the content of, or meanings implied by, the artistic work or text being engaged [41, 42]. Arousal can be increased when properties of a stimulus are novel, surprising, complex, ambiguous, or puzzling – when existing schema cannot be used to easily understand the stimuli. Like curiosity's uncertainty or novelty, the discrepancy between schema and text results in an initial rise in arousal. This increased arousal, which can be termed *arousal boost*, can be pleasurable. However, higher levels of arousal can also be overwhelming and unpleasurable. For example, if a narrative is too difficult to understand then the arousal state becomes excessive and interpreting the narrative can become unpleasant. However, reducing high levels of arousal, which can be termed *arousal reduction*, is also pleasurable (potentially due to the removal of displeasure). Thus, the interpreter of the work derives pleasure from both forming (i.e. arousal boost) and resolving (i.e. arousal reduction) interpretations and expectations of narrative. The experience of arousal boost and arousal reduction, specifically in the pursuit of pleasure, has been further evidenced in psychological experiments that monitored physiological responses of participants while engaging with media such as literature [43, 44], television [45], film [46], and music [47].

When relevant schema are more easily determined and accessed in familiar situations and in response to familiar stimuli, a quicker, automated, 'habitual' processing occurs which Berlyne implies provokes less arousal boost. Berlyne therefore outlines various factors of 'dishabituation' that aim to discourage 'habitual processing' and cause access to relevant schemas to become more difficult, with the intent to increase arousal boost. These factors are novelty, expectations, complexity, conflict, ambiguity, and instability. Adopting Piaget's [48] perspective on assimilation and accommodation of schema, Oatley [25] also discusses how pleasure can be experienced through the easy assimilation of new information into existing schema, and the more challenging accommodation of information via substantive (re)construction of schema. Douglas & Hargadon [17] similarly explain a difference between the enjoyment when schema are easily accessed (which they align with the pleasures of 'immersion' in a text) and when access to schema is more challenging (which they align with the pleasures of 'engagement' with a text).

Brewer [49, 50] adopts the concepts of arousal boost and arousal reduction when proposing additional perspectives for the manipulation of arousal. Brewer suggests that narrative consists of a 'discourse structure' that communicates the underlying story's 'event structure', in which the same event structure (i.e. the story) can be represented in multiple forms of discourse structure (i.e. the storytelling). For example, the numerous retellings of Romeo and Juliet may be considered as variable discourse structures using the same event structure. Brewer suggests variations of discourse structure that facilitate either surprise, curiosity, or suspense. In each, the same events are communicated at different times in the narrative so that expectations are influenced and/or subverted in order to instigate changes in arousal. Adopting Hitchcock's example of a bomb under a table at which two characters are conversing [51], Brewer suggests surprise would involve subverting expectations with unforeseen events or information later in a narrative (e.g. the bomb suddenly explodes and harms the characters), whereas suspense and curiosity involve providing some information earlier on in order to elicit uncertainty throughout a narrative (e.g. the audience is told that a bomb is under the table, unbeknownst to the two characters).

# 4   A Theoretical Model of Arousal Regulation in Interpretive Play

Bringing together the body of psychological literature discussed previously, narrative enjoyment as a function of level of arousal and proximity to optimal arousal can be summarily understood as a cycle of arousal regulation (Fig. 1).

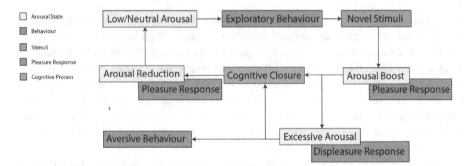

**Fig. 1.** Theoretical model of optimal arousal regulation in interpretive play

Starting with *low/neutral arousal*, *novel stimuli* trigger an initial *arousal boost* and consequent *pleasure response*. Theories of curiosity suggest that, depending on the mood of an individual, novel stimuli may be actively sought out through *exploratory behaviour* in pursuit of this arousal boost. Until *cognitive closure* is achieved, and the novel stimuli are resolved, arousal may continue to rise and fall as the player forms expectations of the narrative's uncertainty. Depending on the arousal potential of the stimuli (i.e. how unfamiliar or novel the stimulus is), this may rise to a level of *excessive arousal* and trigger a *displeasure response*, which may result in *aversive behaviour* (e.g. disengagement with stimuli). Regardless, once the stimuli are familiarised or resolved, *arousal reduction* occurs and triggers another *pleasure response*.

The threshold for unpleasurable arousal, and therefore the arousal-potential of stimuli, differs between individuals. As theories of curiosity and cognitive closure also suggest, individual tolerances for ambiguity differ, meaning some may be more comfortable with a certain degree of ambiguity, whereas others would be uncomfortable or dissatisfied. Either of these may result in more, or less, curiosity-seeking behaviour; individuals comfortable with ambiguity may consequently enjoy seeking our more uncertainty, but also may be less motivated to resolve uncertainty due to their comfort. Uncomfortable individuals conversely may be more motivated to resolve uncertainty and reduce their discomfort, or may disengage entirely to avoid further discomfort.

This psychological understanding of narrative interpretation, and how pleasure is derived from narrative, can firstly help understand contemporary approaches to storytelling in digital games and secondly, can also provide a psychologically grounded approach to design for story-focused digital games. These two aspects are examined in the following sections.

## 5    Arousal Regulation in Contemporary Narrative Design

Aspects of this psychological understanding of narrative interpretation and enjoyment via arousal regulation can be seen in contemporary practice. A broader, implicit, 'gut' understanding of audience psychology may inform the practice of many writers and game designers already, which is reflected in the psychological validity of methods that are typically employed and recommended in creative writing more widely. For example, Hemingway's iceberg theory [52], in which details and events are often omitted to strengthen story, can be argued to discourage easy accessing of schema by requiring readers to infer the missing aspects. However, there are examples of more explicitly intentional consideration of player psychology to inform the writing and design of story-focused digital games; specifically discussed here are the documented approaches to Barlow's *Her Story* [6] and Pinchbeck's *Dear Esther* [5].

Sam Barlow, writer of *Her Story* and *Telling Lies* [53], discusses "telling the story using the player's imagination" [54]. Barlow notes that audiences are increasingly "genre and story-literate", in which they are aware of "every possible combination of plot and character", suggesting that this literacy and familiarity with specific genres and story-structures is part of a player's toolkit that can be leveraged by designers. Also citing Hemingway's Iceberg theory, Barlow argues for the omission of pieces of a narrative and suggests that a story is "all about what you don't show". Moreover, Barlow argues that this method is about "leveraging the imagination" and "engaging the imagination by not showing things". Barlow suggests that depriving content of clear context encourages players to infer their own interpreted context, describing *Her Story's* one-sided video clips and how players must infer the other, missing half of an interrogation scenario. Barlow also explains that the video clips are displayed non-sequentially, thus requiring players to further interpret how the interview clips relate to one-another chronologically. This method of non-chronological storytelling can also be found in games such as *Thirty Flights of Loving* [55] and *Virginia* [56], further suggesting a possibly unintentional application of audience psychology in games more broadly.

Barlow also discusses twists, and how they force a "reboot of the simulation" (perhaps comparable to mental/situation models), requiring the player to reconsider previously interpreted information to account for new information. Following this, Barlow also suggests a manner in which the player's "immersed state is pushed back", stating that due to the player's imagination "working so hard to believe that this is real", the player's imagination will consequently push back to reassert the player's belief of the fictitious. Barlow's suggestion is to momentarily cast doubt over the player's presence in the fictional world, thus encouraging the player to resituate themselves or "engage even harder to believe this is real". One way in which Barlow achieves this is through the reflection of the player-character on the in-game computer monitor, where an occasional strike of lightning reveals a glimpse of a young woman's face.

Barlow's approach is comparable to the psychological foundation of narrative interpretation. The leveraging of players' established knowledge of genre and story reflects the concept of a schema in long-term memory and expectations formed from prior experience of similar phenomena. The consequent omission of details from *Her Story's* video clips, and the non-chronological order in which they are viewed, discourages easy access to and use of these expectations. Barlow's discussion of twists also compares to situation models and similarly suggests that introducing significant, unexpected, or discontinuous information may result in global updating (or 'rebooting the simulation').

Pinchbeck's approach to the design of *Dear Esther* is more explicitly evidenced as compared to Barlow's discussion of *Her Story*, originating with research regarding the application of cognitive psychology in understanding the effect of narrative on the experience of presence [57]. Further research also investigated story first-person shooters (FPS) specifically; for example, in observations of player behaviour in an FPS, Pinchbeck found that whilst players prioritised attention towards humanoid or moving objects, players seemed to care little for narrative during play, ignoring story-elements such as environmental storytelling [58]. However, further research identified that digital games with an emphasis on story enabled players to better recall and order their own experiences [59]. The influences of this research can be seen to be applied to *Dear Esther*; for example, after finding that players seem to prioritise humanoid characters and moving objects, Pinchbeck emphasises that *Dear Esther* presents a "sparse environment with no embedded agents" and notes the use of a humanoid figure (often interpreted as a ghost) to direct player attention [60].

Consequently, Pinchbeck specifically identifies ambiguity and abstraction as methods for "engaging the player's imagination" [61] and argues that "there's nothing more powerful than your own imagination, [it is] the most powerful tool you have at your disposal as a designer and as a writer". Indeed, *Dear Esther* "actively resisted" any direct interpretation, with an intentional lack of a final, 'correct' reading for the story, leading to an "enormous number of interpretations" posited by players.

Speaking in regards to the original version of *Dear Esther*, a *Half-Life 2* [62] modification, the game relies "… purely on the player's engagement with and interpretation of a narrative delivered through semi-randomised audio fragments" [60], demonstrating the priority of interpretation as the player's primary form of engagement. Pinchbeck facilitates this interpretation during gameplay by being 'incredibly ambiguous and abstract'. For example, the story of Dear Esther involves no action; different characters are described, though none explicitly interact. Pinchbeck adopts this approach to avoid providing explicit information to the player and instead "suggests things that could have happened". For example, while players are only given six or seven pieces of information about the character Paul, who is also not visually represented, players' interpretations of the character are "phenomenally complicated". Hemingway's iceberg theory is again adopted, with Pinchbeck noting that this approach would "create tips of icebergs floating above the ocean of action".

A careful balance of abstraction and ambiguity is proposed to better engage players with story, suggesting that players "will automatically create a plot as they go through" and "if presented with something that looks and feels enough like a story, people are likely to interpret the action in a 'storied' way" [61]. For example, if at one point players are told 'Paul was drunk', then at another point it must also be implied that Paul may not have been drunk in order to maintain Paul's ambiguity. Similarly, Pinchbeck notes the use of abstraction through the mention of the biblical story of Lot's wife, intended to be analogous to various storylines and characters in Dear Esther; for example, Lot's wife is at times also implied to be Esther herself.

Pinchbeck emphasises that "if you increase ambiguity, if you increase abstraction, players will invest more heavily" as they are "not necessarily able to drop into that schematic way of doing things". This again suggests that the intended use of ambiguity and abstraction is to reduce players' reliance on established schema, again comparable to dishabituation [40].

Both Pinchbeck and Barlow present methods that focus on engaging the player's 'imagination', with various similarities. For example, both discuss the notion of inference and implication over explication, particularly in regard to Hemingway's iceberg theory. Similarly, the acknowledgement of a player's existing understanding of genres and stories and general narrative schema is considered in both Barlow's 'story literate' audiences and Pinchbeck's explicit discussion of schema. However, the psychological foundation of narrative interpretation can also be seen in digital games that aren't explicit in intentionally discouraging easy access to relevant schema.

## 6    Empirical Study of Player Behaviour and Response in Gone Home

While intentional methods of facilitating more effortful interpretation of narrative can be found in certain games, an analysis of play of a game with no documented intentional use of psychology (*Gone Home* [7]) demonstrates the relevance of the proposed structure of player psychology.

Fifteen participants each played fifteen minutes of *Gone Home*. Via a stimulated recall methodology [63], the participants viewed the recording of their gameplay and reported on their thoughts and feelings at particular moments, providing detailed descriptions of experience. These descriptions were explored via inductive thematic analysis in-line with the process outlined by Braun & Clarke [64], identifying twenty themes from which connections to the psychological foundation proposed previously can be made. Some themes were significant due to their frequency of discussion across the entire participant group, whereas others were significant due to the frequency of discussion by a subset of participants.

The most prevalent theme identified was the formation of expectations. Participants frequently made predictions and voiced their expectations of the story ("maybe someone's dead, or some other tragedy has befallen the family") and of potential events that might occur within the game ("there might be, you know, a secret passage or a key beneath a rug"). Further emergent themes suggest how these expectations were informed, such as general prior knowledge ("… because it was like a caution or warning, a radioactivity sign, I knew that it was important, or, to go in there" or "obviously it says dark room, so I know a dark room is all about photo, photography"), or personal experiences ("… I always leave my keys under plant pots, I'll go look at the plant pots", "sort of brought me back to my childhood" and recalling memories of "constantly having to make new friends"). Expectations were also informed by prior understanding of similar games ("I guess, just, um, player bias in that I've played video games before", "I have played games before, and uh, the door is locked, there's nowhere else out for me to explore, the answer is in this room…"). This ranged from specific titles to broader genres, with many participants attempting to categorise *Gone Home* themselves, typically into an existing genre ("the door right at the beginning, my first thoughts were, uh, it could be a horror game, based on the atmosphere", "I don't like horror games so, I was always a bit hesitant about like a jump scare"). The prominence of the discussion of prior expectations in players of *Gone Home* demonstrates how often players rely on their established schema to understand their experience and form further expectations.

These expectations were often abductive in their reasoning, with various potential outcomes considered – "Did she take it with her or is it somewhere else? Did she throw it away?", "So my, I guess, was she either died, or... she.... was kidnapped or possessed", "...so it could be either a boy or a girl".

Many of the discussions of expectations also coincide with situations that participants found uncertain ("Well something has happened and I don't know what it is") or strange and unfamiliar – such as in response to finding a school locker in a teen girl's bedroom (" to find that combination lock because like you know, it was a bit weird seeing a locker in her room ") or the television being left on in the living room ("who leaves a tv on when they leave the room, especially on like the static channel, like that's very strange to me"). This is similar to theories of curiosity and cognitive closure, and supports the idea that individuals are drawn to uncertain, novel stimuli.

Filtering of irrelevant information was also a common theme, with many participants noting information they had encountered that was unnecessary, with comments such as "...even though it's like such an irrelevant thing and irrelevant piece of information" or "there's little bits of things that I keep finding everywhere which primarily don't have any use other than just to show you what your family is like". This last participant suggests that whilst a piece of information has no immediate relevance to the story, it's general implication (what the family is like) is still considered and perhaps retained – therefore, not all irrelevant information is completely disregarded and forgotten.

One participant in particular clearly demonstrates how they used their prior experiences with games more generally to inform how they approached *Gone Home*; "from previous experience from these sorts of games, my frustration in the past has been that I haven't looked at everything and I've missed something". This is another common theme that emerged – that participants were often systematic and thorough in their approach, often in the explicit pursuit of more narrative information with concern over missing vital details. This typically resulted in participants interacting with as much of the environment as possible, thoroughly examining their environments with great scrutiny; "trying to examine the environment with a magnifying glass, just trying to find that little bit that you missed", "I knew it was going to be one of those games where you had to look at everything", "we loot everything!".

This systematic and investigative approach also shows how participants often navigated the house of *Gone Home* more widely; "the stairs obviously looking all inviting, and there's a little light at the top, but no, I'm going to read everything first". Again, this reflects the careful systematic approach, but also shows how participants determined when each room should be searched; in this case, this participant felt that they were being encouraged to go upstairs, but wanted to complete their search of downstairs. This behaviour occurred frequently amongst eight of the participants; "now here you'll see me not take the obvious direction", "I didn't know whether I was exploring the house in the sort of correct way", "at least the developers want you to go in that direction". This differed between participants, but generally involved consideration of a 'correct' route through the house. While some voiced that they were trying to determine the developer/designer's intent, others only note that they were trying to go in the 'right direction'. Various cues are considered by some participants when deciding which way is the correct way; lighting, whether the path forward was visible (such as through an open door), and one participant noted the size of the staircase. However, Steve Gaynor, lead designer and writer of *Gone Home*, emphasised that while there are two possible routes at the start of the game, either up the stairs or through the left hallway, there is no preferred direction – to progress through the game, player's still need to find a key to unlock another portion of the house, but the specific route the player takes to find this key doesn't matter. This suggests that neither of these paths were 'signposted' or emphasised to players, which may indicate various environmental cues that players seek out when navigating an environment or that the participants retrospectively justified choices in navigation during stimulated recall. This has been discussed previous in regards to critical path design for story games (Higgins, 2019).

Common themes also suggest what kind of information participants retained from the story of *Gone Home*. *Gone Home's* story focuses on the missing family and involves uncovering pieces of information about their lives – therefore, as can be expected, participants frequently demonstrate their depth of understanding for *Gone Home's* characters. Much of this typically pertains to the relationships between characters and establishing how each character is connected. Earlier on in the game, this is focused on identifying the protagonist and player-character Katie ("I don't know who Katie is, I don't know if we're, I don't think we are Katie", "another reminder about um, Katie, which I assume is our character"). As participants acquire more information about the family, the more they are able to identify how they then relate to one-another – for example, Katie's sister Sam ("so, OK, I'm Katie, my sister's Sam", "so Sam, Katie... yeah Sam and Katie are sisters then"), their mother Janice ("I'm realising now that Janice is probably the mother", "I got the idea that she was the mother from a second marriage").

Themes found in the study of players of *Gone Home* reflect the current discussion of cognitive psychology and narrative interpretation. Constant recall and formation of expectations is comparable to discussion of schema theory, particularly in how participants often used their experiences of other games to inform their expectations. The recollections of narrative, particularly around characters, also reflects the discussion of situation models, and individuals' ability to retain a large amount of potentially relevant narrative information. However, these findings also suggest that individuals filter stimuli to determine how they might fit into current schema and situation models. The frequency at which participants were drawn to novel, confusing, uncertain stimuli also supports the propositions made in theories of curiosity, in addition to Berlyne's arousal-increasing factors (i.e. 'novelty, surprisingness, complexity, ambiguity, and puzzlingness'). Observations of participant behaviour also identified aversive behaviour in response to potentially excessive arousal, particularly when participants were scared, with some participants lifting the headphones from their ears to distance themselves from the game.

While the processing of narrative information may be similar across different media, observation shows how these processes mediate behaviour in digital games specifically. Further research into similar story-focused digital games would be beneficial to further testing the reliability of these cognitive psychological models and whether these behaviours and patterns of thought continue in other contexts.

## 7 Conclusion and Future Work

Adopting the perspective that the process of interpreting a narrative can be considered play, a psychological foundation of that process and how it may be pleasurable has been proposed and contextualized in contemporary practice in narrative design. Primary research of players in Gone Home reflects much of the proposed cognitive psychological model for narrative interpretation and arousal regulation and provides a potentially suitable basis for future research of psychology in the context of interpretive play.

A psychological foundation of interpretive play can be used to examine current approaches to narrative design in digital games, as well as inform new approaches. Whilst the primary research so far supports the proposed understanding of narrative interpretation and arousal regulation, further examination in varied game contexts is necessary to determine the consistency of these behaviours. Further to this, it would also be advantageous to measure physiological arousal using biometric feedback during play to examine how it may change during exposure to different narrative stimuli. For example, changes in arousal may help indicate the efficacy of specific design methods or could be used to determine general thresholds for unpleasant arousal.

Approaches to narrative design for digital games informed by cognitive psychology are also recommended to be tested in practice, primarily through development of commercial digital games. Similar psychological approaches to game design have been previously tested in this way, primarily in *Amnesia: A Machine for Pigs* [14, 16]. Potential approaches to narrative design specifically, adopting the proposed psychological basis, are thus being tested in the development of smaller commercial titles, the first of which being *White Lake* (with an early proof-of-concept demo currently available [65]), a story-focused game set in an abstract white void in which an environment constructs itself around the player as they explore and progress. Methods to facilitate arousal regulation through the discouraging of easy assimilation of schema and increased reliance on more effortful inference and interpretation shall be applied in the game's design and development. Following *White Lake*'s release, player responses shall also analysed to determine the impact of the psychological approach on player experience. The ongoing aim of this work is to further investigate interpretive play in the context of digital games and continue to develop a cognitive psychological foundation of narrative interpretation, with a broader goal to contextualise the research and findings in commercial games development.

## References

1. Upton, B.: The Aesthetic of Play. MIT Press, Cambridge (2015)
2. Bozdog, M., Galloway, D.: Worlds at our fingertips: reading (in) what remains of edith finch. Games Cult. 1555412019844631 (2019)
3. Sparrow, G.: What Remains of Edith Finch. Annapurna Interactive, Los Angeles (2017)
4. Boyd, B.: On the Origin of Stories. Harvard University Press, Cambridge (2009)
5. The Chinese Room: Dear Esther. The Chinese Room, Curve Digital, Brighton, United Kingdom and London, United Kingdom (2012)
6. Barlow, S.: Her Story. Self-published (2015)

7. The Fullbright Company M.C.: Gone Home. The Fullbright Company and Majesco Entertainment, Portland (2013)
8. Baddeley, A.: Working memory. Science **255**, 556–559 (1992)
9. An, S.: Schema theory in reading. Theory Pract. Lang. Stud. **3** (2013)
10. Mandler, J.M.: Stories, Scripts, and Scenes: Aspects of Schema Theory. Psychology Press (2014)
11. Bartlett, F.C.: Remembering: An Experimental and Social Study. Cambridge University, Cambridge (1932)
12. Mercier, P., Kalampalikis, N.: Repeated reproduction: back to bartlett A French replication of narrative and an extension to proverbs. Cult. Psychol. **26**(3), 500–527 (2019). https://doi.org/10.1177/1354067X19871197
13. Rubínová, E., Blank, H., Koppel, J., Ost, J.: Schema and deviation effects in remembering repeated unfamiliar stories. Br. J. Psychol. (2020)
14. Howell, P.: Disruptive game design: a commercial design and development methodology for supporting player cognitive engagement in digital games. Creative Technologies, Doctor of Philosophy. University of Portsmouth (2015)
15. Howell, P.: A theoretical framework of ludic knowledge: a case study in disruption and cognitive engagement. In: 10th International Conference in the Philosophy of Computer Games, Valletta, Malta, October 2016
16. The Chinese Room: Amnesia: A Machine for Pigs. Frictional Games, Helsingborg (2013)
17. Douglas, J.Y., Hargadon, A.: The pleasures of immersion and engagement: schemas, scripts and the fifth business. Digit. Creat. **12**, 153–166 (2001)
18. Van Dijk, T.A., Kintsch, W.: Strategies of discourse comprehension (1983)
19. Zwaan, R.A., Radvansky, G.A.: Situation models in language comprehension and memory. Psychol. Bull. **123**, 162 (1998)
20. Zwaan, R.A., Langston, M.C., Graesser, A.C.: The construction of situation models in narrative comprehension: an event-indexing model. Psychol. Sci. **6**, 292–297 (1995)
21. Zacks, J.M., Speer, N.K., Swallow, K.M., Braver, T.S., Reynolds, J.R.: Event perception: a mind-brain perspective. Psychol. Bull. **133**, 273 (2007)
22. Zacks, J.M., Swallow, K.M.: Event segmentation. Curr. Dir. Psychol. Sci. **16**, 80–84 (2007)
23. Newtson, D., Engquist, G.: The perceptual organization of ongoing behavior. J. Exp. Soc. Psychol. **12**, 436–450 (1976)
24. Dream, Q.: Detroit: Become Human. Sony Interactive Entertainment, San Mateo (2018)
25. Oatley, K.: A taxonomy of the emotions of literary response and a theory of identification in fictional narrative. Poetics **23**, 53–74 (1994)
26. Csikszentmihalyi, M., Csikzentmihaly, M.: Flow: The Psychology of Optimal Experience. Harper & Row, New York (1990)
27. Oliver, M.B., Bartsch, A.: Appreciation of entertainment. J. Media Psychol. **23**, 29–33 (2011)
28. Cohen, A.R., Stotland, E., Wolfe, D.M.: An experimental investigation of need for cognition. J. Abnorm. Soc. Psychol. **51**, 291 (1955)
29. Cacioppo, J.T., Petty, R.E.: The need for cognition. J. Personal. Soc. Psychol. **42**, 116 (1982)
30. Cacioppo, J.T., Petty, R.E., Feng Kao, C.: The efficient assessment of need for cognition. J. Personal. Assess. **48**, 306–307 (1984)
31. Litman, J.: Curiosity and the pleasures of learning: wanting and liking new information. Cogn. Emot. **19**, 793–814 (2005)
32. Edelman, S.: Curiosity and exploration (1997). Accessed 11 May 20
33. Litman, J.A., Jimerson, T.L.: The measurement of curiosity as a feeling of deprivation. J. Personal. Assess. **82**, 147–157 (2004)
34. Litman, J.A.: Interest and deprivation factors of epistemic curiosity. Personal. Individ. Differ. **44**, 1585–1595 (2008)

35. Costikyan, G.: Uncertainty in Games. MIT Press, Cambridge (2013)
36. To, A., Ali, S., Kaufman, G.F., Hammer, J.: Integrating curiosity and uncertainty in game design. In: Digra/fdg (2016)
37. Kruglanski, A.W., Webster, D.M.: Motivated closing of the mind: seizing and freezing. Psychol. Rev. **103**, 263 (1996)
38. Webster, D.M., Kruglanski, A.W.: Individual differences in need for cognitive closure. J. Personal. Soc. Psychol. **67**, 1049 (1994)
39. Hiel, A.V., Mervielde, I.: The need for closure and the spontaneous use of complex and simple cognitive structures. J. Soc. Psychol. **143**, 559–568 (2003)
40. Berlyne, D.E.: Aesthetics and Psychobiology. Appleton-Century-Crofts. Meredith Corporation, New York (1971)
41. Gaver, W.W., Mandler, G.: Play it again, sam: on liking music. Cogn. Emot. **1**, 259–282 (1987)
42. Reisenzein, R., Horstmann, G., Schützwohl, A.: The cognitive-evolutionary model of surprise: a review of the evidence. Top. Cogn. Sci. **11**, 50–74 (2019)
43. Nell, V.: Lost in a Book: The Psychology of Reading for Pleasure. Yale University Press, New Haven (1988)
44. Matsubara, M., Augereau, O., Sanches, C.L., Kise, K.: Emotional arousal estimation while reading comics based on physiological signal analysis. In: Proceedings of the 1st International Workshop on coMics ANalysis, Processing and Understanding, pp. 1–4. (2016)
45. Gregersen, A., Langkjær, B., Heiselberg, L., Wieland, J.L.: Following the viewers: investigating television drama engagement through skin conductance measurements. Poetics **64**, 1–13 (2017)
46. Bhattacharjee, T., Datta, S., Das, D., Choudhury, A.D., Pal, A., Ghosh, P.K.: A heart rate driven kalman filter for continuous arousal trend monitoring. In: 2018 40th Annual International Conference of the IEEE Engineering in Medicine and Biology Society (EMBC), pp. 3572–3577. IEEE (2018)
47. Hirokawa, E.: Effects of music listening and relaxation instructions on arousal changes and the working memory task in older adults. J. Music Ther. **41**, 107–127 (2004)
48. Piaget, J.: Piaget's Theory. Piaget and His School, pp. 11–23. Springer, Heidelberg (1976). https://doi.org/10.1007/978-3-642-46323-5
49. Brewer, W.F.: The nature of narrative suspense and the problem of rereading. In: Suspense: Conceptualizations, Theoretical Analyses, and Empirical Explorations, pp. 107–127 (1996)
50. Brewer, W.F., Lichtenstein, E.H.: Stories are to entertain: a structural-affect theory of stories. Center for the Study of Reading Technical Report; no. 265 (1982)
51. Truffaut, F., Hitchcock, A., Scott, H.G.: Hitchcock. Simon and Schuster (1984)
52. Smith, P.: Hemingway's early manuscripts: the theory and practice of omission. J. Mod. Lit. **10**, 268–288 (1983)
53. Barlow, S.: Telling Lies. Annapurna Interactive, California (2019)
54. Game Developers Conference. https://www.gdcvault.com/play/1023430/Making-Her-Story-Telling-a
55. Games, B.: Thirty Flights of Loving. Idle Thumbs, San Francisco (2012)
56. Variable State: Virginia. 505 Games, Milan, Italy (2016)
57. Pinchbeck, D., Stevens, B.: Presence, narrative and schemata. In: Proceedings of Presence 2005: The 8th International Workshop on Presence, pp. 221–226 (2005)
58. Pinchbeck, D., Stevens, B., Van Laar, S., Hand, S., Newman, K.: Narrative, agency and observational behaviour in a first person shooter environment. In: Proceedings of Narrative AI and Games Symposium: Society for the Study of Artificial Intelligence and the Simulation of Behaviour (AISOB 2006), pp. 53–61. SSAISB (2006)
59. Pinchbeck, D.: Story and recall in first-person shooters. Int. J. Comput. Games Technol. **2008**, 6 (2008)

60. Pinchbeck, D.: Dear esther: an interactive ghost story built using the source engine. In: Spierling, U., Szilas, N. (eds.) ICIDS 2008. LNCS, vol. 5334, pp. 51–54. Springer, Heidelberg (2008). https://doi.org/10.1007/978-3-540-89454-4_9
61. Game Developers Conference
62. Valve Corporation: Half-Life 2. Self-published, Bellevue (2004)
63. Pitkänen, J.: Studying thoughts: stimulated recall as a game research method. Game research methods, pp. 117–132 (2015)
64. Braun, V., Clarke, V.: Using thematic analysis in psychology. Qual. Res. Psychol. **3**, 77–101 (2006)
65. Higgins, M.: White Lake. Self-published (2015)

# The Procedural Nature of Interactive Digital Narratives and Early Literacy

Cristina Sylla$^{(\boxtimes)}$ (iD) and Maitê Gil (iD)

Universidade do Minho, 4710-057 Braga, Portugal
cristina.sylla@ie.uminho.pt

**Abstract.** Interactive digital narrative (IDN) has characteristics that challenge the traditional assumptions about narratives, in this sense IDN is defined as composed of system, process, and product, in a model which highlights the procedural nature of IDN as a reactive and generative system [14]. In this paper, we argue that educational applications of IDN can be enhanced by placing the emphasis on the procedural nature of IDN given by the specific framework. We present an authoring tool for IDN to support early literacy practices in pre- and primary school children and discuss how the preliminary findings benefit from an analysis oriented by the Specific Theory for IDN. We propose that the inclusion of system, process, and product in the analysis and the pedagogical use of IDN bring up two crucial aspects of young children's language development: embodied cognition (specially supported by the *system*) and interaction (specially benefited by the *process*). Finally, we argue that the procedural nature of IDN can provide a learning opportunity in educational applications of IDN, whereby we highlight the prominent role of the *user* within the proposed IDN framework.

**Keywords:** Interactive digital narrative · Authoring tools · Early literacy · Children · Storytelling

## 1   Introduction

Interactive digital narrative (IDN) has characteristics that challenge the traditional assumptions about narratives, for instance, the role of the author, the active role of the audience, and the malleability of the narrative itself. Based on these aspects, some authors have argued that analysing IDN with theoretical frameworks created to describe narrative in traditional media does not properly explore the nature of IDN [15]. Different answers to this demand were developed, one of them through a Specific Theory of Interactive Digital Narrative, which aims to overcome the output-centred view of legacy theoretical frameworks, recognising the importance of all elements of IDN, such as the computer system and the participatory process involved [14].

In this paper we argue that educational applications of IDN can be enhanced by placing the emphasis on the procedural nature of IDN [14, 16], and present results from Mobeybou, a research initiative to develop an authoring tool for IDN to support early literacy practices in pre- and primary school children.

© Springer Nature Switzerland AG 2020
A.-G. Bosser et al. (Eds.): ICIDS 2020, LNCS 12497, pp. 258–270, 2020.
https://doi.org/10.1007/978-3-030-62516-0_23

We begin by presenting the key concepts proposed by [14] and providing a summarized review of relevant aspects of the role of narratives in language development. We then establish a dialogue between the specific theory of IDN and early literacy, exploring the procedural nature of IDN as an element which enhances young students' linguistic competences. Finally, we describe Mobeybou, a digital manipulative authoring tool for IDN designed to pre- and primary school children.

## 2 Interactive Digital Narratives: System, Process, and Product

An important contribution to the theoretical model of IDN is the distinction between the material artefact and its output proposed by Nick Montfort in his investigation of Interactive Fiction (IF) works. The assertion that "an IF work is an interactive computer program, but not directly a narrative" [19] is productive because it leads to the understanding of an IF or IDN artefact/system as something bigger and more complex than the narrative itself, as it contains the system, the process and the outcome. Another important characteristic of IDN is that it requires an interactive process to produce the output. Considering these premises, while classical narratology methods focus only on the output (the narrative), an adequate framework to IDN must also account for the combination of the software/hardware and the user's interaction process with it, which together result in a narrative output [14].

Based on these assumptions, IDN is understood as "comprised of system, process, and product" in a model which "takes into account the procedural nature of IDN as a reactive and generative system" [14:97].

In this definition, system refers to the digital artefact, including the executable programming code and virtual assets, as well as the connected hardware. In other words, the IDN system contains potential narratives, which are structured through protostory, narrative design and narrative vectors. The author uses the term protostory to denote a prototype that defines the space of potential narrative experiences; the term narrative design is used to refer to the structure within a protostory that enables a flexible presentation of a narrative; and the term narrative vectors is related to the substructures that provide a specific direction to the story. The second element, the process, is intrinsically interactive and can engage one or several participants. The process is defined by the opportunities the system provides and shaped by the user's actions. The interactions performed during this phase are fundamental to the output and represent a key distinction between IDN and narrative in traditional media. The third element, the product, is classified as an instantiated product, because the participatory process and the procedural nature of IDN make different narrative outputs possible.

Considering these definitions, IDN can be defined as "an expressive narrative form in digital media implemented as a computational system containing potential narratives and experienced through a participatory process that results in products representing instantiated narratives" [14:98]. Outgoing from Koenitz's model, we propose to give to the user a more evident role in the interactive process that takes place between user, system, process, and product. In this sense, a full analysis of IDN needs to include the three elements discussed by the author: system, process and product, as well as the user, who is a cross-cutting element in IDN.

The main difference between a specific theory of IDN and the applications of narrative theories to IDN [17, 1, among others] is the shift from an output-centred view to a procedural account. This shift is fundamental to this paper, once we argue that educational applications of IDN can benefit from it.

## 3 Narratives and Language Development

Children assimilate and produce narratives in connection with their own embodied experiences in real life and in other narratives, in other words, narratives are a form of human thinking that is fundamental in making sense out of one's social experiences, as well as in the development of one's emotions and cognition [5, 7, 9]. Regarding the development of language abilities, the propriety of creating new experiences and knowledge through temporal and causal organization enhances narrative to a privileged place in literacy development.

Storytelling is acknowledged as an effective instrument to boost early literacy, increasing children's active participation in the language learning process [18]. Studies have revealed that children's early exposure to narratives has a major influence on the development of early literacy skills, being a creative and playful way of linguistic exploration [6, 23]. The frequency and the variety of narratives to which a child is exposed also impact the complexity of the vocabulary as well as the syntactic complexity in oral language [23]. Besides, retelling or creating stories implies a mental reconstruction of the story events, which fosters the development of metanarrative consciousness, and the emergence of more advanced language skills, enhancing grammar, vocabulary, and sentence formation [6].

However, narratives are more demanding for children than the discourse they use in daily life, presupposing, for instance, the use of different verb tenses and a more elaborated and structured language, implying decontextualized use of the language, as the narrator always places himself at a distance from the related events [8].

Concerning the scope of this paper, it is relevant to mention that although there are well established evidences of the role played by narratives in language development, most of them focus on the product, namely, on the narrative itself and its structure, not on the system and the process that result in a narrative output. This does not diminish the value of these contributions, as they are aligned with the classical narratology theory and therefore mainly related to narrative in traditional media. However, it shows that investigations about the specific characteristics of IDN and its relation to educational settings are a fruitful area for new contributions.

## 4 The Procedural Nature of IDN and Early Literacy

Interactive process-based narrative has been pointed out as a powerful tool in a variety of situations, such as: technology-enhanced learning for children with autism [20] or cardiac illness [4], health promotion research and practice [11], vocabulary development practices [27] and 21st century literacy skills development [22]. Barendregt et al. define 'collective storytelling' as "the combination of cooperative technologies with storytelling in order to coordinate different authoring efforts" [3]. The authors present digital storytelling and interactive storytelling as related concepts, arguing that collective storytelling differs from them because it puts a focus on the enriched collective authoring experience. Despite the specific particularities of each of these concepts and contributions, our core argument here is that, just as the IDN analysis benefits from the proposition of a specific theory, educational applications for fostering early literacy can also benefit from being designed taking into account the aspects in which IDN differs from other narrative forms. In this sense, the shift from an output-centred view to a procedural account moves the core contribution of IDN to language development from the narrative itself to the interactive process through which it is built.

While in more traditional narrative forms only the output (in the form of a text) is available for analysis - and it is merely possible to speculate about the author's thoughts and her writing process - with IDN, it is possible to record and analyse the output, as well as two additional elements: the system and the interaction process. So, instead of the established theoretical narrative framework used in traditional media, which is composed by an author-writing-output (fixed), a specific IDN framework should be composed by a system-interaction-output (which can be fixed) [14]. This means that an IDN analysis would allow to look at the system's configurations and observe the participant's exploratory process of creating a narrative. In this scenario, the analysis of the instantiated narrative can reveal not only aspects of its structure but also how particular interactions shape the outcome.

Within this framework, the procedural nature of IDN as a reactive and generative system becomes prominent. This is an important contribution to educational applications, because while traditional narrative approaches merely focus on the product, the obligatory interactive process when producing the output of a specific IDN makes the activity of planning and creating stories more concrete and transparent, as well as the activity of teaching how to plan and how to create stories.

Regarding early literacy practices, while the process of creating a narrative can be a challenging and abstract task for young children, the procedural nature of IDN enables a participatory process which is concretely guided by the system's configurations. The inclusion of these elements in the analysis and the pedagogical use of IDN brings up two crucial aspects of young children's language development: embodied cognition (supported by the system) and interaction (promoted by the process).

Children, both in their understanding and production of narratives, refer back to their own experience of reality. When a child narrates a story, she places herself at a distance from the momentary situation, imagines something, remembers, and participates in the portrayed reality. This is not an easy process, and research has called attention to children's need of structures that scaffold them in these tasks, which are intrinsically related to the embodied cognition thesis [2]. Knowing that children assimilate and produce narratives in connection with their own embodied experience in real life and in other narratives, it is possible to argue that the system's configurations aligned with the user's bodily and social interactions are a way to foster the development of storytelling competences. In this context, an IDN system can provide scaffolding structures to young children by: (i) structuring the space of potential narratives through the proto-story; (ii) guiding flexible presentations of a narrative through the narrative design; and (iii) determining possible directions to the story through the narrative vectors.

Considering the participatory nature of the IDN process, the obligatory interaction (whether with the system or with the system and other individuals at the same time) to produce the output is aligned with the sociocultural theory. Vygotsky (1979) accentuated the mediative nature of learning, either by means of signs or by means of human mediation. According to this author, the development of thought is determined by language, that is, by the linguistic instruments of thought and by the socio-cultural experience of the child. In consonance with this approach, it is possible to argue that the IDN interactive process accentuates the role of mediation as an important semiotic mechanism of learning. Here, it is particularly relevant to consider the role of the user not just in the creation process, but also in his interaction with the system. The user is, therefore, the central element that articulates the IDN as a meaningful whole and potentiates IDN as a learning tool. This is a relevant aspect to be considered in IDN educational applications, supported by recent research that has identified the need of fostering interaction with and through the artefact as a more knowledgeable other [10].

Bears et al. first introduced interactive storytelling at the CHI conference in 1998, since then IDN has been widely applied in the educational domain and many fruitful investigations have been done in this area, however not all of them highlight the aspects in which IDN differs from other forms of narrative. In this sense, in this section, we established an initial dialogue between a specific framework of IDN [14] and language development. In the following section, we introduce Mobeybou, an authoring tool for fostering early literacy and outline some aspects of its application to education aligned with the theoretical model for IDN.

# 5    Mobeybou: A Storytelling Authoring Tool for Pre- and Primary School Children

Here we present Mobeybou [26], a digital manipulative aimed at scaffolding the creation of multicultural stories among young children, enhancing the development of narrative competences. The reason for presenting Mobeybou is two-fold. On the one hand, we aim at illustrating how the IDN theoretical approach has an impact on the study, design and development of analytic methods regarding educational settings. On the other hand, we aim at analyzing the potential of this specific digital manipulative as an authoring tool for IDN.

Digital manipulatives are physical representations, materials or objects with embedded computational properties that allow interacting with and manipulating digital content [21]; they are often also named Tangible User Interfaces [12]. These tools are especially adequate for young children because they provide opportunities for exploratory physical embodiment, collaboration, verbalization, exchange of ideas and negotiation [24].

The development of Mobeybou followed an iterative and participatory design methodology, involving children and teachers along its development, thus undergoing several iterations.

### 5.1    The System

The digital manipulative is composed of a series of physical blocks that act as an interface for manipulating the digital content. A previous hardware version of the system is composed of an electronic board that connects to a computer or tablet via USB. The board has six slots for placing blocks, which adhere to it through magnets located on the board and on the bottom of each block (see Fig. 1, left). A more recent hardware version of the system uses blocks that communicate with a computer or tablet via Bluetooth, and with each other through magnets embedded on the sides (see Fig. 1, right).

**Fig. 1.** The System: previous version (left), recent hardware version (right).

The software is the same on both systems. Each physical block embodies a story element having the respective visual representation on the upper face. Placing a block on the board or connecting the blocks to each other triggers its digital representation on a device's screen. Children can create their narratives by connecting the various blocks to each other, or by placing the blocks on the board (depending on the system's version they are using). Removing a block from the board or from the block chain makes its virtual representation disappear from the screen.

Presently, the blocks represent eight cultural sets, namely, India, Brazil, China, Portugal, Germany, Angola, Turkey and Cape Verde. Each set represents the respective culture and is composed of a landscape, two protagonists, an animal, an antagonist, a musical instrument and a magical object. There are also five atmospheric conditions blocks (rain, snow, wind, thunder, night), as well as ambient and background sounds.

Each block element has specific animations that display different actions. The visual narratives unfold according to the combination of blocks that the users place on the board, or connect to each other, while they verbalize their stories. A recording button allows recording/playing children's narratives.

**Protostory.** Considering that the protostory can be understood as a pre-story containing the necessary ingredients for any given walkthrough, the protostory in Mobeybou contains the space of possible stories embedded in the contents of the narrative elements, the narrative preconditions and definitions, as well as the possibility to let the users actively interact with, explore and mix elements from different cultures. These are provided by the programming code and the interactive interface.

**Narrative Design.** The narrative was designed through behaviour trees (BTs), a concept well known in the field of computer games to model character behaviour, reactive decision-making and control of virtual characters [13]. The BTs describe general actions of entities; thus, each entity interacts with the environment according to a set of predefined rules that define its behaviour. The narrative design comprises following entities: environment (scenarios, weather conditions); Items (objects; instruments) and Characters (protagonists, antagonists, animals). The entities behave according the following rules: The antagonists attack the protagonists; The animals defend the latter; The protagonists and the animals can join forces to defend themselves from the antagonists; The antagonists can also join forces to attack the former; The musical instruments and the magical objects have magical properties and can be used by the protagonists to help the protagonists and the animals. When an element is defeated (depending on the system's version being used), the physical block needs to be disconnected from the others and reconnected or removed and replaced on the board, in order to bring it to life again.

Since the behaviour triggered for each entity depends on the other entities that are also present in the scene (on the board or connected), and the properties of those entities, there is a certain degree of unpredictability in the outcome of a given situation. When the users connect the blocks to each other or place the blocks on the platform, the BT of each element gets the inputs of the entities that are present in the scene. Regularly at a predefined time stamp, the BTs perform updates to check the scene and the defined priorities before triggering any actions. As a result, there are no predefined stories, nor a linear narrative. The users create their own narratives according to the sequence of blocks and the order in which they connect them/place them on the electronic platform. This way the narrative design opens up a space for experimentation and agency. So, in their story creation with the digital manipulative, the children are incentivized to find creative solutions for the situations that unfold by attending to the constraints given by the rules, which they therefore must infer and understand.

**Narrative Vectors.** Narrative vectors in the digital manipulative are combinations of elements and the constraints given by the underlying behaviour rules that are designed to create specific experiences, for example the usage of a particular instrument to protect a protagonist after the child has gathered additional knowledge about its properties.

Understanding the digital manipulative in this way facilitates the examination of aspects which are beyond the focus of traditional narrative studies. The participatory possibilities provided by the authoring system and its cultural sets can, for instance, be analysed as part of the protostory in terms of environment definitions and settings.

### 5.2   The Process

Similar to other IDN systems, the storytelling process with the digital manipulative is intrinsically interactive and it can engage one or several participants. The digital manipulative offers a space for exploring storytelling within a multimodal (verbal, visual and auditory) embodied (through manipulation) collaborative process, moving beyond creativity processes based on individual mental imaginary. In other words, it challenges individual-mind-and-mouth narrative construction transforming it into a process in which mind-hands-eyes-and-ears attune in shared embodied, multimodal and collaborative processes of narrative creation [25].

### 5.3 The Output

The digital manipulative offers the possibility to record the resulting product of the interactive digital narrative walkthrough, that is, the instantiated narrative. In this sense, another relevant contribution of this model is that the instantiated narrative can be analysed considering the specificity of the digital manipulative's narrative design, which is defined by certain narrative vectors, instead of applying "the output-centred view of legacy theoretical frameworks" [14:97]. This means that the analysis is no longer constrained by the need to adapt legacy theoretical positions and can instead fully focus on describing the particular narrative strategies of each IDN [14].

## 6   A Pilot User Study: Preliminary Notes on the Educational Application of the Theoretical Model for IDN

In this section, we briefly present a pilot user study carried out with Mobeybou, aimed at receiving feedback from the children about the IDN system in order to validate and inform future developments, as well as at understanding if the manipulation of· the system and the interaction rules between de story elements were well thought and easy to understand by the target users. This study was carried out with the system's version that uses the electronic platform connected to the computer via USB.

The study was carried out at a local public school, with twelve, eight-years-old children from a class of 3rd graders. The children were grouped in pairs by the teacher. A researcher started by giving a brief explanation of the functioning of the IDN system. After that, each pair interacted and explored the tool for around 20 min. Following the exploratory phase, the researcher invited each pair to tell a story using the digital manipulative. The data was collected by two researchers (that stood in the background) through observation and written notes. A third researcher accompanied the children in their storytelling. All the interactions were audio-video recorded using a video camera on a tripod with a fixed focus and zoom. The video camera was placed behind the children focusing on the manipulation of the blocks. At the end of the intervention, the researcher carried out a semi-structured interview with the teacher. Considering the scope of this paper, we focus our discussion on the interaction of just one pair, in order to argue that the preliminary findings benefit from an analysis oriented by a specific theory for IDN.

### 6.1   Analysing the Interaction with Mobeybou Through the Lens of a Specific Theory of IDN

Here, we illustrate representative interaction behaviour of a pair of girls with the tool through two vignettes and one research note, selected for their relevance as representative of children' interaction with the digital manipulative. The vignettes and the research note focus on three major contributions from the theoretical model for IDN to early literacy practices that came up in the analysis, namely: (i) the contributions of the interactive process to the instantiated narrative; (ii) the system's contributions to the instantiated narrative; and (iii) the procedural nature of IDN as a learning opportunity. As we have previously argued, both the vignettes and the note show the user as the central element that articulates the IDN (and IDN experience) as a meaningful whole.

The first vignette illustrates what we have identified (i) as the contributions of the interactive process to the instantiated narrative. It is relevant to say that this relation between the interactive process and the output (the narrative itself) cannot be considered or discussed by applying a traditional narrative theory when analysing the children's IDN production.

**Vignette 1.** A girl starts telling a story: "On a full moon night, it was snowing a lot in India, a little girl was playing ...", she places the pipa-block (Chinese instrument) on the board and looks at the researcher asking for the name of the instrument; the researcher answers: "this is a pipa"; so, the girl continues: "she was playing pipa. And the girl had an elephant and there was a boy. It stopped snowing (she removed the snow-block) [...], the girl stopped playing the pipa and started playing the flute. All of a sudden, a very strong wind started blowing" (she removes the snow-block from the board and places the wind-block and removes the pipa-block and places the pungi-block (Indian instrument). The researcher asks her: "do you know the name of that flute? It's pungi". The girl continues her story: "The boy went home [...] the girl played the pipa again, the wind stopped and it started raining. To stop the rain the girl started playing the ... pingi" (she tries to remember the word and says pingi, instead of pungi).

*Relevance.* V1 exemplifies how the interactive process promoted by the IDN creates a mediative learning environment, accentuating the role of mediation as an important semiotic mechanism of learning. The interaction with the story elements triggered the child's curiosity providing an opportunity to learn new vocabulary. This curiosity was intrinsic and not imposed from the outside and the child immediately put the acquired knowledge into practice using it in her storytelling. Also, it provided an opportunity for a more knowledgeable person (here the researcher) to naturally introduce new vocabulary (the word pungi). The interaction during the story creation opened up a space for learning new vocabulary, which the child immediately and spontaneously used in her narrative (her effort to learn new words was visible when she tried to remember and use the name of the Indian instrument). The possibility to look at this kind of process represents a relevant aspect to be considered in IDN educational applications, since it helps teachers to understand and to access the students' learning process.

The second vignette illustrates (ii) a behaviour that we have identified as the system's contribution to the instantiated narrative. Again, this dimension can only be considered or discussed using the specific theory of IDN when analysing the child's production.

**Vignette 2.** A girl places the panda-block (the Chinese animal) and the snake-block (the Indian antagonist) on the board and observes the screen. According to the rules of the system, the panda and the snake started to fight. As she visualizes the fight between the two animals, the girl gets very stressed, saying: "Oh my God, poor panda!". Some moments later, the girl places the panda-block and the lion-block (the Chinese antagonist) on the board and observes the screen. As they started to fight, the girl places the pipa (Chinese instrument) on the board, saying "the girl wanted to play the pipa so that they did not fight" (when a musical instrument is on the board the animals and the antagonists stop fighting and begin to dance).

*Relevance.* V2 exemplifies how the child defined the introduction of new elements after understanding the relations between certain story elements, that is, scaffold by the possible directions of the story determined by the narrative vectors within the protostory. The decision of introducing a musical instrument was consciously made by the student in order to stop the animals fight (this choice was provided by the protostory, which contains potential narratives, and by the flexible narrative design). Besides, this is an example of a particular interaction that shapes the outcome, and paying attention to it can help the teacher to analyse the instantiated narrative.

Finally, the research note is a starting point to the characterization of the procedural nature of IDN as a learning opportunity, and consequently as a major aspect to be explored in IDN educational applications.

**Research Note.** At the end of the interaction the researchers carried out a semi-structured interview with the teacher, who told that one of the girls of the group above described had major difficulty in reading and was one of the less accomplished students in her class. However, during the interaction with the digital manipulative, she stood out, taking a leading role and narrating most of the story. She used connection expressions in her storytelling (for instance: "On a full moon night, it was snowing a lot […]"; "All of a sudden, a very strong wind started blowing"), asked questions about vocabulary and quickly applied what she had learned. She also quickly understood the rules behind the system, applying the offered strategies in her storytelling, e.g.: "the snake ate the elephant" while removing the elephant-block from the electronic board, because she knew it would disappear.

*Relevance.* This research note shows how IDN considered as a whole, that is, the triad of system, process, and product, triggers fundamental dimensions that foster language development, such as embodied cognition and interaction, and doing so, it creates an environment that encourages learning. Again, by giving attention to the participatory process, it was possible to perceive some narrative competences that the child was not able to demonstrate in a fixed narrative or through a traditional output-centred approach.

The vignettes and the research note illustrate some contributions from the theoretical model for IDN to early literacy practices. The extension from an output-centred analysis to a comprehensive analysis of the system, the process and the output represents an opportunity to inform the design of pedagogical applications of IDN. Moreover, the evident role of the user in the interactive process that takes place between user, system, process, and product opens up a window into the student's learning process, enabling researchers and educators to guide and to better understand the development of the students' language and narrative skills.

268    C. Sylla and M. Gil

## 7 Conclusion

By synthesizing the key concepts of a specific theory of IDN [14] and reviewing the role of narratives in language development, we aimed at establishing a dialogue between the framework of IDN and early literacy. We argued that educational applications of IDN can be enhanced by placing the emphasis on the procedural nature of IDN.

The description of Mobeybou and the preliminary findings of a pilot user study, brought some evidence to the potential of the dialogue between the IDN theoretical framework and the educational context proposed in this paper. It also provided valuable insights for future developments of IDN's authoring tools for young children and, specially, for new educational applications relating IDN to early literacy and digital manipulatives devices.

In short, we proposed that the inclusion of system, process, and product (and the user) in the development of educational applications of IDN, especially the ones designed to early literacy practices, reinforce embodied cognition and interaction as relevant acting factors during young children's language development. We argued that the procedural nature of IDN offers different learning opportunities from the ones offered by narratives in traditional media and this aspect must be thoroughly explored in IDN's pedagogical uses. Finally, rather than a specific theoretical innovation, we aimed to illustrate how two bodies of literature can inform one another, producing novel insights.

**Acknowledgments.** This work has been financed by national funds through the Portuguese Foundation for Science and Technology (FCT) - and by the European Regional Development Fund (ERDF) through the Competitiveness and Internationalisation Operational Program under the reference POCI/01/0145/FEDER/032580.

## References

1. Aarseth, E.: A narrative theory of games. In: FDG 2012 Proceedings of the International Conference on the Foundations of Digital Games, pp. 129–133. ACM, New York (2012). https://doi.org/10.1145/2282338.2282365
2. Baranauskas, M.C., Posada, J.E.: Tangible and shared storytelling: searching for the social dimension of constructionism. In: Proceedings of the IDC International Conference on Interaction Design and Children, pp. 193–203. ACM Press, New York (2017). https://dl.acm.org/doi/10.1145/3078072.3079743
3. Barendregt, W., Torgersson, O., Eriksson, E., Börjesson, P.: Intermediate-level knowledge in child-computer interaction: a call for action. In: Proceedings of the 2017 Conference on Interaction Design and Children (IDC 2017), pp. 7–16. Association for Computing Machinery, New York (2017). https://doi.org/10.1145/3078072.3079719
4. Bers, M.U., et al.: Interactive storytelling environments: coping with cardiac illness at Boston's Children's Hospital. In: CHI 1998, pp. 603–610. ACM Press/Addison-Wesley Publishing Co., Los Angeles (1998)
5. Bruner, J.S.: The narrative construction of reality. Crit. Inquiry **8**(1), 1–21 (1991). https://doi.org/10.1086/448619
6. Collins, F.: The use of traditional storytelling in education to the learning of early literacy skills. Early Child Dev. Care **152**(1), 77–108 (1999). https://doi.org/10.1080/0300443991520106

7. Dadalto, E., Goldfeld, M.: Características comuns à narrativa oral de crianças na pré-alfabetização. Rev. CEFAC **11**(1), 42–49 (2011). http://dx.doi.org/10.1590/S1516-184620 09005000013

8. Dehn, M., Merklinger, D., Schüler, L.: Narrative acquisition in educational research and didactics. In: Hühn, P., et al. (eds.) The Living Handbook of Narratology. Hamburg University, Hamburg (2014)

9. Eagle, S.: Learning in the early years: social interactions around picturebooks, puzzles and digital technologies. Comput. Edu. **59**(1), 38–49 (2011). https://doi.org/10.1016/j.compedu. 2011.10.013

10. Fadeev, A.: Vygotsky's theory of mediation in digital learning environment: actuality and practice. Punctum **5**(1), 24–44 (2019). https://doi.org/10.18680/hss.2019.0004

11. Gubrium, A.: Digital storytelling: an emergent method for health promotion research and practice. Health Promotion Practice **10**(2), 186–191 (2009). https://doi.org/10.1177/152483 9909332600

12. Ishii, H., Ullmer, B.: Tangible bits: towards seamless interfaces between people, bits and atoms. In: Proceedings of the Conference on Human Factors in Computing Systems, pp. 234–241. ACM Press, New York (1997)

13. Kapadia, M., Zund, F., Falk, J., Marti, M., Sumner, R.W., Gross, M.: Evaluating the authoring com- plexity of interactive narratives with interactive behaviour trees. In: Proceedings of the 10th International Conference on the Foundations of Digital Games, FDG 2015. Pacific Grove, CA, USA (2015)

14. Koenitz, H.: Towards a specific theory of interactive digital narrative. In: Koenitz, et al. (eds.) Interactive Digital Narrative. Routledge, NY (2015)

15. Koenitz, H.: Towards a theoretical framework for interactive digital narrative. In: Aylett, R., Lim, M.Y., Louchart, S., Petta, P., Riedl, M. (eds.) ICIDS 2010. LNCS, vol. 6432, pp. 176–185. Springer, Heidelberg (2010). https://doi.org/10.1007/978-3-642-16638-9_22

16. Lambert, J.: The Digital Storytelling Cookbook. Digital Diner Press/Center for Digital Storytelling, Berkeley (2010)

17. Laurel, B.: Computers as Theater, 2nd edn. Addison-Wesley, Reading (1993)

18. Lucarevschi, C.R.: The role of storytelling in language learning: a literature review. Working Papers Linguistics Circle Univ. Victoria **26**(1), 24–44 (2016)

19. Montfort, N.: Toward a Theory of Interactive Fiction (2003). http://nickm.com/if/toward. html. Accessed 09 June 2020

20. Parsons, S., Guldberg, K., Porayska-Pomsta, K., Lee, R.: Digital stories as a method for evidence-based practice and knowledge co-creation in technology-enhanced learning for children with autism. Int. J. Res. Method Educ. **38**(3), 247–271 (2015). https://doi.org/10.1080/ 1743727X.2015.1019852

21. Resnick, M., et al.: Digital manipulatives: new toys to think with. In: Proceedings of the Conference on Human Factors in Computing Systems, pp. 281–287. ACM Press, New York (1998). https://doi.org/10.1145/274644.274684

22. Robin, B.R.: Digital storytelling: a powerful technology tool for the 21st century classroom. Theory Practice **47**(3), 220–228 (2008). https://doi.org/10.1080/00405840802153916

23. Speaker, K.M., Taylor, D., Kamen, R.: Storytelling: enhancing language acquisition in young children. Education **125**(1), 3–14 (2004)

24. Sylla, C., Coutinho, C., Branco, P.: A digital manipulative for embodied "stage-narrative" creation. Entertain. Comput. **5**(4), 495–507 (2014). https://doi.org/10.1016/j.entcom.2014. 08.011

25. Sylla, C., et al.: Mobeybou - a digital manipulative for multicultural narrative creation. In: Extended Abstracts of the 2019 CHI Conference on Human Factors in Computing Systems (CHI EA 2019), Paper VS15, pp. 1–2. ACM Press, New York (2019). https://doi.org/10.1145/ 3290607.3311769

26. Sylla, C., Pereira, I.S., Sá, G.: Designing manipulative tools for creative multi and cross-cultural storytelling. In: Proceedings of the International Conference on Creativity and Cognition (C&C 2019), pp. 396–406. ACM Press, New York (2019). https://doi.org/10.1145/332 5480.3325501

27. Vaahtoranta, E., Lenhart, J., Suggate, S., Lenhard, W.: Interactive elaborative storytelling: engaging children as storytellers to foster vocabulary. Front. Psychol. (2019). https://doi.org/ 10.3389/fpsyg.2019.01534

28. Vygotsky, L.: Mind in Society. Harvard University Press, Cambridge (1979)

# Vim: A Tangible Energy Story

Skye Doherty$^{(\boxtimes)}$ ⓘ, Stephen Snow ⓘ, Kathleen Jennings ⓘ, Ben Rose,
Ben Matthews ⓘ, and Stephen Viller ⓘ

The University of Queensland, Brisbane, Australia
s.dohert@uq.edu.au

**Abstract.** Vim is a tangible narrative about energy futures. It is designed to illustrate how a story about a public issue could be designed for physical interaction and whether that interaction can encourage participation in that issue. To date, much research into tangible narrative has focused on fiction and childhood education. Energy, as a wicked problem, provides a challenging context for exploring how tangible elements could be used to tell public interest stories. In this paper, we offer an overview of key energy issues in Australia and the role of design in addressing community concerns. We describe Vim and outline how our design research approach informed decisions about form and interaction. An initial critique of our prototype suggests that public interest stories have qualities that diverge from fictional tangible narrative. In particular, factors such as where a story exists and the role of the reader need to take account of the real-world context and role of 'characters' and 'settings' outside of the story.

**Keywords:** Design · Energy · Journalism · Public interest · Tangible narrative

## 1 Introduction

Vim is a tangible narrative about energy futures. It is designed to illustrate how a story about a public issue could be designed for physical interaction and whether that interaction can encourage participation in that issue.

While broadly positioned within journalistic practice and its desire to tell public interest stories [1], the project challenges journalistic conventions around truth [2] and time. In doing so, it draws on the idea that design things play a role in addressing matters that concern communities [3–5]. Vim also aims to explore tangible interfaces in a non-fiction, public-interest context. While tangible interfaces have long been of interest to the interactive narrative community, this attention has largely been directed at childhood education and fictional storytelling [6]. The opportunities for, and implications of, tangible non-fiction and public interest storytelling have received less attention: projects that deal with factual stories tend to focus on history [7], personal stories [8, 9] or cultural preservation [10]. Public interest stories, by contrast, aim to balance the information needs of public and private interests [11, 12]. Telling such stories using tangible interaction presents particular challenges such as the dominance of established narrative forms (e.g.: the inverted pyramid) and strong ties to current real-world events.

© Springer Nature Switzerland AG 2020
A.-G. Bosser et al. (Eds.): ICIDS 2020, LNCS 12497, pp. 271–280, 2020.
https://doi.org/10.1007/978-3-030-62516-0_24

In journalism, narrative conventions privilege reporting of facts, which are assumed to provide an objective view of current events.

In this paper, we examine our design response to energy as a public issue, including our approaches to system and story design. In the next section, we introduce the issue of energy policy and how it has been communicated. We then introduce Vim, a research prototype designed to explore how tangible interaction could be used to tell public interest stories. We discuss key features and how these were informed by contextual research involving professional journalists. In particular, we outline how the prototype aims to experiment with physical input and output mechanisms; to encourage readers to act in relation to a public issue; and to understand the value of physical technology in the context of journalistic storytelling. The project is a work in progress.

## 2 Energy Narratives

Energy policy is a contested social, political and economic issue. In Australia in recent years successive governments have unsuccessfully sought to balance public and private interests in the transition to a low-carbon economy. The process has revealed deep divisions about the 'right' mix of renewables and fossil fuels, the role of government in supporting industries and jobs, public subsidies for renewable energy, taxes on carbon emissions, and the possibility of private consumer choice with respect to sources of energy production.

The dominant arguments around energy have often reflected the classic environmental philosophical divide of Cornucopians versus Malthusians [13]: that advances in technology and efficiency negate natural limits to growth and enable ever-increasing consumption (Cornucopian), versus over-consumption of a finite base of natural resources that leads to environmental catastrophe, requiring urgent changes to the way we live (Malthusian) [14]. In debates about energy futures, this argument is demonstrated in discussions about the correct balance of renewables and how involved consumers should be in managing energy demand, e.g. voluntary curtailment vs further investment in generation assets.

In Australia, public discourse about renewable energy has focused on technical and economic debates with a lack of substantive discussion about mixed generation or the consequences of more widespread uptake of renewable energy [15, 16]. Coal has shaped the identity of several mining regions [17] and the country's abundant fossil fuel reserves have helped drive economic growth. Yet the move towards cleaner energy sources threatens to redistribute wealth away from industry and individuals.

Within a wicked and highly politicised issue such as this, journalistic reporting, however objective it may attempt to be, is easily perceived and quickly labelled as politically biased and motivated by special interests, whether progressive or conservative. By contrast, design projects have adopted novel forms and interactions in an attempt to tell public stories of private energy consumption [18, 19], or make public factual information about emissions [20]. These projects use light, space and household items to create novel narratives. This prompts our exploration of how journalistic storytelling might exploit ambient and tangible interfaces.

**Fig. 1.** Main interface

**Fig. 2.** Energy profile

**Fig. 3.** Writing table

**Fig. 4.** Printed story feed

**Fig. 5.** Readers can respond to questions

## 3 Vim: Story Concept

Vim is a wooden box featuring a solar panel. It prints out stories about energy based on the reader's preferences, along with a question for them to answer. It incorporates several physical computing technologies including LED lights, a thermal printer, buttons and a dial. A 3G-connected microcontroller manages the system, accessing a database of stories, and logging interactions. The box is powered by a battery that can be charged by the sun via the solar panel, or by physical effort using a crank. The box has four sides: on the front is the main interface (Fig. 1); on the right is the crank and a profile of Vim's energy use (Fig. 2); the left face features a writing table (Fig. 5); and the back face has information about the project (Fig. 3). Readers can interact with Vim in three ways: by using dials and buttons; by donating energy via the crank; or by returning written responses.

The stories and interactions are a focus of Vim's design, as they reflect the two philosophical positions: either that technology will resolve issues around energy, or that we need to change the way we live. Stories—designed as news briefs—are organised into four categories, including technology, policy, economy and society. The main interface gives readers several options:

1. Choose a feed generated by the reader (human) or by Vim (the machine);
2. If human-generated:

   a. first choose to 'make more' or 'live with less';
   b. then choose a topic: policy, technology, society or economy;
   c. the feed produced is tailored to these parameters

3. If machine-generated, produce a feed.

The feed produced by Vim (Fig. 4) includes three stories: one each from the past, present and future. The stories are drawn from a bank of 48, each two or three sentences long, with headline and dateline stating the location and year. There are 12 stories in each of the four categories, with six under each philosophical position. When a reader selects a position and category Vim produces one of two feeds that match that combination. The question at the bottom of the feed alternates each time a feed is produced. Readers are asked either: 'What is the worst that can happen?' Or 'What is the best that can happen?'

## 4  Design Considerations

Design, as a research discipline, is in transition. Its original set of concerns were directed towards understanding (and optimising) the process by which people could and should create new artefacts [21]. More recent developments in the field have critically appraised the role of design in late capitalism. This has generated a new set of concerns about the prospects and roles that artefacts can play in social change. As a result, design research began investigating how processes can be engaged as a means to challenge the status quo [22], to derive new conceptual and material insights [23], to mobilise publics [5, 24], and to provide alternative ways of thinking about, and engaging with, wicked and social problems [25, 26]. Because of this, design things can play a role in addressing matters that concern communities [3, 4].

In the context of energy futures, our aim is to develop a design prototype that engages people with the issues associated with energy, provoking them to think about the problems from alternative perspectives and encourage them to consider the longer-term implications of personal and policy decisions.

In keeping with a design research approach and our goal to understand the potential of tangible interaction to tell public interest stories, our design was informed by the practices and aspirations of professional journalists. Prior to developing the prototype, seven people were interviewed about their storytelling practices. They were also invited to speculate on how physical computing might change the way they told stories. The seven participants all took an experimental approach to their own journalistic practice. They included the editor of a digital-only daily news site (P5); a science reporter for a national broadcaster (P1); two freelance journalists (P4 and P7); a television current affairs producer (P2); a data journalist (P3); and the president of an international news design organisation (P6).

Interviews focused on the process of storytelling; how journalistic values impact story judgement; and how technology impacts storytelling practices. After the interviews, each person was sent an exercise focused on how they might reimagine telling a news story through objects or ambient technologies. The exercise was contained in a slim A5, blank-page notebook into which was glued instructions and 14 questions, each on a separate page with space for responses. The questions prompted participants to think of a story, identify the people and objects involved, and then consider how they might tell that story by moving it to a different location and using physical computing technologies such as RFID tags, sensors and lights, among other things. Of the seven, four completed and retuned the design workbooks. Insights from the interviews revealed several themes that influenced the design of Vim's stories and interactions.

## 4.1  Time

Time was mentioned by several participants. Comments related to time as both a driver of narrative and a production constraint: stories needed to be timely and produced quickly. This meant that *"Things aren't being uncovered because no one's got the time"* (P4). A lack of time was also seen as an impediment to exploring alternatives: *"I can't spend forever experimenting"* (P3).

Designing Vim, we wanted to play with time, in particular the journalistic focus on immediacy. We extended the narrative timeline, writing stories set in the distant past (850CE when windmills were used to grind grain) through to a distant but not remote future (2085 when black hole technology is used to trap thermal energy from bush fires). A sample story feed for a reader who chooses 'generate more' and 'policy' spans 101 years. The stories cover the development of new coal mines in the UK from 1947; the closure of coal mines in China in 2019; and job losses at the Adani Carmichael mine in 2048. Playing with time in this way enables the design to take a complex topic and project it backward for context and forward to prompt readers to consider the consequences. This breaks with journalistic practices focused on reporting current events and reaction to them, instead resonating with imaginative methods from design such as future scenarios [27] and design fictions [28, 29].

## 4.2  Facts and Fiction

Journalism emphasises reporting facts and representing situations in a balanced way. Because of this, verifying information is a core practice [30]. Interviewees explained it this way: *"Often, I'll have to get three sources to check something"* (P4); *"The basic journalistic tenets remain the same, like factual reporting, remaining balanced and unbiased, not letting as much of my opinions through"* (P1).

However, there is a view that notions of detachment and objectivity embodied in these practices are not sufficient in an online environment and that journalists need to become interested and active participants in stories [31]. One of our participants explained that a news designer she knew wanted the news media to take an active role in addressing the issues it reported on: *"[...] he wants to be able to figure out how to use media to [...] work with healthcare technology to solve the healthcare [issue]"* (P6). She believed the importance of journalism was to effect change.

Our decision to write future news was inspired by critical design practices that seek to offer alternative, or speculative, views of how things are, or how they could be [22]. Vim's future stories describe nuclear-powered cars and towns; laws that require all new buildings to generate power; and a multiplayer game that encourages people to vote against politicians who do not use their position to limit climate change. These scenarios aim to illustrate how today's actions might impact tomorrow.

### 4.3 Participation

Our participants saw a role for physical artefacts and ambient media as a way to enable readers to participate in stories. One of the workbooks described *"a more personal experience being surrounded by images and sound and the physical presence of [...] artefacts"* (P2). Another wanted to *"engage multiple senses"* (P5) and two (P1 and P5) imagined moving storytelling to locations. Yet informing readers was privileged over emotional engagement. One participant lamented a lack of context in journalistic storytelling, saying readers were not given enough information to put stories in context: *"All that's being asked of them is an emotional response, and people can't keep running on emotion"* (P7).

Vim aims to enable participation via physical inputs by the reader. The printed stories reflect the choices readers make via tangible interaction with the machine. This produces a personalised experience to the extent that the printed news feed reflects their choices. The need to physically input preferences contrasts with the passive, algorithm-driven news feeds of social media. Even if a reader wants Vim to decide their news, they need to physically make that choice. In this way, Vim's interaction was designed to encourage participation with the issue of energy futures and to act in relation to it: by choosing a perspective, donating energy, or answering a question.

### 4.4 Impact

Journalism aims to have social impact. The nature of that impact varies greatly and can be as simple as informing communities about things that are important or as ambitious as exposing systemic corruption or injustice. Much journalism reports incremental developments in ongoing issues and often the bigger picture and longer-term consequences can be lost. Our speculative stories aim to address this, but we also want readers to be able to participate in addressing the energy issue. The design does this in two ways: readers can help power Vim through manual effort by turning the crank, and they can respond to the questions. These two questions are open and invite diverse responses. The box is designed to collect responses—via a writing table and slot to return the note, and via a web page, where we plan to collate readers' views.

## 5   Critique

Like many tangible narrative systems, Vim uses physical interaction to drive story experience, but Vim's public-interest goals mean the interaction is directed toward engagement with the underlying issue. The framework for tangible narrative developed by Harley and co-authors [6] provides a useful way to critique Vim's design.

*Primary User.* Vim's primary users are people interested in, or impacted by, energy policy. While those most aware of the effects of power generation on policy, society and economy are most likely to be adults, children are not precluded from Vim's design. Indeed, by adopting a journalistic writing style, Vim's news feed should be accessible to a cross-section of readers.

*Media.* Vim is a multimedia system, encompassing analogue and digital interaction and outputs. In the design, the tangible interface determines the feedback and constrains narrative choice: readers can make three choices in relation to stories: philosophical position; category; or the machine's choice.

*Narrative Function of the Tangible Objects.* Rather than supporting storytelling characteristics such as plot, character or setting, the tangible objects in this prototype primarily communicate information about the system, for instance, the energy being used and generated, or how story components are organised. These objects facilitate user choice and interaction.

*Diegetic Tangibles.* Vim's story world is the real world, both lived and speculative. The narrative exists in the time and place that the box is located and in the interactions of the people who use it then and there. The design does not represent a story component, nor is it the story. The story is in the actions of the public, politicians, energy companies and researchers, among others.

*Narrative Creation.* This system constrains a user's ability to create stories by offering a limited number of pre-written narratives that are organised based on choice. Although a reader can personalise the feed, they would not be considered authors. However, the system also encourages involvement in future narratives by answering questions.

*Narrative Choice.* Vim offers implicit narrative choices as part of the available interactions and readers discover the consequences of their choices after the interaction.

*Narrative Position.* According to Ryan's [32] taxonomy, a reader's position would be considered external, as they are outside the narrative—in this case, their lived experience of energy use. However, the design enables them to both explore and make decisions about the story: they can make choices that impact the content and they are asked to speculate on the future. Because of this, the system does not fit neatly into the four narrative positions.

This brief analysis suggests public interest stories have qualities that diverge from fictional approaches to tangible narrative. In particular, factors such as where a story exists and the role of a reader within the narrative need to take account of the real-world context and role of 'characters' and 'settings' outside of the story. Unlike many tangible story projects, story creation is not the key goal. Rather, the aim is to engage publics on issues that concern them. Storytelling is a way of communicating information and interaction enables people to participate in the issue.

## 6  Conclusion and Next Steps

Vim is a work in progress, however, our design process and story concept suggest there is scope to explore the potential of, and design implications for, tangible public-interest storytelling. As a collection of physical computing components, Vim enables us to explore the potential of light-touch interaction and visceral reactions in relation to a wicked problem. The design challenges people to make a deliberate choice regarding the philosophical divide that permeates public debate about energy, but it also asks them to consider the consequences of decisions. In this way, the design asks the public to participate in energy as a matter of community concern [33].

As a computer system, Vim can capture reader choices and responses. The system logs reader inputs and story outputs, as well as energy donated or generated via the sun. Reader responses to questions are collected in the box. This means Vim can gather insights into perceptions of energy futures as well as insights into the relationship between tangible interaction, stories and responses.

We are mindful that interest in storytelling via objects such as gloves [34], three-dimensional shapes and flat surfaces [35–37] has more recently given way to a focus on immersive storytelling experiences, such as those made possible with mixed reality systems [38]. In journalism, in particular, virtual reality is seen as a way to give people a first-person experience of an event or situation [39]. However, Vim along with projects such as [X]PC [37] and Instabooth [9], which seek to facilitate human interaction and discussion on social issues, or to encourage community engagement, suggests there is more to learn about the use of objects and storytelling in public debate.

We are currently waiting to deploy the prototype in user evaluations. As social distancing restrictions related to the coronavirus outbreak lift, we plan to install Vim in a range of public spaces. We will capture and analyse data on reader's interactions with the system as well as their written responses to questions about the future and how they imagine the issues surrounding energy policy will play out. We are particularly interested in how interaction intersects with the notion of balancing interests, which underpins thinking on the public interest, and what this tells us about story form.

**Acknowledgements.** This research was funded by through a University of Queensland Early Career Researcher Grant.

## References

1. Nerone, J.: The historical roots of the normative model of journalism. Journalism **14**, 446–458 (2013). https://doi.org/10.1177/1464884912464177
2. Broersma, M.: The unbearable limitations of journalism: on press critique and journalism's claim to truth. Int. Commun. Gazette **72**, 21–33 (2010). https://doi.org/10.1177/174804850 9350336
3. Binder, T., De Michelis, G., Ehn, P., Jacucci, G., Linde, P., Wagner, I.: Design Things. MIT Press, Cambridge (2011)
4. Bjögvinsson, E., Ehn, P., Hillgren, P.-A.: Design things and design thinking: contemporary participatory design challenges. Des. Issues **28**, 101–116 (2012). https://doi.org/10.1162/DESI_a_00165

5. DiSalvo, C.: Adversarial Design. MIT Press, Cambridge (2015)
6. Harley, D., Chu, J.H., Kwan, J., Mazalek, A.: Towards a framework for tangible narratives. In: Proceedings of the TEI 2016: Tenth International Conference on Tangible, Embedded, and Embodied Interaction - TEI 2016, pp. 62–69. ACM Press, Eindhoven (2016). https://doi.org/10.1145/2839462.2839471
7. Matias, J.N.: Philadelphia fullerine: a case study in three-dimensional hypermedia. In: Proceedings of the Sixteenth ACM Conference on Hypertext and Hypermedia - Hypertext 2005, p. 7. ACM Press, Salzburg (2005). https://doi.org/10.1145/1083356.1083360
8. Weibert, A., Aal, K., Oertel Ribeiro, N., Wulf, V.: "This is my story...": storytelling with tangible artifacts among migrant women in Germany. In: Proceedings of the 2016 ACM Conference Companion Publication on Designing Interactive Systems - DIS 2017 Companion, pp. 144–149. ACM Press, Edinburgh (2017). https://doi.org/10.1145/3064857.3079135
9. Caldwell, G.A., Guaralda, M., Donovan, J., Rittenbruch, M.: The InstaBooth: making common ground for media architectural design. In: Proceedings of the 3rd Conference on Media Architecture Biennale – MAB, pp. 1–8. ACM Press, Sydney (2016). https://doi.org/10.1145/2946803.2946806
10. Smith, A., Reitsma, L., van den Hoven, E., Kotze, P., Coetzee, L.: Towards preserving indigenous oral stories using tangible objects. In: 2011 Second International Conference on Culture and Computing, pp. 86–91 (2011). https://doi.org/10.1109/Culture-Computing.2011.24
11. Finkelstein QC, T.H.R.: Report of the Independent Inquiry into the Media and Media Regulation. Independent Inquiry into the Media and Media Regulation, Canberra, Australia (2012). https://parlinfo.aph.gov.au/parlInfo/search/display/display.w3p;query=Id:%22library/lcatalog/00380162%22
12. Johnston, J.: Public Relations and the Public Interest. Routledge, London (2016)
13. Myers, N., Simon, J.L.: Scarcity or Abundance? A Debate on the Environment. WW Norton & Company, New York (1994)
14. Bailey, R.: The End of Doom: Environmental Renewal in the Twenty-first Century. St. Martin's Press, New York (2015)
15. Yang, M., Sandu, S., Li, W., Khalid, M.T.: Renewable energy in Australia: a wider policy discourse. Chinese J. Population Resources Environ. 17, 241–253 (2019). https://doi.org/10.1080/10042857.2019.1638730
16. Djerf-Pierre, M., Cokley, J., Kuchel, L.J.: Framing renewable energy: a comparative study of newspapers in Australia and Sweden. Environ. Commun. 10, 634–655 (2016). https://doi.org/10.1080/17524032.2015.1056542
17. Eklund, E.: Mining Towns: Making a Living, Making a Life. UNSW Press, Sydney (2012)
18. Bird, J., Rogers, Y.: The pulse of tidy street: measuring and publicly displaying domestic electricity consumption. In: Proceedings of Workshop on Energy Awareness and Conservation through Pervasive Applications, p. 6. ACM, New York (2010)
19. Broms, L., Katzeff, C., Bång, M., Nyblom, Å., Hjelm, S.I., Ehrnberger, K.: Coffee maker patterns and the design of energy feedback artefacts. In: Proceedings of the 8th ACM Conference on Designing Interactive Systems - DIS 2010, p. 93. ACM Press, Aarhus (2010). https://doi.org/10.1145/1858171.1858191
20. Nuage Vert "Green Cloud" Illuminates Emissions. https://inhabitat.com/green-cloud-hehe-helsinki-environmental-art/. Accessed 27 Aug 2020
21. Simon, H.A.: The Sciences of the Artificial. MIT Press, Cambridge (1969)
22. Dunne, A., Raby, F.: Speculative Everything: Design, Fiction, and Social Dreaming. MIT Press, Cambridge (2013)
23. Dorst, K.: The core of "design thinking" and its application. Des. Stud. 32, 521–532 (2011). https://doi.org/10.1016/j.destud.2011.07.006
24. Le Dantec, C.A.: Designing Publics. MIT Press, Cambridge (2016)

25. Margolin, V., Margolin, S.: A "social model" of design: issues of practice and research. Des. Issues **18**, 24–30 (2002). https://doi.org/10.1162/074793602320827406
26. Buchanan, R.: Wicked problems in design thinking. Des. Issues **8**, 5–21 (1992)
27. Kensing, F., Madsen, K.H.: Generating visions: future workshops and metaphorical design. In: Design at Work: Cooperative Design of Computer Systems, pp. 155–168. L. Erlbaum Associates Inc., USA (1992)
28. Bleecker, J.: Design fiction: a short essay on design, science, fact and fiction. http://blog.nea rfuturelaboratory.com/2009/03/17/design-fiction-a-short-essay-on-design-science-fact-and-fiction/. Accessed 08 June 2020
29. Sterling, B.: Design fiction. Interactions **16**, 20 (2009). https://doi.org/10.1145/1516016.151 6021
30. Kovach, B., Rosenstiel, T.: The Elements of Journalism: What Newspeople Should Know and the Public Should Expect. Three Rivers Press, New York (2001)
31. Ryfe, D.M.: Can Journalism Survive? An Inside Look at American Newsrooms. Polity Press, Cambridge (2012)
32. Ryan, M.-L.: From Narrative games to playable stories: toward a poetics of interactive narrative. Storyworlds: A J. Narrative Stud. **1**, 43–59 (2009). https://doi.org/10.1353/stw. 0.0003
33. DiSalvo, C., Lukens, J., Lodato, T., Jenkins, T., Kim, T.: Making public things: how HCI design can express matters of concern. In: Proceedings of the SIGCHI Conference on Human Factors in Computing Systems, pp. 2397–2406. ACM Press, Toronto (2014). https://doi.org/ 10.1145/2556288.2557359
34. Tanenbaum, J., Tanenbaum, K., Antle, A.: The Reading Glove: designing interactions for object-based tangible storytelling. In: Proceedings of the 1st Augmented Human International Conference on - AH 2010, pp. 1–9. ACM Press, Megève, France (2010). https://doi.org/10. 1145/1785455.1785474
35. Mazalek, A., Davenport, G., Ishii, H.: Tangible viewpoints: a physical approach to multimedia stories. In: Proceedings of the tenth ACM international conference on Multimedia, pp. 153–160. Association for Computing Machinery, Juan-les-Pins (2002). https://doi.org/10.1145/ 641007.641037
36. Ryokai, K., Cassell, J.: Storymat: a play space for collaborative storytelling. In: Extended Abstracts on Human Factors in Computing Systems, pp. 272–273. ACM Press, New York (1999). https://doi.org/10.1145/632716.632883
37. Jaasma, P., Dijk, J. van, Frens, J., Hummels, C.: On the role of external representations in designing for participatory sensemaking. In: Alonso, M.B., Ozcan, E. (eds.) Proceedings of the Conference on Design and Semantics of Form and Movement - Sense and Sensitivity, DeSForM 2017. InTech (2017). https://doi.org/10.5772/intechopen.71207
38. Bucher, J.: Storytelling for Virtual Reality: Methods and Principles for Crafting Immersive Narratives. Routledge (2017). https://doi.org/10.4324/9781315210308
39. de la Peña, N., et al.: Immersive journalism: immersive virtual reality for the first-person experience of news. Presence: Teleoperators Virtual Environ. **19**, 291–301 (2010). https:// doi.org/10.1162/PRES_a_00005

# Tale of T(r)ails: The Design of an AR Comic Book for an Animal Welfare Transmedia

Mara Dionisio[1,2(✉)], Paulo Bala[1,2], Sarah Oliveira[3], and Valentina Nisi[2,4]

[1] FCT, Universidade Nova de Lisboa, Lisbon, Portugal
[2] ITI-LARSyS, Lisbon, Portugal
{mara.dionisio,paulo.bala,valentina.nisi}@iti.larsys.pt
[3] Universidade da Madeira, Funchal, Portugal
[4] IST, Universidade de Lisboa, Lisbon, Portugal

**Abstract.** Storytelling is a fundamental component of a child's early development stages, informing their world view and promoting self-growth. Comic books are a common medium in these development stages, for their power of communication and expression. Inspired by narrative branching structures and technological advances in Augmented Reality (AR), we developed *Tale of T(r)ails*, an AR branching comic book, targeting pre-teenagers (10–12 years old). This paper's contribution focuses on the design of an AR comic book aiming at critically engaging pre-teens with Animal Welfare and motivating them for real-world actions.

**Keywords:** Branching narrative · Interactive storytelling · Augmented reality · Transmedia storytelling · Educational narrative

## 1 Introduction

Stories are a natural and vital element of our lives, imprinting messages in our subconscious and eventually in our belief system [4]. Fictional and non-fictional storytelling allows us to understand and critique our world [4], and through narrative persuasion, to actively educate its audience and promote change in the real world [5]. Stories told or read by children can make a difference as they not only develop literacy but also convey values, beliefs, attitudes and social norms, shaping children's perceptions of reality [1]. However, designing effective digital products for playing and learning requires an understanding of the child's cognitive development stages [3], together with narrative and technological skills.

Inspired by the Transmedia for Change framework (T4C) that focuses on stimulating change in individuals and communities [8], we developed *Tell a Tail*, a bespoke T4C experience, aimed at adolescents (10–19 years old), dealing with Animal Companion Welfare in Madeira Island, specifically, on the (re)education of the public regarding the effects and actionable measures to overcome animal

---

M. Dionisio and P. Bala—Contributed equally.

© Springer Nature Switzerland AG 2020
A.-G. Bosser et al. (Eds.): ICIDS 2020, LNCS 12497, pp. 281–284, 2020.
https://doi.org/10.1007/978-3-030-62516-0_25

abandonment. For that purpose, *Tell a Tail* is composed of two initial proto-types: (1) *Tell a Tail 360°*, an immersive webVR documentary on the different stakeholders of rescue missions (e.g. kennels, veterinarians, non governmental organizations, etc), and (2) *Tale of T(r)ails*, a branching comic book with Aug-mented Reality (AR). Comic books are an expressive medium for storytelling due to its combination of visuals and language [7] and have been previously used in classroom settings [9,11]. Based on previous attempts to redesign comics extend-ing its traditional paper-based format [2,6], this work investigates the potential merging of branching narratives, AR and comic books, therefore, its contribution lies in the artifact description of the *Tale of T(r)ails* T4C component.

## 2   Design of *Tale of T(r)ails*

*Tale of T(r)ails* combines the traditional experience of reading a comic book with AR's potential for agency and immersion. Participants can read the comic as a traditional branching narrative following a "choose your own adventure" struc-ture. Furthermore, along with the comic book, AR scenarios can be triggered at specific points of the narrative. These AR scenarios bring the fictional charac-ters of the comic book into the real-world (as over imposed computer-generated characters and environments), allowing participants to build a stronger rela-tionship with the characters and deeper immersion in the story world. Figure 1 shows the overall flow of interaction of the participants with the comic book and the mobile application that triggers the AR scenarios. In this section, we delve into the details of the narrative design, the comic book design and AR mobile application design.

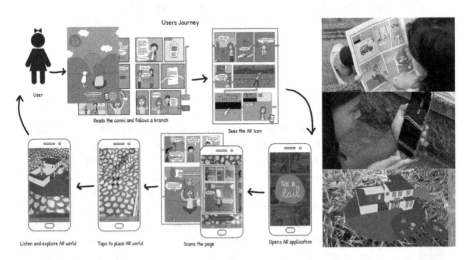

**Fig. 1.** Flow of interaction with the comic book enhanced with AR scenarios.

The story recounts the adventures of Chris, who after a long wait is finally allowed to own a dog, Penny. Chris is a pre-teenager struggling to fit in school, burdened with self-esteem problems and easily influenced by her peers while searching for their approval. By reading the comic book in the format of a branching narrative, the audience is able to uncover and make choices regarding how Chris handles the inherent responsibilities of owning Penny. The narrative was strongly inspired by a contextual research regarding Animal Welfare in Madeira Island, where data exposed the main issues being: overpopulation of animal shelters; domestic animals mistreatment; lack of awareness to the importance of sterilization; and lack of responsibility/education of owners regarding the basic care. Hence, the story branches were designed to raise the reader's awareness about animal abandonment, how to train and take care of a pet and the importance of sterilization. At the very beginning of the comic book, the story branches into two paths: "Path A – Adoption" of Penny from the kennel and "Path B – Purchase" of Penny from a shop. The two paths never intertwine and the story trails culminate into four different endings (two for each path, A and B). The story shows how dogs, independently of the breed, do not come pre-disciplined and how sterilization is important in controlling the abandoned animal population.

The visual style and graphical decisions were matched to our target audience as we opted for joyful visuals to keep pre-teens interested, despite the seriousness of the message. The initial pages give the audience instructions on how to follow the branches of the narrative. The graphical style of the comic book was carefully designed so that the reader can rely on the colors to guide him/her through the choices, while minimizing the visual clutter. Along the comic, story branches are color coded differently, and the border of each panel also is highlighted by the corresponding color, inspired by [10].

There are twelve AR scenarios throughout the whole comic book. These scenarios complement the story from Penny's perspective, showing Penny's feelings and fears towards the events that are happening in the comic book. The AR application is a vital part of making a stronger connection between the reader and Penny. The AR scenarios also contain an educational message regarding Animal Welfare. To further illustrate the nature of the content, we will describe two scenarios. In the first "The Kennel", Penny introduces herself, thanks the reader for adopting her and explains the kennels' adoption system. Furthermore, she highlights the importance of adopting and shows that kennels are almost always overpopulated, hence the dogs do not receive the amount of care that they need. In the other AR scenario "Veterinary", we see Penny behaving nervously as she does not understand where she is going. At the vet, Penny gets a vaccine, and hates the experience but she is rewarded with a treat, calming her down. This intends to show the importance of going to the vet even when the pets get anxious and the power of positive reinforcement.

To uncover the AR scenarios, the reader utilizing the camera view of the AR application scans the comic book page. This will trigger the placing of a pop-up scenario into the real-world. These scenarios are comprised of a mix between a 3D background environment and a 2D model of characters. In the AR scenarios, Penny dialogues with the reader, using a tone and narrative structure suitable for the target audience. The graphic style of the AR application matches the comic book style, bringing the comic and its characters to life. In this way, the reader does not need to be confined to what is shown in the comic book panels, giving them the ability to move around freely and explore the fictional world. The whole AR application was developed in Unity 2019.3.0a11, with ARCore v1.10.0, along with Fungus SDK to handle the narrative flow.

## 3    Conclusion

During the development of *Tale of T(r)ails*, it become evident that comics offer a rich design space, full of potential interaction possibilities when AR is applied to traditional mediums such as branching comic books. In the future, using this prototype, we will investigate the potential of combining comics, branching narratives and Augmented Reality in creating experimental and novel ways to tell a story, by conducting formal evaluations studies focusing in distilling lessons for designers and uncovering limitation of comics as a design space.

**Acknowledgments:.** This work has been supported by MITIExcell (M1420-01-0145-FEDER-000002), LARSyS-FCT funding (UIDB/50009/2020) and FCT Ph.D. Grant PD/BD/128330/2017 and PD/BD/114142/2015.

## References

1. Albers, P.: Why stories matter for children's learning (2016). http://theconversation.com/why-stories-matter-for-childrens-learning-52135
2. Eisner, W., Eisner, W., Eisner, W.: Comics and Sequential Art: Principles and Practices from the Legendary Cartoonist. W.W. Norton, The Will Eisner Library, New York (2008)
3. Gelman, D.L.: Design for Kids: Digital Products for Playing and Learning. Rosenfeld Media, Brooklyn, NY (2014)
4. Green, M.C., Brock, T.C.: The role of transportation in the persuasiveness of public narratives. J. Pers. Soc. Psychol. **79**(5), 701–721 (2000). https://doi.org/10.1037/0022-3514.79.5.701
5. Green, M.C., Brock, T.C., Kaufman, G.F.: Understanding media enjoyment: the role of transportation into narrative worlds. Commun. Theory **14**(4), 311–327 (2004). https://doi.org/10.1111/j.1468-2885.2004.tb00317.x
6. McCloud, S.: Reinventing comics: how imagination and technology are revolutionizing an art form. Perennial, New York, NY, 1. ed., [nachdr.] edn. (2000)
7. McCloud, S.: Understanding comics. William Morrow, an imprint of Harper Collins Publishers, New York, reprint edn. (2017)
8. Pratten, R.: Getting Started with Transmedia Storytelling: A Practical Guide for Beginners - 2nd edition (2015)
9. Versaci, R.: How comic books can change the way our students see literature: one teacher's perspective. Engl. J. **91**(2), 61–67 (2001)
10. Ward, P., et al. (eds.): Adventure time. KaBOOM, Los Angeles, CA (2012)
11. Yıldırım, A.H.: Using graphic novels in the classroom. Dil ve Edebiyat Egitimi Dergisi **2**(8) (2013)

# The Interactive Narrative Research Discipline and Contemporary Practice

# Circuits, Cycles, Configurations: An Interaction Model of Web Comics

Alessio Antonini[1] ⓘ, Sam Brooker[2] ⓘ, and Francesca Benatti[1(✉)] ⓘ

[1] The Open University, Milton Keynes MK7 7LX, UK
{alessio.antonini,francesca.benatti}@open.ac.uk
[2] Richmond University, London TW10 6JP, UK
sam.brooker@richmond.ac.uk

**Abstract.** We are accustomed to thinking about multimedia technologies as a coming-together: consider the convergence of still images and sound in film, for example. This approach, however, struggles to accommodate the slippery distinction between different components in a digital space. This paper approaches new technology as a perceptually-generated matrix holding discrete components in relation to one another. These temporary formation of interacting components facilitate a unique structure which is *other* than the sum of its component parts. It outlines the unique lifecycle of the webcomic, and its relationship with infrastructures both of feedback and distribution, through the systematic evaluation of the specific calibration of technology-based interaction found in the medium.

**Keywords:** Webcomics · Interactive narrative · Content technology

## 1 Introduction

Gestalt, from the German word meaning *form*, refers to a pattern or shape – the sense of something being whole. This name was adopted by predominantly Austrian and German psychologists of the early 20th century, to explain (among other things) our perception of individual components as forming part of a pattern. One famous example shows what appears to be an abstract field of black marks; upon recognising it as a dog, the entire image resolves itself in the mind of the viewer. This coming-together of individual components to form a gestalt is embodied in psychologist Kurt Koffka's well-known phrase "the whole is other than the sum of its parts".

Well-known but often mis-translated, with *greater* substituted for *other*. The whole is not *greater* than the sum of its parts - "this is not a principle of addition," as Koffka adds - but something different. This new form has a being apart from the individual elements, one recognised by the drawing-together of single components into one perceptual system.

This approach provides us with a convenient way to talk about new technologies. We are already accustomed to thinking about multimedia technologies as a coming-together: consider the merging of still images and sound in film, for example. We are also acquainted with media convergence more generally, "a situation in which multiple media systems coexist and where media content flows fluidly across them" [1]. If transmedia

© Springer Nature Switzerland AG 2020
A.-G. Bosser et al. (Eds.): ICIDS 2020, LNCS 12497, pp. 287–299, 2020.
https://doi.org/10.1007/978-3-030-62516-0_26

storytelling represents "a process where integral elements of a fiction get dispersed systematically across multiple delivery channels for the purpose of creating a unified and coordinated entertainment experience" [2], one in which "the distinction between the message and the work of art, envisaged as a microterritory attributed to an author, is fading" [3] then our approach seeks to codify the resultant media landscape.

What constitutes an "integral element" in a fluid, fragmented space where unified and coordinated experiences are hard to identify? Transmedia models sometimes struggle to accommodate the slippery distinction between different components found in a digital space. Web technologies, for example, facilitate fast-paced generative spaces in which tools and approaches are continuously combined and recombined, and where static or formalist definitions of a particular configuration seem obsolete. Instead this paper outlines an ontology which positions new technology as a perceptually-generated matrix holding discrete components in relation to one another. The distinction between media systems and media content becomes less profound, since these integrate in a temporary configuration in which the paratextual becomes textual. These temporary formations of interacting components facilitate a unique structure which is *other* than the sum of its component parts. It is a framework general enough to describe the technology-mediated interactions between actors involved in the content lifecycle whilst remaining agnostic to specific platforms.

By way of illustration this paper situates the webcomic not as a discrete entity, a JPEG on a screen, or as a transmedial component in a greater distributed story. Instead it sees the webcomic as a formation of discrete interactions which take place in a variety of spaces. These interactions blend together in a continuous experience that manifests across multiple platforms: reading apps, mailing lists, comment forums, funding platforms, conventions etc. They also exist between the user and the content, in operations which exist solely in the narrative spaces. The affordances of the "digital first" reading experience facilitated by webcomics in turn permits the formation of this integrative, aggregate model.

The specific configuration of the current webcomics ecosystem creates a new interaction space that in turn configures the relations between all actors (readers, authors, editors etc.) The value of this investigation is threefold:

1. It permits a better understanding of a web-native models of interaction, which goes beyond speculation about specific platforms. Understanding the limitations represented by a particular configuration of elements (social and technological) provides a predictive model for fledgling authors looking to identify how a particular technological circumstance will affect their work.

2. It explores the combination of diegetic (within) interaction with non-diegetic (out) interaction combining reading and authorial space. This is of particular relevance to scholars and authors seeking to understand how technological and social externalities impact and shape narrative content, and the manner in which expectations produced by a certain configuration may impact their creative work.

3. It is beneficial both to readers and authors of webcomics: readers are recognised for the ways in which the discrete components of their experience are drawn together, while authors can better understand the relationship between readers and funders, an essential part of the content creation experience. Authors seeking to thrive in a world

where the traditional publishing value chain is being "disrupted and disintermediated at every stage" [4] would do well to understand the osmosis between the construction of narrative and that of audience. Reader-response as a technologically mediated process deserves this recognition.

This contribution presents a technological analysis of webcomics as an integrated ecosystem of authorial, editorial, funding and reading tools, mediating a complex network of interrelation between the key actors of the webcomics life cycle. The analysis highlights the technology-mediated interactions within the specific anatomy of webcomics, breaking the traditional separation in phases of the content industry, and the differentiation between the diegetic space of content experience and the nondiegetic spaces of content creation. The study of webcomics provides the opportunity to outline a general framework of analysis that can be used to guide the design and assessment of content technologies.

## 2 Background

The differences between the communication circuit of print comics and webcomics have been discussed in Benatti [5]. In print comics and by extension in digital versions of print comics, the agents invested with the most significant amount of influence are publishers and distributors. Webcomics by contrast develop a different communication circuit that enables the emergence of alternative genres, formats, authors and readers. This broadening of the audience of comics is also enabled by webcomic creators' preference for microtransactions. Unlike print comics, webcomics are often free to read and employ crowdfunding platforms such as Kickstarter and Patreon to support creators through small voluntary transactions. These often use as an enticement additional interaction possibilities, such as pre-release access to new content or more direct involvement in the content creation process, from naming new characters to having the reader's likeness included within the narrative. Additionally, webcomics also allow readers to interact with other readers by inscribing their views as comments in the margin of the page or even upon the page itself (such as in Japanese tsukkomi). Finally, webcomics experiment with digital-native page layouts optimised for mobile interfaces, such as the vertical strip of the Korean platform Webtoons, which enable new haptic interface possibilities (see Fig. 1).

One consequence of this shift to a more creator-centric approach to publication is a desire for immediacy in the interactions between consumers and creators of content, which is also evident in other sections of the digital literary sphere [6]. Maintenance of an online persona becomes a de facto requirement as webcomics creators take responsibility for what might previously have the role of a publisher, including marketing. Combined with a frequent posting schedule (daily or weekly) and the emotional investment that often comes with financial ones, webcomics producers become obvious candidates for the formation of parasocial relationships, imagined relationship consumers have with the producers of content. The formation of these relationships represents a significant part of our conversation around online media, where consistency of persona permits the relationship to form.

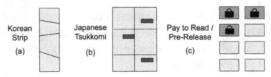

**Fig. 1.** Korean long-strip (a) is optimised for continuous scrolling; Japanese tsukkomi (b) enable comments on the comic boards; micropayments (c) grant sponsors pre-release access.

In his exploration of audience types, theorist Gamson identifies five ways to experience celebrity, of which four position the relationship as antagonistic to some degree [7]. Audiences are seen as probing or testing the reality of the celebrity persona as articulated either through their work or behaviour (the former being a component of the latter) in a relationship analogous to the play between comic creator and audience. Audiences both test the persona, seeking inconsistency in identity, but also seek to define (or redefine) the persona, policing the identity presented by the creator. This tension between the demands of the reader and the willingness of the author to acquiesce in turn manifests itself in the nature and form of interactions resulting from that tension.

### 2.1 Content Lifecycle

As theorised by Darnton [8], the "communications circuit" of print book production has a clear distinction between phases. Once printed, works cannot be amended unless published in a new edition. The work requires significant production time and a material outlet (bookshops) for distribution, after which the reader's role in the feedback mechanism is historically confined primarily to indirect sources (such as sales). Print comics have a shorter life cycle, which is dominated by their serial publication, usually through monthly issues. Further periodicity also exists, for example through annual conventions such as Comic-Con, Lucca Comics and the Angoulême Festival.

Digital technology does not introduce new elements to the content life cycle, but it can blur its shape and distinctions between phases. It is worth highlighting that the current model we consider as a baseline is the result of the industrialisation of content creation, which rationalised phases and roles so that they achieve predictable outcomes. In general, we generalised at least three different lifecycle models (see Fig. 2):

1. A book-like life cycle is distinguished by long creation and distribution phases; book writing can take a span of years, and its fruition can span decades or centuries
2. A serialization-like life cycle is distinguished by a long creation phase and a distribution broken-down in periodical issues, i.e. weekly or monthly episodes
3. A webcomics-like life cycle is distinguished by a broken-down creation phase which generates small units of interdependent contents, that are distributed before the ending of the overall creative process

The differences between the first two models concern mostly the distribution channels and media used. On the one side, books are expensive to produce and their distribution through a network of bookshops and libraries is relatively slow. On the other side,

**Fig. 2.** Life cycles of (a) books, linear creation and linear content experience, (b) series, a linear creation and experience in episodes, and (c) web series creation and experience.

magazines have a lower cost of production and they can rely on the distribution network of newsagents.

In contrast, the model of webcomics is justified by the need to support the ongoing creation process, by monetization and rapid assessment of the validity of the creative work. Webcomics are not usually like magazine strips, short and self-conclusive works, but often lengthy works of hundreds or thousands of issues. As independent publications, webcomics are not overseen by professional editors, but supported by self-organised volunteers or para-professional groups. Thus, both the author and the support groups are limited and cannot sustain years or months necessary to "complete" a work, but must monetize as soon as possible by publishing on a weekly basis.

In a short time, a new issue is created, translated, distributed, monetised, read, commented and discussed. Readers can play multiple roles: contributing to translations for the benefit of other communities, funding the author, providing feedback, publicising the contents through social media, recommending and rating contents, commenting on the issue or commissioning new issues. While reading, users contribute both indirectly (through generation of ad revenue, for example) and directly (through micro-payments, rating, comments, commissions and suggestions). The parasocial relationship developed by an author discussing their lives and motivations with an interested audience deepens the engagement, a positive feedback loop. Such interactions can be detrimental, of course: the emotional labour of addressing fans, for example, or the scraping of new content for distribution in other platforms (with the author attribution removed.) All form part of the aggregate technology of the webcomic.

Overall, the webcomics life cycle has two distinct circuits: a reciprocal circuit in which rapid switching of roles and phases is necessary to support creation, and a terminal circuit more akin to magazines in the mid-term and books in the long term (see Fig. 3). Indeed, webcomic issues are collected in arcs which can be seen as major narrative milestones or partially independent storylines, which in the long term constitutes a coherent work in the light of an overall plot.

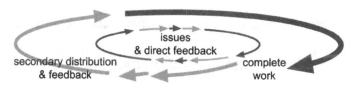

**Fig. 3.** Webcomics life cycle.

## 2.2  Content Technology

The disruptive, disintermediating effect of web technologies create the conditions under which webcomics can exist. The activities of each actor (author, reader, editor, publisher) is to an extent regulated by aggregate components of this technological gestalt. The combination of interactions represented by webcomics can be aligned with what this paper considers the four components of the mainstream content industry:

1. *Publishing systems*, in which the content is published first to the core reader base
2. *Distribution systems*, in which new content propagates across portals, newsfeeds and notification systems to secondary pool of consumers, which recontextualises the material
3. *Reading systems* (or consumer system), represented by multimodal, multi-channel web reading structures
4. *Feedback systems*, which connect authors, publishers and readers. This might be through comments, for example, or mechanisms of micro-funding based on early access to content and on ads.

This rather linear model can be simplified to consider the way in which a content technology "infrastructures" the content lifecycle. This in turn simplifies our understanding to something more akin to the traditional model of distribution and feedback found in the study of communications (see Fig. 4) which highlights two main phases:

1. *Distribution infrastructure*, in which content is delivered to users. This accommodates shops, websites, e-reader software, collected volumes etc.
2. *Feedback infrastructure*, which delivers resources necessary for the creative process: comments, ideas, criticism and (crucially) payment.

*Content creation* is motivated by the author but constrained by the resources provided by the feedback infrastructure. *Content experience* is instead motivated by reader curiosity but constrained by the resources provided by the distribution infrastructure.

In summary, the content life cycle is defined by two components: the infrastructures of distribution and of feedback.

**Fig. 4.** Distribution and feedback infrastructures.

## 3  A Framework for Content Technologies

A particular configuration of distribution and feedback infrastructures supports a particular content life cycle, which in turn exerts an influence over the actors participating in that life cycle. This drawing-together represents in some respects a causality dilemma: are webcomics creators more engaged with fans because technology encourages this behaviour, or because it permits it? Would the current configuration which we recognise as the common webcomics experience exist, were these technologies transplanted to a century ago?

Such questions are beyond the scope of this paper. What can be considered, however, is the particular circumstances which the current configuration of technology-mediated interactions creates. The frenetic lifecycle of the webcomic (combined with tools for social interaction) permit readers to develop a close relationship with the work, for example. What likely forms of interaction arise from the alignment of different actors within this matrix?

As discussed above, the content lifecycle involves a wide range of interactions: author-editor, editor-distributor, user-user, user-distributor and user-author. These interactions are supported either by feedback or distribution infrastructures. Focussing first on the former, it is possible to split interactions into two parts: diegetic interactions, which concern elements of the narrative world; non-diegetic, which concerns elements tangential to it. Which a reader favours has an impact on the manner in which they interact with the author. Some readers, for example, may object to Patreon announcements or the author's discussion of their personal politics – issues which they feel are unrelated to the world of the narrative. Digital technologies often place all user-to-user interactions within the same physical space, resulting in the interleaving of these conversations, much as game chat interrelates conversations about in-game currencies, difference-based bullying and more mundane social matters [9].

Interactions may be classified as regarding the narrative (N); tangential to the narrative (NN); part of the content experience (E); part of content creation (P). Each of these categories may befit a different actor (editors are more likely to be involved in content creation, for example) and each is likely to perceive object of study in a different way. See Fig. 5.

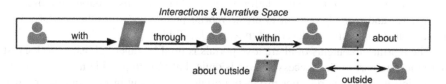

**Fig. 5.** Features of interactions: (N) about the narrative, (NN) not about the narrative, (E) part of the content experience, (P) part of the content creation.

As a content technology, webcomics mediate a wide range of interactions. In this regard, we can identify at least five main types of actors: author, reader, publisher, editor and patron. This results in 25 points of potential interaction between actors and a relative set of interactions (see Appendix[1], Table 1 [10]).

The language for these interactions is derived from an earlier work on the nature of technology mediated interaction [11] which seeks to identify appropriate binary dimensions which can be used to calibrate expectations around a particular technology (see Fig. 6 [10]). These dimensions are used as scales in describing in which direction the technology is pushing the interaction (see Appendix, Table 2 [10]).

**Fig. 6.** Dimensions of mediation of technologies-based interactions. (The original work of Antonini & Brooker identifies twelve dimensions, this contribution extends this list with three extra dimensions: negotiate/declarative, one-time/recurrent and structured/unstructured.)

By way of illustration, we may consider three examples of interactions between identified agents:

**Example 1: Author to Reader/Diary of a Serial**

The *diary of a serial* is an appendix included at the end of a webcomic issue. In these extra panels, authors share with readers their plan for the progression of the comic, the timing of the next issues and the difficulties they are facing.

The diary also provides a view on the sources of inspiration for the story, doubts and other insights which enrich the reading experience. The diary is coupled by the comment features and contacts of the author, such as upcoming convention appearances, which are used by readers to engage with the author.

The diary exploits the same publishing mechanism of the comic. This interaction is configured as described in Appendix, Table 3 [10].

**Example 2: Publisher to Publisher/Reprint**

Content is published on a main platform while other specialised publishers monitor for updates and extracts content to create reprint publications on other portals. This interaction is configured as described in Appendix, Table 4 [10].

The reprint of contents of alternative portals is used by other publishers to harvest and monetize part of the success of a webcomic, but also to provide new contents to the audience of their portal. For instance, portals specialising in Korean authors may replicate successful contents from Chinese or Japanese portals.

---

[1] Appendix published as a separate CSV file https://doi.org/10.21954/ou.rd.12936596.v2.

While in some cases the reprint does not add any value to the content, in other cases it requires a form of editing, such as translation of the comic.

### Example 3: Patron to Reader/Payment for Early Release

Webcomics issues are often free to read, but additional features or preferential early access may be locked under a pay to read condition. This interaction is configured as described in Appendix, Table 5 [10]. Payment for early release is a mechanism provided to readers who want to support an issue. Readers can take turns supporting the author knowing that their contribution to the community will be compensated by other members. Furthermore, this mechanism creates over time a fan club of readers sharing the burden of supporting the author.

In summary, narrative-mediated interactions between users (with the narrative and through the narrative) are likely to be diegetic interactions, while interactions within the narrative may or may not concern the narrative. Lastly, interactions outside the narrative are likely to be non-diegetic, but could still concern aspects of the narrative (e.g. critique, translations, or editorial contribution).

The preceding section considered one way in which interactions are regulated by a specific feedback infrastructure. We now move to consider how distribution infrastructure can impact on content distribution.

As discussed above, the webcomics technology ecosystem supports a frenetic life cycle. Phases that require years in print publication take place in weeks but are followed by a commensurate long tail of other activities. For instance, payment for early release accelerates the distribution to readers and the creation of new contents, while reprints broaden the distribution outside the author's channels. These interactions occur either during the creation or experience of contents, as input or output of the distribution or feedback infrastructures (see Fig. 7) with a commensurate effect on the speed of distribution.

The lifecycle is the result of numerous interactions between different subset of actors. The overall functioning of this technology-enhanced lifecycle is the result of the quality of the interactions, which the technology can support or hinder. Each activity requires alignment and compatibility between actors, specifically in regard to:

1. *Power structure* between the actors
2. The interviewing of actors' *Activity Schedules*
3. *Resource management*, i.e. access and use of resources among actors
4. Synergies between actors' *Goals*

Indeed, the features of the technology-mediated interaction provide a specific configuration for each activity. For instance, in **Example 1**, there is an alignment of goal and schedule between author and readers. The technology is reflective and negotiative, recurrent and about control, supporting the author in iteratively managing the alignment between their views and audience expectations. Both reading goal and production schedule are therefore kept in a tight engagement. In **Example 2**, there is an asymmetry in the power structure, which eventually reaches a balance. Even the publishers whose comics are reprinted are in turn capable of reprinting other publishers' comics. There is an exchange between subjects, who change their role. The technology is actionable and

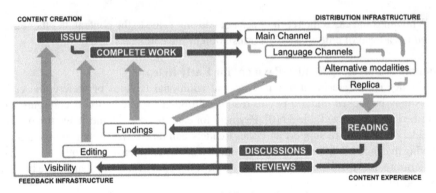

**Fig. 7.** Lifecycle activities in web comics

synchronous, resulting in a mutual enrichment of publishers' catalogues and an expansion towards new reader communities. In **Example 3**, the technology enables readers to take turns in sharing the burden of providing resources to the author. This happens by establishing a temporary power structure where readers take on the role of patron temporarily. No content creation, distribution, experience and feedback is possible without interaction, and with its lack of oversight, webcomics is an emblematic example.

Webcomics development becomes profoundly open, even where the author does not wish it to be so. If we see webcomics not as images on a website, but a complex ecosystem of interaction modalities held in matrix, then the various pressures exerting themselves upon the creator become manifest. Tensions emerge between the author as autonomous creative and an invested audience with a desire to shape the content. The non-diegetic element of the author's persona becomes enmeshed with the diegetic components of the story, in a manner which would likely distress Roland Barthes. The author in turn seeks to actively shape their audience both diegetically (through the content of their work) and non-diegetically (their online persona). By way of illustration we may consider the case of webcomic Ctrl-Alt-Del.

Ctrl-Alt-Del is a long-standing webcomic by artist and writer Tim Buckley [12]. A videogames-oriented webcomic in a model popular in the early 2000s (see also Penny Arcade [13] and PVP Online [14]) the tone was initially irreverent - and disinterested in longer-standing narrative. A contemporary reviewer described his work as consisting of "catty Warcraft jokes and the monkey-cheese-ninja random wackiness of manchild main character Ethan" [15].

On June 2nd 2008 Buckley posted a comic entitle *Loss* [16], which wordlessly depicted the miscarriage of main character Ethan's fiancée Lilah. This transition to a storyline which the same reviewer described as "excruciatingly slow, melodramatic, ham-handed" was met with significant negative response within the wider community. "I know that everybody has their own idea of what Ctrl + Alt + Del [15] is "supposed" to be," explained Buckley in a contemporary blog post, and this was certainly the case. Fellow webcomics creators jokingly described him as "the antichrist" and the comic received such widespread derision that it became a widely popular meme – one which Buckley subsequently engaged with. The comic returned to its roots, emphasising single-page arcs and narratives drawn from video games. Buckley sought to challenge his audience, and lost.

## 4   Discussion and Conclusions

"It is important," write Paul Duguid, "to think not idealistically about information, but materially" [17]. The novel emerged as the first print-native literary genre in the seventeenth and eighteenth centuries, simultaneously constrained and enabled by the technologies of print production and distribution [18]. In the nineteenth century Charles Dickens attempted to take control of the communications circuit by publishing his novels in the periodicals that he owned and edited, *Household Words* and *All the Year Round* [19]. However, the technological circumstances of print limited the opportunities for rapid response to reader feedback. Dickens sought to engage with his audience through an extensive programme of public readings, which spanned several countries and forced him into punitive workloads, potentially hastening his death. The rapid production, distribution and feedback infrastructures of webcomics are establishing the motivated cycle that eluded content creators like Dickens, who sought to cultivate those types of audience interaction that would better suit their needs. At the same time, readers become central to the distribution and feedback infrastructure, intervening into the storytelling process by taking over the roles of editors, translators and funders. The content experience of webcomics is therefore permeated by the diegetic and non-diegetic interactions enabled by this unique technological configuration.

Webcomics are a web native genre innovating mainstream comics from several perspectives, such as disintermediating the author/reader relation, enabling user-driven editorial processes, self-organised distribution of contents, multi-modal and multi-channel redistribution and micro-payments. The most relevant distinguishing results of this setting are the fragmentation of the communications circuit, as there is no centralized oversight by any organisation, and the blending of creation and experience, for example combining reading with publishing, publishing with engaging readers and reading with social media activity.

With this work, we want to raise awareness of different types of diegetic and non-diegetic interactions and use webcomics as an example of how technologies can be used to promote (or hinder) them. A limitation of this contribution and a clear line of future work is the analysis of the interplay between narrative and audience reaction. Several possible approaches present themselves: detailed semi-structured interviews with web comics creators, in which this relationship is explored; empirical explorations of fan communities and their fragmentation following significant evolution in the creator's work; a conscious reconfiguration of the communication circuit and study of its long-term consequences. Each of these approaches would require significantly more context – intellectually, biographically, socio-politically – than this technically-focussed paper can afford. The shift in tone and political consciousness of long-running "slice of life" webcomic Questionable Content, for example, presents an ideal model for exploring the fragmentation of its community – but would require significantly more space to evaluate. While the emphasis of this paper has not been on application, it is hopefully clear that there is substantial scope in this regard, at least sufficient to justify its presentation to this community.

Further work will also reflect on how certain configurations of aggregate technologies precipitate certain kinds of interaction. The gestalt of integrated technologies that we call webcomics is held together in part by the perception of its audience as having a form. Cultural perceptions of a certain configuration of technologies then impose their logic on the environment and influence criteria for success, as discussed for example by Floridi on the ethics of infrastructure [20]. We need a system to study these functionalities in general, abstracting their effects in the interactions between actors, both diegetic and non-diegetic. This speaks to a potential area of discussion – that this paper assumes a financial imperative, which is used a proxy for the wider motivations felt by the author.

A particular configuration of distribution and feedback infrastructures supports a particular content life cycle, which in turn exerts an influence over the actors participating in that life cycle. In this view technology is not neutral – rather it configures a specific field for interaction which may facilitate or impede communication, collaboration or competition between actors. The image-based format of webcomics, for example, permits forms of predatory publishing which erode the income of the author, but also supports the reader base in providing translations and pushing the content to different communities. The combination of impression-based advertising, with the limited cost of content crawling and replication, pushes toward a competition between platforms for the fastest and more reliable service.

Identifying the outcome of a particular technological configuration poses significant social and technological challenges. The interaction between an array of components, technologies, actors and social structures frustrates such efforts. Developing a model for evaluating the mediating effects of technology-based interaction would be helpful in developing a better understanding of how unique technological configurations can generate commensurate interaction configurations.

# References

1. Jenkins, H.: Convergence Culture: Where Old and New Media Collide. New York UP, New York (2006)
2. Jenkins, H.: Transmedia storytelling 101. Confessions ACA-Fan **22**(03) (2007)
3. Jenkins, H.: Art form for the digital age. Technol. Rev.-Manchester NH- **103**(5), 117–120 (2000)
4. Murray, P.R., Squires, C.: The digital publishing communications circuit. Book 2.0 **3**(1), 3–23 (2013)
5. Benatti, F.: Superhero comics and the digital communications circuit: a case study of *Strong Female Protagonist*. J. Graphic Novels Comics **10**, 306–319 (2019). https://doi.org/10.1080/21504857.2018.1485720
6. Murray, S.: The Digital Literary Sphere. Johns Hopkins University Press, Baltimore (2018)
7. Gamson, J.: Freaks Talk Back: Tabloid Talk Shows and Sexual Nonconformity. University of Chicago Press, Chicago; London (1998)
8. Darnton, R.: What is the history of books? Daedalus **111**, 65–83 (1982). https://doi.org/10.2307/20024803
9. Sengün, S., Salminen, J., Mawhorter, P., Jung, S.G., Jansen, B.: Exploring the relationship between game content and culture-based toxicity: a case study of league of legends and MENA players. In: Proceedings of the 30th ACM Conference on Hypertext and Social Media, pp. 87–95, September 2019

10. Antonini, A., Benatti, F., Brooker, S.: Appendix to "Circuits, Cycles, Configurations: an Interaction Model of Web Comics" (2020). https://doi.org/10.21954/ou.rd.12936596.v2

11. Antonini, A., Brooker, S.: Mediation as calibration: a framework for evaluating the author/reader relation. In: Proceedings of HyperText 2020. Orlando, Florida, July 2020. In print

12. Buckley, T.: Ctrl + Alt + Del Comic - A comic about video games!. https://cad-comic.com/. Accessed 09 June 2020

13. Holkins, J., Krahulik, M.: Penny Arcade. https://www.penny-arcade.com/. Accessed 09 June 2020

14. Kurtz, S., Meconis, D.: PVP Online. http://pvponline.com/. Accessed 09 June 2020

15. Clark, S.: Ctrl + Alt + Del's Winter-een-mas spontaneously aborts', 29 January 2010. http://blog.thephoenix.com/blogs/laserorgy/archive/2010/01/29/ctrl-alt-del-s-winter-een-mas-spontaneously-aborts.aspx via http://archive.org

16. Buckley, T.: Loss (2008). https://cad-comic.com/comic/loss/

17. Eliot, S., Rose, J. (eds.): A Companion to the History of the Book. Blackwell Pub, Malden (2007)

18. Duguid, P.: Material Matters: Aspects of the Past and Futurology of the Book. In: The Future of the Book, edited by Nunberg, pp. 63–102. University of California Press, Berkley (1996)

19. Patten, R.L.: Charles Dickens and His Publishers. Oxford University Press, Oxford, New York (2018)

20. Floridi, Luciano: Soft ethics and the governance of the digital. Philos. Technol. **31**(1), 1–8 (2018). https://doi.org/10.1007/s13347-018-0303-9

# Archiving Interactive Narratives at the British Library

Lynda Clark[1] , Giulia Carla Rossi[2] , and Stella Wisdom[2(✉)]

[1] InGAME, University of Dundee, Seabraes Ln, Dundee DD1 4LN, UK
lclark001@dundee.ac.uk
[2] The British Library, 96 Euston Road, London NW1 2DB, UK
{giulia.rossi,stella.wisdom}@bl.uk

**Abstract.** This paper describes the creation of the Interactive Narratives collection in the UK Web Archive, as part of the UK Legal Deposit Libraries Emerging Formats Project. The aim of the project is to identify, collect and preserve complex digital publications that are in scope for collection under UK Non-Print Legal Deposit Regulations. This article traces the process of building the Interactive Narratives collection, analysing the different tools and methods used and placing the collection within the wider context of Emerging Formats work and engagement activities at the British Library.

**Keywords:** Interactive Narratives collection · New media collection management · Digital storytelling · Emerging Formats · Web archiving · Digital preservation

## 1 Introduction: The Emerging Formats Project and the UK Web Archive

With the introduction of new digital media in the publishing landscape [1], cultural heritage institutions need to consider how new formats and their technical dependencies are shaping their collection policies, and how they can ensure meaningful collection and preservation of current digital outputs over the long term.

In order to address these issues and successfully represent the breadth of today's digital offer in their collections, the British Library (BL), together with the other five UK Legal Deposit Libraries (LDLs) set up the 'Emerging Formats Project' [2].

The UK Legal Deposit Libraries (Non-Print Works) Regulations 2013 [3], which extended legal deposit to include non-print publications alongside print works, provide the context for the Emerging Formats Project. The main objective of these Regulations was to help ensure comprehensive collection of UK publications, as well as safeguard born-digital publications against the risk of disappearance. Since 2013, the UK LDLs have been collecting a variety of born-digital material, mainly comprising eBooks, eJournals and archived UK websites [4]. All six UK LDLs, as a collaborative effort, are now looking at digital publications that are in scope for collection under Non-Print Legal

© Springer Nature Switzerland AG 2020
A.-G. Bosser et al. (Eds.): ICIDS 2020, LNCS 12497, pp. 300–313, 2020.
https://doi.org/10.1007/978-3-030-62516-0_27

Deposit (NPLD) Regulations, but whose formats, structure and content are more complex than those currently in their collection, and could pose a challenge to their existing collecting practices.

For this purpose the Emerging Formats Project was launched in 2017. Emerging formats were defined as born-digital publications with no print counterpart that have strong software and hardware dependencies, and often consist of more than one media type. They are created within a continuously changing marketplace, and most of these new formats are already at risk of rapid obsolescence [5].

In order to correctly identify user needs, The BL conducted targeted UX research into user behaviour and expectations for access to emerging formats. The research identified a strong interest in the added value of a curated collection of emerging formats, as well as support for the collection of contextual information around publications [6]. The anticipated need was for researchers - from a variety of fields, e.g. literature, digital humanities, history of science, social sciences, programming - and for creators of emerging formats. With regards to access, support from reference and curatorial staff was viewed as important, as was the idea of new types of library environment in which to use complex digital publications. These findings helped us shape the collection management methodology for emerging formats, including what and how we collect complex digital objects, and informed plans for future access.

The main goal of the Emerging Formats Project was to devise a system to identify, collect, describe, preserve and make available complex publications within scope of NPLD in a timely manner. This was to be achieved by means of different resources and collaborations (with creators, users, researchers, etc.) The UK LDLs chose to prioritise specific formats to begin their research: Book as mobile apps and web-based interactive narratives. The former refers to digital books published as mobile apps - they tend to have strong hardware and software dependencies and often make use of interactive features characteristic of mobile technology. The latter are online text-based stories, which require the reader's active input to determine how the narrative unfolds.

While the collection of mobile apps was uncharted territory for the LDLs, capturing web-based interactive narratives could be supported by workflows and tools already employed by the UK Web Archive (UKWA). The UKWA was originally founded at the beginning of 2005 as a consortium (UKWAC), and only operated on a permission basis, with curators carefully selecting websites and asking domain owners for permission to archive their work [7]. With the introduction of NPLD Regulations in 2013, the UKWA moved to archiving the UK web under Legal Deposit Regulations on behalf of all six UK LDLs. This includes an annual automated crawl of all UK websites (those that have either a UK top-level domain or can be identified as hosted or based in the UK), as well as the curation of special collections around specific topics and themes. This results in an archive of many millions of websites and hundreds of special collections.

## 2   Experiments and Engagement Activities that Enabled the British Library to Better Understand the Interactive Narratives Landscape

The BL established a Digital Scholarship department in 2010, with the aim to promote new methods of research using born digital and digitised library collections [8]. From its inception, this department fostered an interest in creative innovation and partnerships. Including seeking opportunities to collaborate with experimental writers and digital makers of narrative games and interactive fiction, to better understand the emerging digital format works, which they were creating.

The Library instigated experiments and initiatives, which included competitions, transmedia writing residencies, interactive writing summer schools and online game jams.

### 2.1   The Off the Map Game Design Competition

An early creative collaboration was the Off the Map competition [9], organised in partnership with GameCity festival and the videogame publisher Crytek. Launched in 2013, this competition set UK higher education students the task of creating videogames and virtual interactive environments using digitised British Library collection items, including maps, views, texts, illustrations and recorded sounds as creative inspiration [10].

A team of students called Pudding Lane Productions from De Montfort University, Leicester, won the first competition with their stunning interpretation of seventeenth century London before the great fire of London in 1666 [11]. Later Off the Map competitions were themed to coincide with BL exhibitions on gothic literature, William Shakespeare and Lewis Carroll's Alice's Adventures in Wonderland. Submissions offered completely new interpretations of the Library's collections and included interactive fiction entries, which had been created using the open source Twine platform.

### 2.2   Transmedia Writing Residencies in the British Library

The BL further learned about interactive storytelling methods, tools and technologies, via hosting creative residencies. Theatre-maker and entertainer Christopher Green was the Library's first writer-in-residence. His research into the history of hypnosis in the Library's collections, inspired him to write a book and a song cycle of original material through his character the Singing Hypnotist, who healed and mesmerised at Library performances and via online videos [12].

Following in these footsteps, Rob Sherman, author of experimental The Black Crown Project [13], undertook a transmedia residency interconnected to the Library's Lines In The Ice exhibition, which displayed collection items relating to Arctic exploration expeditions, including John Franklin's ill-fated voyage to find the Northwest Passage in 1845.

In a hybrid physical/digital installation On My Wife's Back, Sherman created a multimedia narrative about the fictional Isaac Scinbank, commissioned to search for Franklin's missing expedition [14]. This residency used many techniques, from songwriting, to baking ships biscuits and writing on them, to book binding, via an artistic collaboration with BL book conservators to make a faux-historical diary, called the "salmon book", which was installed in the gallery as an 'exhibit' and which Sherman updated with Scinbank's diary entries [15].

Sherman's residency included public workshops, where he taught attendees how to use the interactive narrative writing open-source programme Twine, to create their own hypertext stories. These workshops were further developed into week long interactive fiction writing summer schools held at the BL in 2017 and 2018. Jonathan Laury, writer of Ostrich, attended the 2018 summer school, mentioning it in the work's credits as being important to the piece's creation [16].

### 2.3 Online Interactive Fiction Writing Jams and AdventureX

Building from the experience of the Off the Map competitions, creative residencies and summer schools, the BL continued learning about web-based interactive narratives, by running online interactive fiction writing jams in partnership with Surrey Libraries and Read Watch Play: a global online reading group.

In 2017 Odyssey Jam was held, in which Lynda Clark created a Twine entry 108 Suitors, retelling the story of Penelope and her 108 suitors [17].

In 2018 a Gothic Novel Jam celebrated the 200th year anniversary of the publication of Mary Shelley's Frankenstein. It received 46 entries from all around the world including the UK, Australia, America and France [18].

The Bitsy game development community engaged with these jams, using their software to create 1980s retro style 2D games. Freya Campbell, whose works are in the UKWA collection, used both Twine and Bitsy to create her gothic novel jam submission THE TOWER [19], a work about trans women, tarot, therapy, and alien abduction. In addition to participating in Gothic Novel Jam, Campbell exhibited works, Superlunary [20] and Perseids, or, All This Will Go On Forever [21] at AdventureX; The Narrative Games Convention, which was hosted by the BL in 2018 and 2019 [22]. This event is dedicated to narrative-driven gaming and interactive storytelling, providing a forum for writers to share and celebrate their work. The AdventureX convention also provides opportunities for the BL to meet with the developer community and make contacts to facilitate collecting some of these works - inkle's mobile app 80 Days [23] was collected as part of the Emerging Formats project thanks to the direct collaboration with the studio, after discussions with co-founder, Jon Ingold, at AdventureX 2018 [24].

### 2.4 Archiving the Outputs of British Library Interactive Writing Experiments, Collaborations and Research Projects

In the early days of these experimental creative and research collaborations, collecting and preserving the digital outputs as Library collection items was not part of project aims for the Off the Map competitions, the online game jams, or the interactive fiction writing summer schools. However, with experience gained from each of these initiatives and events, the Library has increased its knowledge and understanding of the technologies and tools, such as Twine and Bitsy, which writers commonly use to create web-based interactive narratives. This reflection led to the development of research questions, which shaped Lynda Clark's BL post-doctoral placement project; investigating whether web archiving methods and web crawling technologies could capture, preserve and effectively play-back, these types of web-based interactive narrative works [25].

# 3   Building the Collection[1]

The Interactive Narrative collection was established as part of a six month post-doctoral placement entitled 'Emerging Formats: Discovering and Collecting Contemporary British Interactive Fiction'. The decision to focus on interactive fiction arose out of the Library's Emerging Formats project, acknowledging that without intervention, many culturally valuable digital artefacts are at risk of being lost. As observed by Joseph Tabbi in 2004, the experimental methods employed by many creators means they do not necessarily subscribe to standardised production practices, and have few centralised locations to share their work, a problem which is yet to be entirely solved [26]. However, this wild experimentation also means that digital interactive fiction is created by and for a wide variety of audiences and creators.

During the UX research mentioned previously, it was found that creators (more than readers) were particularly concerned about their work becoming unavailable in the future. Therefore, a creator-centric approach was adopted for the project. Selection was initially based on searches for British interactive fiction using a variety of specially selected websites, e.g. the Interactive Fiction Database (IFDB), and the entries of key interactive fiction competitions, e.g. The Interactive Fiction Competition (IFComp), plus submissions to various jams, including those organised by the BL. A callout was also issued via the BL's Digital Scholarship blog requesting that creators submit their own eligible work. In order to comply with LDL regulations and take ethical and technical considerations into account, the collection criteria specified that items must: be digital and web-based (e.g. not downloadable files); contain at least one interaction mechanic which advances the story; be a work of fiction (although it was acknowledged that the collection should later be expanded to include non-fiction works); be complete (e.g. have at least one beginning, middle and end - this was to address ethical concerns around inadvertently collecting texts which were not in the final release version intended by the creator); be made by an individual creator or small team, not a major studio; and be easily discoverable (e.g. hosted on a public site or entered into a competition, this was to avoid accidental inclusion of games, which creators did not intend to be widely shared). Items consisting purely of moving or static images; audio; or which were purchasable, or behind a login screen were excluded (due to the additional technical difficulties associated with collecting content of this nature).

## 3.1   Collection Tools

Tools used were W3ACT and Conifer (formerly Webrecorder). W3ACT, or ACT, the Annotation Curation Tool is Open Source software designed by the Library to help

---

[1] This section is an amalgamation of extracts from two reports originally produced for internal use at the British Library during the research project: https://doi.org/10.23636/1193 & https://doi.org/10.23636/1192.

librarians, curators and subject specialists curate specific parts of the Web [27]. It interfaces with the Heritrix crawl engine built by the Internet Archive. Both ACT and the Heritrix crawl engine are web archiving tools geared towards crawling the web at scale rather than in high fidelity. Rhizome's Conifer specialises in content which relies "on complex scripting, such as embedded videos, fancy navigation, or 3D graphics" [28] and had already been successfully used to collect a variety of complex content in the Net Art Anthology [29]. It was therefore adopted as a secondary capture method for items which could not easily be crawled due to multi-media content.

Conifer's capturing tool hosts collections of works online, which can also be downloaded as WARC files (although it should be noted that they are actually WARC.GZ). Conifer is also able to emulate older browsers, allowing capture of works which use older versions of javascript and Flash (Flash becoming obsolete was a key concern for some creators in the UX research). In order to get the best captures from Conifer, pre-planning is necessary, with an initial exploration of the work to determine how much needs to be captured, and to determine the best route to take through the work in the event that capturing in its entirety would prove too time-consuming. In an effort to ensure clarity of metadata for this project, each work was downloaded as an individual WARC file, although the tools do allow for combining multiple items (even entire collections) into single WARC files.

Broadly speaking, Conifer and ACT were each suited to capturing different types of works, although there were some works which neither could capture and some which worked well with both. Works which included YouTube videos could only be captured with Conifer, although this proved time consuming, as it seemed videos had to be played fully in order to guarantee good capture.

### 3.2 Categorising Collection Items

As this was a community-driven project, categories were developed from terms most often used within the community [30] and which could be easily explained to Library staff unfamiliar with IF: parser-based (works in which '[t]he player reads textual descriptions of the world and takes action by typing commands') [31]; choice-based (works in which the reader-player makes decisions as to the direction and/or outcome of the story at various branching points), hypertexts (primarily link-based and often non-linear) and multi-modal (works which 'link together many forms of communication: text, graphics, animation, sound, video, etc.') [32].

However, works made with Bitsy proved a challenge to categorise, as they often have a strong visual and textual element, but do not fall neatly into these existing categories. Therefore an additional category was adopted to refer to works created with Bitsy and similar tools: avatar-driven. Bitsy titles were considered within scope for this study because Bitsy creators tended to self-identify as creators of interactive fiction, as was seen both in how they categorised their work on itch.io and their entries into the Library's online jams.

It should also be noted these categories are not discrete and may overlap. As observed in previous BL studies of the form: 'Authors, readers, and technological development are all combining to create new kinds of literature, and thus fresh digital preservation challenges' [33]. Therefore, some works may arise which do not fit any of the aforementioned categories, or which recombine them in unexpected and challenging ways.

### 3.3 Findings

For the most part, Conifer is the best option for parser-based works. Inform 7 works can be captured very quickly – for the vast majority, visiting the title page and pressing space bar was sufficient to capture the entire work. They are then fully replayable in the capture, with users able to type any valid commands in any order. As many Inform 7 works use an emulator to run, most could not be captured with ACT. However, there were exceptions. Robin Douglas Johnson's Aunts and Butlers is a parser-based game created with his bespoke Versificator engine which captured successfully with ACT in a fully-playable state [34]. Similarly, 1k Cupid, an Inform 7 work by Elizabeth Smyth [35] uploaded to the Itch.io platform also captured successfully with ACT, which suggests the way the creator has structured and/or uploaded their work is of greater importance than the tool used, when it comes to how easily the work might be archived. One format which could not be captured by Conifer or ACT was Quest. Reasons for this are unclear, but as most Quest games are available both online and as downloadable files, and the Quest Software is open source, it may be possible to archive these files in a different manner [36].

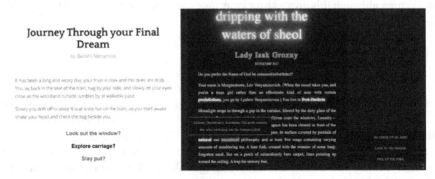

**Fig. 1.** Standard format Ink (l) vs customised format Ink with hover text and other styling (r)

Plain text works created with Ink, capture well in ACT and are fully playable [37]. Ink works with customised interfaces, such as Isak Grozny's dripping with the waters of SHEOL, would not capture with ACT, but captured well with Conifer [38] (see Fig. 1). This was more time-consuming than capturing parser-games, as each page was visited to ensure good capture. Visiting only the title page captured all links, but not any images or dynamic content on individual pages. Therefore each page should be visited to ensure good capture, which may not be actionable for large, multi-branching works. Obtaining walkthroughs may help direct captures, or serve as alternatives to capturing entire works, but are unlikely to be available for many works.

Works created with ChoiceScript can be captured with Conifer using its Firefox v49 emulator, although this is not without errors. However, experimentation showed that problems with capture in ACT appear to be due to the fact that many ChoiceScript authors host their files (even for complete, finished works) in an 'unfinished' state. When the files are finalised and compiled into a single html file, ChoiceScript works can be captured equally well with any version of Conifer and ACT. As ChoiceScript's standard output is a single html file, it should be possible to obtain these files from creators and archive them with relative ease, or suggest that creators host their files in this format prior to capture.

The majority of hypertext works capture well with ACT, although images are often missing. However, as with parser works, there are exceptions - Sleepless by Natalia Theodoridou was captured with all backgrounds and dynamic text. Only audio was missing, and this was successfully captured with Conifer [39]. Missing images in Twine games are generally due to use of the standard Twine file structure for images: http://game-name/images/image-name, while the game itself is usually kept at something along the lines of http://game-name/game. This can be resolved by adding the image URLs as separate seeds. (Right clicking the image or using a tool such as Link Klipper will generally yield the URL for the image). Some Itch embedded works made with Twine will not capture with ACT - this seems to be related to whether the creator has used a clickable 'run game' button to start the game – as works with autorun enabled (and therefore no button present) are less likely to capture. Twine works which use extensive Javascript are best captured with Conifer using the Firefox v49 emulator.

**Fig. 2.** Winnipeg captured in Conifer (l) vs ACT (r). In both cases, the coloured text remains dynamic, but in ACT, background images and additional moving text is lost.

The vast majority of Bitsy works captured well with ACT, despite functionality being primarily based around the use of arrow keys. As with other itch.io works, those with the auto run feature enabled did not capture with ACT, but captured successfully with Conifer. Only one work made with RPG Maker was found during the course of this study, but this also captured with ACT and retained full functionality including point-and-click and arrow key controls, although not without some technical problems. For example, skipping the title sequence sometimes causes a crash in the captured version. Increasing the capture limit in ACT seemed to improve the capture – the work was fully playable from beginning to end without error, even if the title sequence was skipped.

Generally, Conifer was most effective for capturing multimodal work due to its versatility with video and audio content, flash and javascript, and its ability to combine several interlinked sites into one WARC file. However, ACT proved surprisingly effective where multimodal works were concerned, depending on their construction, and provided they didn't contain Flash. Maria Mencia's The Winnipeg captured reasonably well with most background images and some animated text obtained (see Fig. 2) [40]. Some of the page's dynamic content failed, as did the browsable archive, since this required typing keywords rather than typical clicking. Similarly, works made with Unity captured unexpectedly well in ACT. Often, where a javascript page capture appears to have failed with ACT, finding the page which incorporates the html index file usually results in a good capture of the fully working piece. (This will generally be the url ending in index.html). This was the case with J.R. Carpenter's Along the Briny Beach [41], where capturing with ACT had the added benefit of capturing each asset used within the work, and the webpage's CSS stylesheet, which could not have been obtained using Conifer. These additional assets are likely to be useful to future researchers. In another of Carpenter's works, This is a Picture of Wind, neither ACT nor Conifer were able to capture the dynamic content present on the website since it uses live wind data to generate poetry [42]. However, during its crawl of urls associated with the site, ACT captured an example thumbnail of one of the poetry fragments. This demonstrates that even when a functioning version of the site cannot be captured, crawling may still be worthwhile.

Itch.io is a hosting site which hosts games of all kinds, including a large number of interactive fiction works. Capturing author's work from their itch page has the advantage of showing their work across different formats, plus any comments reader-players may have left for them, plus any development notes they themselves may have left. Works on these pages tend to be updated with greater regularity than those hosted on author's personal sites, and therefore may be useful to future researchers as a means of examining how interactive works are developed over time, or how creators evolve their work across different tools and projects.

ACT usually manages to capture multiple works from an itch page, although as mentioned previously, if the creator has used the 'auto run' button on any of work, this may result in a partial capture containing only the itch.io 'frame' and not the embedded content. As mentioned above, capturing with ACT may still be valuable regardless because of the other contextual information provided. Conifer (using Firefox javascript & Flash emulation where necessary) can successfully capture embedded itch works in all formats (at least, all those tested – Inform 7, Bitsy, Ink, Twine, Texture, Unity & compiled ChoiceScript), although it is necessary to click through each work in one single recording session in order to have a fully replayable capture. For some works, this took upwards of 30 min per work, and required QA of a comparable duration, which may not be feasible for Library staff where larger works, or larger collections of works are concerned. This also has the additional issue that any captures will only be a single instance of a work, with no method to see the work develop over time, aside from undertaking additional manual captures at later dates. Therefore, as Montfort and Wardrip-Fruin stress, it is important to encourage creators to capture their own work, and provide them with the means to do so [43].

Perhaps unsurprisingly, there is no single solution for capturing interactive narrative content on the web. Generally, works which are primarily text-based (with the exception of parsers) are best-captured with ACT, while those with images, video, Flash and javascript elements are best captured with Conifer. Some works (for example, those made with Bitsy) capture equally well with either method. Ideally Itch pages would be captured with ACT due to the likelihood of updates, but in reality, each must be considered individually to ensure good capture. A summary of which tool to use for which type of work can be found below in Table 1.

**Table 1.** Tool Usage Recommendations

| Creation tool | Notes | Recommended capture tool |
|---|---|---|
| Any | Works containing significant video, audio, or visual elements | Conifer (any browser) |
| Any | Works which require a button press or text entry to start rather than a click | Conifer (any browser) |
| Twine | Most images in Twine works capture successfully with ACT, particularly if image URLs are added. Some may require Conifer if javascript or dynamic images are used | ACT in the first instance, Conifer with any browser to eliminate issues with images, Conifer with Firefox v49 to eliminate issues with javascript |
| RPG Maker | | ACT |
| Bitsy | If the work has an opening page which can be started by clicking, ACT will be able to capture successfully, if not, use Conifer | Click to start: ACT<br>Arrow keys to start: Conifer |
| Inform 7 | While Conifer is generally recommended for Inform 7, ACT can work equally well depending on whether it is click to start, or space bar to start, and where and how it has been uploaded | Conifer (any browser) |
| Emulated BBC Micro (online) | | Conifer (any browser) |
| Adventuron | | ACT |
| Ink/Inklewriter | Basic Ink works capture well with ACT, those which have been heavily customised may require Conifer | ACT in the first instance, Conifer with any browser to eliminate issues with styling such as dynamic or hover text elements |
| Texture | | ACT |
| ChoiceScript | Only compiled works can be captured fully, although any CS works can be captured to some degree with Conifer (Firefox v49) | ACT (compiled)<br>Conifer (uncompiled – errors likely) |
| Flash | | Conifer (Firefox v49) |
| Quest | | Cannot be captured with either tool. |
| Genarrator | | Cannot be captured with either tool. |
| Construct 2 | | ACT |
| Unity | | ACT |
| Javascript Website | Depending on the nature of the dynamic content, it may be best to run the site through ACT to ensure CSS code, images, html index files etc are captured and follow up with Conifer to see if more of the 'feel' of the site can be obtained | ACT & Conifer |

For those works where it is difficult to identify the tools used in creation, using the Chrome Web Developer Plugin to 'view source' may provide this information. Creating sample works with some of the tools was invaluable for testing purposes. Sample pieces were created in Twine and ChoiceScript to facilitate testing of creator-applied settings and how this affects webcrawling. Collaborating with creators to obtain sample works in other formats, experimenting with different settings and uploading methods is likely to be highly beneficial as the project continues. While large scale collection of such works is unlikely due to their labour-intensive nature, it is possible that in the future further crowd-sourcing activities may be possible, an approach recommended for archiving complex resources in the Digital Curation Centre's State of the Art report [44].

## 4  Conclusions

The Interactive Narratives collection is a living and growing collection, counting almost 200 websites (190 at the moment of writing [45]). It includes a variety of web-based works, created with different tools and exhibiting different interaction patterns. Many websites containing contextual information (e.g. author websites, project blogs, press kits, promotional material, etc.) have also been added to the collection, to "fill in the gaps" for what couldn't be captured and to provide context to the collected publications.

This research also provided the basis for a new collection of interactive digital works: the New Media Writing Prize collection, which will be added to the UKWA, and will include shortlisted and winning entries to the prize since its launch in 2010. The New Media Writing Prize (NMWP) is a UK-based prize awarded annually to interactive digital works that use technology in innovative and often experimental ways [46]. While adopting methods and workflows already established during the work on the Interactive Narratives collection, the NMWP collection introduces new challenges - for example, the worldwide nature of the prize means that works by non-UK artists can only be captured on a permission basis (authors are being contacted with the help of Bournemouth University, organiser of the award). Further challenges are presented by the fact that not all works are web-based, but often include a variety of formats (from interactive fiction created using Adobe Flash, to augmented reality pieces requiring physical elements to be activated), many of which have already disappeared from use or are about to become obsolete (Adobe Flash, among others [47]). Collecting and curating contextual information around these publications is especially valuable in these cases: as an alternative to collecting the original artefact, when the object itself could not be collected or there are no access options available. This type of descriptive material can also help give a sense of the original "look and feel" of a publication; it clarifies authorial intent and context and provides instructions on use, especially when a specific format becomes obsolete.

The research findings from the UX testing and the work conducted on the Interactive Narratives collection confirmed that there is value in libraries collecting and preserving complex born-digital publications. The knowledge and expertise gained with this project can be shared with other cultural institutions dealing with new media types and rapid technological change, whether it's collecting time-based media art, video game preservation, or other challenges. Likewise, we can learn from other projects and researchers tackling similar challenges: The BL is one of the founding members of the subject specialist network Videogame Heritage Society [48] and actively participates in events organised by the Digital Preservation Coalition [49]. In a rapidly evolving landscape, cultural heritage institutions need to adjust the way they collect and manage born-digital material, in order to provide meaningful user experiences, and to successfully represent the changing nature and cultural diversity of the UK digital landscape.

# References

1. Mod, C.: The 'Future Book' Is Here, but It's Not What We Expected. WIRED (2018). https://www.wired.com/story/future-book-is-here-but-not-what-we-expected/. Accessed 22 June 2020
2. The British Library: Projects - Emerging Formats (2018). https://www.bl.uk/projects/eme rging-formats. Accessed 22 June 2020
3. Parliament of the United Kingdom: The Legal Deposit Libraries (Non-Print Works) Regulations 2013 (2013). https://www.legislation.gov.uk/uksi/2013/777/contents/made. Accessed 22 June 2020
4. The British Library: Legal Deposit. https://www.bl.uk/legal-deposit. Accessed 22 June 2020
5. Smith, C., Cooke, I.: Emerging formats: complex digital media and its impact on the UK Legal Deposit Libraries. Alexandria: J. Natl. Int. Libr. Inf. 27(3), 175–187 (2018). https://doi. org/10.1177/0955749018775878
6. Bunnyfoot: Emerging Formats Report (2019). (The British Library internal circulation only)
7. Webber, J.: 15 Years of the UK Web Archive - The Early Years. UK Web Archive blog, The British Library (2020). https://blogs.bl.uk/webarchive/2020/03/15-years-of-the-uk-web-archive.html. Accessed 22 June 2020
8. British Library. Digital Scholarship. https://www.bl.uk/subjects/digital-scholarship. Accessed 26 June 2020
9. Wisdom, S.: Taking library collections Off The Map. Research Information (2015). https://www.researchinformation.info/feature/taking-library-collections-map. Accessed 26 June 2020
10. Cieslak, M.: British Library's old maps become 3D virtual worlds. BBC News (2013). https://www.bbc.co.uk/news/av/technology-24865099/british-library-s-old-maps-become-3d-virtual-worlds. Accessed 26 June 2020
11. Dempsey, J., et al.: Pudding lane: recreating seventeenth-century London. J. Digit. Hum. 3(1) Spring (2014). http://journalofdigitalhumanities.org/3-1/pudding-lane-recreating-sevent eenth-century-london/
12. Wilcox, Z.: Goodbye to the Singing Hypnotist. British Library English and Drama blog (2013). https://blogs.bl.uk/english-and-drama/2013/03/goodbye-to-the-singing-hypnot ist.html. Accessed 26 June 2020
13. Sherman, R.: I Did a Thing on A Hill: On Meaning And Purpose in Games. Rock Paper Shotgun (2014). https://www.rockpapershotgun.com/2014/11/03/i-did-a-thing-on-a-hill/. Accessed 26 June 2020
14. Wisdom, S.: Research Reflections: A Transmedia Residency at the British Library. CWL News Archive (2015). http://www.creativeworkslondon.org.uk/cw-news/research-reflections-a-tra nsmedia-residency-at-the-british-library/. Accessed 26 June 2020
15. Arts and Humanities Research Council: Creative collaborations: Creative Entrepreneur in Residence. https://ahrc.ukri.org/research/readwatchlisten/features/creative-collaborations-creative-entrepreneur-in-residence/. Accessed 26 June 2020
16. Laury, J.: Ostrich (2018). https://borntopootle.itch.io/ostrich. Accessed 20 Aug 2020
17. Clark, L.: 108 Suitors (2017). https://notagoth.itch.io/108-suitors. Accessed 26 June 2020

18. Green, G.: 46 fantastic entries submitted Gothic Novel Jam #GothNovJam #classicread (2018). https://readwatchplay.wordpress.com/2018/08/29/46-fantastic-entries-submitted-got hic-novel-jam-gothnovjam-classicread/. Accessed 26 June 2020

19. Campbell, F.: The Tower (2018). https://communistsister.itch.io/the-tower. Accessed 26 June 2020

20. Campbell, F.: Superlunary Episode 1.0 (2019). https://communistsister.itch.io/superlunary-ep-1. Accessed 26 June 2020

21. Campbell, F.: Perseids, or, All This Will Go On Forever (2018). https://communistsister.itch.io/perseids. Accessed 26 June 2020

22. AdventureX The Narrative Games Convention. http://adventurexpo.org/. Accessed 26 June 2020

23. Inkle: 80 Days (2014). https://www.inklestudios.com/80days/. Accessed 02 Sept 2020

24. Rossi, G.: Collecting Emerging Formats (2019). https://blogs.bl.uk/digital-scholarship/2019/04/collecting-emerging-formats.html. Accessed 02 Sept 2020

25. British Library: Lynda Clark: Case Studies (2019). https://www.bl.uk/case-studies/lynda-clark. Accessed 03 Sept 2020

26. Tabbi, J.: Preface: acid-free bits and the ELO PAD project. In: Montort, N., Wardrip-Fruin, N. (eds.) Acid-Free Bits: Recommendations for Long-Lasting Electronic Literature. ELO (2004). http://eliterature.org/pad/afb.html. Accessed 20 Aug 2020

27. Github: W3ACT User Guide (2015). https://github.com/ukwa/w3act/wiki/W3ACT-User-Guide#introduction. Accessed 25 June 2020

28. Rhizome: Conifer – About (2020). https://conifer.rhizome.org/_faq. Accessed 25 June 2020

29. Rhizome: Net Art Anthology (2016–2019). https://anthology.rhizome.org/. Accessed 20 Aug 2020

30. Interactive Fiction Technology Foundation: Frequently Asked Questions About Interactive Fiction (ND). https://iftechfoundation.org/frequently-asked-questions/. Accessed 20 Aug 2020

31. Mateas, M., Wardrip-Fruin, N.: Personalized and interactive literature. In: Bainbridge, W.S., Roco, M.C. (eds.) Handbook of Science and Technology Convergence, pp. 501–515. Springer, Cham (2016). https://doi.org/10.1007/978-3-319-07052-0_75

32. Howell, G., Yellowlees Douglas, J.: The evolution of interactive fiction. Comput. Assist. Lang. Learn. **2**(1), 93–109 (1990). https://doi.org/10.1080/0958822900020108

33. Day, M., Pennock, M., Smith, C., Jenkins, J., Cooke, I.: Preservation planning for emerging formats at the British Library. In: iPRES 2018, Boston, 24–27 September 2018. https://osf.io/58pjv/. Accessed 25 June 2020

34. Johnson, R.D.: Aunts and Butlers (2006). http://versificator.net/aunts-and-butlers/. Accessed 25 June 2020

35. Smyth, E.: 1k Cupid (2018). https://untiltheygo.itch.io/1k-cupid. Accessed 29 May 2019

36. Textadventures.co.uk: Quest 5 Documentation (2018). http://docs.textadventures.co.uk/quest/. Accessed 25 June 2020

37. Narramore, S.: Journey Through Your Final Dream (2018). https://narramoreart.itch.io/finaldream-inkjam18. Accessed 14 Oct 2020

38. Grozny, I.: Dripping with the waters of SHEOL (2017). https://ladyisak.itch.io/sheol. Accessed 25 June 2020

39. Theodoridou, N.: Sleepless. Sub-Q Magazine (2015). https://sub-q.com/play-sleepless/. Accessed 25 June 2020

40. Mencia, M.: The Winnipeg: (El barco de la esperanza/The boat of hope) (2018). https://winnipeg.mariamencia.com/. Accessed 25 June 2020

41. Carpenter, J.R.: Along the Briny Beach (2012). http://luckysoap.com/alongthebrinybeach/. Accessed 25 June 2020

42. Carpenter, J.R.: This is a Picture of Wind (2018). http://luckysoap.com/apictureofwind/. Accessed 25 June 2020
43. Montfort, N., Wardrip-Fruin, N.: Acid-Free Bits: Recommendations for Long-Lasting Electronic Literature. ELO (2004). http://eliterature.org/pad/afb.html. Accessed 20 Aug 2020
44. Ball, A.: Digital Curation Centre State of the Art Report: Web Archiving (2010). http://www.dcc.ac.uk/sites/default/files/documents/reports/sarwa-v1.1.pdf. Accessed 20 Aug 2020
45. UKWA: Interactive Narratives collection. https://www.webarchive.org.uk/en/ukwa/collection/1836. Accessed 22 June 2020
46. The New Media Writing Prize. https://newmediawritingprize.co.uk/. Accessed 22 June 2020
47. Adobe.com: Adobe Flash Player EOL General Information Page. https://www.adobe.com/products/flashplayer/end-of-life.html. Accessed 22 June 2020
48. VHS - Videogame Heritage Society: A Subject Specialist Network. https://vhs.thenvm.org/. Accessed 24 Aug 2020
49. Digital Preservation Coalition: Web Archiving & Preservation Working Group: Social Media & Complex Content. https://www.dpconline.org/events/past-events/wapwg-subtopic-dec2019. Accessed 24 Aug 2020

# Gated Story Structure and Dramatic Agency in Sam Barlow's *Telling Lies*

T. M. Gasque[✉], Kevin Tang, Brad Rittenhouse, and Janet Murray

Georgia Institute of Technology, Atlanta, GA 30332, USA

{tgasque,ktang39,bcrittenhouse,jmurray}@gatech.edu

**Abstract.** Sam Barlow's story-based video game *Telling Lies* (2019), like his previous game, *Her Story* (2015), is based on an interaction mechanic in which the player searches a fixed archive of videoclips using keywords found in the dialog of the fictional characters. This storytelling strategy can be situated within traditions of epistemic narratives in which the interactor navigates through a set of unchanging narrative segments, motivated by the desire to increase knowledge of the story. Such stories offer the pleasure of revelation, and they hinge on hiding information so that it is later revealed in a way that maximizes the experience of dramatic agency. This paper explores the expressive potential of Barlow's signature database search mechanic for creating the experience of dramatic agency through managed revelation. By mapping our own experience and examining Barlow's development documents and code, we describe how the artfully gated search mechanic creates temporal disjunctions that provide glimpses of narrative situations that pique curiosity while suppressing explanatory revelations. Using *Telling Lies* as an example, we identify some characteristic design challenges and opportunities afforded by the constrained database search approach and point to unexplored design opportunities that could make this strategy the basis of a more widely-practiced genre.

**Keywords:** Interactive narrative · Epistemic immersion · Dramatic agency

## 1 Dramatic Agency in Epistemic Narratives

In recent years, interactive narrative has been recognized as a distinct genre independent of, though often overlapping with, video games [1, 2]. As such it has its own aesthetics and can be assessed by how well the mechanics of interaction reinforce the narrative experience. To the extent that they diverge, they display ludo-narrative dissonance [3]; to the extent that they converge, the interactor experiences dramatic agency, in which the mechanics of interaction map tightly to the experience of arousing and satisfying narrative curiosity. Dramatic agency need not entail affecting the events of a story; it can be produced by navigating a story through a set of choices that engage the intent of the interactor to actively investigate a particular narrative thread [4]. Much of the controversy over ludology versus narratology has reflected the awkwardness of interrupting gameplay and suspending agency in order to introduce story content, as with cut scenes. But it

© Springer Nature Switzerland AG 2020
A.-G. Bosser et al. (Eds.): ICIDS 2020, LNCS 12497, pp. 314–326, 2020.
https://doi.org/10.1007/978-3-030-62516-0_28

is also true that the wrong game mechanics can become a jarring distraction from a compelling interactive story. In order to reinforce the experience of dramatic agency, the mechanics must be transparent and congruent with the narrative situation.

Marie-Laure Ryan has identified one form of narrative as "epistemic", which describes stories in which our engagement is "driven by the need to know" [5]. Detective stories are the model for epistemic storytelling. Within the diverse meta-genre of interactive narrative, epistemic narratives allow interactors to enact their narrative curiosity through the navigation of fixed narrative fragments of an unchangeable event. They may take the form of detective stories like the Frogware Sherlock Holmes games [6] or Capcom's Phoenix Wright: Ace Attorney series [7], in which the interactor is assembling incriminating elements, confronting the murderer, and achieving closure by bringing a villain to justice. Or they may refuse closure, like the postmodern hypertext rhizomes of the late 20th century (e.g. Michael Joyce's Afternoon [8]) that have no clear ending, as an affirmation of the epistemic openness of all systems of meaning.

Since human experience is temporal, and there is usually something that happens last in any sequence of events, it is hard to write a story or to experience even the most labyrinthian story structure without imposing a temporal sequence of beginning-middle-end. A database or video archive, however, is the opposite of a temporally-ordered sequence. It exists in the misnamed "random" access present. That is, we can separate the sequence in which we call things up from their linear order (which is what we mean by "random") by calling them up through metadata (which is highly specific and opposite of the ordinary meaning of "random"). Lev Manovich has pointed out "As a cultural form, database represents the world as a list of items and it refuses to order this list. In contrast, a narrative creates a cause-and-effect trajectory of seemingly unordered items (events)" [9]. Despite this opposition, Sam Barlow has created two well-received fixed story interactive narratives that use database search of a video archive as the predominant game mechanic. This approach poses two related design challenges. First, how can the designer allow access across the temporal restructure without cutting short the satisfying experience of narrative curiosity by rewarding it prematurely? Second, how can the designer constrain access to some segments while maintaining the transparency of interface mechanics that makes for the successful experience of dramatic agency?

## 2   Closure and Gating Strategies in Epistemic Narrative

The 169 component narrative video segments of Telling Lies cover more than a year of telephone conversations (with each side recorded separately), along with a few social media posts and surveilled group encounters. Together they fall into four storylines, all of which center around the downward trajectory of the protagonist, David, an undercover FBI agent. David begins as a faithful husband, loving father, and idealistic law-enforcement officer charged with investigating eco-activists. He then commits a series of betrayals that culminate in a violently destructive and suicidal act of eco-terrorism.

The video archive the player character is charged with exploring contains conversation David has with his FBI handler, and with 3 women with whom he has sexual relationships: Ava, a young activist; Maxine, a sex-cam worker who performs under multiple personas; and David's wife Emma who is with their young daughter and his ailing mother-in-law in another state. There is also a real-time frame story of Karen, a fellow FBI agent exploring the video archive. It is her role that the player turns out to be enacting.

As in Her Story [10], in Telling Lies [11] the interactor is presented with a rigidly constructed archive that can only show five items at a time in response to text-based queries. The returned videos represent fragments of longer scenes. In Her Story the scenes are from successive police interrogations in what may be a murder investigation. In Telling Lies, a more complex and better funded story-game, the fragments come from government surveillance of telephone calls and meetings. Telling Lies adds the further conceit that each side of any individual phone call is recorded separately. The interactor plays only a small diegetic role within each of these stories, but the experiential role in both is quite clearly that of detective.

Telling Lies situates the narrative on a fictional computer desktop with a specialized search interface. One of the first things to strike a player upon starting Telling Lies is the game's visually-faithful emulation of a Linux-type operating system. The buttons, menu bars, and icons all clearly allude to the distinctive design of the open-source OS favored by digital power-users. The flexibility of Linux systems provides computationally-skilled users relatively unfettered user agency to manipulate information compared to more tightly controlled commercial operating systems like Apple's iOS and Microsoft's Windows. Telling Lies' pseudo-Linux is much more limited in functionality than any off-the-shelf system, forcing the player to work within constrained game mechanics.

The game limits the five video results by when they fall in the hidden timeline of the narrative, with only the earliest videos being returned for any one keyword. As a result, even if you know that a word appears in a late-story video, you will not be able to retrieve and review that video if five videos prior to it also use that word. This design element was also present in Her Story. The benefit of this artificial search limitation is that it serves as a gate to prevent players from jumping to certain carefully hidden late-story videos that reveal deeper backstory or the climax of one of the plot threads. To reach these hidden videos, the player must have found specific or even unique words that are only revealed at the end of long word-trails. Since videos are only available by keyword search there is no way to get around this artificial limitation. There is no way to navigate directly to a video by typing in its name, or navigating through a file directory as one might in the standard Windows desktop GUI, or by a command line cd as in the Unix-like shell environment of Hacknet [12].

The limitation of search returns, then, violates our expectations of the operating system, but it serves the narrative experience by fulfilling the same purpose as the locked doors or hidden entries in an epistemic adventure-style game. We can think of this structure as a gating system in which parts of the narrative are unreachable until certain conditions are met. Gating systems are an important part of murder mysteries, escape rooms, and level design in games, and they are crucial to creating dramatic agency in interactive narrative because without gates you could see the story in any order. The search limitations in Telling Lies serve the function of these figurative gates, preventing players from accessing later narrative sequences prior to obtaining some requisite information. However, their presence and function are opaque. Unlike other interactive narratives, where gates might be literally represented as locked doors for which you must find a key, the gates in Telling Lies are never explicitly explained to interactors and one must instead infer their mechanics, the way one would infer the workings of a puzzle. According to Manovich, "While computer games do not follow database logic, they appear to be ruled by another logic – that of an algorithm. They demand that a player executes an algorithm in order to win". In obscuring not only the game mechanics but also the narrative itself, Barlow makes a step toward creating a game that is both database and algorithm.

It is a common mistake to think of interactive narratives as "non-linear" or merely subversive of meaningful sequencing of legacy narrative forms. But digital structures offer the opportunity to create more complex structures with multiple coherent sequences, and are therefore more helpfully thought of as "multi-sequential", as distinguished from traditional "unisequential" stories [4, 13]. In order to support this complexity, designers often provide a unisequential structure that serves as a spine for the story, or a "rail" that forces the learning of information in a fixed order similar to the levels in a videogame. The story is provided with gates that do not allow passage into a new set of narrative revelations until prior segments have been experienced.

Sometimes these "gates" are physical barriers within the fictional space. For example, the Fullbright Company's well-received Gone Home [4] is set in an abandoned house that the player explores to uncover a story told in fragments associated with objects within rooms. The spatial exploration seems to be quite open: you can go where you like in the large Gothic house. But in actuality, the story is structured as a clue trail in which access to later events is cut off until you have literally unlocked specific rooms and containers. The story that is hidden in Gone Home turns out not to be murder mystery or a horror story as the initial Gothic conventions (dark and rainy night, deserted house, disorder and unexplained disappearance of the protagonist's family) lead us to expect. Instead it is a teenage love story between the protagonist's younger sister and another woman, and a story of estrangement and renewed commitment in the marriage of the player character's parents. The story fragments are contained within documents like notes and photographs found in the house, and in a voice-over diary triggered by these spatial discoveries.

The experience of Gone Home is therefore one of unlocking a space in order to uncover a story. Hannah Wood [15] describes a subgenre of Story Exploration Games that shifts the player perspective from the traditional view of story protagonists to "experience protagonists". Wood sees story games like Gone Home as moving away from giving the player a central self-goal and toward giving the player a more empathic engagement with the goals expressed by the active characters in the narrative. The story is experienced from the perspective of an older sister returning to a mysteriously empty family home, but the actions we care about belong to the other members of the family whose struggles are revealed through artifacts within the many rooms of the house:

*"As experience protagonists, players [of Gone Home] operate as detectives trying to decipher the story. The central mechanics (or player verbs) of 'searching' and 'exploring' enable decisions on how the story is pieced together and parallel the search for meaning and identity central to the stories of Sam, Jan and Terry"* [15].

In Telling Lies, the player embodies a similar "experience protagonist", of a named character, the FBI agent Karen, who is mostly an observer. Instead of occupying the more specific career or personal goals of that character, the player is motivated to soak in the stories told within the database, to form emotional bonds with the dramatized characters, and have those bonds motivate us to uncover more of the story about them. There is a brief temporal ending to the story based on Karen's actions, but all the codas to the story wrap up the stories of the surviving active characters, and only one is shown for each play-through based on which of the women characters—Ava, Maxine, or Emma—the interactor followed the most closely.

Another recent example of an epistemic narrative driven by an enticing mystery, and one closer to the detective framework than either Gone Home or Telling Lies, is Lucas Pope's follow-up to Papers, Please [16], Return of the Obra Dinn [17]. In this adventure-style game, the player is in the role of an insurance investigator attempting to discover the fates of 60-odd ship passengers missing from a recently-reappeared ghost ship. There is a ghost ship to spatially navigate, filled with hidden corpses, but the story revelations are significantly organized by an interactive object, a 135-page notebook complete with "Table of Contents," art plates, and chapter sections separating the game's narrative into individual arcs. Like the diary in Gone Home or the operating system in Telling Lies, the notebook in Obra Dinn does not behave like an ordinary paper object. It is the interface through which the player manipulates information, providing templates with multiple choices to fill in about who perished (or disappeared), how, and at whose hands. The notebook provides some expected forms of digital affordances, allowing players to surface all vignettes containing specific characters with a single click, to bookmark important flashbacks, and to easily link characters as they appear physically in the game world with the information recorded about them in the log. Matthew Weise's observes that Obra Dinn does "not [skimp] on real deduction and non-linearity in adventure game design", instead providing him with robust mechanical tools "to create a timeline so I could paint a clear picture in my head of how the story happened. Obra Dinn understands this kind of pleasure, the pleasure of un-watered down detective work. Rather than reducing the forensic expectation put on the player, it makes the game openly, unabashedly about forensic collection of information. Except, unlike System Shock, it makes the note-taking the core mechanic" [18]. Information retention, management, and manipulation, then, become central mechanics for navigating, both spatially and epistemically, these database games.

In Obra Dinn physical corpses are the gates to greater story content. It is finding another corpse that triggers the recorded interactive vignette that makes up a segment of each chapter of the larger story. To review previous segments, players must remember which corpse triggered it. While this makes story navigation a bit clunky, the note-book, which in which the player records their steadily growing knowledge and insight, serves as a consistent anchor for the player in the story, allowing them to reorient them-selves repeatedly as they find the need to backtrack and re-examine evidence. For those who successfully unearth all the vignettes and make the right deductions through the corpse-and-notebook navigation, it does offer narrative closure in explaining all the mysteries (albeit supernaturally, as befits the genre) and in a final "secret" scene which provides recognition that the player character has successfully solved all the mysteries.

In materializing player knowledge in game mechanics, and connecting the perfection of the player's knowledge with narrative unity, Pope offers a compelling model for ludo-narrative design in the mystery/database game genre.

One strategy common to all of these stories is the bifurcation of the story between the interactive element which is represented by the present-tense action of a solitary detective figure and a fixed set of story segments describing a past set of actions by multiple characters. Todorov pointed out that this bifurcated structure is the essence of the detective genre which consists of "two stories: the story of the crime and the story of the investigation" Todorov [19]. Or as Wood suggests, echoing Todorov:

> *"Casting players as story protagonists does not allow them to know their own fate and do nothing about it without being dramatically dissatisfying; but, an alternate viewpoint as experience protagonists provides the opportunity to manipulate time and allow players to see the fate of story protagonists, a hook which can generate narrative drive and motivate them to actively uncover why it ended that way"* [15].

In the epistemic story, the dramatic agency belongs to the least dramatic actions – not the seductions and betrayals of Gone Home, but the unlocking of the doors that lead to the revelation of the next fragment of the story; not the deceits, seductions, and political entrapments of Telling Lies but the typing in of the right keywords to reveal those plot points.

## 3   Gated Keyword Trails in *Telling Lies*

In two design documents that Sam Barlow shared with the authors of this paper, the story elements are ordered in a table with dramatic scenes (in temporal order) forming the rows, and 4 columns for each of the main characters, David and the three women he is involved with: his wife Emma and the mother of his young daughter; Ava, the young activist David seduces and impregnates; and Maxine, a sex cam performer with whom he has salacious conversations. (They have other names in the design document and the plot developments are different from the final version, but the characters and major events are the same). The conversations are divided into 8 sections labeled A-H, each of which asks a question in each of the story threads (see Fig. 1). The final story provides a date and time stamp for all of the conversations, creating a linear timeline that runs from August 2017 through November 2018.

The scenes are skillfully written, directed, and acted to elicit narrative curiosity about what is being said on the other end, so as to prompt the interactor to further investigation. For example, the game begins with a preloaded search term "LOVE" which pulls up a clip of David talking with his FBI hander, Mike, and clips of Emma, Max, and Ava talking with David. All of these sequences happen at the beginning of the story in August 2017, a wise design choice, serving to orient the player at the start of the narrative. From this initial set of videos, new players are expected to be interested in a spoken word and investigate the keyword in the database, unlocking a new set of videos from different story threads and chronologically different points on the timeline. In one of the initial videos, David uses the word "romantic" to describe himself (in his undercover persona) and if you feed this word into the search engine you will find two early clips and one from July

2018 which marks a climax in Emma's story and offers a disturbing revelation on David's violent nature. Navigating through the database is full of these jumps across characters and time, providing an epistemic detective task in which the player is constantly trying to reconstitute the underlying temporal and narrative order.

To illustrate the prevalence of these kinds of disjunctions, we mapped our own experience of one playthrough of the game. In Fig. 1 the x-axis represents time covered by all the videoclips and the y-axis shows the five speakers on the videos. David is in the center since he is present in all conversations. In addition to Emma, Ava, and Maxine, we have a row for David's FBI handler Mike and some minor characters associated with the FBI plotlines which provide the momentum for the major story events.

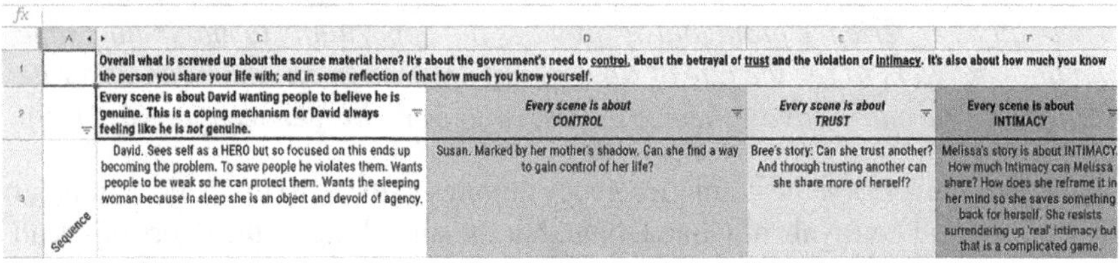

**Fig. 1.** Barlow's design documents: outline showing story segments ordered by time, theme, and character

The Fig. 1 chart is limited to key scenes and searches and does not include our whole player experience or all 169 possible scenes. Our paths took the form of long runs of keyword chains. For instance, Path 1 is the blue line that starts with the initial "LOVE" search provided at the game's start. From that initial briefing between David and Mike, we investigated the word "convergence" which sent us barreling from August all the way to April, and from the FBI timeline to Ava's. The resultant video then hinted at the existence of Karen, who we also investigated in the database as a keyword. This cycle of discovery and investigation would continue until we ran out of productive searches for new videos. At that point, we would need to reference our notes and memories for potential keywords until we discovered a new chain of videos. Path 2 (in red and enlarged in Fig. 2) shows our next successful run, which circles around the middle of the time frame, and Path 3 (in dark green) takes us to the events that end the story. We did other searches as well but these summarize the major paths we took through the archive to reveal the key plot points and visit all the parallel strands of the story (Fig. 3).

Throughout the session, we spent the bulk of our time in the temporal middle of the story, following keywords that looped us around across characters and back and forward in time in a circular and zigzag fashion. At the same time, the team's overall progression follows a clear trajectory towards the timeline's final video, driven by narrative curiosity to learn the conclusion to David's story. David's fall follows an Aristotelian tragic arc, including a moment of recognition of his sins and a final act of violence that takes his life. Whichever path we take, we are aware of irreconcilable conflicts and rising tensions in his life, which cause us to look for resolution. This desire propels us to the chronological end of the story and his rather pathetic attempt at redemption and catharsis by committing suicide.

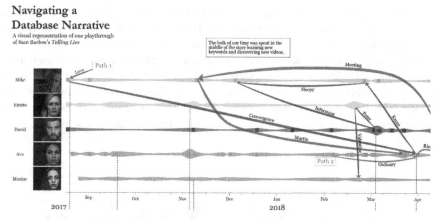

**Fig. 2.** Navigating a database narrative: first half (Color figure online)

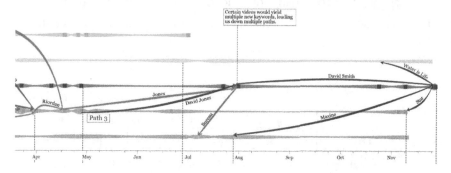

**Fig. 3.** Navigating a database narrative: second half

It is important to note that the visualization shows only one possible traversal of the narrative, and every node could have led in other directions since we were selecting one of several possible keywords from one of up to five different videos that were returned for each search. Other playthroughs might focus on different words in the game's dialogues as search terms, leading to different paths through the database, and would lead to videos that we never got to see.

This potential for multiple player narratives through the constructed narrative is by design. The algorithm driving the search engine only returns five videos with the search term and does not show or hide specific videos based on player progression. It is not trying to show you new things. It is trying to hide chronologically later videos using the same search term. The search terms that reveal later sections are like Easter eggs hidden in select segments – they are unique terms that you are not likely to guess unless you have gone through a lot of the story. For example, we don't find out that David Jones' real name is David Smith until a very late scene, and "Smith" is the only keyword we personally found to unlock the final suicide scene.

This gating technique uses unique search terms the same way that *Gone Home* uses hidden keys and secret locker combinations, but it differs in how the gates are constructed and enforced. In *Gone Home*, the gates are enforced by the system's code; in *Telling Lies*, the gates are enforced by the design of the script. The design documents that Sam Barlow shared with us included an elaborate spreadsheet cross-listing every word in the script and every video segment. It makes clear that the game's script, its entire gating mechanic, was intentionally designed so that earlier segments have more successful search terms than later ones. Figures 4 and 5 show the Hits values for early and late segments.

| fx | | | | | | | | | | | |
|---|---|---|---|---|---|---|---|---|---|---|---|
| | A | B | C | D | E | F | G | H | I | J | K |
| 1 | | 1 | 2 | 3 | 4 | 5 | 6 | 7 | 8 | 9 | 10 |
| 2 | **Hits** | 168 | 81 | 86 | 161 | 52 | 124 | 91 | 41 | 97 | 44 |
| 4 | **Clip** | mirr | prin | hug | dad | hey | how | hey | you | oka | hi |

**Fig. 4.** From Barlow's development documents: unique word scores from segments early in the timeline

| fx | | | | | | | | | | | |
|---|---|---|---|---|---|---|---|---|---|---|---|
| | A | FD | FE | FF | FG | FH | FI | FJ | FK | FL | FM | FN |
| 1 | | 159 | 160 | 161 | 162 | 163 | 164 | 165 | 166 | 167 | 168 | 169 |
| 2 | **Hits** | 2 | 10 | 7 | 1 | 35 | 6 | 12 | 95 | 6 | 13 | 16 |
| 4 | **Clip** | ton | hey | hey | you | wha | hey | why | i mi | it s | my | mill |

**Fig. 5.** From Barlow's development documents: unique word scores from segments late in the timeline

Hits represents the number of unique keywords that, when searched in the database, will return that video segment as one of the first five videos to include that keyword in its dialogue. For instance, video segment 1 is the first video in the narrative, a conversation between David and Mike detailing David's undercover mission and alibi. During the briefing, David describes himself as a "loyal friend". The keywords "loyal" and "friend" each contribute to the Hits value, and they would reveal video segment 1 when searched in the database. In total, there are 168 total keywords that would return video segment 1.

On the other end is video segment 169, the final video in the chronological narrative that shows David's public apology and subsequent suicide. The video acts as a conclusion to David's story and has an appropriately low Hits value of sixteen, meaning only sixteen keywords would reveal this final video. This list was curated in such a way that an interactor would have already spent significant time investigating the narrative before searching these keywords. For example, searching the word "David" would not return the final video, as his first name is a common piece of information. However, David's real last name, "Smith", is one of the sixteen keywords to the final video, and the information on his name is appropriately hidden in harder to reach videos later in the narrative. That is not to say an interactor will not find later videos early in a playthrough, but that situation is less likely to happen due to the way the story's information is structured.

The dramatic satisfaction comes then, as in the traditional detective story, from revealing the underlying sequence of events and the chain of causation that is otherwise hidden. The skipping around across time actually reinforces this pleasure by offering many mysteries. Every scene revealed out of temporal order raises a question of "why did this happen?" which leads us to want to explore backwards in the story as well as forwards. Showing half of every conversation creates a desire to move vertically in the story – to find the other half of the conversation. But at the same time we are motivated as we would be in a unisequential presentation of a narrative to wonder "how will this end".

## 4  Design Issues for Archive Narratives

In narratological terms we can think of the events on the parallel timelines of Fig. 1 as the fabula (plot) and the paths through the archive as the syuzhet (discourse or telling). Each playthrough of the game creates a unique instance of Wood's "dynamic syuzhet", an instantiation of all the potential narratives implicit in Hartmut Koenitz's "protostory" [13]. The events on the timeline make up four stories, each with their own climax and all four main characters emerge from the events in a dramatically different place than they are in at the beginning. The women's stories are all survivor tales, and David's story, which takes up 96 of the 169 segments, is, as we said above, similar to a classic Aristotelian tragedy. But one might argue that one effect of the database structure is to undermine the sense of catharsis and closure that David's story might otherwise have produced. David is a deluded, arrogant hero who goes from a high position to total destruction by way of a series of crises and revelations that lead to devastating self-knowledge. But we don't finish the story when we experience his suicide. We know that we are finished when we have explored the situation from every angle, creating the experience Murray identified as "saturation", Murray [4] or as Alex Navarro described it in a "Quick Look" for the Giant Bomb website, "You will know when you are satisfied when you know you are satisfied" [11].

Furthermore each of these women whom David has exploited gets an epilogue after the ending of the game, showing how their lives turned out years later, and all three pointedly say that they refused to look at the video with his final message to them, because of their disgust with his patterns of betrayal. The player sees only one of these epilogues on any one playthrough, based on which woman's videos they spent the most time with, but this teaser motivates replay, encouraging us to return to the game and watch more videos in order to see them all and experience all the epilogues. There are therefore four different "last" endings to the action of the story, but none of them closes off the possibility of further explorations of the archive, and while they all exist within the fabula of the narrative, only one exists within the experiential syuzhet of a playthrough.

In All Data Are Local Yanni Loukissas warns us that vast databases often decontextualize information, but data always belong to specific places and social structures and are influenced by how they were collected and by whom:

*"Data are useful precisely because they provide unfamiliar perspectives, from other times, places, and standpoints that we would not be able to access otherwise. The strangeness of data is its strength"* [20].

The strangeness of data is well-suited to fictional narrative. Furthermore the process of exploring datasets prompts an investigative mindset as individuals try to find contextualization for the sea of information in which they are submerged. Telling Lies invites the player into the experience with no overt guides or direction, allowing the player to stumble into its robust dataset. Once encountered the player is then drawn to investigate the contextless information and build connections between the data to solve the inherent mystery of the dataset.

The ending of the game does not provide the conventional satisfaction of a detective game. At 5 AM Karen, our player avatar, inserts a flash drive that requires the user to upload their videos to a government whistle-blower site. This prompt provides the users with a moral question not raised yet in the game: Do you reveal David's actions to the world? Up to this point, despite the implicit investigative nature of the experience, the user is merely a witness, and at times an uncomfortable voyeur, of a series of betrayals as David's life slowly unravels. The whistleblower prompt provides a moment of reflection and active participation that re-contextualizes the experience. Or it would if the button was an actual choice in the experience. But in fact the button is merely a trigger to end the game. When either the in-game clock reaches 6 am or you choose to send the data, the final cut-scene plays and the game ends.

This moment suggests other design opportunities for database narratives. The interactor could be given the task of assembling a selection of sequences that taken out of the larger context of the archive to incriminate or exonerate a particular person. There could be multiple possible sequences and a limited time to discover them. The notebook, which is underdeveloped in Telling Lies as compared to Obra Dinn's, could be turned into an editing table or evidence bin where interactors create their own interpretation of the situation. Her Story suggested this sort of approach in its support of alternate interpretations of the subject of the interviews as a single person or twins, sane or insane, murder or victim. Sherlock Holmes [21] and L.A. Noire [22] use this technique to invest the accusation with dramatic import. The Telling Lies scenario suggests the possibility of a politically-themed twist on this strategy in which there is a single level of reality but multiple patterns of complicity.

Another powerful design feature of the Telling Lies gated archive structure that could be further exploited by future designers is the removal of David, the protagonist, from 73 of the 169 videos. Watching so many videos in which people are conversing with the protagonist but his part is missing reinforces the theme of David's elusive and deceptive character. His removal allows the player's investigation of the database to only be informed by how other characters within the narrative react to David. In essence, David becomes a ghost or myth that the users only understand through the perceptions of the character in the narrative. This ghosting allows for David to be different for each play-through depending on how he is seen through the reactions of the other characters. A player who only views videos containing Maxine and Mike, for instance, might create a David that is struggling to complete his mission and turns to a parasocial relationship for guidance. While players who only saw videos of people reactive to David's violent actions might see him as a violent rabble-rouser. Others might see him as a responsible husband and father, or a caring boyfriend.

All of these potential enhancement are based on the central expressive strategy of the video archive story, which is the creation of the experience of dramatic agency through narratively-motivated strategic actions (selecting keywords) that lead to results that expand narrative motivation and multiply coherent paths forward. The essential pleasure of the form is the epistemological quest, the discovery of more information about a series of complex events in which the paths reflect specific acts of narrative curiosity on the part of the interactor, and the fragments can be assembled in multiple coherent sequences.

Barlow and his team have proven that the exploration of a video archive can produce narratively satisfying play-throughs given a careful structuring of the underlying fabula and the design of a mechanic that shapes the paths of the interactor into meaningful dynamic syuzhets. It is also clear that the form has more design possibilities that Telling Lies hints at but does not deliver on, and that remain for potential exploitation, perhaps by a wider range of practitioners.

# References

1. Koenitz, H.: Thoughts on a discipline for the study of interactive digital narratives. In: Rouse, R., Koenitz, H., Haahr, M. (eds.) ICIDS 2018. LNCS, vol. 11318, pp. 36–49. Springer, Cham (2018). https://doi.org/10.1007/978-3-030-04028-4_3
2. Murray, J.H.: Research into interactive digital narrative: a kaleidoscopic view. In: Rouse, R., Koenitz, H., Haahr, M. (eds.) ICIDS 2018. LNCS, vol. 11318, pp. 3–17. Springer, Cham (2018). https://doi.org/10.1007/978-3-030-04028-4_1
3. Hocking, C.: Ludonarrative dissonance in bioshock: the problem of what the game is about, Click Nothing, 7 October 20087. https://clicknothing.typepad.com/click_nothing/2007/10/ludonarrative-d.html. Accessed 20 May 2020
4. Murray, J.H.: Hamlet on the Holodeck: The Future of Narrative in Cyberspace. Updated Edition. MIT Press, Cambridge (2017)
5. Ryan, M.-L.: Interactive narrative, plot types, and interpersonal relations. In: Spierling, U., Szilas, N. (eds.) ICIDS 2008. LNCS, vol. 5334, pp. 6–13. Springer, Heidelberg (2008). https://doi.org/10.1007/978-3-540-89454-4_2
6. Fernández-Vara, C.: The Game's afoot: designing sherlock holmes. In: DiGRA '13 - Proceedings of the 2013 DiGRA International Conference: DeFragging Game Studies, Atlanta (2013)
7. Capcom Production Studio 4. Phoenix Wright: Ace Attorney Series, Osaka, Japan (2001)
8. Joyce, M.: Eastgate Systems. Afternoon: a story (2016)
9. Manovich, L.: Database as symbolic form. Millenium Film J. (34) (1999)
10. Barlow, S.: Her Story (2015)
11. Navarro, S.: Telling lies: quick look. https://youtu.be/t8FjXPpXUF0. Accessed 20 May 2020
12. Team Fractal Alligator: Hacknet. Fellow Traveller (2015)
13. Koenitz, H.: Toward a Specific Theory of Interactive Digital Narrative: Interactive Digital Narrative. Routledge, New York (2015)
14. The Fullbright Company: Gone Home (2013)
15. Wood, H.: Dynamic syuzhets: writing and design methods for playable stories. In: Nunes, N., Oakley, I., Nisi, V. (eds.) ICIDS 2017. LNCS, vol. 10690, pp. 24–37. Springer, Cham (2017). https://doi.org/10.1007/978-3-319-71027-3_3

16. Pope, L.: Papers, Please (2013)
17. Pope, L.: Return of the Obra Dinn (2018)
18. Weise, M.: How return of the Obra Dinn pushes environmental storytelling forward. Outside Your heaven: Writings on storytelling at the crossroads of new and old media. http://outsideyourheaven.blogspot.com/2018/11/how-return-of-obra-dinn-pushes.html. Accessed 20 May 2020
19. Todorov, T.: The Typology of Detective Fiction: The Poetics of Prose. Cornell University Press, Ithaca (1966)
20. Loukissas, Y.A.: All Data are Local: Thinking Critically in a Data-Driven Society. MIT Press, Cambridge (2019)
21. Frogwares: Sherlock Holmes (2002)
22. L.A. Noire Team Bondi: Rockstar Games (2011)

# Magic and Immersion in VR

Ágnes Karolina Bakk[(⊠)] [iD]

Moholy-Nagy University of Art and Design, Zugligeti Street 9-25, Budapest, Hungary
bakk@mome.hu

**Abstract.** The rise of the notion of "immersion", thanks to interactive VR productions, provokes creators and experiencers to think of new design frameworks. The concept of immersion is frequently mentioned together with the notion of illusion. In this paper I will outline a way to think of the sense of immersion in VR that is based on the science of magic. Based on this particular view of immersion as a magical experiment I will present an outline of a possible parallel between experiencing immersion in VR and in a magic trick.

**Keywords:** VR · Psychology of magic · Immersion

## 1 Content for VR

### 1.1 Introduction

The current re-birth of the medium of Virtual Reality brought with itself a new era in narrative studies and a longing for immersion that resulted in a boom in immersive businesses.

In this paper I will argue that in the centre of interactive VR productions is the concept of embodiment of the experiencer, as this assures the promise of interactivity and immersion. The level or intensity of the interaction of the experiencer's body with its environment is based on the sense of embodiment, and also on how this embodiment can surprise the experiencer and how can it create unfamiliar bodily feelings. I will provide a definition of the sense of immersion in VR by drawing a parallel with the science of magic, focusing on the effects that immersion has on the experiencer's brain and how the audiences perceive a magic trick, especially conjuring tricks.

### 1.2 The Concept of Immersion

As Zhang et al. define: "Immersion is a complex phenomenon that demands multiple levels of neuro-psychological involvement such as perception, attention and emotion" [1]. The complexity of the concept of immersion can be observed in its inconsistent usage, too [2]. In video games, immersion is about the various levels of attention and engagement [3] or presence in virtual environments [4]. Based on their systematic literature review, Nilsson et al. suggest a new typology for the concept, which consists of the following: "(a) immersion as a property of the system, (b) immersion as a response

© Springer Nature Switzerland AG 2020
A.-G. Bosser et al. (Eds.): ICIDS 2020, LNCS 12497, pp. 327–331, 2020.
https://doi.org/10.1007/978-3-030-62516-0_29

to an unfolding narrative, the diegetic space, or virtual characters, and (c) immersion as a response to challenges demanding use of one's intellect or sensorimotor skills" [2]. In the area of research in virtual environments, the term immersion has been widely used with various and disparate meanings by different authors and an important distinction is the one between psychological and perceptual immersion [5]. In this paper, I will be using the concept of immersion "as a property of the system" and I will tackle both the psychological and perceptual types.

There are many scientific experiments that deal with bodily illusions or illusions in virtual reality experiences. Liam Jarvis, partly explaining this new trend of experiment, argues that "mounting evidence in body-ownership, the integration of body illusions as a mode of immersive 'spectatorship' and emergent/experimental technologized forms of cultural practice are modifying our perception of the world in radically new ways." [6]. Immersive VR environments enable the illusion to transport the experiencing subject into another environment, as the system offers a high-level immersion state. Due to its illusionistic character, this transportation can be perceived as an impossible act. In 2007, Bowman has already stated about VR that it engages and entertains the user "by producing an experience that's usually impossible to achieve in the real world." [7]. In the case of interactive VR experiences that I am focusing on, this transportation is experienced by the user as an almost impossible event, and after the experiencer gets used to the sudden state of change she can find her body in a responsive immersive environment. This *sensory-type of immersion* [8] lets the experiencer's imagination to stay on stand-by and let the sense of embodiment take over the consciousness into the flow [9]. This stage is when the body and the sense of embodiment act as the agent on the behalf of the experiencer.

### 1.3   The Sense of Embodiment (SoE), or How to Be Present

What conditions are needed to feel with the body of the other in a suddenly changed environment? Kilteni et al. define this strong sense of presence with the notion of "sense of embodiment" (SoE) [10]. Based on their analysis, we can point out several requirements for VR to support a SoE. The sense of self-representation required for SoE is characterized by:

1. The Sense of Self-Location, defined as one's spatial experience of being inside a body and which is related to "the relationship between one's self and one's body", while presence is "the relationship between one's self and the environment";
2. The Sense of Agency, defined as having "global motor control, including the subjective experience of action, control, intention, motor selection and the conscious experience of will" [11];
3. The Sense of Body Ownership, defined as the feeling of the body as being the source of the experienced sensation and one's self-attribution of a body [12].

## 2   The Science of Magic

For a very long time, cognitive science has overlooked how magic tricks affect the human mind. Even though Binet was already studying magicians back in 1894 by using the most sophisticated methods of that time, but only in mid-1980's researchers (including some of the earliest pioneers in psychology such as Hyman) started to look more closely into magic tricks and their cognitive and perceptual effects [13]. In the recent years, researchers started to give more attention to the science of magic in pursuit of finding a new approach for studying various functions and processes of the mind [14].

According to Jason Leddington, magic is "a form of theater that apparently presents impossible events and *at the same time* represents them as impossible" [15]. This specific definition suggests that the experience of magic is a counterintuitive experience, where the magic does not take place on the stage, but rather in the perception of the spectator of the magical act. We can agree with Rensink and Kuhn's suggestion that the science of magic can be a suitable framework for using magic "to investigate human perception and cognition" [14]. Indeed, the science of magic can offer us new perspectives on several levels in analyzing phenomena such as immersion. First of all, "adaptation of traditional magic techniques" might offer us possibilities to scrutinize current research issues. Secondly, it can help us investigate various psychological phenomena such as "the sense of wonder induced by an apparently impossible event". Also, the science of magic can offer us the possibility of finding out large-scale patterns among magic tricks. And, importantly, science of magic can help us better understand the workings of ordinary human cognition. As Smith et al. put it, investigations into conjuring tricks that "routinely and reliably bring about radical failures in how people make sense of the world, might open a new window into how that sense is normally achieved" [16]. They write that "an important starting point for [their] account is to see the effect of a magic trick as an impossible state transition in which a situation passes impossibly from one state to another. We focus on tricks that fit this conception, describing them as *happenings*. In happenings, there is nothing intrinsically impossible, nor even anomalous, about the final state of objects on display (e.g., the non-existence of a coin in a purse, or the existence of a ball under a cup). Rather, the impossibility lies in how the present situation came about from the immediate history of witnessed events" [16]. The magic trick as an impossible state transition is similar to immersive experiences, where the experience of being transitioned from environment A (initial environment) to environment B (immersive environment) which we have via sensory stimuli (especially via visual, auditory and proprioceptive stimuli) can be compared to the sense of wonder.

The science of magic has also started to be discovered by human-computer interaction and game design researchers [18, 19] (see Tognazzini 1993 and Kumari, Deterding and Kuhn 2018). Researchers such as Kuhn have taken up the idea that we can use the science of magic to study different complexities such as video games, while, on the other hand, the media of VR has started to be used by magicians, as in Derren Brown's VR ghost train [17].

## 3   Magic and Immersion in VR

In perceiving a magic trick, a subject, even if she believes at the rational level that she is spectating an event that is meant to be illusory, still produces cognitive and behavioral responses that is caused by a surprising, counter-intuitive violation of physical law. This is similar to the cognitive state where the user of an immersive VR experience understands rationally that he or she is in an immersive environment, but her body can give different reactions on the level of senses, such as muscle reactions. That is, even if the experiencer is fully aware of the illusory nature of the immersive environment, she nevertheless produces some responses as if she took the environment as not virtual but real.

When discussing the act of putting on the VR headset elsewhere, I have argued that "by the combination of the use of "human interface" with the ritualistic situation of taking on the virtual reality headset, participants can be part of an initiation ceremony, a rite of passage." [21]. These rites of passage are characteristic to the situation of switching between worlds, between immersive environments. The very act of starting or finishing a VR-production and the movements that are accompanying this act can have a performative effect, which is a characteristic of the medium of performance. The participants of a VR production here enter the "magic circle", to borrow a concept used in LARP design practices referring to the participants' entering the storyworld of a LARP. While presenting an actual magic trick, it is essential for the magician to convey relevant information about the conditions, that are, seemingly, raising the chances of something impossible being about to happen [22] and this way the magicians are also embedding the trick into a storyworld that enables the audience to perceive the trick as an impossible act. This embedding is an initiation stage of an experience that takes place in an immersive environment.

Continuing with the parallel between magic and immersion, another similarity that can be pointed out between the two is a similarity concerning the nature of beliefs that are held when undergoing experiences of magic. Encountering magic does not involve passive "suspension of disbelief" but rather an active disbelief [15]. The magical experience is not unexpected; the audience's attention is guided in a way that creates expectations about what will happen. The attention of the participants of VR experiences are similarly drawn to what they should anticipate: they can understand that putting on the VR headsets and controllers will enable them to be in an immersive artificial world, a simulation, the truthfulness of which depends only on their imagination.

## 4 Conclusion

The discussions about the sense of immersion in VR will probably continue for a longer time, as long as interactive VR experiences are in the stage of "media of attraction". In this paper I offered a possible framework about how the experience of immersion in VR can be compared to encountering a magic trick. The study of magic tricks and the empirical work that has been done on their presentation and perception is one such field that carries the potential for VR production creators to design new types of immersive works.

## References

1. Zhang, C., Perkis, A., Arndt, S.: Spatial immersion versus emotional immersion, which is more immersive? In: Ninth International Conference on Quality of Multimedia Experience (QoMEX), Erfurt, pp. 1–6 (2017). https://doi.org/10.1109/QoMEX.2017.7965655

2. Nilsson, N.-Ch., Nordahl, R., Serafin, S.: Immersion revisited: a review of existing definitions of immersion and their relation to different theories of presence. Hum. Technol. **12**(2), 108–134 (2016)
3. Brown, E., Cairns, P.: A grounded investigation of game immersion. In: CHI 2004 Extended Abstracts on Human Factors in Computing Systems, pp. 1297–1300 (2004)
4. Slater, M.: A note on presence terminology. Presence-Connect **3**(3). http://s3.amazonaws.com/publicationslist.org/data/melslater/ref-201/a%20note%20on%20presence%20terminologogy.pdf. Accessed 26 June 2020
5. Skarbez, R., Brooks Jr, F.P., Whitton, M.C.: A survey of presence and related concepts. ACM Comput. Surv. **50**(6) (2017). Article 96. https://doi.org/10.1145/3134301
6. Jarvis, L.: Immersive Embodiment. Palgrave Macmillan, Basingstoke (2019)
7. Bowman, D., McMahan, R.: Virtual reality: how much immersion is enough? Computer **40**(7), 36–43 (2007). https://doi.org/10.1109/MC.2007.257
8. Ermi, L., Mäyrä, F.: Fundamental components of the gameplay experience: analysing immersion. In: Worlds in Play: International Perspectives on Digital Games Research, pp. 15–27. Peter Lang Publishing, New York (2005)
9. Csíkszentmihályi, M.: Flow: The Psychology of Optimal Experience. Harper & Row, New York (1990)
10. Kilteni, K., Groten, R., Slater, M.: The sense of embodiment in virtual reality. Presence Teleoperators Virtual Environ. **21**(4), 373–387 (2012)
11. Blanke, O., Metzinger, T.: Full-body illusions and minimal phenomenal selfhood. Trends Cogn. Sci. **13**(1), 7–13 (2009). https://doi.org/10.1016/j.tics.2008.10.003
12. Tsakiris, M., Prabhu, G., Haggard, P.: Having a body versus moving your body: how agency structures body-ownership. Conscious. Cogn. **15**(2), 423–432 (2006). https://doi.org/10.1016/j.concog.2005.09.004
13. Hyman, R.: The psychology of deception. Ann. Rev. Psychol. **40**, 133–154 (1989). https://doi.org/10.1146/annurev.ps.40.020189.001025
14. Rensink, R., Kuhn, G.: The possibility of science of magic. Front. Psychol. **5**, 1508 (2015). https://doi.org/10.3389/fpsyg.2015.01576
15. Leddington, J.: The experience of magic. J. Aesthet. Art Crit. **74**(3), 253–264 (2016)
16. Smith, W., Dignum, F., Sonenberg, L.: The construction of impossibility: a logic-based analysis of conjuring tricks. Front. Psychol. **7** (2016). Article 748
17. Kuhn, G.: Experiencing the Impossible, 1st edn. MIT Press, Cambridge (2019)
18. Tognazzini, B.: Principles, techniques, and ethics of stage magic and their application to human interface design. In: Proceedings of the INTERACT 1993 and CHI 1993 Conference on Human Factors in Computing Systems, pp. 355–362 (1993)
19. Kumari, S., Deterding, S., Kuhn, G.: Why game designers should study magic. Paper presented at Foundations of Digital Games – FDG, Malmö, Sweden (2018)
20. Dixon, S.: Digital Performance, 1st edn. MIT Press, Cambridge (2007)
21. Bakk, Á.K.: Sending shivers down the spine: VR productions as seamed media. Acta Univ. Sapientiae Film Media Stud. **17**, 143–156 (2019)
22. Lamont, P.: A particular kind of wonder: the experience of magic past and present. Rev. Gen. Psychol. Am. Psychol. Assoc. **21**(1), 1–8 (2017)

# Demonstrations

# Honey, I'm Home: An Adventure Game with Procedurally Generated Narrative Puzzles

Lilian Morgan$^{(\boxtimes)}$ and Mads Haahr

School of Computer Science and Statistics, Trinity College Dublin, Dublin, Ireland
{limorgan,haahrm}@tcd.ie

**Abstract.** We present *Honey, I'm Home*, a short 2D adventure game which makes use of the SPHINX framework for procedurally generating narrative puzzles. The player guides the protagonist, a journalist for a local newspaper, through four game areas, interacting with numerous characters and objects along the way. The player must solve puzzles to complete each area, combining objects and interacting with characters in the game. The procedural generation of puzzles ensures that while the gameworld remains largely identical between replays, the puzzles encountered are different. The aim of *Honey, I'm Home* was to serve as a tool for our two-fold evaluation of the SPHINX algorithm, from its functionality in game development, as well as its effect on player experience. To this end a small user study was also conducted on *Honey, I'm Home*.

**Keywords:** Procedural content generation · Puzzle games

## 1   Introduction

Story Puzzle Heuristics for Interactive Narrative eXperiences (SPHINX) was developed by Barbara de Kegel and Mads Haahr [1] and aims to provide an alternative to other systems for procedural generation of narrative puzzles, such as the Puzzle-Dice system [2]. As presented at the ICIDS 2019 conference, the system is focused on narrative puzzles, i.e., puzzles that require the player to examine their surroundings, and to interact with objects and characters to progress in the story.

At the core of the SPHINX framework is an algorithm based on an extended context-free grammar. The puzzle designer provides the algorithm with three core elements: items, rules and areas. To allow for further freedom and expressivity, optional information such as properties can also be defined on items and rules. The format of the rules is given below (1), as well as an example rule using properties (2).

$$Main\ Output\left[By-products\right]\ ::=\ Action\ Input(s) \tag{1}$$

$$Radio\left[ison:True\right]\ ::=\ SwitchOff\ Radio\left[ison:False\right] \tag{2}$$

The puzzle generation happens at runtime on a per-area basis. Each area is associated with at least one goal, from which a form of backwards substitution creates a puzzle

© Springer Nature Switzerland AG 2020
A.-G. Bosser et al. (Eds.): ICIDS 2020, LNCS 12497, pp. 335–338, 2020.
https://doi.org/10.1007/978-3-030-62516-0_30

"tree" (see Fig. 1). This same information is also used during puzzle solution, where the tree is traversed in the opposite direction. This method of generation helps guarantee the solvability of a puzzle, a consideration that is critical to player satisfaction. In addition to this feature, the SPHINX framework also aims to provide a large amount of expressive freedom to puzzle designers, as well as the possibility of using the algorithm across numerous game genres. As the system can function independently of core game mechanics and game worlds, it could, for example, be modified and integrated into open-world games or, potentially, into games that are already at a later stage in development. These possibilities could be explored further in future projects.

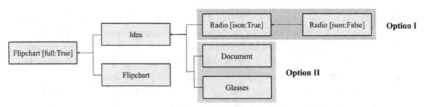

**Fig. 1.** An example puzzle tree from *Honey, I'm Home* showing an area with goal *Flipchart[full:True]* where the generator chooses randomly between options I and II to get the *Idea* item.

During initial conceptualization and implementation of the SPHINX framework within the Unity game engine, a small proof-of-concept game was developed. To further evaluate the overall framework, it was suggested SPHINX be integrated into another, larger game and tested within a small user study [1]. For the purpose of this two-fold evaluation, the story-based adventure game *Honey, I'm Home* was created. This demonstration aims to present how the SPHINX framework can be used to enrich aspects of gameplay, using *Honey, I'm Home* as an example.

## 2  Design and Development

In *Honey, I'm Home*, an atmospheric 2D side-scrolling adventure game, the overall objective for the player is to guide the protagonist, a journalist for a local newspaper, home. In order to progress in the game, the player must interact with objects and characters in four different game areas. Starting in the journalist's *Office*, the player is asked to help disguise the fact that the day was rather unproductive. Then, in the *Landing*, an ID card needs to be acquired to be able to call the elevator and finally leave the office building. Once outside, the journalist visits the *Pub* down the road: either to find a story to submit to the newspaper or find a present to bring home. After having completed one of these tasks, all that remains is for the player to get home – be that via the park, a car or a taxi in the *Street* (see Fig. 2).

The intended time to finish *Honey, I'm Home* is between 10–15 min and is available to play online[1]. On average, the puzzles associated with each game area increase in

---

[1] *Honey, I'm Home* is hosted on simmer.io: https://simmer.io/@honeyimhome/honey-i-m-home

length and difficulty as the player progresses, such that it should take the least amount of time to complete the *Office* area puzzle and the most for the *Pub* or *Street* areas. This setup aims to provide a more natural learning curve, allowing the player to get used to the game mechanics.

Aesthetically, *Honey, I'm Home* aims to create a slightly alternative art deco/mid-century world, where the odd occurrence of a UFO in the night sky is not entirely surprising. All artwork and animations were created specifically for the game. A number of audio tracks and effects were sourced to support the overall atmosphere and also provide feedback to the player. On the completion of an area, for example, an old-fashioned oven timer goes off.

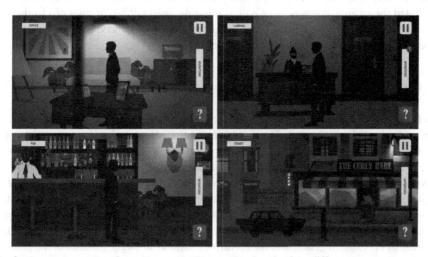

**Fig. 2.** Screenshots taken from *Honey, I'm Home*, showing the four different game areas; top to bottom, left to right – *Office, Landing, Pub* and *Street*.

The elements used during puzzle generation by the SPHINX system, include four game areas, 59 puzzle items and 84 puzzle rules. In addition to this, some minor modifications were made to the SPHINX framework in order to refine the experience for both the puzzle designer and the player:

- A basic "selection" system, as used in many adventure or puzzle games such as the *Rusty Lake* game series [4], was added such that the player needs to select specific items from their inventory to interact with others.
- The *Player* puzzle item was also designated to be used as a progress tracker, when needed. This is useful when the result of an action does not necessarily logically correspond to a directly interactable item.
- Certain items in the game world react when properties are changed following player interaction. This may affect the appearance of the game object, play or stop localized music (e.g., on switching on/off the *Radio*) or give access to other areas.
- A transcript for reviewing dialogues – or monologues – can be found in the pause menu, as inspired by *L.A. Noire* [3].

- A simple randomizer allows for a game object to have a list of prefabs, one of which is then chosen randomly and spawned at runtime. For example, the cars on the street make use of this function and differ in colour, depending on the random prefab selected.

While the overall level of variation in puzzles generated from one playthrough of *Honey, I'm Home* to the next is successful, the algorithm's random choice relies heavily on the breadth of the grammar provided by the puzzle designer [1]. Unfortunately, this does not guarantee maximal puzzle variation, resulting in the some of the same puzzles being chosen in successive playthroughs, despite other options being available within the grammar. In an attempt to lessen this effect, a basic memory system was recently added to keep track of rules chosen in a playthrough. The next time a puzzle is then generated for an area, the generator will, if possible, select different rules. To further be able to objectively evaluate the degree of variation in the produced puzzles, the puzzle for each area is saved to a text file during runtime.

## 3  Conclusion

The focus of the overall project was to put the SPHINX approach to procedural generation of narrative puzzles to the test. The resulting creation, *Honey, I'm Home*, demonstrates that SPHINX can be used to add complexity and range to puzzles. To further support this, the results from a small user study conducted online were generally very positive. Players felt that the variation in puzzles from one playthrough to the next contributed positively to the overall game experience and resulted in improved re-playability of the game, as well as a better understanding of the game world and mechanics. Approaching future possibilities, participants of the user study also showed a lot of interest in the addition of procedural generation for narrative elements in larger games. As the general concept of the SPHINX system allows for modifications and adaptations to the needs of specific games, the potential for integration across genre boundaries is promising.

## References

1. De Kegel, B., Haahr, M.: Towards procedural generation of narrative puzzles for adventure games. In: Cardona-Rivera, R.E., Sullivan, A., Young, R.M. (eds.) ICIDS 2019. LNCS, vol. 11869, pp. 241–249. Springer, Cham (2019). https://doi.org/10.1007/978-3-030-33894-7_25
2. Fernández-Vara, C., Thomson, A.: Procedural generation of narrative puzzles in adventure games: the puzzle-dice system. In: Proceedings of the Third Workshop on Procedural Content Generation in Games, p. 12. ACM (2012)
3. Bondi, T., Games, R.: LA Noire (2011)
4. Rusty Lake B.V. Ex.: Rusty Lake Series (2015–2019)

# A Natural History Museum Experience: Memories of Carvalhal's Palace – Turning Point

Vanessa Cesário[1]([✉]) [iD], Sandra Olim[1] [iD], and Valentina Nisi[1,2] [iD]

[1] ITI/LARSyS, Lisbon, Portugal
{vanessa.cesario,sandra.olim,valentina.nisi}@iti.larsys.pt
[2] Instituto Superior Técnico, University of Lisbon, Lisbon, Portugal

**Abstract.** Teenagers are a large pool of potential museum audiences. This age group is identified as an audience group that is often excluded from a museum's curatorial strategies [1] and appears to be generally disinterested in what museums might offer [2]. Without some degree of digital interactivity, it is challenging for a museum to remain interesting and relevant to a young tech-savvy audience [2]. Our application is a location-specific gamified narrative deployed at the Natural History Museum of Funchal (Madeira island, Portugal) which embraces the potential of mobile interactive technologies and digital storytelling to promote engaging tours for teenage visitors, encouraging more active, enriching and tailored experiences. Through our interactive story app, the audience is challenged to explore the museum to unlock fragments of a narrative that relates to the main story.

**Keywords:** Museums · Teenagers · Digital storytelling · Augmented Reality

## 1 Museums and New Mobile Interventions

There is an increasing concern about traditional exhibition and communication style of museums, which often fails to engage teenagers and denies the potential of museums to be a fundamental institution in a society which values cultural heritage [3]. Today museums are starting to embrace mobile applications and digital content as new modes of communication and have reconfigured the traditional narrative subject. These mobile interventions can engage visitors through memorable experiences [4] combining gaming and storytelling, requiring minimal space of reorganization of the exhibits and presenting options that can be tailored individually to suit particular exhibits. Moreover, location-based experiences are also valuable when applied to cultural heritage as a way to display historical content [5].

## 2 Natural History Museum of Funchal (NHMF)

The museum building, dating back to the 18th century, was originally a distinguished palace of Victorian style (wooden floors and ample doors in order for women to move

A.-G. Bosser et al. (Eds.): ICIDS 2020, LNCS 12497, pp. 339–343, 2020.
https://doi.org/10.1007/978-3-030-62516-0_31

around in their ballroom dresses). The NHMF is the oldest museum of the island and does not currently use any digital or interactive technology to enhance the visitors' experiences. With the goal of contributing to fill in the gap regarding teenage engagement in museums [1], we designed the *Memories of Carvalhal's Palace* dual experience, a storyfied game *(Haunted Encounters)* and gamified story *(Turning Point)*. These two experiences make use of the same characters and similar content, but employ different engagement strategies, geared towards better understanding teenagers' preferences and needs in museum contexts. The scope of this contribution is to describe the gamified story experience in details. The *Memories of Carvalhal's Palace – Turning Point* (Fig. 1) has been designed exclusively for the NHMF and based around the museum's permanent exhibition of taxidermied animals and aromatic plants of its garden, and it takes around 30 min to complete it.

**Fig. 1.** Envisioned interaction of *Turning Point*.

## 3 Fictional Plot

After consulting with the museum's staff and director about the museum goals and offerings, an original story plot and fictional characters were created in order to ground the experience onto the NHMF's exhibits. The museum collection includes a great taxidermied monk seal, one of the most endangered species of the Atlantic Ocean. Such species found shelter in the Madeira archipelago, which finally established a protected nature sanctuary devoted to the surviving monk seal in late 1980. This taxidermied species is also one of the most striking exhibits of the entire collection due to its size. This exhibit prompted our creative team to seek inspiration from the northern European legend of the Selkies, or women seals, in order to create the characters and a mystery plot to engage a teenage audience. Selkies are said to live their lives partly as animals, and partly as women, who shed their seal skin to become human and live, marry and procreate on land. The call of the sea will always haunt them, but they need to keep their seal skin at hand in order to be able to slip back in it to fulfill this need. The aim of this fictional plot is not only to familiarize teenagers with the marine and terrestrial natural wealth of the island, but also to use this legend to stimulate awareness towards rare and disappearing species, and conservation of the natural patrimony, in particular of the endangered monk seal exemplars. The fictional plot of *Turning Point* revolves around one of the heirs of the aristocratic Madeiran family that owned the palace, where the museum is currently located. The young heir falls in love with a Selkie woman, but she disappears in myste-rious circumstances leaving him waiting at the altar. He never comes to terms with the grief caused by this loss and, as restless ghosts often do, he lingers around the museum's rooms as an angry spirit. The audience becomes aware of the ghost's drama by collect-ing fragments of the story that unfolds in the museum's garden. After empathizing with the fictional characters, the audience is then prompted to help them find the truth by interacting with the museum's taxidermied species.

### 3.1  Mechanics

With *Turning Point,* users are encouraged to go to specific physical locations of the museum to unlock the story plot points and solve the mystery behind it. The basic mechanic relies on finding Augmented Reality (AR) markers that indicate the presence of story content, and unlocking story fragments that progress the plot. The story is narrated through photorealistic images of the characters accompanied with dialogues rendered as voice over audios and text (Fig. 1). The user is also presented with several historical and scientific facts woven into the story, such as the existence of the Madeiran tradition of whale hunting and the inherent massacre of the seals as a threat to the old fishing industry. In the second part of the experience, which happens inside the museum, each interaction with a taxidermied species will yield scientific facts about the fauna and flora of the island together with key elements that will help the audience put together the truth behind the bride's disappearance. The story is divided into four acts, containing 16 audio visual fragments in total and is presented in the form of a gamified narrative. Its first part, unveiling the couple's drama, is structured linearly: the app asks the user to search and interact with specific species at a time. In its second part, designed as five non-linear interactions, the audience can choose the species they would like to interact with to help the protagonists uncover the truth. This non-linear part does not change the unfolded story as a result of the order of the markers the users scan. Still, users must go to all the species to proceed in the experience. They will finish with the same amount of information if they had chosen other order to listen to these story fragments, then no computational approaches are used.

**Interface.** Upon starting the app, the audience is presented with a tutorial indicating how to interact with the app and how to use its interface. A custom-made map of the museum will help them orient themselves in the real space and find the story content.

The audience can also find out how far they have progressed into the story content according to the main timeline and where to look for markers and species in the physical premises.

**Game Play: Choosing Storylines.** After the tutorial, the user is asked to choose one of the two main storylines, and follow the story from the point of one of the two main characters – the couple Xavier and Marina. Depending on which one of the two they decide to follow, the events will follow a different point of view and involve different animal species in the museum.

**Augmented Reality Markers.** In order to unlock the story plot sequence, the app will guide the user through various sections of the museum, where they can find AR markers, each of which unlocks a new story fragment and is connected to a species of plant or animal. Markers can be scanned using the app, and each story fragment emerges after each marker is scanned.

**Rewards.** Upon completing the story, the user can restart the experience and follow the other character's point of view and reinforce their knowledge of the story, while interacting with different exhibits. Care has been taken not to repeat content inside the museum, and to have the user interact with different species from those encountered through the previous experience. Furthermore, users are also rewarded with the possibility of taking a picture with the story character whose point-of-view they have experienced through the app.

## 4   Concluding Remarks

In *Turning Point* teenagers are challenged to interact with the flora and taxidermy fauna of the Natural History Museum of Funchal while following a multiple-point of view gamified story plot. After the users select which point of view they want to follow, they are guided through the museum to scan AR markers in order to unlock parts of the story embedded with historical and scientific information. The teenage visitor not only learns about the species of aromatic plants and animals represented in the museum but also about its historical significance, which was once the palace of a noble Madeiran family.

**Acknowledgements.** Sense&Tell team from the ITI/LARSyS based in Madeira island.

## References

1. Tzibazi, V.: Participatory action research with young people in museums. Mus. Manag. Curatorship. **28**, 153–171 (2013). https://doi.org/10.1080/09647775.2013.776800
2. Cesário, V., Coelho, A., Nisi, V.: teenagers as experience seekers regarding interactive museums tours. In: Proceedings of the 1st International Conference on Design and Digital Communication, pp. 127–134. IPCA - Instituto Politécnico do Cávado e do Ave, Barcelos (2017)

3. Hooper-Greenhill, E.: Communication and Communities in the Post-museum: From Metanarratives to Constructed Knowledge. University of Leicester, Copenhagen (2001)
4. Bailey-Ross, C., Gray, S., Ashby, J., Terras, M., Hudson-Smith, A., Warwick, C.: Engaging the museum space: mobilizing visitor engagement with digital content creation. Digit. Scholarsh. Humanit. 689–708 (2016). https://doi.org/10.1093/llc/fqw041
5. Haahr, M.: Creating location-based augmented-reality games for cultural heritage. In: Alcañiz, M., Göbel, S., Ma, M., Fradinho Oliveira, M., Baalsrud Hauge, J., Marsh, T. (eds.) JCSG 2017. LNCS, vol. 10622, pp. 313–318. Springer, Cham (2017). https://doi.org/10.1007/978-3-319-70111-0_29

# Ares 2036: Exploring the Space of Rapid Prototyping for Transformative Interactive Storytelling

Christian Roth[1](✉) and Julie Dacanay[2]

[1] HKU University of the Arts Utrecht, Nieuwekade 1, Postbox 1520,
3500 BM Utrecht, The Netherlands
christian.roth@hku.nl

[2] Seabiscuit Creative Solutions, Julianaplein 12A, 1097 DN Amsterdam, The Netherlands
jules.dacanay@seabiscuitcreative.com

**Abstract.** Ares 2036 is a visual novel prototype exploring the circumstances, factors and cognitive biases that come into play in the process of forming opinions. The sci-fi scenario revolves around a potential pandemic on Earth, experienced from the distance of a spaceship on its way to Mars Station Ares. Players experience a situation in which communication is unclear and various factors and motives influence the quality of available information. As the main character, Ikeda, players talk to other crewmembers and try to make sense of varying information and perspectives before forming their own opinion. The prototype was developed over a 4-day sprint and entered into *Complexity Jam*. As proof of concept, Ares demonstrates how a basic visual novel prototype can create an atmospheric, thought-provoking experience.

**Keywords:** Transformative design · Interactive narrative design · Infodemic · Cognitive bias · Communication · Complexity · Learning · Reflection

## 1 Introduction

This paper describes the rapid prototyping approach used to design and implement a ludonarrative concept in a matter of days. Ares 2036 is a visual novel prototype created to immerse players in an interactive narrative experience focusing on the topics of communication and fact finding when factual information cannot be easily obtained. With Ares we explore the circumstances, factors and cognitive biases that come into play in the process of forming opinions during a crisis. Our scenario revolves around a central character, Raven Ikeda as she seeks to understand the cause of sudden radio silence from mission control. As Ikeda, players are confronted with speculation about an alleged catastrophe and varying perspectives and theories, based on which they must then make their own decisions. The first published prototype of Ares 2036 was developed by a team of two within 4 days as part of the first *Complexity Jam* [1].

© Springer Nature Switzerland AG 2020
A.-G. Bosser et al. (Eds.): ICIDS 2020, LNCS 12497, pp. 344–348, 2020.
https://doi.org/10.1007/978-3-030-62516-0_32

## 2   Development

Within the context of a game jam, ideas must lead to working prototypes within a short development window, limiting the amount of possible design attempts and iterations. Using a *rapid prototyping* workflow, which consists of ideation, prototyping, and testing phases, the team was able to test the technical feasibility of the Ares concept early on. See development timeline in Table 1.

**Table 1.** Development timeline of Ares 2036

| Day 1 *Ideation* | Day 2 *Prototyping* | Day 3 *Prototyping* | Day 4 *Testing* |
|---|---|---|---|
| • Look at authoring tools, select Ren'Py<br>• Set narrative theme, draft synopsis<br>• Define core experience<br>• Develop first ideas for opening scene and flesh out dialogue | • Learn Ren'Py<br>• Do a short prototype consisting of only a few scenes<br>• Define basic structure<br>• Select assets<br>• Divide tasks: script and visual lead; programming, audio, playtesting | • Iterate ideas from previous day<br>• Work on script<br>• Finalize ludonarrative experience and ending<br>• Adjust structure for faster implementation<br>• Implement remaining content | • Playtesting and fine tuning<br>• Research nice-to-have additions<br>• Implement latest changes in script<br>• Prepare project page on itch.io<br>• Submit to game jam |

### 2.1   Ideation

The goal for the game jam was to create an insightful, thought-provoking experience on the topic of an infodemic. The coronavirus pandemic has sparked debates on the so-called infodemic, which refers to the flood of misinformation, conspiracy ideologies, and fear mongering that comes as a result of uncertainty. The topic posed a complex challenge for the team as there were many possibilities but limited time and resources. We began ideating by asking ourselves questions about the theme and premise, discussing insights and opportunities for reflection, possibilities for player engagement, and the appropriate authoring tools. As our options and decisions were weighed against practical considerations such as skills, desired outcomes and resources, we made a conscious decision to streamline and simplify our workflow, focus on clarity of thought and intention and, in a sense, allow our limitations to create parameters within which we could design efficiently and effectively.

Doing research on the topic and identifying key aspects, we generated a list of keywords, including "communication failure", "opinion", "fake news", "information vacuum", "cognitive bias", "skepticism", and "group think". These concepts formed a springboard, allowing us to draft the synopsis that would guide the project: A mission to Mars loses radio contact with Earth and the lead character is confronted with hazy information and rumors about a new disastrous pandemic.

Starting with this premise, we created profiles, which included specializations, nationalities, and traits, designed to make each character distinct and believable. From there, the storyline was developed to facilitate interactions between the player and the other characters in the story, designed as a psychometric diagnostic, rating player choices on three dimensions: impressionability, skepticism, and rationality. Implemented as intradiegetic feedback, it is revealed to the player that the space agency is in fact conducting an evaluation of their responses, thus creating a narrative twist and potentially inducing reflection, or in some cases, even transformation.

As creating a 3D environment using *Unity* or *Unreal* was not feasible given the time constraints, we found Ren'Py – a free and versatile visual novel scripting tool based on Python – to be a suitable authoring system, giving us sufficient functionality to tell our story. We decided that a visual novel would be the most appropriate format given the nature of the story and the dialogue-heavy interaction that we envisioned taking place between the characters.

## 2.2  Prototyping

The popular game developer slogans "It is not the idea; it is the execution" [2] and "Ideas are cheap. Execution is everything" show that the value of a concept lies in its implementation. No matter what concept we could have come up with, we needed to be aware of the development reality. This meant assessing our design decisions from different practical perspectives, as creative lead, as narrative designer, and as developer. This shifting dynamic of weighing ideas not just for potential impact, but also against our capability to program them into a tangible experience, guided us through the prototyping phase and, indeed, throughout the entire process.

Efficiency being a prime consideration tasks were divided into segments that would allow us to work in parallel and in cycles. Thus, after the overall flow of the story was decided, one team member would work on scripting dialogue and interactions, while the other realized the scenes within the authoring tool. One member would edit and composite graphic assets while the other would focus on sound design to enrich ambience.

Script readings were used for continuous improvement, allowing us to discuss changes before implementing scenes in Ren'Py. Playtests were integrated at intervals to ensure that we were on the right track. We identified areas where our workflow could be streamlined, even deciding to integrate pseudo-code or cues into the text of our script to make the fine-tuning of dialogue, pacing and transitions more expedient. Finally, we found that integrating checkpoints was an effective strategy for alignment as well as motivation. Our iterative process turned out to be similar to agile development [3].

## 2.3  Playtesting

For the user testing we created an online questionnaire based on the measurement toolbox that had been provided as part of the game jam [4] and linked to it on itch.io to invite jam participants as well as non-participating testers to try the visual novel.

Feedback from 8 testers indicated that our imagery, music and sound design created a cinematic appeal, which heightened the sense of immersion. This was supported by the use of dialogue-driven storytelling, as well as the design of the characters and their personalities.

"The music worked very well with the theme, the graphics are amazing. The storyline is brilliant!", "I am hooked! How does the story go on?".

In addition, we interviewed four testers via chat to ask follow-up questions revealing further feedback. "The characters need more exposition; the beginning is too short." Next prototypes can include better scripting of the interactors by integrating scenes allowing the player to inhabit the character earlier on.

The majority of play testers understood the intention and twist. "I liked the reflective moment of discovering that I was being played while I thought I was playing." "I found it interesting that my personality can be analyzed by an algorithm when I play games." Some feedback indicated that some choices belonging to the preferable rational dimension are rather easy to spot. Future versions can include time pressure and different cognitive biases to make this aspect more challenging.

Some participants wished for more agency and autonomous decisions. We decided to keep the level of player agency rather low with a strict foldback structure. Yet, every decision counts for the assessment in the end. Flags are used to unlock achievements like encountering "The Elephant Poem", which are revealed at the end.

## 3  Conclusion

Creating a meaningful, engaging interactive narrative is a challenging, multifaceted task requiring ideas to be generated, quickly assessed and then implemented and tested. Dialogue and interactions get adjusted as the storyline gets fleshed out. Some materials get discarded and replaced as some design decisions are prioritized over others. All these require decisiveness and speed while staying true to the core concept.

During the course of development, many of our decisions were made on the basis of practical considerations, including the use of dialogue-driven storytelling, still images, and Ren'Py which was simple enough to deliver quick results and yet complex enough to enable advanced interactive storytelling techniques. But perhaps more importantly, many of our design decisions were informed by the desire to create information while simultaneously withholding the confirmation thereof, which we found to be aligned with the lack of perceivable emotion or intent. Without animation to show bodily actions or spatial contexts, and without visible facial expression or audible voice inflection, the players had a lot of room to interpret intent and hence veracity. This served to heighten the sense of uncertainty which was a strong element of the experience.

Overall, we have found that a deliberately designed minimal interactive narrative can create an immersive atmosphere and storyline capable of engaging players. Ares 2036 demonstrates how a team of two designers without prior programming knowledge can prototype a visual novel in 4 days following a rapid-prototyping framework and well-articulated design goals. This project provides a reference that can be used for interactive narrative design workshops and seminars, including rapid prototyping of visual novels for students with limited programming knowledge.

# References

1. Complexity Jam. Ares 2036. https://itch.io/jam/complexityjam/rate/663174
2. Kultima, A.: Game Design Praxiology. University of Tampere, Finland (2018)
3. Petrillo, F., Pimenta, M.: Is Agility Out There? Agile Practices in Game Development. SIGDOC (2010)
4. Roth, C., Koenitz, H.: Evaluating the user experience of interactive digital narrative. In: Proceedings of the 1st International Workshop on Multimedia Alternate Realities, pp. 31–36. ACM (2016)

# The Story Maker - An Authoring Tool for Multimedia-Rich Interactive Narratives

Ektor Vrettakis[1,2], Christos Lougiakis[1,2], Akrivi Katifori[1,2(✉)], Vassilis Kourtis[1,2], Stamatis Christoforidis[1,2], Manos Karvounis[1,2], and Yannis Ioanidis[1,2]

[1] ATHENA Research Center, Artemidos 6 & Epidavrou, 15125 Maroussi, Greece
{ekvre,chrislou,vivi,vkourtis,stachris,manosk,yannis}@di.uoa.gr
[2] Department of Informatics and Telecommunications, National and Kapodistrian University of Athens, Panepistimioupolis, Ilissia, Greece

**Abstract.** In our previous work, we have experimented with branching narratives in cultural heritage, seeking to validate the efficacy of such narratives in this context and identify best practices in their creation. In this work we present the Story Maker, an authoring tool designed as a result of an iterative co-design process with heritage domain experts. The tool is situated within the domain of Interactive Digital Narrative (IDN) authoring tools and was created to support both the design and the production of multimedia rich interactive narratives. We briefly present the motivation for the creation of the tool and describe its main features concluding with the future directions of our research.

**Keywords:** Interactive digital storytelling · Authoring tool · Branching narratives · Cultural heritage

## 1 Introduction

The *Story Maker* is a web-based authoring tool to promote the creation of digital multimedia-rich interactive narratives for cultural heritage. Story authors in this domain typically have limited experience with IDN and programming. The tool has been tailored to support them from the story structure design phase to production. In this way they can create ready to use experiences available through the web or as an Android application for mobile devices to their intended audience, on-site or virtual museum visitors.

Based on the IDN authoring tools classification work in [3], we situate our tool within the area of interactive fiction tools and more specifically within the "Hypertext" category. The *Story Maker* is written in JavaScript on top of the Angular framework and backed by a document store. Any communication between the app and the backing store is made through a RESTful interface.

In this work we briefly present our motivation for the creation of the tool and then focus on its two main structural components, the Story Design Editor and the Storyboard Editor.

© Springer Nature Switzerland AG 2020
A.-G. Bosser et al. (Eds.): ICIDS 2020, LNCS 12497, pp. 349–352, 2020.
https://doi.org/10.1007/978-3-030-62516-0_33

## 2  Background and Motivation

The Story Maker is the result of an iterative co-design process with the domain experts that started in the context of the project CHESS [4] and continued through a series of collaborations with different cultural heritage sites as well as during the EMOTIVE project [2]. It was designed to provide an intuitive way for experimentation with the use of branching narratives for cultural heritage, to validate the efficacy of such narratives and identify best practices for IDN in this domain [1].

In our previous work working with domain experts in the context of the CHESS project with the CAT authoring tool [4], a graph based authoring tool to produce the digital experience, and later on in the context of the EMOTIVE project with the Storyboard Editor, which offered a folder like visualization to navigate the story structure [5], we observed that the authors prepared the structure and textual content of the experience in word processing software and then used the authoring tools only for the production of the content. Sometimes, especially when their story structure had many branching points, they created representations of the story graph, on paper or with tools like Microsoft PowerPoint. Taking into account these observations, we designed the Story Maker as an integrated tool that would support authoring from conceptualization, to the design of the story structure and then to the final production. Our tool integrates in a simple and intuitive interface, the Story Design Editor, used as a first step to define the structure and concept of the branching narrative in a text-editor like format, and the Storyboard Editor which can then be used to transform this concept into the final experience offering built-in template support to create different types of multimedia activities. The added value of the tool for the specific domain, in comparison with similar tools like inklewriter [6] and Twine [7] is the possibility to create complex multimedia experiences from conceptualization to production in an integrated tool and intuitive for its intended user group.

## 3  The Story Design Editor

The Story Design Editor (SDE) can support the design of the story concept and structure with a simple text editor, very similar to common word processors (e.g. Microsoft Office and Google Docs) and enhanced with additional features to support branching narratives. The narrative text can be organized in *Parts*, defined as coherent parts of the narrative, and *Branches* that connect them. The story graph functionality offers a visual interactive overview of the experience structure, generated automatically, while editing the experience description (Fig. 1). Parts and branches are sufficient to support the creation of a variety of interactive stories, from very simple, linear narratives, to very complex branching ones that may also use *tags* and *conditions*. Tags can be associated with Parts or Branches, and then they can be used in a Branch condition to show or hide the specific Branch. The conditions are determined by enforcing boolean constraints on the tags encountered so far, defining whether a tag has been met during an experience, or not.

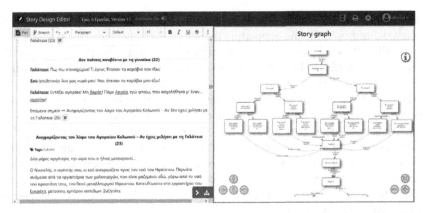

**Fig. 1.** The *Story Design Editor text editor* with the slide-in *graph view* visible.

# 4   The Storyboard Editor

While the SDE supports the first steps of the authoring process (conceptualization & scripting), the *Story Maker's Storyboard Editor (SBE)* covers the production of the final visitor experience. During the production phase, all *Parts* of the script are materialized through the creation of a set of *Screens* that give "flesh and bone" to each story snippet (Fig. 2).

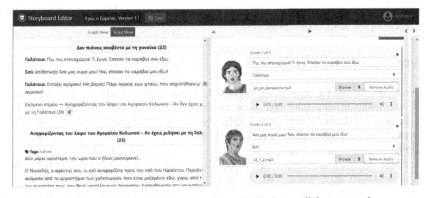

**Fig. 2.** The *Storyboard Editor text editor* - Voiced-over dialogue template.

To create, one or more, *Screens* that will implement a *Part*, the authors are provided with a predefined set of templates, that allow the production of the content without having to design and program user interface features. The available templates range from simple ones, used to present a combination of text, images and audio, to more complex, designed to address common needs of the creators of cultural heritage experiences. These include a) Simple, b) Voiced-Over Dialogue, c) Quiz, d) Video, e) Interactive Images, f) Interactive Books, g) Near-Field Communication Interactors, h) Question Prompts and i) Navigation Maps.

Additionally, to the *Screens*, the authors are able to create *Menus* to implement the branches defined in SDE, thus supporting the selection of alternative paths of the plot. In short, SBE offers templates for menu functionalities and appearance, that include the following: a) Tiles/List, b) Interactive Images, c) Near Field Communication Interactors, d) QR-Code Interactors and e) Jumps.

The experience created with the *SBE* can be made available in a web based view mode as well as through a mobile application for Android devices. After producing an interactive storytelling experience, the result becomes available to be downloaded on the corresponding smartphone application. The end-users (the visitors) are able to view and interact with the various *Screens*, created using the available templates. The story branches that affect the way the narrative unfolds can be made available to the user through *Menus* or selected automatically according to conditions that are set while the user proceeds in the experience.

## 5   Conclusions and Future Steps

In this work we presented the Story Maker, a web-based authoring tool for the design and production of multimedia rich, interactive narratives for cultural heritage, where story design and production functionalities are tightly coupled to support codelss and intuitive authoring.

We continue the evaluation of our tool in real life applications for cultural heritage aiming to transform it into an effective means for promoting and experimenting with IDN in this field. We are also working towards supporting the concrete need for multi-user interactive storytelling experiences that has been identified during our research in the context of the EMOTIVE project [2].

## References

1. Katifori, A., Karvounis, M., Kourtis, V., Perry, S., Roussou, M., Ioanidis, Y.: Applying interactive storytelling in cultural heritage: opportunities, challenges and lessons learned. In: Rouse, R., Koenitz, H., Haahr, M. (eds.) ICIDS 2018. LNCS, vol. 11318, pp. 603–612. Springer, Cham (2018). https://doi.org/10.1007/978-3-030-04028-4_70
2. Katifori, A., Roussou, M., Perry, S., Drettakis, G,. Vizcay, S., Philip, J.: The EMOTIVE project – emotive virtual cultural experiences through personalized storytelling. In: CIRA@ EuroMed 2018, pp. 11–20. IEEE, Ireland (2019)
3. Shibolet, Y., Knoller, N., Koenitz, H.: A framework for classifying and describing authoring tools for interactive digital narrative. In: Rouse, R., Koenitz, H., Haahr, M. (eds.) ICIDS 2018. LNCS, vol. 11318, pp. 523–533. Springer, Cham (2018). https://doi.org/10.1007/978-3-030-04028-4_61
4. Vayanou, M., et al.: Authoring personalized interactive museum stories. In: Mitchell, A., Fernández-Vara, C., Thue, D. (eds.) ICIDS 2014. LNCS, vol. 8832, pp. 37–48. Springer, Cham (2014). https://doi.org/10.1007/978-3-319-12337-0_4
5. Vrettakis, E., Kourtis, V., Katifori, A., Karvounis, M., Lougiakis, C., Ioannidis, Y.: Narralive – creating and experiencing mobile digital storytelling in cultural heritage. Digit. Appl. Archaeol. Cult. Herit. **15**, e00114 (2019)
6. Inklewriter. https://www.inklestudios.com/inklewriter/. Accessed 28 Aug 2020
7. Twine. https://twinery.org/. Accessed 28 Aug 2020

# Using Reverse Interactive Audio Systems (RIAS) to Direct Attention in Virtual Reality Narrative Practices: A Case Study

Aletta J. Steynberg[(⊠)] [iD]

Berklee College of Music, Boston, MA 02115, USA
asteynberg@berklee.edu

**Abstract.** Game audio is widely implemented as being reactive to player actions and environmental influences. However, with virtual reality narratives, there is a growing need to be able to direct audience attention. ArrivalVR is the first nationally co-created storytelling project presenting curated immigration/migration stories of Americans in virtual reality (VR). In this paper, we discuss how reverse interactive audio systems could direct audience attention using ArrivalVR as a case study.

**Keywords:** Virtual reality · Digital narrative · Spatial audio · Audio interaction

## 1 Introduction

ArrivalVR is the first nationally co-created VR storytelling project that gathers and curates immigration/migration stories of Americans (pre-1620 through 2019) and incorporates them into a timeline in a narrative VR platform. The project tells the stories of immigrants to the United States, ranging from the 1600s to 2018. We aim to facilitate dialogue on what it is like to be an American.

In ArrivalVR, we sought to overcome mere engagement, surpass engrossment, and take the user on a journey of full immersion [4]. Immersion is defined as the engagement of all senses through cognitive processing and natural attention direction [4]. This engagement results in an illusion of embodiment [10] in a non-physical space through the emotional response that influences attention [7]. Player immersion results in greater emotional connection and internalization of digital narrative [6].

In ArrivalVR, we approached immersion from a sonic viewpoint. According to O'Keeffe, "The physicality of sound can alter our perception of the space in which we hear it, expanding or contracting the landscape and shaping our psychological and sociological response to space" [9]. Additionally, according to Berndt et al., sound is processed subconsciously and therefore has a direct effect on the limbic system [1]. This causes sound to engage the players emotionally, which is a crucial step in leading to player immersion [7]. Considering this, and the thought that sound creates the sense of another person's presence and of activity [10], we explored ways in which sound can direct audience attention in Virtual Reality (VR).

© Springer Nature Switzerland AG 2020
A.-G. Bosser et al. (Eds.): ICIDS 2020, LNCS 12497, pp. 353–356, 2020.
https://doi.org/10.1007/978-3-030-62516-0_34

## 2  Directing Audience Attention to Support Narrative in VR

Narratives in virtual reality are unique because the player is immersed in the environment in which the story takes place [12] and this improves the emotional connection the player forms with the story. However, it is exceedingly hard to predict where players will be looking [8]. This creates a problem when designing the flow of the narrative [5], as players might miss important details of the story [13]. With ArrivalVR, we took it a step further in relying solely on gaze-interaction to direct the narrative. Gaze interaction has merit in that it simplifies navigation, but it also means that many of our players might never experience the full narrative if they do not look at and initiate elements of the story. Therefore, until the player looks at an interactive object in the environment, the narrative will not unfold.

In current virtual reality and cinematic virtual reality practices, visuals such as illumination of the area, the changing of colors, and movement are used to direct attention [5]. This is effective on 2D screens, but it poses a problem in a 360-degree environment such as VR, because it requires the player to turn his or her head and look in the direction of the interaction. However, using spatial audio, humans have a 360-degree perception of sound in which we can sense the direct position of audio sources [9]. Blesser et al. expand on this, arguing that space becomes revealed to us through its "aural architecture" [3]. In ArrivalVR, we used spatial audio to make the player aware of the full virtual environment, stretching beyond the visual representation of the scene. We implemented audio invoking environmental presence [5] (neighbors talking, the street below, far-off clock tower), as well as the sounds originating in the apartment (radio, water pipes, floor creaks, and human sounds). This engages the player's imagination to fill in the gaps of the world and creates a sense of placement in the world [2]. Within this soundscape, we have background sounds as well as sounds designed to stand out and grab the player's attention. Through the architectural design of the soundscape, we have managed to guide the audience's attention through the narrative while allowing the player to move at their own pace and interact with the scene.

## 3  Setting up Reverse Interactive Audio Systems (RIAS) Using Arrival as an Example

Currently, interactive game audio is reactive to player actions. With ArrivalVR, we sought to use audio not only to improve immersion and as a source of confirmation of action, but also to direct audience attention and initiate action. To accomplish this, our team designed a method that we call Reverse Interactive Audio Systems (RIAS). RIAS is based on a timeline of events that prompt player interaction, setting up a structure for the narrative [13], while preserving the player interactivity. This is where our system is unique from commercial game audio – instead of actions triggering audio, the system is reversed where sounds prompt action. For example, when the player first enters the environment, they are free to look around and interact with anything. However, after 15 s, the storyteller in the scene shifts their weight and the floorboards creak. For a player not engaged with an element in the scene, this alerts them to the social presence [5] of the other person in the room. If the player is engaged with something else in the scene, the timeline progresses into the next phase – the storyteller clears their throat, sighs, and then gives verbal interaction such as 'Hello' and 'I'd like to tell you my story'. The player is able to look at the person at any time which triggers the Gazebutton [11]. This trigger stops all other sounds ('stop all' event) and starts the storyteller's audio sequence. Through the audio system, the player's attention is guided towards the next phase in the narrative while relying on the player to initiate the transition.

We created this system by combining Audiokinetic's audio-middleware, Wwise, with a timer sequencer in Unity. We set up events in Wwise that trigger audio sample groups selecting from a list of randomized audio files. Each event is then linked to a specific point on the timeline sequence within Unity. In contrast to other systems, the player's interaction with a specific area results in a reverse event being triggered. For example, the 'waiting storyteller' sequencer continues playing until the player looks at the person, triggering an event in Wwise – the 'stop all' event. However, the effectiveness of this system relies entirely on the accuracy of the audio spatial mapping.

## 4 Spatial Audio Mapping Using ArrivalVR as an Example

Spatial audio mapping is essential in establishing the virtual space, the accuracy of which has a direct impact on the user's psychological response to the space [9]. When using audio cues to guide audience attention, this mapping has to be flawless. In ArrivalVR, we used the attenuations built into Audiokinetic, Wwise, and plugins such as Wwise Reflect and Convolution to ensure accuracy of not only the direct audio sources but also the reflections in space. The range of possible settings made it possible for us to customize each sound source, and make tiny adjustments for the best results.

## 5 Conclusion

In conclusion, in virtual reality, it is difficult to predict where players will be looking which creates a problem when designing the flow of the narrative. In ArrivalVR, we implemented reverse interactive audio systems that guide player attention through natural audio cues in the environment. We believe that this resulted in enhanced player immersion, stretching beyond the visual representation of the scene, and created the potential for increased emotional connection and internalization of the digital narrative.

## References

1. Berndt, A., Hartmann, K.: Directing for cinematic virtual reality: how the traditional film director's craft applies to immersive environments and notions of presence. In: Spierling, U., Szilas, N. (eds.) Interactive Storytelling, ICIDS, Erfurt, DE, vol. 8, pp. 126–131 (2008). https://doi.org/10.1080/14682753.2017.1305838
2. Bhide, S., Goins, E., Geigel, J.: Experimental analysis of spatial sound for storytelling in virtual reality. In: Cardona-Rivera, R.E., Sullivan, A., Young, R.M. (eds.) ICIDS 2019. LNCS, vol. 11869, pp. 3–7. Springer, Cham (2019). https://doi.org/10.1007/978-3-030-33894-7_1
3. Blesser, B., Salter, L.: Spaces Speak, Are You Listening?: Experiencing Aural Architecture. MIT Press, Cambridge (2009). https://doi.org/10.7551/mitpress/6384.001.0001

4. Jennett, C., et al.: Measuring and defining the experience of the immersion in games. Int. J. Hum. Comput. Stud. **66**, 641–666 (2008). https://doi.org/10.1016/j.ijhcs.2008.04.004
5. Mateer, J.: Directing for cinematic virtual reality: how the traditional film director's craft applies to immersive environments and notions of presence. J. Media Pract. (5), 14–25 (2017). https://doi.org/10.1080/14682753.2017.1305838
6. Mendanca, R.L., Mustaro, P.N.: Immertion: immersion and emotion in digital games. In: Brazilian Symposium on Computer Games and Digital Entertainment, P.P.G.E.E., Brazil, pp. 103–113 (2012)
7. Nacke, L.E., Grimshaw, M.: Game interaction through affective sound. Game Sound Technology and Player Interaction: Concepts and Developments, University of Bolton, pp. 264–285 (2011). https://doi.org/10.4018/978-1-61692-828-5.ch013
8. Nielsen, L.T., et al.: Missing the point: an exploration of how to guide users' attention during cinematic virtual reality. In: Proceedings of the 22nd ACM Symposium on Virtual Reality Software and Technology, Munich, DE, pp. 229–232 (2016). https://doi.org/10.1145/2993369.2993405
9. O'Keeffe, L., Grimshaw, M.: Sound is not a simulation. Game Sound Technology and Player Interaction: Concepts and Developments, University of Bolton, UK, pp. 44–59 (2011). https://doi.org/10.4018/978-1-61692-828-5.ch003
10. Parker, J.R., Heerema, J.: Audio interaction in computer-mediated games. Int. J. Comput. Games Technol. **5**, 1–8 (2008). https://doi.org/10.1155/2008/178923
11. Radiah, R., Abdrabou, Y., Mayer, T., Pfeuffer, K., Alt, F.: GazeButton: enhancing buttons with eye gaze interactions. In: Kreitz, K., Sharif, B. (eds.) Proceedings of the 11th ACM Symposium on Eye Tracking Research & Applications 2019, ETRA, vol. 11, pp. 1–7. Association for Computing Machinery, Colorado (2019). https://doi.org/10.1145/3314111.3318154
12. Steedm, A.J.: Defining interaction within immersive virtual environments. Game Sound Technology and Player Interaction, University of Bolton, UK, pp. 44–59 (2011)
13. Syrett, H., Calvi, L., van Gisbergen, M.: The oculus rift film experience: a case study on understanding films in a head-mounted display. In: Poppe, R., Meyer, J.-J., Veltkamp, R., Dastani, M. (eds.) INTETAIN 2016 2016. LNICST, vol. 178, pp. 197–208. Springer, Cham (2017). https://doi.org/10.1007/978-3-319-49616-0_19

# Tell a Tail 360°: Immersive Storytelling on Animal Welfare

Paulo Bala[1,2(✉)], Mara Dionisio[1,2], Tânia Andrade[3], and Valentina Nisi[2,4]

[1] FCT, Universidade Nova de Lisboa, Lisbon, Portugal
[2] ITI-LARSyS, Funchal, Portugal
{paulo.bala,mara.dionisio,valentina.nisi}@iti.larsys.pt
[3] Universidade da Madeira, Funchal, Portugal
[4] IST, Universidade de Lisboa, Lisbon, Portugal

**Abstract.** Immersive technologies aligned with storytelling can create novel and powerful tools to inform and ponder on social issues. This demo paper describes a cinematic virtual reality project, Tell a Tail 360°, on the rescue of abandoned companion animals. *Tell a Tail 360°* was designed targeting teens (13–19 years old) and its inclusion in a classroom setting. By using 360° videos of a rescue kennel, animal hospital and the field work of non-governmental organizations, we intend for the target audience to be exposed to different animal welfare issues relevant to their context.

**Keywords:** Cinematic VR · Storytelling · Animal welfare

## 1 Introduction

Meaningful play [2], where playful interactions are used to inform and critique social issues, offer a new lens from which to design storytelling and immersive experiences. Aligned with XR technologies (eXtended-Reality, encompassing: VR, Virtual Reality; CR, Cinematic Reality; AR, Augmented Reality), stories with a social focus have the potential to bond users to virtual environments and characters. As an example, Peña et al.'s seminal work on Immersive Journalism "Hunger in L.A." [4], emerges as a pillar of VR nonfiction experiences [1]. A preferred medium for VR nonfiction experiences is 360° video, since it offers realistic visuals grounded in reality and low-cost overhead in terms of production and consumption. Vishawanath et al. [5] take advantage of this opportunity when integrating low-cost smartphone-based 360° videos in a co-design, co-creation and co-learning process with students and teachers. Bolstered by this intersection of immersive storytelling, social causes and education, in this paper, we introduce *Tell a Tail 360°* prototype, an immersive documentary focused on the rescue of abandoned companion animals (dogs and cats).

P. Bala and M. Dionisio—These authors contributed equally.

## 2    Animal Welfare in Madeira Island

Concerning animal welfare worldwide, one of most urgent intervention target is the abandonment of companion animals. One of the strategies adopted is public (re)education, specifically within school curricula. An example of such an intervention is Kim and Lee's work [3], a socio-scientific program for middle school students, including classroom activities and engagement in the community (e.g. visit kennels). Since on-site tours might not be possible for a myriad of reasons (e.g. economic, scalability to larger programs, proximity, etc.), virtual tours could be a successful alternative. Furthermore, they do not fully portray the rescued animal experience and the specific context of where they happen. For example, in Madeira Island, although there is enacted legislation (for criminalization of cruelty and abandonment) and support programs (for sterilization and microchipping), "No Kill" shelters are unable to handle the overpopulation of stray animals. Many times, private citizens, organized into NGOs (nongovernmental organizations), coordinate rescue missions and make arrangements for care, documenting their work through social networks like Instagram.

## 3    Design and Prototype of *Tell a Tail 360°*

*Tell a Tail 360°* follows a documentary narrative approach portraying different stakeholders' views of the companion animal abandonment issue in Madeira Island. Our goal was to create an experience targeting teenagers (13–19 years old), that could be included in classroom activities as a prompt to discuss the social issue and raise interest for out-of-classroom activities like volunteering. As such, the content was structured in three main topics (see Fig. 1): content supporting the *navigation* in the prototype, content related to the kennel, and content related to NGO. The *Kennel Tour* branch (blue in Fig. 1) is an alternative to the on-site tours and would allow the audience to learn about the kennel's daily routines. *Chico's Rescue* branch (purple in Fig. 1) offers a novel experience for the audience, following the NGO volunteers rescuing an abandoned dog, Chico. This branch shows different stages of the rescue including consultation/treatment at the Veterinary Hospital and adoption through the NGO's Instagram posts. Table 1 includes a description of the different story nodes, grouped by branches.

Initially developed in Unity 2019.3.0a11 for Oculus Go and Gear VR devices, the prototype was re-implemented as an interactive web application using web-based VR framework A-frame[1], making it compatible for web viewing (computer/smartphone), as well as HMD devices with 3 degrees of freedom controllers (e.g. Oculus Go). The prototype was optimized for web viewing using 360° videos (in webm format), images/360° panoramas (in jpg and png formats) and audio (in mp3 format). Video and equirectangular images are projected on a sphere, around a virtual camera (see Fig. 2 left); if viewing in a computer, clicking and dragging rotates the camera and its corresponding viewport; viewing

---

[1] https://aframe.io.

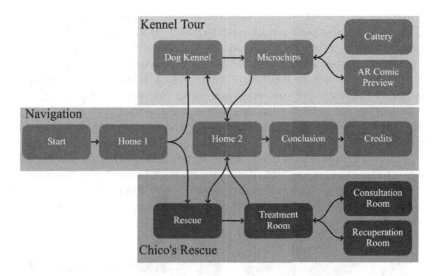

**Fig. 1.** Story structure (Color figure online)

**Table 1.** Story nodes, including 360° type (V: video; P: panorama; V→P: video finishing in a panorama) and a description

| | Node | 360° | Description |
|---|---|---|---|
| **Navigation** | Start | P | Instructions on interaction and how to start the experience. |
| | Home 1 | V→P | Kennel entrance with rescued animals and the kennel director welcoming the user to the experience. |
| | Home 2 | V→P | Kennel entrance with rescued animals and the kennel director. |
| | Conclusion | V | Kennel director ends the visit. This is triggered if both branches have been visited. |
| | Credits | P | Production credits and restart option. |
| **Kennel Tour** | Dog Kennel | V | Tour of dog kennel facilities and the work done by the auxiliary staff. |
| | Microchips | V→P | Veterinarian microchips a rescued animal. |
| | Cattery | V | Tour of the cat's play area. |
| | AR Comic Preview | P | Preview of AR branching comic for children on adoption and animal care. |
| **Chico's Rescue** | Rescue | V | NGO volunteers rescue an animal, Chico, from poor living conditions, with the help of the police. |
| | Treatment Room | V→P | Chico is brought to a Veterinary Hospital. |
| | Consultation Room | V | Excerpt of veterinarian consultation, where Chico is diagnosed with multiple cancerous growths. |
| | Recuperation Room | V→P | Chico and Serrinha, another rescued animal, are recuperating. The NGOs Instagram posts are over imposed showing the adoptions of the two animals. |

in a smartphone or HMD device, uses the device's sensors to adjust this camera. Throughout the experience, interactive points (IPs), represented by outlined characters (see Fig. 2 right) and buttons, appear signaling a user choice and work as hyperlinks to other story nodes; if viewing in a computer/smartphone, these IP are reactive to click or touches; if viewing in a HMD, IPs are reactive by being pointed at with the controller and using the trigger. Depending on the story nodes, certain actions (like skipping and going back) are available; these options appear by double-clicking/triggering the remote and disappear when a choice is made or after a period of inactivity. Future works include testing with teenagers in a school setting, addressing different research goals, such as (1) how effective the intersection of storytelling with immersive technologies can be to raise awareness to social causes and (2) to explore how the prototype can be expanded to include other types of media (e.g. websites, news and 3D recreations).

**Fig. 2.** *Tell a Tail 360°* prototype

**Acknowledgments.** This work has been supported by MITIExcell (M1420-01-0145-FEDER-000002), LARSyS-FCT funding (UIDB/50009/2020) and FCT Ph.D. Grant PD/BD/128330/2017 and PD/BD/114142/2015.

# References

1. Bevan, C., et al.: Behind the curtain of the "ultimate empathy machine": on the composition of virtual reality nonfiction experiences. In: Proceedings of CHI 2019, pp. 1–12. ACM Press, Glasgow (2019). https://doi.org/10.1145/3290605.3300736
2. Flanagan, M.: Critical Play: Radical Game Design. MIT Press, Cambridge (2013). oCLC: 935016500
3. Kim, G., Lee, H.: A case study of community-based socioscientific issue program: focusing on the abandoned animal issue. J. Biolog. Educ. 1–15 (2019). https://doi.org/10.1080/00219266.2019.1699150
4. de la Peña, N., et al.: Immersive journalism: immersive virtual reality for the first-person experience of news. Presence: Teleoper. Virtual Environ. **19**(4), 291–301 (2010). https://doi.org/10.1162/PRES_a_00005
5. Vishwanath, A., Karusala, N., Wong-Villacres, M., Kumar, N.: Engaging lived and virtual realities. In: Proceedings of CHI 2019, p. 1–15. Association for Computing Machinery, New York (2019). https://doi.org/10.1145/3290605.3300580

# Digital Narrative, Documents and Interactive Public History

Tristan Revells[1]([⊠]) and Yuzhu Chai[2]

[1] East Asian History, Columbia University, New York, USA
ter2121@columbia.edu
[2] School of the Art Institute of Chicago, 36 S Wabash Ave., Chicago, IL 60603, USA
ychai2@saic.edu

**Abstract.** To date, the implications and potential of interactive digital narrative have had a limited effect on history as an academic discipline. This project is an attempt to form a dialogue between the practice of historians and the rich scholarship on interactive narrative already undertaken by literary theorists, researchers of interactive systems, scholars of media studies, and practicing creative technologists. Probing the narrative devices common to the production of historical work, this VR project uses Maya, Unity, and a range of visual and aural historical sources from Republican-era China (1912–1949) to offer a digital demonstration of the possibilities of combining interactive digital narrative with long accepted materials and modes of historical production. Specifically, our project focuses on making accessible to a global audience the stories of several scientists and historical factories key to the rise of the renewable energy industry in China during the 1940s. In turn, we hope that we can offer participants in the interactive digital storytelling community a few thoughts on the potential of collaboration with historians via the avenue of "public history".

**Keywords:** Digital humanities · VR · Public history · Modern Chinese history

## 1 Relevance and Significance of the Work

### 1.1 Repositioning Archival Sources

Traditionally, historical documents are preserved in archives, often accessible only to qualified specialists. It is then the work of the historian to select, analyze, and boil down masses of archival documentation, enrich them with pre-existing secondary sources, and then produce a legible historical narrative for a wider public. This is of course something of a simplification – historians of cultures and regions that do not rely on written records often prioritize oral sources, while historians of art or material culture focus on physical objects. Yet the archive remains a dominant aspect of historical production, both in terms of the authority its inclusion confers on historical work and in structural terms – simply put, many sources of funding for the discipline revolve around the use of institutional archives.

© Springer Nature Switzerland AG 2020
A.-G. Bosser et al. (Eds.): ICIDS 2020, LNCS 12497, pp. 361–364, 2020.
https://doi.org/10.1007/978-3-030-62516-0_36

In recent years, historians themselves have called attention to the "epistemic anxieties" [1] imbricated in the production and maintenance of archives. And scholars in adjacent fields have pushed the point further. Expanding on reader-response theory, media scholars like Lisa Gitelman [2] suggest that "individual genres aren't artifacts... they are ongoing and changeable practices of expression and reception." Building on this point, Gitelman argues for understanding "the document" as a genre itself. Much like a novel or serialized sitcom, the historical document is a "mode of recognition instantiated in discourse", which for all of its subgenres (tax records, government memo, draft treaty) is recognizable by its institutional framing and its preoccupation with systematized, bureaucratic knowledge.

If Gitelman is correct, it is worthwhile for historians to deeply consider the relationship between the archive, the source document and the completed historical work. In other words, if the sources that historians commonly use to construct historical work cannot be regarded as fixed, timeless entities preserved unchanging in archives, it is worthwhile rethinking the balance between the source material and authorial voice in historical work. Given the possibilities available via digital formats [3], could the source not become more visibly and accessibly a part of the final work?

Meanwhile, scholars of electronic literature like Scott Rettberg [4, 5] increasingly question the idea of the "work" itself - - many digital projects can appear as installations, apps, and websites without the need for a fixed form. And a digital project reliant upon audience input seems to exist in a different state of "completion" than say a printed detective novel. What might this mean for the possibilities of non-print historical work?

## 1.2  History and Narrative

If the "historical" document can be interpreted as a genre, and the concept of a fixed "work" is increasingly problematic, can historians afford to rely solely on the static, text-based format that characterizes the majority of contemporary historical production? The discipline's relatively limited engagement with alternate formats is not simply indicative of disinterest on the part of academic historians toward anything "digital". On the contrary, for well over a decade, venues like the Journal of Digital Humanities have welcomed initial efforts by historians to reconceptualize the production of historical work in a non-print format. Meanwhile, professional organizations like the American Historical Association have sponsored conferences and grants aimed at promoting consideration of digital output for tenure and increasing training in digital tools for graduate students. If anything, younger scholars of history are anxious to produce work that is increasingly categorized under the larger rubric of "digital humanities" [6].

Rather, it may be that the historical discipline has yet to fully come to terms with scholarship in media studies, critical theory, electronic literature, and other fields which for several decades have critiqued and disassembled classical modes of understanding narrative. In other words, "narrative" is as much an obstacle as "digital" in deterring the full engagement of historians with the potentialities of incorporating interactive digital narrative into the production of historical works. As early as the mid-1970s, influenced by structuralist linguistics and reader response theory, the philosopher of history Hayden White published widely read and acclaimed critiques of the process of historical production, arguing that historians emulate novelists in adhering to the tropes of drama, tragedy, and so on to chart the rise and fall of leaders and nations: in short, while the historical work references "real life" archival sources, it conveys levels of meaning beyond "information" found in a scientific text via devices most commonly associated with the literary arts. Yet as Herman Paul [7] concluded in a recent study of White's work, more than three decades later, White's critiques have altered less than might be expected in the field of historical work. Meanwhile, social history, post-colonial history, and histories of gender and sexuality have each marked turns in the historical field over the last three decades. But while the expansion of voices and viewpoints has been both needed and welcome within the discipline, historical work is still largely output in text format via monograph and academic journals, offering little chance for a general public audience to see, much less interact with, the issues and materials a historian grapples with on a daily basis.

Our demo is an attempt to address a few of these issues by presenting sources and digitized material artifacts alongside a historical narrative within the context of a reader-centered immersive environment. We are particularly inspired by the challenges of the present moment, when geopolitical events in Xinjiang and Hong Kong as well as the COVID-19 pandemic have limited the abilities of researchers to conduct on the ground research in China. Nor can the accessibility of historical sites and material artifacts be taken for granted, as the domestic political situation can quickly impact scholars' ability to access materials vital to their work. Beyond the challenge of obtaining archival documents, rapid economic growth in the past few decades has spurred development which while in many respects positive has also endangered historical sites and buildings deemed unviable for renovation or preservation. Sustained exploration of digital mediums as legitimate formats for historical production, and more importantly, attention to the insights of adjacent fields in the arts and digital humanities, are vital steps in confronting these challenges.

## 2 Design and Development: "China's First Biofuel Factory"

### 2.1 Digital Modeling as a Complement to the Archive

While the intended output is a viewer-centered immersive experience, creating historically accurate 3D models and developing methods for making source material accessible enriches the process of scholarship as well. The project began as a series of photos, architectural blueprints, engineering documents, and the crumbling remains of an ethanol factory located in southwest China, about 1 h south of Chongqing. The materials were discovered during archival research on the origins of a biofuel program initiated by the Chinese government during the late 1930s and early 1940s in order to preserve fuel supplies during World War II. Millions of gallons a year of ethanol-based biofuel supplied not only Chinese troops but US army troops stationed in the China theater throughout the war. Wartime conditions as well as the social and political tumult in mid-20th China resulted in many of the factories involved failing and gradually being forgotten, as was much of the documentation related to their existence. Recreating the equipment digitally was made possible by researching early 20th century journals of industrial machinery and applied chemistry, and consulting with experts at the Science History Institute in Philadelphia over a six month period.

Our project uses the game engine Unity to enable significant interaction between the viewer and digitized archival material (maps, blueprints, and scientific notes) as well as digitalized material artifacts (industrial distilling equipment) that would be impossible in a text-based format. Using an interactive UI "field book", the viewer can choose to read and explore the documents and machinery prior to encountering a historical narrative which places it within a framework. Additionally, mouse click events and keyboard commands have been implemented allowing free movement around the factory environment, interaction with visual sources, animation of the distilling equipment, and so on. Naturally, there is a process of selection which is an interpretative act in and of itself. But by elevating the visibility of sources and digitized material artifacts within the immersive work, we hope to remind viewers that writing history is very much an act of construction.

### 2.2  Public History and Collaboration

After incorporating feedback from the demo, we plan to present the project as a public installation in several cities in western China where factories in the biofuel network were located. In turn, if the public installation generates additional documents, photos, or recollections from viewers, we will aim to include these in the digital environment as well, creating a feedback loop between project and public. In our project documentation online, we have included photos taken in November 2019 at one of the few remaining ruins, which is located on the edges of a landfill in the city of Zunyi. Images from the working demo of our project have been included in an online project folder, which will be updated over fall and spring 2020–2021.

## References

1. Stoler, A.: Along the Archival Grain: Epistemic Anxieties and Colonial Common Sense. Princeton University Press, Princeton (2010)
2. Gitelman, L.: Paper Knowledge: Toward a Media History of Documents. Duke University Press, Durham (2014)
3. Spierling, U., Winzer, P., Massarczyk, E.: Experiencing the presence of historical stories with location-based augmented reality. In: Nunes, N., Oakley, I., Nisi, V. (eds.) 10th International Conference on Interactive Digital Storytelling 2017. LNCS, vol. 10690, pp. 49–62. Springer, Cham (2017). https://doi.org/10.1007/978-3-319-71027-3_5
4. Madsen, J.B., Madsen, C.B.: Handheld visual representation of a castle Chapel Ruin. J. Comput. Cultural Heritage 9(1), Article 6 (2015)
5. Rettberg, S.: Electronic Literature. Polity Press, Cambridge (2018)
6. Gardiner, E., Musto, R.G.: The Digital Humanities: A Primer for Students and Scholars. Cambridge University Press, New York (2015)
7. Paul, H.: Hayden White. Wiley, Oxford (2013)

# Author Index

Alinam, Mortaza 75
Andrade, Tânia 357
Anne Brown, Sarah 229
Antonini, Alessio 287
Arnds, Peter 83

Bakk, Ágnes Karolina 327
Bala, Paulo 281, 357
Barbara, Jonathan 120
Basaraba, Nicole 83
Benatti, Francesca 287
Bernstein, Mark 3
Bosser, Anne-Gwenn 3
Bouchardon, Serge 221
Brooker, Sam 287
Brown, Sarah Anne 125

Cardona-Rivera, Rogelio E. 133
Cesário, Vanessa 339
Chai, Yuzhu 361
Charles, Fred 102
Christoforidis, Stamatis 349
Chu, Sharon Lynn 125
Ciotoli, Luca 75
Clark, Lynda 300
Conlan, Owen 83

Dacanay, Julie 344
Debus, Michael S. 133
Dighe, Mayank 44
Dionisio, Mara 281, 357
Doherty, Skye 271

Echeverri, Daniel 15
Edmond, Jennifer 83

Gasque, T. M. 314
Gibson, Steve 92
Gil, Maitê 258
Green, Craig Paul 92
Green, Daniel 102

Haahr, Mads 178, 335
Hales, Chris 149

Han, Vanessa 229
Hargood, Charlie 102
Higgins, Matthew 243
Holmquist, Lars Erik 92
Howell, Peter 243
Hubbard-Cheuoua, Aleata 111

Ioanidis, Yannis 349

Jennings, Kathleen 271
Jhala, Arnav 44

Karanam, Pratyusha 229
Karvounis, Manos 349
Katifori, Akrivi 349
Koceva, Frosina 75
Koenitz, Hartmut 3
Kourtis, Vassilis 349
Kway, Liting 164

Louchart, Sandy 3
Lougiakis, Christos 349
Lynn Chu, Sharon 229

Martens, Chris 3, 44
Matthews, Ben 271
Middleton, Stuart E. 58
Millard, David E. 3, 58
Miller, Chris 44
Minogue, James 111
Mitchell, Alex 164, 190
Morgan, Lilian 335
Mott, Bradford 111
Murray, Janet 314

Nack, Frank 3
Nielsen, Thomas Lund 30
Nisi, Valentina 281, 339, 357

Olim, Sandra 339
Oliveira, Sarah 281
Oliver, Kevin 111

Palamas, George   30
Palosaari Eladhari, Mirjam   3

Quek, Francis   125

Rafferty, Eoin Ivan   30
Resch, Cheryl   229
Revells, Tristan   361
Revi, Ashwathy T.   58
Rezk, Anna Marie   178
Ringstaff, Cathy   111
Rittenhouse, Brad   314
Rose, Ben   271
Rossi, Giulia Carla   3, 300
Roth, Christian   344

Schoenau-Fog, Henrik   30
Smith, Andy   111
Snow, Stephen   271

Steynberg, Aletta J.   353
Sych, Steven   203
Sylla, Cristina   258

Tan, Kenneth   190
Tang, Kevin   314
Taylor, Sandra   111
Thue, David   212
Torre, Ilaria   75

Vaishnavi Surampudi, Srividya   229
Viller, Stephen   271
Vrettakis, Ektor   349

Wei, Huaxin   15
Wisdom, Stella   300

Zagal, José P.   133
Zarei, Niloofar   125

Printed in the United States
By Bookmasters